CliffsTestPrep®
Foreign Service Officer Exam

PREPARATION FOR THE WRITTEN EXAM AND THE ORAL ASSESSMENT

An American BookWorks Corporation Project

Contributing Authors

Deborah Barrett, Ph.D.

Elaine Bender, M.A.

Phillip Gay, Ph.D.

Freddy Lee, Ph.D.

Val Limburg, Ph.D.

Tandy McConnell, Ph.D.

Edward Miller, Ph.D.

Nafelie Monsour, B.A.

Deborah Grayson Riegel, M.A.

Sharon Saronson, M.F.A., M.A.

Brice Sloan, B.A.

Jonathan Weber, B.A.

Mark Weinfeld, M.A.

Houghton Mifflin Harcourt
Boston   New York

Publisher's Acknowledgments

Editorial

Acquisitions Editor: Greg Tubach

Project Editors: Tere Stouffer, Marcia Larkin

Technical Editor: Clifford Hull

Composition

Proofreader: Debbye Butler

CliffsTestPrep® Foreign Service Officer Exam

Copyright © 2006 Houghton Mifflin Harcourt

ISBN 978-0-7645-9646-9

1B/RV/QV/QY/IN

For information about permission to reproduce selections from this book, write to Permissions, Houghton Mifflin Harcourt Publishing Company, 215 Park Avenue South, New York, New York 10003.

Trademarks: Houghton Mifflin Harcourt, CliffsNotes, the CliffsNotes logo, Cliffs, CliffsAP, CliffsComplete, CliffsQuickReview, CliffsStudySolver, CliffsTestPrep, CliffsNote-a-Day, cliffsnotes.com, and all related trademarks, logos, and trade dress are trademarks or registered trademarks of Houghton Mifflin Harcourt and/or its affiliates. All other trademarks are the property of their respective owners. Houghton Mifflin Harcourt is not associated with any product or vendor mentioned in this book.

Library of Congress Cataloging-in-Publication Data
Grayson, Fred N.
  CliffsTestPrep foreign service officer exam / by Fred Grayson / contributing authors Deborah Barrett . . . [et al.].
     p. cm. -- (CliffsTestPrep)
  "An American BookWorks Corporation Project"--CIP t.p. verso
  Includes bibliographical references and index.
  ISBN-13: 978-0-7645-9646-9 (pbk. : alk. paper)
  ISBN-10: 0-7645-9646-2 (alk. paper)
1. Diplomatic and consular service, American--Examinations, questions, etc. 2. Civil service--United States--Examinations, questions, etc. I. Title: Foreign service officer exam. II. American BookWorks Corporation. III. Title. IV. Series.
  JZ1480.A82G72 2006
  327.73'0076--dc22
                                                2005023490

Printed in the United States of America

DOH 12 11 10 9

Table of Contents

PART I: WRITTEN EXAM: THE JOB KNOWLEDGE TEST

PART II: WRITTEN EXAM: THE ENGLISH EXPRESSION TEST

PART III: WRITTEN EXAM: THE BIOGRAPHIC INFORMATION QUESTIONNAIRE

PART IV: WRITTEN EXAM: WRITTEN ESSAY

PART V: ORAL ASSESSMENT

Introduction

Welcome to this review of the Foreign Service Officer Examination (FSOE). This book has been written to help you prepare, in-depth, for the examination that can lead to a career as a Foreign Service Officer. We present you with everything you have to know about the test: the different parts of the exam, what to expect, how to answer the different questions, plus almost 800 practice questions that cover every subject area on the exam.

In order to use this book effectively, we suggest you follow it step-by-step. In each of the individual parts of the book, you'll be given a complete overview of that test section, plus sample questions so that you will be fully prepared when you take the actual test.

About the FSOE

The FSOE consists of five major sections. These sections include:

- **The Job Knowledge test:** The 90 questions you encounter on this portion of the exam are multiple-choice questions that cover the eight following topics. See the first chapter for an overview of this test; see the rest of Part I for specifics about each topic area.
  - United States Government
  - United States Society
  - World History and Geography
  - Economics
  - Mathematics and Statistics
  - Management
  - Communication
  - Computers
- **The English Expression test:** Part II of this book provides an in-depth chapter on grammar and usage, which is what the English Expression test covers.
- **The Biographic Information Questionnaire:** Part III of this book discusses the Biographic Information Questionnaire, which includes questions that are all about you.
- **The Written Essay:** Part IV of this books helps you understand the elements of good writing, which is tested on the Written Essay, a portion of the test that's graded only if you pass the other three sections of the written exam.
- **The Oral Assessment:** If you pass the four written exams, you're asked back for the Oral Assessment. Part V of this book tells you what to expect.

As you study for these portions of the FSOE, you'll find that some areas will be easier than others. For example, you may be an excellent writer, and the Written Essay will present no problem to you. If that's the case, go through Part II so that you get an idea of the types of questions you may encounter but don't spend too much of your time there.

Of course, it depends on how much time you have to prepare before the test. The more time you have, the better. However, if time is limited, we suggest that you put together a study plan. Because there are eight major subject areas in the Job Knowledge test, it would probably be valuable to concentrate on those that you have the least knowledge about. If, for example, you were a history major in college, you might have a strong background in subjects like history, society, economics, and government, which means you may want to spend more time studying mathematics and statistics. Only you can determine which sections need your in-depth attention.

However, in order to be successful on the FSOE, you need to be familiar with a wide range of subjects. In addition to bringing your knowledge and background to the test, try to read as much as possible on all of the subjects that are presented in this book.

Commonly Asked Questions about the Foreign Service Officer Exam Test-Taking Strategies

In order to score well on any exam, you must have a basic understanding of the subject matter. There's no getting around that, and especially with a test like the FSOE, as you should be able to tell from the subjects tested. However, there are certain ways to increase your ability to do well on tests in general, and this test, specifically.

Q. **What kind of test is the Job Knowledge test?**

A. The Job Knowledge test is a multiple-choice test that requires you to have a fairly comprehensive knowledge of eight subject areas, each discussed in the Part I chapters.

Q. **What type of questions will be asked on the English Expression test?**

A. The English Expression test is also a multiple-choice test, but it demands a strong ability to understand proper grammar and usage. Part II helps you review and gives you practice tests to hone your skills.

Q. **How can I prepare for the Biographic Information Questionnaire?**

A. Take a look at Part III of this book to familiarize yourself with the questions. Keep in mind, however, that these are questions about yourself, so there's no right or wrong answer. This section of the FSOE is designed to provide an overview of your experience based on past interests and activities in which you've participated. Although most of the questions are multiple-choice questions, some of the questions may ask you to elaborate on your answers.

Q. **What if I can't answer all of the questions on the Biographic Information Questionnaire?**

A. Use your time wisely, because it is important to respond to all of the questions on this section in order to provide a clear picture of your experiences separate and apart from your educational background.

Q. **How can I improve my chances with the multiple-choice questions?**

A. Most of the standardized tests you've taken throughout your educational career have contained multiple-choice questions. For some reason, these types of questions give a large percentage of test-takers a difficult time. If you approach these questions carefully, however, they should be easier than you think. Keep in mind that these questions are created to test your abilities to recognize the correct answer from four choices. From the start, you should be happy that there are only four choices, not five, as there are on many exams, because this reduces the available choices. Questions are comprised of several parts.

- The question stem
- The correct choice
- Distracters

As test-item writers create questions, they normally approach it as follows:

- One choice is absolutely correct.
- Once or two choices that are absolutely incorrect (distracters).
- Once or two choices that may be similar to the correct answer, but might contain some information that is not quite accurate or on target, or even may not answer the specific question (distracters).

How should you approach the questions? First, read the question and see whether you know the answer. If you know it automatically, you can look at the choices and select the correct one. Here's an example.

---

1. The first group of English who established a permanent colony in Virginia in the early seventeenth century consisted mostly of

    A. Younger sons of the gentry who faced limited options at home
    B. Families
    C. Royal family members
    D. Wealthy investors

Do you know the correct answer? If so, what is your choice? If you don't, start with the process of elimination. Right now, if you don't know the answer and can't even guess at it, you have a one in four chance of guessing it correctly: 25%. But you can increase your odds by eliminating some of the choices.

Choice A could be correct, as could choice B. Royal family members could be a possibility, but as the ruling class, there was no reason for them to leave home to explore the New World. So, you can eliminate choice C, and now you have a one in three chance, or 33%, which is better than 25%.

Next, look at choice D. Wealthy investors were not needed at this point in history, because there was nothing in which to invest. Investors did put up the money but generally did not make the grueling trip. So you can eliminate choice D, and now you have a 50% chance of making a correct guess—one out of two choices. You've quickly improved your odds, and if you still can't figure out the answer, take a guess.

The correct answer is A. Under the practice called primogeniture, oldest sons inherited everything. Thus, their younger brothers had an incentive to relocate to America. Very few families made the journey during the early years in Virginia, because conditions were so primitive. How did your guessing turn out—or did you already know the answer?

The process of elimination is a time-honored technique for any multiple-choice test, one that works well if you don't know the answer as soon as you read the question.

Q. Is there anything else I should look for that will give me a clue to the answer?

A. Pay attention to words like *always, never,* and *not.* Most things in the world are not *always* or *never,* so be careful if a question asks you to choose which of the choices is not . . . ! And make sure you read questions carefully that say, "All are correct except . . . !"

Q. How can I do well on the Written Essay?

A. Some people have a knack for writing, and for them, the essay will come easily. If you don't have that strength, take the time to go through Part IV of this book. It'll help you get a handle on how to organize your thoughts, think them through, put them on paper, and then proofread them to make sure you've present a clear and cogent sample of your writing ability.

Q. What else do I have to do to improve my score on the FSOE?

A. There are probably dozens of little things you can do, but of course, the most important is to have the basic knowledge of these subject areas so that you can take this exam with confidence. Read as many newspapers and magazines as possible. Watch the news on television. And make sure you get a good night's sleep the night before the exam. The test will take a full day, and you should have as much energy as possible to go through this.

Q. What's left to do?

A. The bottom line is that if you feel comfortable with these subjects on the Job Knowledge test, you should be able to do well on the exam. Spend the time reading through the various parts of this book. It has been divided into sections of the test, and we've presented the material in a unique way. In Part I, the review section for each topic is presented as a series of questions and answers. Read each question and try to answer it quickly. The correct answer immediately follows the question, so you can find out whether you were right or wrong and try to understand why the answer was correct—and the other choices were incorrect.

At the end of every subject review section, we've also presented you with some mini-tests in order to give you a quick view of what you know and what you don't.

Then take the individual full-length simulated Job Knowledge and English Expression tests. Part III gives you sample questions for the Biographic Information Questionnaire. For the Written Essay, you don't need to write an actual essay, but it is worth going through the samples in Part IV and creating an outline for yourself based on the topic. And before sitting for the Oral Assessment, go through the material in Part V.

Good luck.

PART I

WRITTEN EXAM: THE JOB KNOWLEDGE TEST

About the Job Knowledge Test

Job Knowledge Topic Areas

The Job Knowledge test was developed to test candidates' knowledge throughout a range of eight subjects. These subjects were determined to be the most important in terms of becoming a Foreign Service Officer. The eight topics are as follows:

- United States Government
- United States Society
- World History and Geography
- Economics
- Mathematics and Statistics
- Management
- Communication
- Computers

What Are the Career Tracks?

The Job Knowledge test is divided into two sections: general, which includes the eight topic areas discussed in the preceding sections, and career track. As soon as you have completed the questions in the general section, you immediately turn to the career track section. The following are the five career tracks and a brief description of what these careers might entail. More in-depth information is found through the U.S. Department of State. You can find specific information about the Foreign Service as a career by pointing your browser to www.careers.state.gov/officer.

- **Management:** A management officer is normally involved in business management within a consular unit or management office of an embassy. You could eventually supervise a Human Resources unit for Americans as well as local staff (within the country you are stationed). At the senior level, you may become an ambassador, head one of the large consulates, and even direct the development of new embassies.
- **Consular:** As a consular officer, you often work in local embassies adjudicating visas, assisting American citizens in emergency situations, and serving as the primary contact people have with the local U.S. embassies or consulate offices. As you grow in the job, you will likely manage sections of an embassy, and eventually, head up an office somewhere in the field.
- **Economic:** As an economic officer, you are involved in negotiating treaties, developing a network of contacts in local communities, and becoming involved in local economic developments in the country in which you are stationed. As a senior officer, you may be responsible for developing U.S. policy for economic and trade issues.
- **Political:** A political officer works with the local society and requires a strong understanding of local culture, the people, and the language. You would be responsible for monitoring the local politics as well as working with local political figures to convey the political views of the United States. Senior officers manage and supervise other political officers, either in the United States or abroad.
- **Public diplomacy:** In this role, the public diplomacy officer is really an information officer whose role it is to influence public opinion and put forth the best view of the United States. You work with local media, local cultural leaders, and so on, eventually managing significant country-wide programs to convey the concepts of democracy and free speech.

The questions in the career track portion of the Job Knowledge test are unique to that section, and the career track portion is equal in length to the general section. The scores, though, are combined. Make sure you take the section that corresponds to the career track you selected earlier. If you take the wrong test, one that does not correspond to the number you marked earlier, you will receive no score, because only the test form number you selected will be graded.

You can complete only one career track section, so make sure you know which one you're going to take long before you take the exam. This is one area that is worth spending time researching, because it relates to the area in which it is likely you will spend your entire career as a Foreign Service Officer.

Both the general and the career track sections have the same types of multiple-choice questions and essentially cover the same eight subject areas. However, in the career track section, the balance of the question subjects is weighted toward that specific career. If you are looking toward a career in public diplomacy, you will likely receive more questions in communications, computers, and management than you will on economics and mathematics.

Note that we've divided Part I of this book into each of the eight Job Knowledge areas. It is important that you go through all of the chapters and learn the material, because these are the types of questions you will find in the general sections. Because you also have to answer a heavier concentration of some of the same subject areas in the career track section, you will have covered all your bases by reviewing all of the questions and answers.

In each subject area, we've presented dozens of review questions, each question followed immediately by the correct answer, plus an explanation of why that answer was correct. This approach provides immediate reinforcement for you. In addition, at the end of the review questions, there are several mini-tests per subject area. As you take each of these tests, treat them as if you were taking the career track sections of the Job Knowledge test, because each mini-test is a concentration of a specific subject.

At the end of Part I, there is a sample exam consisting of 90 questions, followed by an explanation of all of the answers. To help you evaluate your strengths and weaknesses by subject, we've also indicated the appropriate subject area (and chapter reference) at the end of each answer. Try to keep track of your incorrect answers, especially by subject area. If you find that you have a weakness in one or two of the topics, consider reviewing those chapters again. And you might want to reevaluate the career track you have selected if you think your weakness in any area may affect your score on that portion of the test.

United States Government

What You Should Know

In both the general and career track sections of the Job Knowledge test, the questions require knowledge of a general understanding of the U.S. federal government — how it functions and how it is comprised. You are also required to understand the history as well as the content of the Constitution. This includes not only the treaties but also the Constitutional influences on U.S. foreign relations. The test also covers the structure of Congress and its role in foreign affairs, such as human rights, trade agreements, and so on. And you are also asked questions about the overall government structure, how government policies are made, and how the United States conducts itself in foreign affairs.

The questions in the following section are for your review. Go through each question and try your best to answer it. The explanation of the answer follows immediately afterward so that you can actually learn new material. After you've completed reviewing these questions and answers, three brief practice review tests at the end of the chapter help you determine how much you know. Of course, there is a full-length exam at the end of Part II that also includes U.S. government questions.

U.S. Government Review Section

Read the following questions and select the choices that best answer the questions.

1. Why did President Franklin Roosevelt recommend expanding the size of the Supreme Court?

   A. Because it had a large backlog of cases.
   B. He wanted the court to represent a greater diversity of the population.
   C. The Court had invalidated many New Deal programs.
   D. He wanted to divide the court into a criminal and a civil panel.

   C. The Supreme Court had ruled against many New Deal programs. He recommended adding members to the court for every member who was over 70.

2. Comparing 1964 to 1994, what happened to Americans' trust in government?

   A. It declined.
   B. It stayed about the same.
   C. It rose.
   D. It rose sharply, and then fell sharply.

   A. Trust in government has declined over the years, although there have also been some years of improvement. For example, more people believe that government wastes money than it did in former years. Trust in government represents an attitudinal index based on several public opinion questions. The most often cited trust index is derived from the regular survey done by the Institute for Social Research at the University of Michigan.

3. President Bush has proposed a constitutional amendment barring same-sex marriage. To have this amendment added to the Constitution, what must happen?

   A. The amendment must be proposed by three-fourths of both houses of Congress and approved by the legislatures of two-thirds of the states.

   B. The amendment must be proposed by two-thirds of both houses of Congress and approved by the legislatures of three-fourths of the states.

   C. The amendment must be proposed by two-thirds of both houses of Congress, signed by the President, and approved by the legislatures of three-fourths of the states.

   D. The amendment must be approved by conventions in two-thirds of the states, and then approved by three-quarters of both houses of the Congress.

   B. Article V gives the method of approval. There are actually two methods, one allowing the states to call for a constitutional convention. The most common method, however, is a proposal by two-thirds of both houses of Congress and approval by the legislatures of three-fourths of the states. (The Congress could select conventions in the states for approval.) The president does not have to approve.

4. If the Office of Vice President is vacant, what happens?

   A. It remains vacant until the next election.

   B. The president's political party holds a mini convention to select a new vice president.

   C. The Senate selects a new vice president.

   D. The president nominates a new vice president, who must be approved by a majority of the Congress.

   D. The 25th Amendment said a new vice president could be appointed by the president and approved by a majority of the Congress to serve out the term. Prior to the 25th Amendment, the office remained vacant.

5. The post–World War II defense policy used to maintain a balance of power in the world is known as

   A. Mutual Assured Destruction (MAD)

   B. Strategic Defense Initiative (SDI)

   C. the Marshall Plan

   D. the Truman Doctrine

   A. Mutual Assured Destruction (MAD) has been the U.S. defense policy. It worked to keep the Soviet Union from acquiring a first-strike capability, which meant that if the Soviet Union struck first, the United States would be able to knock out an effective retaliation. The MAD doctrine said that if a nation struck first, the other side would be able to retaliate and inflict unacceptable damage. Based upon this policy, the international system was said to be in balance.

6. What is the theory that suggested that U.S. democracy is based on many groups, each pressing its own interest?

   A. elitism

   B. pluralism

   C. entrepreneurial politics

   D. conflict resolution

   B. Robert Dahl and others have written about the American political system as being pluralistic.

7. Conference Committees are

   A. permanent Joint Committees for dealing with serious national concerns, such as 9/11

   B. temporary Committees of House and Senate members to resolve bill differences between the chambers

   C. special Committees that study issues but have no power to report legislation

   D. meetings between members of Congress and the Executive departments

B. Conference Committees are used when differences exist between House and Senate bills. Each house's conferees vote separately and both sets must agree to approve a provision. Ultimately, the floors of each chamber must approve a Conference Committee's report.

8. The President may veto

    A.   the entire bill and items in an appropriations bill
    B.   the entire bill and items in a tax bill
    C.   the entire bill and items in any bill
    D.   the entire bill only

D. The president, unlike many governors, does not have an item veto. There was an attempt to give him the equivalent of one through legislation, but the Supreme Court ruled that attempt unconstitutional.

9. One consequence attributed to malapportionment was that

    A.   Urban areas were overrepresented.
    B.   Urban areas were underrepresented.
    C.   Suburban areas were overrepresented.
    D.   The minority party was concentrated, resulting in fewer minorities being elected than their percent in the population.

B. Malapportionment prior to the Supreme Court decision ordering reapportionment resulted in rural areas being overrepresented and urban areas underrepresented. The apportionment of congressional and state legislative districts did not keep pace with the movement of people from rural areas to cities (and, subsequently, to suburban areas) and immigrants who came primarily to cities.

10. The function of the Office of Management and Budget to review all legislative proposals by the departments of government for consistency and conformity with the president's policies is termed

    A.   central clearance
    B.   review and comment procedure
    C.   legislative oversight
    D.   bottom-up review

A. Started to make sure that policy proposals from the departments did not conflict with the president's budget, it has been extended to all policy proposals made by the departments to ensure conformity to the administration's policy. Central clearance function began after the president received executive budget authority in the Budget and Accounting Act of 1921.

11. The marble cake theory of federalism implies

    A.   the establishment of separate functions for the national and state governments
    B.   the sharing of functions between the national government and the states
    C.   the reservation of all non-delegated powers to the states
    D.   the establishment of a federal form rather than a confederational form of government

B. The marble cake theory of federalism was described by Morton Grodzins. It is frequently used to describe the sharing of functions between the federal government and the states.

12. The Constitution requires that members of the Supreme Court

    A.   be a member of a state bar
    B.   be at least 25 years old
    C.   be born in the United States
    D.   No specific requirement is mentioned.

D. The Constitution does not include any requirements for a Supreme Court justice. There are also no requirements in the judiciary statutes.

13. The courts are inundated with *habeas corpus* writs. The courts turn to Congress for help and ask them to suspend the writ for one year to allow them to get caught up. Can Congress do this?

    A. Yes. Article I gives the Congress the right to do this.
    B. No. Only the president can do this.
    C. No. Congress can suspend the writ but only in cases of rebellion or invasion.
    D. No. *Habeas corpus* is a fundamental right and cannot be suspended.

C. *Habeas corpus,* which requires that someone who is arrested be taken before a judge, can be suspended by the Congress but only when there is a rebellion or invasion. President Lincoln tried to suspend the right during the Civil War, but the Supreme Court said only Congress may do so.

14. A writ of *certiorari* is employed when

    A. appealing to the Supreme Court
    B. the police want to search one's home
    C. obtaining an injunction to stop the implementation of a law
    D. the president wants to send a judicial nominee to the Senate for confirmation

A. The writ of *certiorari* is the main way that cases go to the Supreme Court. The writ asks for Supreme Court review. Only a small percent of writs received by the Court are granted.

15. Judicial review

    A. is clearly supported in the *Federalist Papers*
    B. was first applied to the Supreme Court in *Marbury v. Madison*
    C. is explicitly defined in the Constitution
    D. was a power given to the Supreme Court by the Judiciary Act of 1789

B. Judicial Review allows the courts to overturn a statute on the basis that it is not constitutional. *Marbury v. Madison* is the famous case in a decision by John Marshall that overturned a portion of the Judiciary Act of 1789 on the basis of its constitutionality, establishing the judicial review precedent for the Court.

16. Which of the following comes closest to defining *stare decisis?*

    A. majority opinion of the Supreme Court
    B. precedent
    C. legislative intent of a statute
    D. dissenting opinion

B. *Stare decisis,* meaning "let the decision stand," are decisions that act as precedent for future decisions. Cases are cited by attorneys as precedents that the decision in their case should follow.

17. Freedom of religion would protect which of the following against state interference?

    A. polygamy practices of Mormons
    B. the refusal of the Amish to allow their children to attend school after 8th grade
    C. the use of deadly snakes in religious ceremonies
    D. the failure of Christian Scientists to seek treatment by an M.D. for their children who have a serious condition

B. The court has ruled in all of these areas. The only one protected are the Amish, who do not have to send their children to school after the 8th grade (*Wisconsin v. Yoder*).

18. Before a case can be heard by a court, it must have *all but one* of the following. The one condition that need *not* be present is

   A. two real parties
   B. parties must have a personal and substantial interest or injury
   C. the case must be a real situation and not a hypothetical situation
   D. the case must be based on the common law

   D. All the conditions in A through C must be present before a court will consider a case. The case need not be a common law case but could be based upon statutory law. Statutory law is a law that is passed by the legislature. Common law is a law that comes from judicial decisions.

19. Someone gets married in Illinois and moves to Wisconsin. On what constitutional grounds is the marriage recognized?

   A. full, faith, and credit
   B. due process
   C. equal protection
   D. right of rendition

   A. States are required to give full, faith, and credit to papers and legal decisions made in other states. Marriage has generally been considered part of the full, faith, and credit provisions. Historically some states had refused to accept mixed racial marriages if their own state did not allow it. Today, states may not accept same-sex marriage. The federal law known as the Defense of Marriage Act explicitly excludes same-sex marriage from the full, faith, and credit provision. However, it still remains to be seen whether the courts will accept this act as constitutional, because it provides an exception to the full, faith, and credit constitutional provision.

20. Which of the following groups was the last to receive the right to vote in the United States?

   A. women
   B. non-property owners
   C. African Americans
   D. Youth ages 18 to 21 years old

   D. Youth received the vote by constitutional amendment ratified in 1971 — the 26th Amendment. Women were granted the right to voted by the 19th Amendment, and African Americans by the 15th.

21. Which of the following taxes would most likely be considered progressive?

   A. property tax
   B. sales tax
   C. income tax
   D. cigarette tax

   C. Progressive taxes are taxes that take a greater percent income from the rich than the poor. They are advocated based upon the principle of the "ability to pay." Of the taxes listed, the income tax with its graduated tax brackets is typically progressive. All the others are regressive. Few sales taxes are progressive — only those that exempt many necessities and also tax services such as attorney's fees that wealthy people use more tend to be.

22. Open market operations in economic policy refer to which of the following?

   A. the buying and selling of securities by the Federal Reserve to affect the economy
   B. the reduction in trade barriers to facilitate trade (for example, NAFTA)
   C. the clearance of checks by the Federal Reserve
   D. the lending by the Federal Reserve to member banks who then make loans

   A. Open market operations involve the buying and selling of securities by the Federal Reserve. An Open Market Committee of the Federal Reserve (also known as the Fed) makes the decision. Securities are sold to counter inflation and are bought to put more money in the economy to counter a recession.

23. The scientific management school of public administration affected the organization of many cities. Its approach was based upon the conception of the city as

    A.   a responsive mechanism; the need of the city to be responsive to all groups in a city

    B.   a representative mechanism; the city must have on the council exact proportions of each major social group in the city

    C.   a service deliverer concerned with efficiency and economy of service provision

    D.   a holding corporation whose purpose is to contract with private businesses to provide services

C. The scientific management school of public administration was aimed at developing organization and management that would achieve the goals of efficiency and economy. (A similar movement can be found in business administraton.) In terms of cities, they viewed the city as delivering services, which would be done as efficiently as possible, and not making the same type of policy decisions found at the state and national levels. The city manager form of government was advocated by this school of thought.

24. Which of the following describes the differences between Temporary Assistance to Needy Families (TANF) and the Aid to Families with Dependent Children (AFDC)?

    A.   TANF is entirely federal, while AFDC was a federal-state cooperative program.

    B.   There was no time limit on receiving AFCD; for TANF, you can only receive funding for five years.

    C.   AFDC did not go to non-citizen immigrants; TANF does include them.

    D.   AFDC included the provision of child care; TANF does not.

B. TANF's main feature is that welfare is limited to five years, although there can be some people exempt from this requirement. AFDC did not have any such time limit. AFDC did go to immigrants, while TANF restricts immigrants who are not citizens from getting funding.

25. Medicare does use tax dollars from the general treasury for some of its programs. Other programs are restricted to amounts in the trust fund. For what are tax dollars used as a portion of the funding?

    A.   hospital payment

    B.   physicians and outpatient services

    C.   nursing homes for custodial care

    D.   experimental procedures

B. Medicare's Part B, which goes for physician and other outpatient services, includes tax dollars. Three-fourths of the cost comes from general taxes. Part A, which pays for hospital care, comes only from money in the trust fund, which people pay into while they are working. Custodial nursing home care is not covered by Medicare, nor are experimental procedures.

26. On what basis does Medicare pay hospitals for the care of those covered by Medicare?

    A.   on the basis of what is charged

    B.   by establishing a grant to the hospital based upon how many Medicare patients are treated

    C.   by a price list for each service rendered (established by a national expenditure committee)

    D.   on the basis of a predetermined amount for the condition for which the person was admitted

D. Since 1983 Medicare pays a specific sum based upon the condition for which the person was admitted. This system is called the Prospective Payment System (PPS) and bases its payment on a classification of illnesses called Diagnostic Related Groups (DRG). With the former system of paying the individual's bill, physicians and hospitals were encouraged to keep patients longer. With the PPS system, early discharge is pushed.

27. Concerning the poverty rate for senior citizens, which of the following is correct?

    A. It has significantly increased over the last 25 years.
    B. It has been reduced primarily because of the indexing of social security.
    C. It has remained the same despite policy efforts to reduce it.
    D. It fell from 1980 to 1990, then rose again, approximating the level in 1980.

    B. The poverty rate for the elderly has been reduced, while the poverty rate for others has increased. The indexing of social security to inflation is considered among the major reasons for this change.

28. Following WWII, the United States instituted a massive effort to rebuild Europe. What is the name attached to this policy?

    A. the Marshall Plan
    B. NATO
    C. SEATO
    D. Point Four

    A. The Marshall Plan called for the reconstruction of Europe to prevent Soviet incursion. Point Four was aimed at developing countries. The other two — NATO and SEATO — were collective security agreements.

29. From recommendations of the 9/11 Commission, what change did Congress make in the U.S. national security structure?

    A. combined the CIA and the NSA
    B. made the National Security Council a cabinet department equal with State and Defense
    C. created an independent office of Director of Intelligence, a job previously performed by the director of the CIA
    D. removed the counter-intelligence function from the FBI and gave it to the CIA

    C. A separate Director of Intelligence was created to coordinate the 15 agencies in the intelligence community. Prior to this time, the Director of the CIA was also the Director of Intelligence. However, it was argued that it was difficult to be director of one agency in the intelligence community while also coordinating all agencies, because, in doing the latter role, the individual had little power. In establishing the new office, there was conflict over whether to give the new director personnel and budget authority. The final bill establishes limited budget authority.

30. Which of the following is not a statutory member of the National Security Council?

    A. vice president
    B. secretary of state
    C. secretary of defense
    D. chairman of the Joint Chiefs of Staff

    D. The National Security Council was established in 1947 to ensure that both military and diplomatic viewpoints were heard in making foreign policy. The statutory membership is limited. Others can be invited by the president to participate. For example, the secretary of the Treasury is often involved although not a statutory member. During the Ford Administration, legislation was enacted to add the Treasury secretary, but President Ford vetoed it, stating that he did not want to make the group too large. The chairman of the Joint Chiefs of Staff and the assistant to the president for national security affairs are both advisory and not statutory members.

31. Which of the following statements is correct regarding the War Powers Act?

  A. The Supreme Court has overturned the act as violating the president's commander in chief powers.

  B. Sanctions for violating the War Powers Act is a fine of $10,000 or imprisonment for not more than ten years.

  C. Presidents must seek a resolution from Congress to continue military action more than 60 days (90 if it is necessary to get the troops out safely).

  D. The act only allows a president to take defensive military actions without a resolution of approval from the Congress.

  C. The War Powers Act was enacted in 1973 over the veto of President Nixon. It allows the president to engage in military actions (also instituted if troops are moved into harm's way) for 60 days (90 to get troops out safely). The Congress must pass a resolution or the troops must come out. The Court has said that an appropriation to support the action constitutes a resolution supporting the engagement. The Supreme Court has never ruled on the constitutionality of the act, and there are no penalties specified in the act. Several presidents have questioned the constitutionality of the act but have followed it.

32. In the war on poverty, what did maximum feasible participation mean?

  A. The poor would serve on Community Action Agency (CAP) boards to develop community programs.

  B. The poor must receive services regardless of race or religion.

  C. Local governments must contribute the maximum percent of the cost of the program in order to be entitled to receive any federal funds.

  D. CAP boards must be elected in community elections with efforts made to maximize turnout.

  A. Maximum feasible participation was one of the most controversial aspects of the war on poverty. Its intent was to involve the clients — the poor — in the development of community programs. It was a fundamental shift in philosophy of having the programs developed for the poor by middle class reformers. The argument was that the poor knew the most about their problems, involvement would encourage a sense of community, and there would be more acceptance of programs they developed themselves. CAP boards challenged local government, which resulted in significant controversy for the program. Daniel Patrick Moynihan, political scientist and later senator from New York, wrote a book on the subject titled *Maximum Feasible Misunderstanding*.

33. What was the purpose of the *Federalist Papers?*

  A. to end slavery

  B. to convince conventions in the states to ratify the Constitution

  C. to serve as the original party platform of Washington and Adams, laying out their plans for the new nation

  D. to propose President Franklin D. Roosevelt's New Deal

  B. The *Federalist Papers* were written by Jay, Hamilton, and Madison. It was a series of newspaper pieces to encourage the ratification of the new constitution.

34. In Congressional elections, party loyalty is a variable that describes the largest percent of the vote. When someone votes for a candidate of the party opposite their party identification, what is the most frequent explanation for that vote?

  A. personality of the candidate

  B. issues raised in the election

  C. incumbency

  D. the state of the economy

  C. Incumbency has been a powerful force in congressional elections. Deviations from party go overwhelmingly to the incumbent. The incumbent typically has more money to spend, has the experience of past campaigns, has performed constituent service, and is better known than the challenger.

35. Concerning national turnout in presidential elections, which of the following is accurate?

    A. It is high, typically around 70 percent of the eligible voters.

    B. It typically is about 50 percent of the eligible voters.

    C. It is typically low, around 30 percent of eligible voters.

    D. It is very low at 15 percent.

B. National turnout in presidential elections is around 50 percent; some years in which the contest is close, the percentage is a bit higher. Turnout in local elections is even lower, sometimes no more than 15 percent.

36. Well known in American political history is the spoils system. What is it?

    A. the allocation of projects to districts of powerful members of Congress

    B. the expiration of programs after a specified time

    C. contracts given to large private corporations

    D. jobs given to supporters of winning candidates

D. The spoils system is based on the idea that jobs are given to supporters of the winning candidate. "To the victor belongs the spoils" is not dead, but such patronage has been reduced on the national level by civil service reforms, beginning with the Pendleton Act in 1883 that followed the assassination of President Garfield by a disappointed office seeker. State and local governments have civil service systems that vary in the completeness of their coverage.

37. Concerning economic inequality in the United States, which of the following is correct?

    A. The distribution of income has become more unequal in the last two decades.

    B. The distribution of income has remained relatively constant over the last two decades.

    C. The distribution of income has become more equal in the last two decades.

    D. The distribution is represented by a cycle — more unequal for a decade, and then more equal for the subsequent decade.

A. Income distribution has become more unequal. This was a focus of a recent American Political Science Association Task Force. Inequality can be shown on a Lorenz curve, which now bows further out, representing greater inequality. The area under the curve is measured by the Gini coefficient, which is an index of income inequality ranging between 0 (perfect equality) and 1 (absolute inequality).

38. The District of Columbia does not have voting representation in the Congress. Because the electoral votes are allocated based upon the number in the Congressional delegate, can they provide votes in the Electoral College?

    A. No. They have argued to be included for many years.

    B. Yes. The district's population is included with Maryland's for the purpose of voting for president.

    C. Yes. They have been given electoral votes equal to that of the smallest state (which is three).

    D. Yes. They are given electoral votes based upon their population, just like a state.

C. The District of Columbia secured the right to vote for president by the 23rd Amendment in 1961. The number of votes is specified as equal to that of the smallest state.

39. President Clinton was impeached by the House of Representatives but not convicted by the Senate. Could the federal prosecutor have indicted him on the same charges on which he was found innocent in the Senate trial?

    A. No. This would amount to double jeopardy.

    B. No. The Constitution specifically prohibits civilian trials of public officials found not guilty at impeachment trials.

    C. Yes. But only if the Senate approves by a two-thirds vote.

    D. Yes. The Constitution specially says that a person found guilty by the Senate can be subject to trial by law. By extension, a person found innocent could as well.

D. The Constitution (Article I, Section 3) specifically allows a person to be charged and tried for a crime even if he has been impeached. This has occurred with federal judges.

40. Concerning affirmative action in college admissions decisions, what has the Supreme Court ruled?

    A. That affirmative action is permissible if done in a systematic way, such as adding points to a minority's application for admission to school.

    B. That affirmative action is discriminatory and cannot be used.

    C. That affirmative action is permissible, and race can be taken into account in making admissions decisions.

    D. Affirmative action is permissible but must be limited to encourage minority applicants to apply and cannot be used for the final admission decision.

C. Since the Bakke case, the Supreme Court has allowed affirmative action. However, they have stated that there cannot be quotas or adding a specific number of points to a minority's application. The latter was a focus of the University of Michigan affirmative action decisions (*Gratz v. Bollinger* and *Grutter v. Bollinger*). D is not correct because the court did not limit affirmative action to simply encouraging applicants; it can be used as a factor in making decisions. In the two University of Michigan cases cited (those involving Bollinger), the Supreme Court said in the law school case that affirmative action could be used as an element in admission decision-making, but in the undergraduate case, where points were added based on race, the Supreme Court said that this method was impermissible.

41. A realigning election means

    A. that groups switch parties, and a new party comes out with a majority

    B. that an election has high turnout

    C. that an election has many competitive states (battleground states)

    D. that a third party wins the election, changing the party system

A. Realigning elections have been extensively discussed in the party literature. Clearly, 1932 was a realigning election. Speculation is that the election of George W. Bush could represent another, but we have not seen the massive change that occurred in previous realigning periods and it is uncertain whether the realignment will be long term. Some political scientists are considering this a realignment, while others are not sure.

42. What is the constitutional reason limiting the regulation of spending by campaigns?

    A. Elections are described in the Constitution and the addition of regulations would amount to adding provisions to the Constitution.

    B. Limiting spending would limit the right of association.

    C. Money is free speech, and you can't limit free speech.

    D. There is no constitutional reason. It is rarely been done because of political opposition.

C. The Supreme Court in *Buckley v. Valeo* limited the regulations of money in campaigns, arguing that to control spending would be tantamount to controlling speech, which is protected by the 1st Amendment.

43. What was the literacy test?

    A. the requirement under the No Child Left Behind Act that must be met for a school not to be labeled a "failing school"

    B. a test that must be passed to vote in a number of states before being outlawed. It frequently was used to deny blacks the right to vote.

    C. legislation that was ruled unconstitutional in 1920 that all individuals elected to Congress must be able read and write

    D. a requirement of immigrants in a number of states to be eligible for several benefit programs. The requirement is that they be literate in English. This is a backdoor method of declaring English as the nation's language.

B. The literacy test, among other means, was used by a number of states to keep blacks from voting. It tended to be implemented in an inequitable way. Whites were given simple tests, while blacks were given tests that required knowing provisions of their state constitutions. The 1965 Voting Rights Act suspended the test in many states, and this was extended in the 1970 Voting Rights Act.

Practice Tests

Directions: Following are three mini-practice tests. Select the choice that best answers each question. Fully explained answers follow each test.

Practice Test 1

1. How many Supreme Court justices are required to be appointed according to the Constitution?

    A. seven
    B. nine
    C. ten
    D. The Constitution does not specify the number.

2. Which of the following describes fiscal policy in the United States?

    A. the use of taxes and expenditures to control the economy
    B. the use of the interest rate by the Federal Reserve to regulate the economy
    C. the use of policy to improve the U.S trade balance
    D. the elimination of regulations to improve industrial competitiveness in the United States

3. How important is party voting in the U.S. Congress?

    A. Party voting was much stronger in the 1950s and 1960s than today.
    B. Party voting has been very weak in the U.S. Congress.
    C. Party voting has been very important in the last decades, much more important than in the 1950s and 1960s.
    D. Party voting has been strong for Republicans but not for Democrats.

4. Majority minority districts have been created, especially in the South, since the 1990s' reapportionment. What has the Supreme Court said about them?

    A. They are not allowed because they constitute a racial gerrymander.
    B. They are acceptable as long as race was not the primary factor in creating them.
    C. They are acceptable because they make up for past discrimination.
    D. They have not been allowed because the districts are not compact.

5. Which of the following gerrymanders has the Supreme Court said would be subject to court review but has never invalidated?

    A. racial gerrymander
    B. gerrymander to benefit incumbents
    C. gerrymanders to increase a city's representation
    D. party gerrymander

6. All proposed rules issued by regulatory agencies and departments must be published where?

    A. Federal Register
    B. Code of Federal Regulations
    C. Congressional Record
    D. U.S. Code

7. Safe Harbor Rules are issued by federal agencies. What are they?

    A. maritime rules
    B. rules on how to provide input into the rule-making process
    C. rules that say that if you follow them you will be in compliance with federal rules and statutes
    D. rules that the military must follow in a conflict

8. If no candidate for president gets a majority in the Electoral College, how is the president selected?

    A. by a majority of the 435 members of the House of Representatives
    B. by a majority of the Senate
    C. by a majority vote in the House of Representatives. Each state has one vote.
    D. by a majority of the House and Senate voting in a joint session

9. What is the difference between block grants and categorical grants?

    A. Block grants go to states, while categorical grants go to cities.
    B. Block grants allow states or cities to use the money as needed, while categorical grants must be used in a specific policy area such as health.
    C. Block grants require matching, while categorical grants do not.
    D. Block grants allow states or cities flexibility to use the money to meet needs in a broad policy area, while categorical grants aim the money at a more specific use.

10. In some states, laws have been passed to protect journalists' sources. What are these laws called?

    A. shield laws
    B. press protection laws
    C. 1st Amendment laws
    D. source protection acts

Answers to Practice Test 1

1. **D.** The Constitution in Article III does not specify the number of justices to be appointed. The Congress through its legislative power determines the number. Currently it is nine but historically, different numbers existed.

2. **A.** Fiscal policy refers to the use of taxes and expenditures to control the economy. These policies typically are recommended by the president but controlled by the Congress. The Congress is the one to change appropriations and taxes. Answer "B" refers to monetary policy, which is determined by the Federal Reserve. Both the trade balance and the economy's competitiveness are important; however, they are not referred to as fiscal policy.

3. **C.** Party voting has been very strong in the United States, especially since the Republicans took control of the majority in 1994. In earlier periods, such the 1950s and 1960s, although party was important, cohesion was far less (significantly less than in the British House of Commons). For the Democrats, party cohesion most notably was reduced by southern Democrats who voted more conservatively than their northern colleagues. Some political scientists thought it important to have strong party cohesion so that the wishes of voters could clearly translate into the Congressional majority, a school of thought known as the Responsible Party Model.

4. **B.** A number of states, especially in the South, created districts where African Americans (the minority) were a majority in the district. Some of these districts have strange shapes, including one that ran virtually the full length of North Carolina. The Supreme Court, in several decisions, especially *Shaw v. Reno,* allowed these districts but said that it must be shown that, although race could be taken into account, it could not be the predominant factor in drawing the district.

5. **D.** Gerrymandering is the drawing of districts to benefit a group. The Supreme Court has disallowed racial gerrymanders. The court has said that political party gerrymanders could be reviewed by the court, and they set up a tough standard. No party gerrymanders have been disallowed. Gerrymanders to benefit incumbents are frequent but have not resulted in court rulings. Gerrymanders to keep a city together in one district have been allowed for state legislatures even if they violate equal population (*Mahon v. Howell*).

6. **A.** All proposed rules issued by federal agencies are published in the Federal Register, allowing comments on these rules to be submitted. Once the rules have been approved, they are codified in the Code of Federal Regulations. The Congressional Record contains debates of the Congress. The U.S. Code is for federal laws (statutes) not rules.

7. **C.** Safe Harbor Rules are issued by regulatory agencies and commissions that say that if you follow them you are considered as abiding by the agency's rules and the applicable statutes. It has nothing to do with the military or maritime law.

8. **C.** The 12th Amendment specifies that the House of Representatives selects the president with voting by state, not by individual member. A majority of the states (26) are needed to elect the president.

9. **D.** Block grants are broad grants that give states or local governments flexibility to meet their needs. Categorical grants are much more specific and must be spent in the specific area (for example, tuberculosis screening) or for a specific project.

10. **A.** In some states, but not all, laws have been passed to allow journalists to protect their sources. These laws are called shield laws. There is not a shield law at the federal level.

Practice Test 2

1. You are a member of your state legislature. Your hometown newspaper has slandered you in an editorial. Can you sue?

   A. Yes. You can sue like any citizen.
   B. No. Public officials are not allowed to sue for newspaper editorials. They must accept accusations made, even if untrue.
   C. Yes, but only if you can prove that the newspaper knew what it said was not true and that you can prove malice in their publication of the falsehoods.
   D. Yes, but as a state public official, you cannot sue in state courts. You must sue in federal court to avoid conflict of interest.

2. What is the difference between an open and closed primary?

   A. In a closed primary, you can vote only in your party's primary. In an open primary, you can vote in either party's primary.
   B. In a closed primary, you can vote only in your party's primary. In an open primary, you can vote in both parties' primaries for the same office.
   C. In a closed primary, you can vote only in your party's primary. In an open primary, you can vote in both parties' primaries for different offices.
   D. In a closed primary, you must have registered to vote before the primary. Open party primaries do not require registration.

3. Political Action Committees (PACs) have increased in the last few decades. What are they?

   A. PACs often demonstrate for a group's interest.
   B. PACs represent groups in giving money to political candidates.
   C. PACs are groups similar to parties but with too few members to get on the ballot.
   D. PACs are committees of legislators promoting a particular bill.

4. Laissez-faire as a governmental philosophy means

   A. The government should regulate monopolies.
   B. The government should allow the market to do the regulation through the invisible hand.
   C. The national government should encourage state regulations rather than national regulation.
   D. The government should join with our trading partners to enact joint regulations.

5. Which one of the following is considered an uncontrollable in terms of federal spending?

   A. the Food Stamp Program
   B. the building of roads
   C. the payment of salary to federal workers
   D. money distributed in the No Child Left Behind Act

6. Job training is most likely to be applied to which of the following types of unemployment?

   A. frictional
   B. structural
   C. inadequate aggregate demand
   D. cyclical

7. Which kind of district system do we use for the election of members of Congress?

   A. multiple-member districts
   B. single-member districts
   C. proportional representation
   D. at-large systems

8. *Gideon v. Wainwright* was a precedent-setting case. What did it require?

   A. an end to segregation of the schools
   B. that public facilities be integrated
   C. that districts be equal in population
   D. that individuals have a right to counsel. If they are too poor, the state has to appoint one.

9. Devolution describes today's federalism. How are powers distributed?

   A. More power is given to the state government.
   B. More federal control is exercised.
   C. Money is given to cooperative regional groups.
   D. Money is given to private groups to administer government programs.

10. There has been a movement for mandatory term limits on legislators. Has it been applied to members of the Congress?

    A. No. The movement was restricted to state legislators.
    B. Yes, they tried, but it was ruled unconstitutional.
    C. Yes, and it is the law in several states.
    D. Yes. There is now a national term limit of 12 years on members of Congress.

Answers to Practice Test 2

1. C. Public figures may sue, but they have to prove that the person making the false statement knew that it was false and it was done maliciously. The requirement to prove slander is greater for those in the public eye, whether officials or actors, than those not. This was the decision in *New York Times v. Sullivan*.

2. A. Open primaries, such as in Wisconsin, allow the voter to vote without declaring a party affiliation but still must vote only in one party's primary. Closed primaries require the voter to declare a party affiliation (in many states, a number of days prior to the primary) and to vote only in his or her declared party's primary (this is true in Maryland). Only the blanket primary in Washington and Alaska allows voters to vote for candidates of different parties for different offices in the primary.

3. B. Political Action Committees (PACs) are formed by groups such as drug companies to contribute money to candidates' campaigns. They are restricted in how much they can contribute. One way around these limits is to form conduits, which bundle money from individual contributions to give to candidates. PACs have been controversial because of a concern that they unduly influence policy.

4. B. Laissez-faire is associated with Adam Smith in his book *The Wealth of Nations*. It indicates that the market will do the regulating and that government should avoid intervention. The invisible hand of the market will regulate.

5. A. The Food Stamp Program is considered an entitlement program, which are known as uncontrollables because those who meet the criteria can participate in the program. All the other types of spending are discretionary. Another uncontrollable is the interest on the U.S. debt.

6. B. Structural unemployment refers to unemployment because individuals lack skills required in the job market. (Structure refers to the structure or job demands of the market.) Frictional unemployment refers to people between jobs, and both inadequate aggregate demand and cyclical refer to unemployment because of a weakened economy.

7. B. Single-member districts are required. In some state legislatures there may be more than one representative from a district. This is called a multimember system.

8. D. This case was the major ruling that defendants had a right to counsel and if they could not afford one, one would be appointed at government expense. Many courts then used appointed counsel from members of the bar for indigent defendants. Public defenders offices were created in many states to provide this representation at the public's expense.

9. A. Devolution refers to the national government giving more power and discretion to the states. TANF (Temporary Assistance to Needy Families), which replaced AFDC (Aid to Families with Dependent Children), is an example.

10. B. The Supreme Court nullified term limits on members of Congress because it said that limits were not specified in the Constitution. To limit the number of terms served would add requirements to the Constitution on what it takes to be elected to Congress, something the Court said could not be done without a constitutional amendment.

Practice Test 3

1. How is much of the business of the Senate conducted?

    A. under a rule issued by the Senate Rules Committee
    B. through unanimous consent
    C. through a motion adopted by a two-thirds vote
    D. without any limitations, because the Senate operates under rules of unlimited debate

2. If the president is disabled and refuses to step aside, what can be done, according to the Constitution?

   A. nothing

   B. the Senate can suspend him from office by a two-thirds vote until they feel he is capable of serving. The vice president takes over as acting president.

   C. The vice president and majority of the heads of the executive departments must declare that the president is unable to discharge the duties of the office. In case the president chooses to dispute this, the Congress can keep the vice president as acting president by a two-thirds vote.

   D. The Congress, through a resolution adopted by a two-thirds vote, can by itself suspend the president.

3. What are 527 groups?

   A. state party committees whose finances are regulated by the states

   B. national party committees, regulated by the Federal Elections Commission

   C. groups not directly associated with political parties that have few campaign finance regulations

   D. conduits that bundle money to be given to candidates as donations

4. Political socialization refers to which of the following?

   A. a command economy

   B. newspaper coverage of political events

   C. Congressional review of administrative policies and practices

   D. learning of attitudes and information about a political system

5. What is political efficacy?

   A. It refers to the extent to which a policy reduces targeted problems.

   B. It refers to the power of the president to get his agenda enacted by the Congress.

   C. It refers to individuals feeling that they can effectively influence the political process and their votes are important.

   D. It refers to support that people have of the political system.

6. *U.S. v. Nixon* is an important case. What was its main point?

   A. The president can withhold some documents from the Congress but cannot simply declare executive privilege as a blanket right.

   B. The president can decide not to turn requested documents over to the Congress. Executive privilege is a fundamental tenet of the separation of powers doctrine.

   C. The president cannot withhold any documents demanded by Congress in furtherance of its constitutionally prescribed roles.

   D. Newspapers cannot be prohibited from publishing material. Prior censorship is not permitted by the 1st Amendment.

7. A rider refers to

   A. the consolidation of appropriations bills into one large omnibus bill

   B. the addition of specific tax exemptions to a general tax bill

   C. an amendment to a bill that is not germane to the subject of the bill

   D. stipulation in a bill that the program being passed must be administered in a particular way

8. What is a class-action suit?

   A. a law suit brought by poor people, where filing fees are waived

   B. a case that charges discrimination by an employer

   C. suits against private firms brought by public officials (for example, state attorneys general)

   D. a suit in which all individuals under similar circumstances are included

9. The initiative refers to

   A. the power of citizens to turn someone out of office prior to the end of his or her term
   B. the power of citizens to put a statute or a constitutional change directly on the ballot, bypassing the legislature
   C. state governments as laboratories of democracy
   D. the power of citizens to suspend a law enacted by the legislature

10. Which of the following best describes the exclusionary rule?

   A. Legislators having an economic interest in legislation are prohibited from voting on it.
   B. Judges must recuse themselves if they have a personal or economic interest in an item before the court.
   C. Groups that have been discriminated in the past are given preference for federal jobs or federal contracts.
   D. Evidence illegally seized cannot be used in court.

Answers to Practice Test 3

1. B. Senate consideration of bills is often done under unanimous consent motion(s). Rules issued by the Rules Committee are the way debate is structured in the House of Representatives.

2. C. The executive departments and vice president declare disability. In case of dispute, the Congress decides, and by a two-thirds vote can continue the vice president as acting president. This procedure was adopted in 1967 in the 25th Amendment.

3. C. 527 groups, named for the section of the Internal Revenue Code under which they fall, are less regulated than either candidate or party committees. These groups played a significant role in the 2004 presidential election. Conduits are groups that bundle campaign contributions from donors as a method to get around the limitations on Political Action Committee (PAC) donations.

4. D. Political socialization is the learning of beliefs and information about the political system. The early agents of socialization are family, school, and peer groups.

5. C. A person who is politically efficacious believes that he or she can have a say in the system. These citizens are confident that their votes count and can make a difference. Therefore, those with a greater sense of political efficacy are more likely to vote.

6. A. This case involved the Watergate tapes that President Nixon did not want to turn over to Congress. The Supreme Court said that executive privilege does exist but is not absolute. It is not clear in what cases it can be applied and what cases it cannot.

7. C. Riders are in order in the Senate but not in the House. They add a provision to a bill that has nothing to do with the bill. A rider may be added to gain the president's signature, save time to get the provision passed, or by-pass a particular committee.

8. D. Many individuals are typically included in a class-action suit. Many suits charge injury by a firm, such as against a medical equipment company, for faulty medical equipment.

9. B. A, B, and D are all methods of direct democracy. A is the recall and D is the referendum. B is the initiative. In some states the ballot measure is referred to as propositions.

10. D. Supreme Court cases recognized the exclusionary rule, excluding evidence that has been improperly obtained. The exclusion is based upon the 4th Amendment. However, in recent years, some exceptions to the rule have been granted where the illegal search was inadvertent. The exceptions are known as good-faith exceptions. The rule was first articulated in *Weeks v. United States* (1914). Good-faith exceptions can be found in two 1984 rulings: *United States v. Leon* and *Massachusetts v. Sheppard*.

United States Society

What You Should Know

In both the general and career track sections of the Job Knowledge test, the questions will require knowledge of a general understanding of U.S. society; that is, the major events that have taken place in U.S. history. You need to know the movements and institutions that were created as the country developed. You also need to understand U.S. political and economic history and recognize the major social issues and trends that have taken place over the years. You should also have an understanding of America's customs and how those customs are indicative of U.S. national culture. Finally, you want to understand how society plays a role in U.S. foreign policy and affairs.

The questions in the following section are for your review. Go through each question and try your best to answer it. The explanation of the answer follows immediately afterward so that you can actually learn new material. After you've completed reviewing these questions and answers, three brief practice review tests at the end of the chapter help you determine how much you know. Of course, there is a full-length exam at the end of Part II that also includes U.S. society questions.

United States Society Review Section

Read the following questions and select the choices that best answer the questions.

1. Which of the following statements regarding the 1924 Immigration Act (often called the Johnson Act) is not true?

   A. It placed annual limits on the number of persons who could legally immigrate to the United States.
   B. It took away the freedom of Asians to legally immigrate to the United States.
   C. It resulted in an increase in the percentages of immigrants from Northern and Western Europe and a decline in the percentages of immigrants from Eastern and Southern Europe.
   D. It resulted in a decline in the number of immigrants to the United States from countries in the Western Hemisphere.

   D. Because it placed no limits on the number of persons who could legally immigrate to the United States from countries located in the Western Hemisphere, the Johnson Act did not result in a decrease in the number of persons immigrating to the United States from countries in the Western Hemisphere. The Johnson Act did, however, place limits on the number of persons who could immigrate to the United States from countries located in other parts of the world, and it took away the freedom of Asians to legally immigrate to the United States. It led to an increase in the annual percentages of immigrants from Northern and Western Europe and a decline in the percentages of immigrants from Eastern and Southern Europe, because it specifically allowed for the annual percentages of immigrants from Western and Northern Europe to be higher than those from Eastern and Southern Europe.

2. Which of the following consisted of a coalition of various liberal and radical groups held together by the common goal of stopping the rise and spread of fascism and Nazism in Europe?

   A. the Wobblies
   B. the Progressives
   C. the Popular Front
   D. the National Front

   C. The Popular Front consisted of a coalition of various liberal and radical groups held together by the common goal of stopping the rise and spread of Fascism and Nazism in Europe. Wobblies was the name given to members of the Industrial Workers of the World, which during the early decades of the 20th century was involved in the mobilization of unskilled and immigrant workers. Members of the Progressive Party, as well as individuals who labeled themselves progressive, were generally in favor of the breaking up of trusts and of more extensive government efforts to improve the life conditions of the working and middle classes. Initially led by Enoch Powell, the National Front consists of British citizens opposed to increased immigration from Africa, Asia, and the Caribbean.

3. The G.I Bill, passed in 1944, is more officially know as the

    A. National Security Act
    B. Servicemen's Readjustment Act
    C. National Industrial Recovery Act
    D. Johnson Act

B. The G.I. Bill was passed (1944) as the Servicemen's Readjustment Act. The National Security Act (1947) placed the Army, Navy, and Air Force under the direction of the newly created Department of Defense. It also authorized the creation of the National Security Council and the CIA. The National Industrial Recovery Act (1933) mandated that codes of fair competitive and labor practices be drawn up for different U.S. industries. The Johnson Act (1924) placed limits on the number of persons who could immigrate to the United States during any given year.

4. Which of the following was not present at the Yalta Conference?

    A. Franklin Roosevelt
    B. Winston Churchill
    C. Charles De Gaulle
    D. Josef Stalin

C. Charles De Gaulle was not present at the Yalta Conference in 1945. Roosevelt, Churchill, and Stalin were present.

5. In 1950, communist-backed forces went from _____ to _____, prompting the United States to call for a United Nations sanction against the invasion.

    A. Cuba to Panama
    B. China to Tibet
    C. the Soviet Union to Poland
    D. North Korea to South Korea

D. In 1950, South Korea was invaded by communist-backed forces from North Korea, prompting the United States to call for the imposition of sanctions against the invaders.

6. _____ was President of the United States during the economic panic of 1929 that led to the Great Depression of the 1930s.

    A. Hoover
    B. Harding
    C. Roosevelt
    D. Coolidge

A. Herbert Hoover was President of the United States during the economic panic of 1929 that led to the Great Depression of the 1930s. Warren G. Harding was president from 1921 to 1923. Calvin Coolidge was President from 1923 to 1929. Franklin D. Roosevelt was President from 1933 to 1945.

7. _____ is the only person to have served as both vice-president and president of the United States without having been elected to either office.

    A.   Chester A. Arthur
    B.   Theodore Roosevelt
    C.   Calvin Coolidge
    D.   Gerald Ford

D. Gerald Ford is the only person to have served as both vice-president and president of the United States without having been elected to either office. He became vice-president upon the resignation of elected Vice-President Spiro Agnew, and president upon the resignation of President Richard Nixon. Arthur, Roosevelt, and Coolidge were each elected to the office of vice-president before becoming president.

8. Which of the following prohibited the manufacture, sale, transportation, import and export of intoxicating liquor?

    A.   the 18th Amendment
    B.   the 19th Amendment
    C.   the 20th Amendment
    D.   the Wagner Act

A. The 18th Amendment prohibited the manufacture, import and export of intoxicating liquor. The 21st Amendment (1933) repealed the 18th Amendment. The 19th Amendment (1920) gave women the right to vote. The 20th Amendment (1933) changed the dates on which members of Congress and the president and vice-president are inducted into office.

9. Which of the following is not true?

    A.   Before 1914, there were no legal controls or restrictions on the sale of opium or heroin.
    B.   Cocaine was an ingredient in early 20th century bottled Coca-Cola.
    C.   Before 1914, in most states, alcohol could be legally sold to persons younger than 14 years old.
    D.   Before the 1930s, there were no legal controls or restrictions on the use or possession of marijuana.

C. It is not true that before 1914, most states permitted the sale of alcoholic beverages to persons under 14 years of age. But it is true that before 1914, there were no legal controls or restrictions on the sale of opium or heroin, and that cocaine was an ingredient in early 20th century Coca-Cola. It is also true that before the 1930s, there were no legal controls or restrictions on the use or possession of marijuana.

10. Which of the following, regarding the CIA, is false?

    A.   It was created in response to the threat of a communist takeover of Greece and Turkey.
    B.   It was an outgrowth of the American policy of containment.
    C.   It was created during the presidency of Harry Truman.
    D.   It was created in response to the Soviet Union's launching of *Sputnik*.

D. The CIA came into existence in 1947; the *Sputnik* satellite was launched ten years later, in 1957. It was created during the presidency of Harry Truman, in response to the threat of a communist takeover in Greece and Turkey and as was, thereby, a direct outgrowth of America's policy of containment (of communism).

11. The _____ were a husband and wife team convicted of espionage on behalf of the Soviet Union.

    A.   Chambers
    B.   Whittakers
    C.   Rosenbergs
    D.   Hisses

C. Julius and Ethel Rosenberg were a husband and wife team convicted of espionage on behalf of the Soviet Union. As a result of charges made against him by Whittaker Chambers (a *Time* magazine employee), former

State Department official Alger Hiss was convicted (in 1950) of having committed perjury by denying that he had once sent copies of confidential state documents to the Soviet Union.

12. Which of the following is not true?

A. By the mid-1950s, R&B (rhythm and blues) had become widely popular among white youth and was banned on some radio stations in the South and other parts of the United States.

B. During the mid-1950s, R&B was picked up and fused with country music by Elvis Presley, Buddy Holly, Jerry Lee Lewis, and other white artists.

C. During the 1950s and 1960s, black artists more commonly covered (that is, recorded) songs first recorded by white performers than did white performers cover songs first recorded by black artists.

D. To call a song an R&B song today tells us much less about the race or ethnicity of the artist than it did during the 1950s.

C. During the 1950s and 1960s, it was more common for white artists to cover songs recorded by black artists than vice-versa. By the mid-1950s, R&B had become so popular among white youth that it was banned on some radio stations in the South and other parts of the country. During the mid-1950s, it was picked up and fused with country music by Elvis Presley, Jerry Lee Lewis, Buddy Holly, and other white artists. During the 1950s, it would have been accurate to state that to label a song R&B was to state that it was recorded by a black artist and was, therefore, popular among African Americans. But this is no longer true because, since the 1950s, there have been many popular white R&B artists — New Kids on the Block and Norah Jones — just to name two.

13. The Berlin Wall was in existence from

A. 1959 to 1988
B. 1961 to 1989
C. 1963 to 1989
D. 1961 to 1991

B. The Berlin Wall was in existence from 1961 to 1989.

14. The New Frontier was a plan for domestic social reform put forth during the presidential administration of

A. Theodore Roosevelt
B. John F. Kennedy
C. Lyndon B. Johnson
D. Ronald Reagan

B. The New Frontier was a plan for domestic social reform put forth during the presidential administration of John F. Kennedy.

15. _____ put forth the creation of The Great Society as one of the goals of his administration.

A. Theodore Roosevelt
B. Franklin Roosevelt
C. John F. Kennedy
D. Lyndon B. Johnson

D. Lyndon B. Johnson put forth the creation of The Great Society as one of the goals of his administration.

16. The Cuban Missile Crisis of 1962 ended when Secretary General of the Communist Party of the USSR, _____, finally agreed to remove nuclear missiles from Cuba under U.N. supervision.

A. Malenkov
B. Krushchev
C. Brezhnev
D. Andropov

B. Nikita Krushchev was the Secretary General of the Communist Party of the USSR who agreed to remove nuclear missiles from Cuba under U.N. supervision. George Malenkov was Krushchev's predecessor. Brezhnev and Andropov were his successors.

17. President John F. Kennedy was assassinated in November of

A. 1962
B. 1963
C. 1964
D. 1965

B. John F. Kennedy was assassinated in November of 1963.

18. _____ invented the first effective polio vaccine.

A. Jonas Salk
B. Albert Sabin
C. Wallace Sabine
D. Margaret Sanger

A. In 1952, Jonas Salk developed the first effective polio vaccine. During the late-1950s, Albert Sabin developed an oral polio vaccine. Wallace Sabin (1868–1919) created the science of architectural acoustics. Thus, a unit of sound-absorbing power is called the sabin in his honor. In 1921, Margaret Sanger founded the Birth Control League, which is now Planned Parenthood.

19. The *Feminine Mystique*, published in 1963, was written by

A. Betty Friedan
B. Bell Hooks
C. Patricia Hill Collins
D. Gloria Steinem

A. *The Feminine Mystique,* published in 1963, was written by Betty Friedan. Bell Hooks (actually she prefers that her name be presented in lower case) is a black scholar and feminist writer. Her first full-length book, *Ain't I a Woman: Black Women and Femininism*) was published in 1981. She has been a member of the faculties of Yale University, Oberlin College, and CCNY. Femininst and scholar Patricia Hill Collins is the author of numerous feminist books and articles, including *Black Feminist Thought: Knowledge, Consciousness, and the Politics of Empowerment.* Feminist author and lecturer Gloria Steinem helped establish the National Women's Political Caucus in 1971 and the Coalition of Labor Union Women in 1972. She also became the founding editor of *Ms.* Magazine in 1972. Among her published books are *Outrageous Acts and Everyday Rebellions* and *Moving Beyond Words.*

20. _____, a Democrat from Arkansas, was the first woman to be elected to the U.S. Senate.

A. Susan B. Anthony
B. Francis Perkins
C. Hattie Wyatt Caraway
D. Margaret Chase Smith

C. Hattie Wyatt Caraway, a Democrat from Arkansas, was the first woman to be elected to the U.S. Senate. Susan B. Anthony was a women's suffragette who, in 1869, along with Elizabeth Cady Stanton, founded the National Woman Suffrage Association, with the goal of obtaining the vote for women. Francis Person became Secretary of Labor in 1933, making her the first woman appointed to a presidential cabinet position. In 1940, Margaret Chase Smith was elected to serve out her husband's term as Congressman from Maine. In 1948, she was elected to the Senate, making her the first woman to serve in both chambers of Congress.

21. Which of the following, regarding the Strategic Arms Limitation Talks (SALT) is not true?

    A. They begin in 1969.

    B. The countries involved were the United States and the U.S.S.R.

    C. They ushered in a period of *détente* between the countries involved.

    D. They ceased to be held after the election of Richard Nixon.

D. It is not true that SALT ceased to be held after the election of Richard Nixon. They began in 1969 during his tenure of office. The countries involved were the U.S.S.R. and the United States, and the talks did usher in a period of détente (during the Nixon years) between the two countries.

22. The U.S. Secretary of Defense in 1967 was

    A. Dean Rusk

    B. William Westmoreland

    C. Robert McNamara

    D. Henry Kissinger

C. Robert McNamara was Secretary of Defense in 1967. Dean Rusk was Secretary of State. General William Westmoreland was in command of military forces in Vietnam. Henry Kissinger was called to serve as Secretary of State by Richard Nixon.

23. _____ was the first African American woman to run for president of the United States.

    A. Shirley Chisholm

    B. Angela Davis

    C. Carol Moseley Braun

    D. Lena Horne

A. Shirley Chisholm, Congresswoman from New York, was the first African American women to run for president. After a gun registered in Angela Davis's name was used during an aborted courtroom escape, the leftist African American activist was placed on the FBI's most wanted list. She did not, however, end up serving prison time. Carol Moseley Braun was an African-American woman who served as one of the U.S. senators from Illinois during the 1990s. During the 2004 presidential campaign, she campaigned to become the Democratic Party's presidential nominee. Lena Horne was a singer whose popularity was at its peak during the 1940s and 1950s.

24. The U.S. Supreme Court decision in *Roe v. Wade* followed from Norma McCorvey's lawsuit against the state of _____ for denying her the right to have an abortion.

    A. California

    B. Texas

    C. Georgia

    D. Mississippi

B. The U.S. Supreme Court's decision in *Roe v. Wade* followed from Norma McCorvey's lawsuit against the state of Texas for denying her the right to have an abortion.

25. Which of the following regarding the Pentagon Papers is not true?

    A. They were made public by Daniel Ellsberg.

    B. They were published in 1978.

    C. They were first published by the *New York Times*.

    D. They revealed that U.S. political and military leaders had been less than totally honest in their reports concerning the progress of the Vietnam War.

B. The Pentagon Papers were made public by Daniel Ellsberg and published in the *New York Times* in 1971. They revealed that U.S. political and military leaders had been less than totally honest in their reports concerning our military involvement in Vietnam.

26. The five burglars of the Watergate Hotel (1972) were attempting to

    A. remove fingerprints

    B. plant false documents

    C. steal documents

    D. bug telephones

    D. The five employees of the 1972 Nixon presidential campaign caught trying to burglarize Democratic Party offices in the Watergate Hotel were attempting to bug telephones.

27. In 1979, the U.S. embassy in_____ was stormed and 90 hostages were taken.

    A. Iran

    B. Iraq

    C. Pakistan

    D. Kenya

    A. In 1979, the U.S. embassy in Iran was stormed and 90 hostages were taken.

28. Operation Desert Storm began when invaders refused to withdraw from_____

    A. Iraq

    B. Iran

    C. Afghanistan

    D. Kuwait

    D. Operation Desert Storm began when invaders refused to withdraw from Kuwait.

29. In 1993, U.S. Black Hawk helicopters flew over _____, which is located in Somalia.

    A. Abijan

    B. Mogadishu

    C. Lagos

    D. Soweto

    B. In 1993, U.S. Black Hawk helicopters flew over Mogadishu, which is located in Somalia.

30. The 1995 Oklahoma City bombing caused the most extensive damage to a

    A. federal office building

    B. U.S. Post Office building

    C. hospital

    D. high school

    A. The 1995 Oklahoma City bombing caused the most extensive damage to a federal office building. No U.S Post Office building, hospital, or high school suffered damage.

31. On September 11, 2001, the World Trade Center in New York City was first hit by a

    A. Boeing 707

    B. Boeing 737

    C. Boeing 747

    D. Boeing 757

    D. On September 11, 2001, the World Trade Center in New York City was first hit by a Boeing 757.

32. Enron was based in which Texas city?

    A. Dallas

    B. Fort Worth

    C. Houston

    D. San Antonio

    C. Enron was headquartered in Houston, Texas.

33. Which of the following translates in English as "Holy War?"

    A. diaspora

    B. *coup d'etat*

    C. jihad

    D. Ramadan

    C. Jihad translates from Arabic into English as holy war. Diaspora is a word of Greek origin that translates into English as scattering or dispersion. *Coup d'etat* is a French language phrase, whose literal translation means attack on the state. Ramadan is the ninth month of the Islamic calendar. It is also the holy month during which faithful religious adherents of the Islamic faith observe a daily fast from dawn until sunset.

34. In December 2004, all of the following suffered extensive property damage and loss of human life from the effects of an earthquake-generated tsunami, except

    A. Sri Lanka

    B. Sumatra

    C. the Philippines

    D. India

    C. Sri Lanka, Sumatra, and India suffered extensive property damage and loss of human life from the effects of a December 2004 earthquake-generated tsunami. The Philippines did not.

35. America's first computer network was designed by

    A. the U.S. Department of Education

    B. the U.S. Department of Defense

    C. the U.S. Chamber of Commerce

    D. a group of Massachusetts Institute of Technology math and physics professors

    B. America's first computer network was designed by the Department of Defense.

36. America's first female Secretary of State was

    A. Margaret Chase Smith

    B. Janet Reno

    C. Madelyn Albright

    D. Condelezza Rice

    C. America's first female Secretary of State was Madelyn Albright, who was appointed to that position in 1997 by President Bill Clinton. Janet Reno was appointed to the office of Attorney General by President Bill Clinton (1992–2000). In 2005, Condelezza Rice became Secretary of State under newly reelected President George W. Bush.

37. Which of the following is not a signatory of the Kyoto Protocols mandating caps on the emission of greenhouse gases within the United States and Europe?

    A. France
    B. Great Britain
    C. Sweden
    D. the United States

    D. The United States is not a signatory of the Kyoto Protocols, which mandate caps on the emission of greenhouse gases within the United States and Europe.

38. Which of the following well-known Americans is not publicly known to have ever been charged with having committed a felonious crime?

    A. Michael Jackson
    B. Robert Blake
    C. Phil Spector
    D. Louis Farrakhan

    D. Louis Farrakan, the current leader of the Nation of Islam, is not known to have ever been charged with having committed a felonious crime. Robert Blake was charged with having murdered his wife. Phil Spector was charged with having murdered actress Lana Clarkson. Michael Jackson was charged with child molestation.

39. _____ constitute America's largest racial/ethnic minority group.

    A. Hispanics
    B. African-Americans
    C. Asian Americans
    D. Native Americans

    A. Persons classified by the U.S. Census Bureau as Hispanic (or Latino/Latina) now constitute America's largest ethnic group. Up until the beginning of the 21st century, persons classified as African American constituted the largest group.

40. Megan's Law requires that officers of the law and members of communities into which a _____moves be given advance notification.

    A. serial murderer
    B. sex offender
    C. person on house arrest
    D. person on community release

    B. Megan's Law requires that officers of the law and members of communities into which a sex offender moves be given advance notification.

41. _____ constitute the largest Hispanic group in the United States.

    A. Brazilian Americans
    B. CubanAmericans
    C. Mexican Americans
    D. Puerto Rican Americans

    C. Mexican Americans constitute America's largest Hispanic group. Approximately two-thirds (63 percent) of all U.S. citizens classified by the U.S. Census Bureau as Hispanic (or Latino/Latina) identified themselves as being of Mexican ancestry. Approximately ten percent are of Puerto Rican ancestry. Approximately eight percent are of Caribbean or other origin. The remainder are either of Cuban (5 percent) or Central and South American ancestry (14 percent).

42. Which of the following, regarding the Nation of Islam, also known as Black Muslims, is not true?

    A. It was brought into existence on the belief that the best way to attain justice for African Americans was to do everything possible to make Caucasians more aware of the immorality and unjustness of racial prejudice and discrimination.

    B. Its leaders have consistently advocated self-defense, self-help, and economic self-sufficiency for African Americans.

    C. During World War II, its leader (Elijah Muhammad) was imprisoned for counseling his followers not to serve in the U.S. Armed Forces.

    D. Its membership recruitment efforts — and consequently, its influence — have always been strongest and most successful among the least educated, culturally assimilated, and economically secure African Americans.

A. The Nation of Islam was founded in the early-1930s by W.D. Fard and Elijah Muhammad; one of its most basic premises was that racism was so deeply ingrained in Caucasian Americans that it was naïve to think that they could be made aware of the unjustness of racial prejudice and discrimination. One of the Nation of Islam's aims was to attain cultural as well as territorial separation from Caucasians. Leaders of the Nation of Islam have consistently advocated that African Americans organize into self-defense groups while working to gain economic independence from mainstream Americans. The Nation of Islam's membership efforts — and, consequently, its influence — have been weakest and less successful among the *most* educated, culturally assimilated, and economically secure African Americans. Its leader during the 1940s, Elijah Muhammad, was imprisoned during World War II for counseling his followers not to serve in the U.S. Armed Forces.

43. Which of the following, regarding the U.S. Supreme Court decision in *Brown v. Topeka Board of Education,* is not true?

    A. Its main objective was to put the United States on a path that would lead to the creation of a truly culturally pluralistic society.

    B. It led to more open racial conflict and hostilities in the South.

    C. Attempts to implement it brought American race relations to the forefront as both a national and international issue.

    D. Attempts to implement it involved a great many Caucasians in efforts to desegregate public schools, as well as in the staging of ride-ins, sit-ins, and voter registration drives.

A. The terms culturally pluralistic or cultural pluralism do not appear in any Supreme Court judge's opinion in the *Brown v. Topeka Board of Education* decision. From all indications, the intent of the decision was not to preserve African American cultural heritage. Its intent appears to have been to make African Americans fully (socially, politically and economically) integrated members of U.S. society — which, if achieved, could actually cause the loss of some distinctly African American linguistic and other cultural characteristics. The decision led to more open racial conflict and hostilities in the South, as some southern Caucasians engaged in violent acts of resistance to attempts to integrate schools and other public accommodation facilities. A great many Caucasians, along with a great many African Americans, were also physically involved in efforts to desegregate public schools, as well in the staging of ride-ins and sit-ins staged to integrate trains, buses, lunch counters, and other public accommodation facilities. The ride-ins, sit-ins, and attempts to desegregate schools received extensive coverage by foreign media, which is one reason Martin Luther King, Jr. was sufficiently well-known abroad to become the recipient of the 1964 Nobel Peace Prize.

44. Unreasonable searches and seizures are prohibited by which of the following amendments to the U.S. Constitution.

    A. 1st

    B. 2nd

    C. 4th

    D. 13th

C. The 4th Amendment makes unreasonable searches and seizures unlawful. The 1st Amendment guarantees freedom of religion, speech, press and assembly. The 2nd Amendment gives citizens the right to bear arms. The 13th Amendment abolished slavery.

Practice Tests

Directions: Following are three mini-practice tests. Select the choice that best answers each question. Fully explained answers follow each test.

Practice Test 1

1. Tobacco was first brought back to Europe from America by

    A. Christopher Columbus
    B. Sir Walter Raleigh
    C. Captain John Smith
    D. Lord Baltimore

2. The first permanent English settlement in the New World was

    A. Jamestown
    B. Plymouth
    C. Roanoke Island
    D. Concord

3. The first group of Puritan separatists (from the Church of England) to land in what is now Massachusetts and establish the Plymouth Colony in 1620 were the

    A. Antidisestablishmentarians
    B. Mennonites
    C. Pilgrims
    D. Quakers

4. Historians generally agree that the first Africans brought to the Americas arrived in 1619 on a _____ ship

    A. Dutch
    B. Portuguese
    C. British
    D. French

5. In 1836, after being banished from Massachusetts due to his advocacy for greater religious freedom, Puritan minister _____ went south, where he established the first settlement in what is now Rhode Island.

    A. John Winthrop
    B. Roger Conant
    C. Roger Williams
    D. Thomas Hooker

6. Which of the following churches traces its origins back to the Puritans?

    A. Presbyterian
    B. Episcopal
    C. Methodist
    D. Congregationalist

7. _____ was the first U.S president to be born after the United States declared its independence from Britain.

   A. Thomas Jefferson
   B. George Washington
   C. Andrew Jackson
   D. Martin Van Buren

8. Which of the following, regarding members of the Federalist Party, is not true?

   A. Alexander Hamilton was one of their early leaders.
   B. They stood as representatives and supporters of urban mercantile interests.
   C. They were in favor of the establishment of a national bank.
   D. They were in favor of the establishment of a strong central government.

9. During the War of 1812, British troops burned down the city of

   A. Philadelphia
   B. Boston
   C. Hartford
   D. Washington

10. Which of the following regarding President Lincoln's Emancipation Proclamation is not true?

   A. It gave rise to the Civil War, causing eleven states to secede from the Union and form the Confederate States of America.
   B. The only slaves it freed were those residing in the states that seceded from the Union.
   C. It was one of the precipitators of the New York City draft riots.
   D. It helped prevent Britain and France from intervening in the American Civil War on the side of the Confederacy.

Answers to Practice Test 1

1. **B.** Tobacco was first brought back to Europe from America by Sir Walter Raleigh, for whom the city of Raleigh, North Carolina, located in America's tobacco belt, was named. Raleigh also established the first British colony in North America, located on Roanoke Island off the coast of North Carolina. John Smith was the military commander (1607–1609) of the Jamestown settlement. After obtaining a charter from King Charles I, Lord Baltimore came to North America, where he founded the colony of Maryland.

2. **A.** Settled in 1607, Jamestown was the first permanent English settlement in the New World. The Roanoke Island colony, established in 1585 by Sir Walter Raleigh, was short-lived, lasting less than two years. The first group of Pilgrims arrived in what is now Massachusetts and established the Plymouth Colony in 1620. Colony status was never conferred on the Massachusetts town of Concord, the scene of a 1775 colonial militiamen victory over the Redcoats.

3. **C.** The first group of Puritan separatists (from the Church of England) to land at what became the Plymouth Colony were the Pilgrims. As the name suggests, an antidisestablishmentarian stands in opposition to the withdrawal of government support or recognition from an established church. The Mennonites trace their origins back to 16th century Europe and are the forefathers of today's Amish, who descend from the followers of Jacob Amman, a 17th century Swiss Mennonite bishop.

4. **A.** Historians generally agree that the first Africans brought to America arrived in 1619 on a Dutch ship. This is so because there exist no records of prior arrivals of Africans.

5. **C.** Roger Williams established the first settlement in what is now Rhode Island. John Winthrop was prominent among the members of the Massachusetts Bay Company, who founded Boston in 1630. Thomas Hooker, a minister whose views were similar to those of Roger Williams, led his followers out of Massachusetts into Connecticut, where they founded the city of Hartford. Roger Conant was the leader of the group of Puritans who founded the city of Salem, Massachusetts.

6. **D.** The present-day Congregationalists are the religious descendants of the Puritans. Present-day Episcopalians are still aligned with the Church of England. The Presbyterian Church was founded in Scotland by adherents to the teachings of John Calvin. The first American Presbyterian congregation was established in 1684, in Snow Hill, Maryland, by Francis Makemie. The Methodist Church was founded by English evangelist John Wesley, who lived from 1703 to 1801.

7. **C.** Born in 1782, Martin Van Buren was the first president to be born after the colonists declared their independence from Britain, and thus was America's first native-born president. Washington, Jefferson, and Jackson were born, respectively, in 1732, 1743, and 1767, and thus came into the world as British subjects.

8. **B.** It is not true that the Federalist Party and its early leaders stood as representatives and supporters of urban mercantile interests. They represented rural agrarian interests. But Alexander Hamilton was one of their early leaders, and they were in favor of the establishment of a national bank and a strong central government.

9. **D.** During the War of 1812, British troops burned down the city of Washington.

10. **A.** It is not true that Lincoln's Emancipation Proclamation caused eleven states to secede from the Union and form the Confederate States of America. The Emancipation Proclamation was issued in 1863; the states seceded and formed the Confederate States of America in 1861. It is true, however, that the only slaves freed by the Proclamation were those residing in the states that seceded from the Union. The Proclamation was also one of the precipitators of the New York City draft riot, as many Irish workers turned against that city's African American population in violent protest of having to fight in the Union Army to free the slaves, so that — in the minds of the rioters — the freed slaves could come north as free men and women and compete for the rioters' jobs. The rioters were also resentful of the fact that because they were too poor to buy their way out the draft, they were disproportionately represented among Union Army troops. The Proclamation helped prevent Britain and France from intervening in the war on the side of the Confederacy, because having freed all slaves residing in their territorial possession, both countries had since become advocates of the abolition of slavery in all parts of the world. The Emancipation Proclamation made the American Civil War a war to abolish slavery, rather than one caused by disagreements as to whether the seceded or any other American states had the Constitutional right to withdraw from the Union.

Practice Test 2

1. One of the results of the Bargain of 1876 was that

   A. Ulysses S. Grant became president of the United States.
   B. Rutherford B. Hayes became president of the United States.
   C. Chester A. Arthur became president of the United States.
   D. James A. Garfield became president of the United States.

2. Which of the following, regarding 19th century American Social Darwinists, such as Herbert Spencer and John Fiske, is not true?

   A. They believed that native intellectual abilities varied among individuals, but not among "races."
   B. The believed that a laissez-faire economic system provided equality of opportunity and guaranteed the survival of the fittest.
   C. The believed that wealthy industrialists contributed more to society than did relatively poor, unskilled workers.
   D. William Graham Sumner was also one of their most influential spokespersons.

3. Which of the following regarding 19th century Populists is not true?

    A. They viewed both the Democratic and Republican parties as servants of the monopolists and finance capitalists.

    B. They saw themselves as representatives of farmers and agricultural workers, as well as factory workers.

    C. By the 1890s, their leaders were supportive of efforts to disenfranchise African Americans and of laws mandating racial segregation.

    D. The believed that America's laissez-faire economic system provided equal opportunity for white Americans, but not for non-white minorities.

4. Which of the following U.S. Supreme Court decisions gave legitimacy to separate but equal schools and other public accommodation facilities?

    A. *Marbury v. Madison*

    B. the Dread Scott decision

    C. *Plessy v. Ferguson*

    D. *Myers v. United States*

5. Which of the following, regarding the No-Nothings, is not true?

    A. The wanted to restrict the immigration of Catholics into America.

    B. They were supporters of the back-to-Africa movement.

    C. In 1856, they ran former president of the United States, Millard Fillmore, as their candidate for president.

    D. They believed in the superiority of a white, Anglo-Saxon culture.

6. _____ was president of the United States in 1883, when Congress passed the Pendleton Act, thereby establishing a Civil Service Commission to administer a merit-based U.S. Civil Service.

    A. Rutherford B. Hayes

    B. James A. Garfield

    C. Chester A. Arthur

    D. Grover Cleveland

7. Which of the following did not occur as a result of the signing of the Treaty of Guadalupe Hidalgo in 1848?

    A. The United States acquired approximately one-third of its present mainland territory.

    B. The United States paid Mexico officials approximately $15 million in gold.

    C. Former Mexican nationals on the land taken over by the United States were given the option of becoming U.S. citizens.

    D. Former Mexican nationals on the land taken over by the United States were granted the right to be educated in Spanish.

8. In order to protect them from formal legal discrimination on the basis of race, in 1917 President Wilson issued a presidential decree designating _____ as Caucasian.

    A. Puerto Ricans

    B. Mexicans

    C. Cubans

    D. Filipinos

9. The American film industry rose to a position of world dominance, producing more than half of all films shown in the world, during

    A. the decade before the beginning of World War 1
    B. World War 1
    C. the 1920s
    D. the decade after World War II

10. The _____ raids, launched in response to the Red Scare of the 1920s, were so-called because they were authorized and overseen by U.S. Attorney General _____.

    A. Wendell Willkie
    B. John Mitchell
    C. John J. Pershing
    D. Mitchell Palmer

Answers to Practice Test 2

1. **B.** One of the results of the Bargain of 1876 (between leaders of the Democratic and Republican parties) was that Rutherford B. Hayes became President of the United States. Ulysses S. Grant occupied the office of president from 1873 to 1877; James A. Garfield from March 4, 1881 to September 19, 1881; Chester A. Arthur from 1881 to 1885.

2. **A.** Social Darwinists believed that native intellectual abilities varied among "races," as well as among individuals. They also believed that a laissez-faire (which literally means to allow to act) economic system provided equality of opportunity and guaranteed the survival of the fittest; and that wealthy industrialists contributed more to society than did relatively poor, unskilled workers. William Graham Sumner was one of their most influential spokespersons.

3. **D.** The Populists did not believe that an unbridled laissez-faire economic system provided equal opportunities to either African Americans or most Caucasians. They viewed both the Democratic and Republican parties as servants of the monopolists and finance capitalists, and they saw themselves as representatives of small farmers and agricultural workers, as well as factory workers. Although they started out as advocates of racial equality, by the 1890s, Populist leaders were in adamant support of efforts to disenfranchise African Americans and of laws mandating racial segregation.

4. **C.** *Plessy v. Ferguson* was the U.S. Supreme Court decision that gave legitimacy to separate but equal schools and other public accommodations. In its decision in *Marbury v. Madison* (1803), the Supreme Court gave itself the right to review the constitutionality of acts of Congress. In the Dread Scott decision, the Supreme Court ruled that African Americans were not citizens and that Congress did not have the right to make laws prohibiting slavery in any territory. In *Myers v. United States* (1926), the Supreme Court ruled that the president had the right to fire executive branch employees, thereby making null and void the Tenure of Office Act of 1867 that was brought forth to impeach Andrew Johnson.

5. **B.** The No-Nothings are not known to have been involved in the back-to-Africa movement of either the 1830s or 1920s. They were, however, in favor of restricting the immigration of Catholics to the United States. Former U.S. President Millard Fillmore was their presidential candidate in the 1856 election. They also believed in the superiority of white, Anglo-Saxon culture.

6. **C.** Chester A. Arthur was president of the United States in 1883, when Congress passed the Pendleton Act, which established a Civil Service Commission to administer a merit-based civil service. Hayes was president from 1877 to 1881. Garfield was president from March 1881 to September 1881. Cleveland was president from1893 to 1897.

7. **D.** The Treaty of Guadalupe Hidalgo did not grant former Mexican nationals residing on the land ceded to the United States the right to be educated in Spanish. But it did result in the U.S. acquiring approximately one-third of its present-day North American continental territory. Implementation of the treaty was also contingent on a $15 million payment to Mexican government officials. Former Mexican nationals on the land taken over by the United States were given the option of becoming U.S. citizens.

8. B. In order to protect them from legal discrimination on the basis of race, President Wilson, in 1917, issued a presidential decree officially designating Mexicans as Caucasians.

9. B. By 1915 — that is, before America's one-year involvement in World War 1 — more than half of all movies shown in the world were produced in the United States. This was partly so because, during the World War 1, film production came to an almost total halt in the warring European countries.

10. D. The Palmer raids were so-called because they were launched under the authority and direction of U.S. Attorney General Mitchell Palmer. John Pershing was the commanding general of the American Expeditionary Force during World War 1. John Mitchell was Attorney General during the Nixon Presidency (1969 to 1974). Wendell Wilkie was the 1940 Republican presidential candidate.

Practice Test 3

1. According to statistics released in 2005, _____ is now the leading cause of death of Americans under 85 years of age.

    A. heart disease

    B. cancer

    C. Alzheimer's disease

    D. emphysema

2. Approximately _____ of all American students who began their first year of college do not return to begin their second year of college.

    A. one-half

    B. one-third

    C. one-fourth

    D. one-eighth

3. Which of the following is the first Latino to serve as U.S. Attorney General?

    A. Cesar Chavez

    B. Alberto Gonzales

    C. Orlando Cepeda

    D. Vincente Fox

4. _____ was the first state to abolish slavery.

    A. Massachusetts

    B. Rhode Island

    C. Pennsylvania

    D. Vermont

5. On February 1, 2003, the NASA space shuttle _____ exploded over the state of Texas as it returned to Earth, killing all seven astronauts on board.

    A. *Columbia*

    B. *Challenger*

    C. *Intrepid*

    D. *Sputnik*

6. There is a nuclear weapons laboratory located in all but which of the following cities?

    A. Los Alamos, New Mexico

    B. Sandia, New Mexico

    C. Livermore, California

    D. Lodge Pole, Nebraska

7. Which of the following, regarding present-day members of the present-day Amish Americans is not true?

    A. They are direct descendants of the Anabaptists of 16th century Europe.

    B. They are largely of Scottish extraction.

    C. They began arriving in America during the early 18th century.

    D. At present the largest numbers reside in Pennsylvania and Ohio.

8. Which of the following American artists (that is, painters) is generally recognized as one of the initiators of action painting or Abstract Expressionism?

    A. Jackson Pollock

    B. Jan Vermeer van Delft

    C. John Singleton Copley

    D. Matthew Paris

9. America's major television networks rely primarily on the _____ ratings to determine the size and demographic characteristics of their nationally telecast television programs.

    A. Nielsen

    B. Arbitron

    C. Gallup

    D. Field

10. According to recent U.S. Census data, which of the following is not true?

    A. The number of women enrolled at four-year colleges is now larger than the number of men enrolled at four-year colleges.

    B. During the past few years, more men than women received associate's (two-year college) degrees.

    C. During the past few years women have received more master's degrees than have men.

    D. During the past few years, the number of men who earned degrees in engineering and the physical sciences outnumbered the number of women who earned degrees in these fields.

Answers to Practice Test 3

1. D. According to 2005 data from the American Cancer Association, cancer is now the leading cause of death of Americans under 85 years old. Heart disease is now the second leading cause. Alzheimer's and emphysema are neither the first nor the second leading cause.

2. B. According to 2004 U.S. Bureau of Census data, one-third of all Americans who begin their first year of college do not return the following year to begin their second year of college.

3. B. Alberto Gonzales is the first Latino U.S. Attorney General. Cesar Chavez was a Latino civil rights activist and founder of the United Farm Workers union. Orlando Cepeda is a former professional baseball player. Vincente Fox is the president of Mexico.

4. C. Pennsylvania was the first state to abolish slavery. Slavery had already been abolished in Massachusetts, Rhode Island, and Vermont before the American Civil War, but Pennsylvania was the first U.S. state to abolish slavery.

5. **A.** On February 1, 2003, the U.S. space shuttle *Columbia* exploded over Texas, thereby killing all seven astronauts on board. The destruction of the space shuttle *Challenger,* killing all seven crew members, occurred on January 28, 1986. There has been no space shuttle named *Intrepid. Sputnik* was the first space satellite launched by the Soviet Union (in 1957).

6. **D.** There are nuclear weapons laboratories in Los Alamos, New Mexico; Sandia, New Mexico; and Livermore, California. There is no nuclear weapons laboratory located in Lodge Pole, Nebraska.

7. **B.** The present-day Amish are not largely of Scottish extraction. They are largely of Germanic-Swiss extraction. They are the direct descendants of the Anabaptist of 16th century Europe who, among other things, rejected infant baptism, advocated complete freedom of religious belief and practice, believed in the separation of church and state, and were pacifists opposed to military service of any kind. They began arriving in American in sizable numbers during the early 18th century, when their first permanent settlements were established in Pennsylvania. The largest local concentrations of Amish are in Holmes County, Ohio, and Lancaster County, Pennsylvania. Although the U.S. Census Bureau does not track the U.S. Amish population, estimates by journalists and scholars place their population as approximately 200,000, spread out across more than twenty states.

8. **A.** According to renowned art historian E.H. Gombrich, American painter Jackson Pollock "is widely recognized as one of the initiators of action painting or Abstract Impressionism." Jan Vermeer van Delft was a 17th century Dutch painter known for his richly colorful still-life paintings. John Ruskin was an influential art critic of the 19th century. Matthew Paris lived during the 13th century and is, among other things, known for having drawn the first elephant — sent by St. Louis, King of France, to Henry III in 1255 — to have been seen in England.

9. **A.** America's major television networks rely primarily on data collected by the A.C. Nielsen organization to determine the size and demographic characteristics of the viewers of its nationally telecast television programs. Arbitron measures the size of radio audiences in local markets. The Gallup organization conducts national polls and surveys of, among other things, political and social attitudes and behaviors, as well as lifestyle trends. Based in California, the Field organization conducts polls and surveys that focus primarily on the social and political attitudes and lifestyle trends of Californians.

10. **B.** B is not true, because during the past several years, more women than men have been recipients of two-year college degrees. But it is true that more women than men are enrolled in four-year colleges. It is also true that more women than men have, during the past few years, received more master's degrees than have men. And it is also true that, at present, the number of men earning degrees in the physical sciences and engineering is greater than the number of women earning degrees in these fields.

World History and Geography

What You Should Know

In both the general and career track sections of the Job Knowledge test, the questions will require knowledge of a general understanding of world history and geography — the major significant events that have taken place in the world. You want to study issues and developments around the world, especially their impact on U.S. foreign policy. You are also required to have a knowledge of world geography and its relationship to U.S. foreign policy. This also includes an understanding of the natural resources throughout the world, and how these resources affect national rivalries and alliances and how they have led to local and international conflicts.

The questions in the following section are for your review. Go through each question and try your best to answer it. The explanation of the answer follows immediately afterward so that you can actually learn new material. After you've completed reviewing these questions and answers, three brief practice review tests at the end of the chapter help you determine how much you know. Of course, there is a full-length exam at the end of Part II that also includes world history and geography questions.

World History and Geography Review Section

Read the following questions and select the choices that best answer the questions.

1. The 1978 Iranian Revolution, which overthrew the shah and resulted in the establishment of an Islamic Republic,

   A. took Western diplomats largely by surprise
   B. was driven by frustration with Iran's lack of economic development and modernization
   C. was sparked by President Jimmy Carter's decision to admit the shah to the United States for medical treatment
   D. put Sunni Muslim clerics in control of the government

   A. Most diplomats were taken by surprise by the depth and swift speed of the revolution. The shah was not admitted to the United States for treatment until after he had fled the country, although this incident did incite the kidnapping of the 52 American hostages at the U.S. Embassy. Iran came to be controlled by Shi'ite rather than Sunni clerics.

2. Although the 1917 Balfour Declaration pledged British support for an eventual Jewish state, Britain strictly limited Jewish immigration to Palestine before 1948

   A. to placate anti-Zionist sentiments in Britain
   B. to encourage Jewish immigration to the less contentious British colony of Uganda
   C. to keep from alienating Arab leaders
   D. to maintain pressure on the United States to accept higher numbers of refugees

   C. The British government had many motives for limiting Jewish immigration to Palestine, but the most compelling was the desire to not antagonize Arab leaders.

3. With the expulsion of the Kuomintang from China in 1949,

    A. the Chinese Communist Party moved quickly to secure its power in China by instituting the Cultural Revolution

    B. Chaing Kai-shek was overthrown as leader of the Kuomintang

    C. the Nationalists withdrew to the Island of Formosa

    D. Chairman Mao initiated conversations with the Truman Administration to normalize relations

    C. The Nationalists, or the Kuomintang Party, led by Chaing Kai-shek, fled to the Island of Formosa.

4. Which of the following countries never belonged to the Warsaw Pact?

    A. Bulgaria

    B. Hungary

    C. Czechoslovakia

    D. Yugoslavia

    D. Yugoslavia's leader, Josip Broz Tito, won power in Yugoslavia with minimal assistance from the Soviets, and thus was able to resist Stalin's pressure to join the Soviet Bloc military alliance.

5. Although it came to symbolize the entire Cold War conflict, the Berlin Wall was built with what narrower purpose?

    A. to stop residents of the Soviet sector of Germany from fleeing to the West

    B. as a preliminary step to imposing the Berlin Blockade

    C. to embarrass President Truman

    D. to undermine efforts by the East German government to improve relations with the West

    A. Throughout the 1950s, residents of the Soviet sector of Berlin had been able to flee to the West by doing little more than crossing the street or catching a bus. In order to stem this embarrassing flow of defectors, the Berlin Wall, cutting off West Berlin from the rest of East Germany, was built in 1961.

6. With international recognition of the Congo Free State by the Berlin Congress in 1885, responsibility for governing the Congo

    A. fell by default to the government of Belgium

    B. was returned to the tribal chiefs of the Congo

    C. was shared by Belgium, France, and Britain

    D. was held personally by Belgium's King Leopold II

    D. Leopold, not the Belgian government, was recognized as sovereign over the Congo Free State until 1908 when, after an international outcry about human rights abuses, sovereignty was transferred to Belgium.

7. The Fashoda Crisis of 1896 brought which two great powers to the brink of war?

    A. Russia and Britain

    B. France and Germany

    C. France and Britain

    D. Britain and the United States

    C. French troops under Marchand, hoping to stymie Britain's plans for a Cape to Cairo railroad, made their stand at the remote Sudanese village of Fashoda. British troops under Kitchener contested their presence until an international agreement defused the crisis and averted war.

8. Cecil Rhodes (1853–1902) advocated what broad goal for British involvement in Africa?

   A. the establishment of autonomous English-speaking dominions, on the model of Australia and Canada, throughout Africa

   B. the creation of a continuous line of British possessions connecting Capetown with Cairo

   C. greater respect for indigenous African institutions

   D. greater cooperation with other European powers

B. The most outspoken of British imperialists, the South African magnate and politician advocated a line of British colonies, eventually linked by rail, connecting the Cape of Good Hope with the Mediterranean.

9. The French decision to support the nascent United States against Britain in the American Revolutionary War was most decisively motivated by

   A. French Enlightenment thinking

   B. French perceptions that an independent United States would counterbalance British power in the Atlantic

   C. French hostility to Britain in the aftermath of the Seven Years War

   D. French confidence that the Americans would win with or without French support

C. The French monarchy was aware of, but not much influenced by, the Enlightenment's political demands. Few in Europe or America thought that the United States could win without French support. France aided the American revolutionaries out of an abiding hostility to England that was reinforced in the Seven Years War.

10. The Seven Years War (1756–1763) went by what name in North America?

   A. King William's War

   B. Queen Anne's War

   C. the French and Indian War

   D. the War of Jenkins's Ear

C. Unlike earlier Continental wars that spilled over into North America and the Caribbean, the Seven Years War was motivated by conflicting colonial aims. Thus, the Americans came to know it as the French and Indian War.

11. During the Tokugawa Shogunate (1603–1868), Japan's government

   A. sought to keep outside influences from reaching Japan as much as possible

   B. was frustrated in its efforts to expand Japanese influence into Asia

   C. encouraged immigration in order to limit population growth

   D. encouraged the efforts of Jesuit and other Christian missionaries

A. The Tokugawa shoguns adopted a policy of cultural, economic, and political isolation and allowed minimal, and very controlled, contacts between Japanese merchants and the outside world. Christian missions were forbidden altogether.

12. A fundamental difference between the colonialism of the 18th century and that of the 19th was that

   A. Nineteenth-century colonial policies, unlike those of the 18th, focused on controlling raw materials and markets.

   B. Nineteenth-century colonial powers, unlike those of the 18th, often claimed land simply to keep it away from a competing power.

   C. Nineteenth-century colonial powers, unlike those of the 18th, established colonies in locations that were unlikely to ever support a substantial European population.

   D. Nineteenth-century colonial policies were more indifferent to the presence of indigenous people than were those of the 18th.

C. Eighteenth century colonies, such as those in North America, Australia, and Cape Colony, were seen as extensions of the home country; indigenous people were swept aside or enslaved. Nineteenth century colonization focused on places such as Africa and Southeast Asia, where Europeans would likely never live in substantial numbers. Most such colonies remained indifferent to indigenous people, but were not more indifferent.

13. The French Revolution bore what relation to the American Revolution?

   A.   It preceded and partially shaped the American Revolution.
   B.   Like the American Revolution, it was inspired by Enlightenment thinking.
   C.   It bore only a superficial relationship to the American Revolution.
   D.   Unlike the American Revolution, which was political and economic in nature, it was a product of the Enlightenment.

   B. Both the American and French Revolutions were inspired and shaped by Enlightenment thinking. The American Revolution started in 1776; the French Revolution began 13 years later. Both were motivated and shaped in part by political and economic factors, as well as Enlightenment ideology.

14. The First Opium War (1839–1842) was a result of

   A.   the Chinese government's efforts to halt the importation of opium into China by British and other merchants
   B.   the British government's efforts to halt the export of opium from China to India
   C.   American efforts to monopolize legal drug imports from China
   D.   the Chinese government's refusal to control the production of opium

   A. During the first decades of the 19th century, British merchants were profiting handsomely from exchanging opium grown in India for tea grown in China. When the Chinese government tried to crack down on this illegal trade, British merchants appealed to the British government, which responded by attacking China in support of the drug trade.

15. The Boxer Uprising, while aimed against Western influence in China,

   A.   won the admiration and support of President Theodore Roosevelt
   B.   was also directed against corruption and incompetence within the Ch'ing government
   C.   was openly supported by Tz'u Hsi, the Dowager Empress
   D.   shared the same progressive goals that the deposed emperor Kuang-Hsu had supported

   C. As Western influences, including Christian missions, pervaded China, a militant organization called the Harmonious Society of Fists — the Boxers — launched attacks on Western missionaries, Christian converts, and other symbols of Western imperialism. The dowager empress, Tz'u Hsi, openly supported the Boxers.

16. America's Open Door Policy toward China

   A.   sought to prevent the partitioning of China by outside powers
   B.   sought to prevent Chinese workers from competing with American labor
   C.   sought to regulate immigration from China
   D.   promised citizenship to Chinese immigrants after a four-year waiting period

   A. The Open Door Policy sought to keep the door open to China for American merchants and missionaries, and thus opposed partitioning. The door for Chinese immigration remained firmly closed.

17. The French colonial presence in Vietnam became unsupportable

   A.   after the establishment of the Fifth Republic in France
   B.   after the Japanese conquest of southeast Asia in 1941
   C.   after the death of President DeGaulle
   D.   after the battle of Dien Bien Phu

   D. After French forces were defeated at Dien Bien Phu, the French started looking for a way out. Eventually, the French recognized the partitioning of Vietnam between north and south, and American advisors replaced French troops on the ground.

18. Relations between the People's Republic of China and the Soviet Union

    A. remained friendly from 1949 until the end of the Soviet Union
    B. although initially friendly, quickly turned hostile and remained so into the 1970s
    C. although initially hostile, quickly turned friendly because both states shared a common enemy
    D. were adversarial at times, but were never hostile

    B. Although the Soviet Union supported the Chinese Communist Party's ascent to power, the two socialist states embodied different visions of how to achieve communism. Sino-Soviet tensions flared into open conflict several times during the Cold War era.

19. The United States and the People's Republic of China started to normalize relations during the

    A. Eisenhower administration
    B. Kennedy administration
    C. Johnson administration
    D. Nixon administration

    D. President Nixon, long an opponent of communism, became the first American president to visit China in 1972, when talks continued over the normalization of relations and an end to China's isolation.

20. In traditional Chinese political thinking, the Mandate of Heaven can be lost

    A. if the emperors lack virtue and can no longer maintain a proper relationship with Heaven
    B. if the people lack virtue
    C. if the emperor dies without a legitimate male heir
    D. if the army suffers a military defeat

    A. The Mandate of Heaven can be lost if the population believes that the emperor no longer maintains right relations with heaven. Thus, a series of bad harvests, drought, floods, or other signs that Heaven is displeased can be enough to bring about the downfall of a dynasty that has, in the eyes of the people, lost the Mandate of Heaven.

21. Augusto Sandino, whose name came to be associated with the left-leaning Sandinistas, became famous for resisting United States military intervention in

    A. Guatemala
    B. Cuba
    C. Nicaragua
    D. the Philippines

    C. Sandino fought for Nicaraguan freedom and resisted American intervention in the 19th century.

22. Although intended as a term of derision, banana republic reflected

    A. the political and economic power of the United Fruit Company in much of Central America
    B. the power of the *lumpen proletariat* in Honduras
    C. the autarkic policies of several Central American countries that restricted the growing of export products, like bananas and coffee
    D. the power of a few wealthy landowning families in many Central American countries

    A. The United Fruit Company so completely controlled the economies in several Central American countries that their governments came to be seen as serving the interests of the company and of American consumers.

23. During the bloodiest phase of the Mexican Revolution, American troops fought a series of cross-border skirmishes with this revolutionary leader.

    A. Pancho Villa
    B. Emiliano Zapata
    C. Alvero Obreson
    D. Lazaro Cardenas

    A. Pancho Villa made several daring cross-border raids into the United States and was pursued fruitlessly for months by American troops.

24. During its first decades, the success of the Monroe Doctrine depended largely on

    A. Britain's desire to keep France and Spain out of the New World
    B. France's desire to regain control of Canada
    C. the failure of the European powers to discover the value of Latin America as a market
    D. the absorption of the European powers with East Asia and Africa

    A. During most of the 19th century, British and American interests in keeping France, Spain, and other European powers out of Latin America coincided, but it was the overwhelming power of the British navy, not the Monroe Doctrine, that enforced the exclusion.

25. The United States emerged as a self consciously colonial power as a result of

    A. the 1867 purchase of Alaska
    B. American intervention in Cuba and Guatemala
    C. the Monroe Doctrine
    D. the Spanish American War

    D. American success in the Spanish American War gave the United States control of the Philippines and Cuba and, for the first time, gave the United States a minor, but quite real, stake in global imperialism.

26. The Japanese attack on the American Pacific fleet at Pearl Harbor had only a limited strategic effect largely because

    A. the American aircraft carriers were at sea and escaped harm
    B. the newest battle ships (with a few exceptions) escaped unharmed
    C. Hawaii proved to be of minimal strategic value
    D. the Japanese failed to take advantage of the attack in the rest of the Pacific

    A. Hawaii was of great strategic value, but was too well defended for the Japanese to have launched a successful invasion. Even the battleships that survived the attack on Pearl Harbor proved to be of limited value. It was the aircraft carrier force that eventually turned the tide of war in the Pacific.

27. The Roosevelt Corollary of 1904 held that

    A. The United States had the right to collect debts and maintain order in countries that failed to do so on their own.
    B. The United States was obligated to protect the sovereignty of Central and South American states.
    C. The United States would refrain from interfering in the internal affairs of its Latin American neighbors.
    D. The United States would intervene in Latin America only if a European power intervened first.

    A. In order to keep European states from gaining influence in Latin America and to assert U.S. dominance in the region, Roosevelt claimed for the United States the right to intervene in Latin America to collect debts and restore order, a policy that came to be known as the Big Stick.

28. The Horn of Africa includes all of the following countries except

    A. Eritrea
    B. Ethiopia
    C. Somalia
    D. Kenya

D. Kenya is farther south and west, and is also culturally different from, the countries in the horn of Africa, the region in West Africa vaguely resembling the horn of a rhinoceros.

29. The modern state of Bangladesh won its independence in 1971 from

    A. Pakistan
    B. India
    C. the British Empire
    D. Indonesia

A. When predominantly Muslim Pakistan separated from India in 1949, its two halves were separated by the bulk of India. In the 1971 revolution, the eastern province of Bangladesh declared and won its independence.

30. Among the sites holy to Islam, this is associated with the Prophet Muhammad's ascension to heaven:

    A. Mecca
    B. Medina
    C. Jerusalem
    D. Baghdad

C. The prophet Muhammad reported that he was elevated into the heavens and returned to earth at the site that had once been the Jerusalem Temple and is now marked by the Mosque of Omar.

31. As a result of the Lateran Treaty of 1929,

    A. the papacy gave up its claims to sovereignty over the city of Rome
    B. the papacy agreed not to interfere in Italian politics
    C. Pope Pius IX agreed to recognize the legitimacy of the Fascist state
    D. the Nazis agreed not to suppress the Catholic Church in Germany

A. The papacy, which had refused to acknowledge its loss of the papal states to the new Kingdom of Italy in 1872, made peace with the Fascists in exchange for guaranteed sovereignty over the Vatican.

32. During the 1980s, the Soviet experience in this country was compared to the American experience in Vietnam.

    A. Uzbekistan
    B. Kazakhstan
    C. Afghanistan
    D. Azerbaijan

C. Soviet troops invaded Afghanistan in 1979 to prop up a failing socialist regime, leading to a debilitating, decade-long conflict from which the Soviets eventually had to withdraw in humiliating defeat.

33. Mutually Assured Destruction (MAD) was the basis of what policy?

    A. nuclear deterrence
    B. chemical weapons ban
    C. biological weapons ban
    D. the Geneva Conventions

A. MAD assumed that as long as neither the Soviet Union nor the United States could hope to survive a nuclear exchange, neither country would be tempted to launch a pre-emptive strike.

34. In the Tiananmen Square protests of 1989, Chinese students called for

    A. a return to traditional Taoist and Confuscianist values
    B. freedom and democracy
    C. a recovery of Maoist Communism
    D. the overthrow of the Chinese Communist Party

    B. The protesters in Tiananmen Square were careful not to call publicly for an end to Communist Party rule, but their demands for freedom and democracy, symbolized by a Chinese version of the Statue of Liberty, appeared to be a fundamental challenge to the Chinese Communist Party's hold on power.

35. After the fall of the Soviet Union, Fidel Castro

    A. attempted to appease American demands without giving up power
    B. softened his hardline commitment to communism
    C. offered to send Cuban troops to replace Soviet forces in Africa
    D. eased restrictions on religion and looked for new trading partners while maintaining one-party control of the state

    D. Having lost the support of his most important trading partner and military guarantor, Castro invited Pope John Paul II to visit Cuba while looking for other markets for Cuban sugar and cigars.

36. The Aral Sea in Central Asia has shrunk dramatically in the last several decades due largely to

    A. irrigation
    B. changing weather patterns
    C. dams and channels that divert the sea's upstream sources
    D. geophysical changes that have raised the sea level in the region

    C. Diversion of the Aral Sea's waters by upstream dams and channels has left much of its former basin a desert.

37. Although they are identified largely with Iraq, the Tigris and Euphrates rivers originate in

    A. Jordan
    B. Iran
    C. Syria
    D. Turkey

    D. The Tigris and Euphrates rivers find their sources in the heights of Turkey's eastern highlands, from which they flow through Iraq into the Persian Gulf.

38. Although three-fourths of the world's surface is covered by water, how much of the world's water is fresh?

    A. 15 percent
    B. 10 percent
    C. 5 percent
    D. 2 percent

    D. Only two percent of the world's water is fresh. Approximately one-quarter of one percent is available for human use.

39. The Basque people are indigenous to

    A. Spain
    B. Italy
    C. Switzerland
    D. Romania

A. The Basque, with a language unrelated to any other, were indigenous to the Iberian Peninsula for a millennia before the Celts, Phoenicians, and Romans arrived.

40. Qat (or khat), a relatively mild stimulant, is most widely used in

    A. Yemen
    B. South Africa
    C. Brazil
    D. Mexico

    A. Qat is increasingly popular in West Africa, but appears to be most widely used in Yemen.

41. The Brezhnev Doctrine was enunciated in response to

    A. the Prague Spring
    B. the Hungarian Uprising
    C. the Polish Uprising
    D. the Cultural Revolution in China

    A. After the 1968 Prague Spring, which attempted to put a human face on socialism, was crushed by Soviet tanks, Brezhnev declared it the obligation of all Socialist states to prevent backsliding.

42. Since its introduction in 2002, which country has not adopted Europe's common currency, the euro.

    A. Britain
    B. Germany
    C. France
    D. Greece

    A. Britain has elected to retain the pound sterling as its currency and has, to date, not accepted Europe's common currency.

43. The Truman Doctrine, which held that the United States would aid any country threatened with communist takeover, was first applied in

    A. Vietnam
    B. Korea
    C. Greece
    D. Cuba

    C. In 1947, the British government informed the Truman administration that they would no longer be able to support the Greek government's struggle against a Yugoslav-backed communist insurgency. President Truman, in an address to Congress, stated that it would be American policy to support free people everywhere in a struggle against communist subversion.

44. In the United Nations Security Council, which country does not have veto power?

    A. the People's Republic of China
    B. France
    C. Japan
    D. Great Britain

    C. The permanent members of the UN Security Council are the United States, Russia, France, China, and Britain.

45. The Hungarian Uprising of 1954 was premised on the hope of American intervention. What American policy made this intervention unlikely?

    A. containment

    B. rollback

    C. non-proliferation

    D. avoidance

A. The policy of containment, first enunciated by George F. Kennan in 1947, was designed to keep communism within its current boundaries while avoiding armed confrontation with the Soviet Union — a confrontation that could lead to nuclear war.

Practice Tests

Directions: Following are three mini-practice tests. Select the choice that best answers each question. Fully explained answers follow each test.

Practice Test 1

  1. The founder of modern Turkey, Mustafa Kemal Ataturk, sought to create

    A. a secular multi-national state

    B. a religious national state

    C. a religious multi-national state

    D. a secular national state

  2. The Wahhabi interpretation of Islam

    A. tends to be more secular than other branches

    B. focuses on encouraging spiritual transformation through meditation

    C. calls for a return to the purity of the earliest years of Islam

    D. tends to be more liberal than other branches

  3. Hong Kong became a British possession as a result of

    A. World War I

    B. World War II

    C. the Seven Years War

    D. the Opium Wars

  4. Although the Dalai Lama claims sovereignty over Tibet, the People's Republic of China has ruled the country since China invaded Tibet in

    A. 1949

    B. 1939

    C. 1849

    D. 1969

5. Beginning in the 1980s, Peru has struggled with a particularly violent, terrorist group that wanted to transform Peru along Maoist lines. This group is called

   A. Tupac Amaru
   B. the Shining Path
   C. FARC
   D. Aum Shinrikyo

6. Blood diamonds refers to

   A. the use of contraband diamonds to fund civil insurgencies and terrorism in Africa
   B. a rare, reddish gem found only in Liberia and Sierra Leone
   C. a diamond-shaped region in western Africa noted for its history of tribal violence
   D. a notorious terrorist organization in Germany

7. Manuel Noriega, who ruled Panama from 1983 to 1989, was toppled and imprisoned in the United States on charges

   A. that he committed crimes against humanity
   B. that he was involved in narcotics trafficking
   C. that he provided cover for terrorist organizations
   D. that he had seized power in Panama illegally

8. The policy of containment, as enunciated by George Kennan, was based on a belief that

   A. Communism would eventually collapse of its own accord.
   B. Global thermonuclear war was inevitable.
   C. China and Russia were uniquely vulnerable to communist subversion.
   D. Few people outside of the intelligentsia would ever find communism attractive.

9. Simon Bolivar was instrumental in freeing all of the following from Spanish rule except

   A. Venezuela
   B. Colombia
   C. Argentina
   D. Bolivia

10. In the 18th century, Botany Bay in Australia served Britain as

   A. an agricultural research station
   B. a penal colony
   C. a base for missionary work among the aborigines
   D. a leprosy colony

Answers to Practice Test 1

1. D. Attaturk envisioned, and largely succeeded, in building a secular, Western-oriented, national state out of the heartland of the old multi-national Ottoman Empire.

2. C. Founded by Muhammad ibn Abd al-Wahab in Arabia in the 18th century, the Wahhabi interpretation of Islam regards all innovations in the faith after about 950 c.e. to be false. The Saudi royal family adheres to the Wahhabi interpretation of Islam.

3. D. Hong Kong first became a British colony as a result of the Opium Wars. China was forced to surrender the territory in 1859.

4. **A.** Chinese Communist forces invaded Tibet in 1949. The Dalai Lama slipped out of China in 1959 and from exile has continued to press his claim for Tibetan independence from China.

5. **B.** The Maoist revolutionary force that has struggled against Peru's government is the Shining Path or Senderao Luminoso. The Tupac Amaru also seeks to overthrow Peru's government, but follows Castro's rather than Mao's example.

6. **A.** Because diamonds tend to be found in some of the most troubled regions of Africa and are difficult to trace, they have been used regularly to fund revolutions and insurrections in Central Africa. Because they often buy guns and bullets, these diamonds are called blood diamonds.

7. **B.** Although he received training at the U.S. Army's School of the Americas and was on the payroll of several U.S. government agencies, Noriega was accused and, after an invasion removed him from power, convicted of drug trafficking.

8. **A.** Kennan was persuaded that, in time, the internal contradictions inherent in communism would lead to its collapse in the Soviet Union. His goal was to prevent the expansion of Soviet influence and communism beyond the Soviet Union and Eastern Europe.

9. **C.** Bolivar was an anti-colonial leader who was instrumental in ending Spanish power in Bolivia, Panama, Colombia, Ecuador, Peru, and Venezuela but not Argentina.

10. **B.** So named for the variety of its plant life, but noteworthy mostly for its hostility to human habitation, Botany Bay served as a place for Britain to dispose of its criminal class from 1788 to 1868.

Practice Test 2

1. The Republic of Panama won its independence from _____ in 1903.

   A. Costa Rica
   B. Mexico
   C. Colombia
   D. Honduras

2. In Mexico, the *Dia del Grito* (Day of the Call) celebrates

   A. Miguel Hidalgo's call for universal freedom
   B. Mexican Independence Day
   C. the Expulsion of the French
   D. Santa Ana's victory at the Alamo

3. As an international athletic competition, the first modern Olympiad was held in Athens in

   A. 1840
   B. 1896
   C. 1888
   D. 1916

4. A fundamental goal of the Concert of Europe was

   A. to maintain a rough balance of power among the European great powers
   B. to encourage democracy within the lesser states
   C. to encourage nationalist movements in the Ottoman Empire
   D. to promote economic liberalism

5. The purpose of mercantilist policies was to

    A. encourage free trade

    B. promote economic self-sufficiency

    C. maintain a favorable balance of trade

    D. encourage standardization

6. The _____ dynasty ruled China from 1644 until it was overthrown in 1908.

    A. Chin

    B. Xin

    C. Ming

    D. Qing (Manchu)

7. Admiral Perry's entry into Yokohama Harbor in 1853 led to

    A. the fall of the Tokugawa shogunate

    B. the opening of Japan to trade with the West

    C. the eventual restoration of power to the emperor

    D. all of the above

8. Bohemia and Moravia are part of what modern state?

    A. Germany

    B. Austria

    C. the Czech Republic

    D. Switzerland

9. The Schlieffen Plan in World War I called for Germany to

    A. defeat Russia first, and then turn on France

    B. invade France by way of Belgium, before attacking Russia

    C. invade Belgium and France before launching a cross-channel invasion of Britain

    D. employ a holding force against France while launching a lightning invasion against Russia

10. The body of water that links Sweden, Lithuania, and Russia is

    A. the Baltic Sea

    B. the North Sea

    C. the Adriatic Sea

    D. the Arial Sea

Answers to Practice Test 2

  1. C. With substantial help and prodding from the United States, Panama separated from Colombia and immediately agreed to sign over the Panama Canal Zone to the United States.

  2. A. Miguel Hidalgo issued the call for universal freedom on what became known as the Day of the Call.

  3. B. The first Olympiad of the modern Olympic movement was held in Athens in 1896.

  4. A. The Concert of Europe aimed at maintaining a conservative order in Europe by suppressing nationalism and discouraging free market liberalism.

  5. C. Mercantilism, the economic basis of 18th-century Europe, aimed at maintaining a favorable balance of trade rather than free trade or self-sufficiency.

  6. D. The Qing (or Manchu) dynasty overthrew the Ming in 1644 and ruled until the early 20th century.

7. D. Admiral Perry's display of power convinced many Japanese that their isolation had rendered them vulnerable to the very forces of imperialism the Tokugawa Shogunate had hoped to protect them from.

8. C. Bohemia and Moravia make up the bulk of the modern Czech Republic.

9. B. Alfred von Schlieffen, Germany's Chief of the Great General Staff before World War II, believed that any war with Russia would inevitably draw France into the war. Therefore, he proposed a surprise invasion of France, via Belgium, that would take France out of action, freeing Germany to turn on Russia with its full might. The plan failed, in part, because Belgium put up unexpectedly stiff resistance.

10. A. The Baltic Sea touches Lithuania, Sweden, and Russia as well as Latvia and Estonia.

Practice Test 3

1. After World War II, the German city of Danzig became

   A. an independent city-state
   B. the Polish city of Gedansk
   C. a victim of Stalin's vengeance and was destroyed
   D. a Russian enclave in East Germany

2. The assassination of the Archduke Franz Ferdinand in 1914, although it sparked the First World War, was motivated by a desire for

   A. Italian unification
   B. Serbian independence from Austria
   C. the unification of Serbia and Bosnia-Herzegovina
   D. Hungarian independence from Austria

3. Among the states of the former Soviet Union, the state with the closest ties to Russia is

   A. Azerbaijan
   B. Belarus
   C. Ukraine
   D. Moldova

4. The Armenian Genocide of 1915–1923 took place in

   A. the Ottoman Empire
   B. Russia
   C. India
   D. East Africa

5. The Vietnamese celebration of Tet marks

   A. Vietnamese independence from French rule
   B. Vietnamese independence from China
   C. Vietnam's victory over the United States
   D. the lunar new year

6. In traditional Chinese thinking, the loss of the Mandate of Heaven justifies

   A. a monk's leaving the monastery to enter secular life
   B. a son abandoning his family
   C. a war of conquest
   D. a rebellion against the emperor

7. Transylvania is part of what European state?

    A. Romania

    B. Bulgaria

    C. Turkey

    D. Greece

8. The October 1917 Revolution (also called the Bolshevik Revolution) overthrew

    A. Tsar Nicholas II

    B. Alexander Kerensky's provisional government

    C. the Menshevik regime

    D. Germany's government of occupation in Moscow

9. Vaclav Havel, a former dissident and playwright, became president of _____ in 1990.

    A. Hungary

    B. Poland

    C. Bulgaria

    D. Czechoslovakia

10. Although it accomplished little, the Evian Conference (1938) was intended to

    A. find refuge for German Jews seeking to escape Germany

    B. settle Germany's claims to the Sudetenland

    C. preserve Ethiopian independence

    D. settle Germany's dispute with France over the Ruhr Valley

Answers to Practice Test 3

1. B. A free city during the interwar period, Danzig's German population was expelled as the city was incorporated into Poland after the Second World War and given the Polish name, Gedansk.

2. C. Franz Ferdinand and his wife were killed by a terrorist organization, Union or Death, that sought to unite the Serbian Kingdom with the Austrian province of Bosnia-Herzegovina.

3. B. Belarus maintains far closer ties to Russia than any other former member republic of the Soviet Union.

4. A. After a Turkish nationalist movement came to power in the Ottoman Empire, the government moved to rid the empire of its Armenian Christian subjects.

5. D. Tet marks the lunar new year. It was the occasion of a major offensive in 1968 by Vietnamese communist forces against American and South Vietnamese troops.

6. D. If the population perceives that an imperial dynasty has lost the mandate of heaven, the dynasty's legitimacy can be challenged and the mandate claimed by another.

7. A. Originally part of Hungary, Transylvania became part of Romania as a result of the 1919 Treaty of Trianon.

8. B. The Bolsheviks overthrew the liberal Provisional government, led by Alexander Kerensky, in 1917. Tsar Nicholas had already abdicated, although he and his family would die at the hands of the Bolsheviks.

9. D. Vaclav Havel, a playwright, had helped organize the influential Charter 77 movement that challenged the legitimacy of the Czechoslovak Communist Party's monopoly on power and sent Havel to prison. Havel was sworn in as president of Czechoslovakia in January 1990.

10. A. Intended to do little more than give the illusion of activity, the stated goal of the conference was to assist Jewish refugees trying to escape persecution in Nazi Germany.

Economics

What You Should Know

In both the general and career track sections of the Job Knowledge test, the questions require knowledge of a general understanding of the economic issues and the economic system of the United States. In addition, you are also required to understand the basic principles of economics, including supply and demand, and the economic relationship the United States has with the rest of the world.

The questions in the following section are for your review. Go through each question and try your best to answer it. The explanation of the answer follows immediately afterward so that you can actually learn new material. After you've completed reviewing these questions and answers, two brief practice review tests at the end of the chapter help you determine how much you know. Of course, there is a full-length exam at the end of Part II that also includes economics questions.

Economics Review Section

Read the following questions and select the choices that best answer the questions.

1. Based on supply/demand economic theory, price controls on the supply of wheat during a famine would result in

   A. an increased supply of low-cost wheat
   B. social unrest
   C. no supply of low-cost wheat
   D. a scarcity of low-cost wheat

   D. According to supply/demand economics, price controls on the supply of wheat during a famine will almost always result in a scarcity of low-cost wheat. Supply/demand economics defines price as the single most important factor. Accordingly, few suppliers will be willing to supply low-cost wheat if consumers are willing to pay higher costs on the black market. Further, if the price does not match the sellers' perception of risk and actual expenses, sellers will withhold the product from the market, thus aggravating the already dire situation.

2. One of South America's OPEC members is

   A. Mexico
   B. Brazil
   C. Bolivia
   D. Venezuela

   D. Venezuela and Ecuador are South America's members of OPEC.

3. In 1898, President _____ launched the trust-busting era, when he appointed the U.S. Industrial Commission on Trusts, which interrogated Carnegie, Rockefeller, Schwab, and other industrial titans.

   A. William McKinley
   B. Theodore Roosevelt
   C. Franklin D. Roosevelt
   D. William Taft

   A. Although Theodore Roosevelt is well known as a trustbuster, it was President William McKinley who appointed the U.S. Industrial Commission on trusts, and thus shaped the United States' modern economy.

4. Since World War II, the agriculture sector's contribution to GDP among first-world nations has generally

    A. stayed the same
    B. fallen
    C. increased
    D. remained immeasurable

    B. As the agriculture's importance in the first world has diminished, its percentage of the GDP has steadily diminished as well.

5. Which of these works first introduced Marxism?

    A. *The Invisible Hand*
    B. *Das Kapital*
    C. *Mein Kampf*
    D. *The Communist Manifesto*

    D. Karl Marx wrote *The Communist Manifesto* in 1848 and then followed it up with *Das Kapital,* written in 1867, thus setting the stage for Marxism as an ideology. Adolf Hitler wrote *Mein Kampf.*

6. An economist who advocates that governments take a laissez-faire approach to the economy is advocating

    A. that the government intervene in markets to protect the vulnerable
    B. that the economy should regulate itself without government intervention
    C. that the government intervene only in regulating the money supply
    D. none of the above

    B. Laissez-faire policies mean a policy of (governmental) non-intervention. In the field of economics, laissez-faire policies such as free trade were persuasively advocated by Adam Smith in his book *The Wealth of Nations* (1776).

7. Adam Smith wrote this landmark book in 1776, called the

    A. *Declaration of Independence*
    B. *The Wealth of Nations*
    C. *Das Kapital*
    D. *The Creation of Wealth*

    B. Written the same year as the Declaration of Independence, Adam Smith's economic opus (much referred to but little read) is called *The Wealth of Nations.*

8. In July 1944, even as World War II still raged, delegates met to sign the Bretton-Woods Agreement, which did not result in the following:

    A. Member countries agreed to combat currency fluctuations by pegging their currency to gold and a reserve currency.
    B. Member countries created the IMF.
    C. Member countries created the International Bank for Reconstruction.
    D. Member countries created the Marshall Plan.

    D. The Bretton-Woods Agreement did everything except launch the Marshall Plan. The Bretton-Woods Agreement provided for the combating of currency fluctuation by pegging their currency to gold and a reserve currency (which became the U.S. dollar by default), created the IMF, and created the International Bank for Reconstruction (later to become the World Bank).

9. In the 17th century, an increased supply of South American gold in Europe caused prices to rise (inflation). In the 21st century, countries experiencing large net inflows of currency must _____ in order to avoid inflationary pressures.

    A. sterilize the inflows by soaking up the currency and purchasing international bonds
    B. sterilize the inflows by issuing domestic bonds
    C. peg their currency to the dominate export market's currency
    D. peg their currency to the dollar

A. In order to avoid inflation, countries sterilize their currency when faced with significant net currency inflows. This is accomplished by parking the incoming currency in foreign currency bonds. That is one reason why countries with strong exports to the United States, such as Japan or China, purchase large quantities of U.S. treasury bonds.

10. If you favor governmental spending to reduce the down portion of an economic cycle, you are most influenced by

    A. Keynes
    B. Smith
    C. Marx
    D. Ricardo

A. Keynes advocated government spending to flatten out the business cycle.

11. Conventional wisdom suggests that as stock values increase, bond yields

    A. increase
    B. stay the same
    C. decline
    D. none of the above

C. Bond yields typically decrease as stock yields increase. As the economy improves (and stock prices rise), companies have an easier time raising money on the stock market; thus, bond issues decline. As the economy declines, bond yields rise as companies look to bond issues to raise capital.

12. It was the dramatic 1911 breakup of this American monopoly that helped set the stage for the modern American economy.

    A. US Steel
    B. Edison Power
    C. AT&T
    D. Standard Oil

D. The breakup of Standard Oil, led by President Theodore Roosevelt, helped set the stage for the modern American economy, because it allowed smaller private companies to pursue oil production. The remnants of Standard Oil became dynamic separate entities, such Exxon and Mobil.

13. Gold frequently increases in value during political or economic instability because

    A. gold is intrinsically valuable
    B. as a respective currency weakens, speculators know that governments will purchase gold to prop up their currency
    C. it is seen as a reliable store of value
    D. none of the above

C. Gold is no longer used to back currency and has little intrinsic value, but in times of crisis, investors tend to gravitate toward gold as a reliable store of value.

14. Which currency is no longer traded?

    A. baht
    B. forint
    C. mark
    D. ruble

    C. The German mark is no longer a currency, because it was replaced by the euro in 2002.

15. In recent years, farmers have plowed under their corn or wheat, rather than harvest it for market. This decision is best explained by

    A. mass irrational behavior
    B. farmers avoiding the variable cost of taking their products to market
    C. farmers attempting to recover their base cost
    D. the rising marginal cost of producing corn or wheat

    D. The rising marginal cost of producing agricultural products best explains this behavior. Marginal costs are the additional costs associated with producing one more unit of output. In other words, the value obtained by adding additional inputs (fertilizer, fuel, time) was not worth a harvest, thus the decision to plow the crop under.

16. In 2003 and 2004, the largest exporter in the world (in dollar terms) was

    A. Germany
    B. China
    C. United States
    D. Japan

    A. Remarkably, Germany remained the largest exporter in the world in 2003 and 2004.

17. The consumer price index (CPI) is

    A. a measure of the average change over time in the prices paid by urban consumers for a market basket of consumer goods and services
    B. a cost of living index
    C. an exact measure of inflation
    D. none of the above

    A. The consumer price index is the measure of change over time in the prices paid by urban consumers for a market basket of good and services.

18. This disease (or diseases) significantly dampened economic growth in some countries.

    A. bird flu
    B. mad cow
    C. AIDS
    D. all of the above

    D. Bird flu had a significant impact on economies in Southeastern Asia, while mad cow has had a significant impact on the U.K., Canadian, and other economies. AIDS has had a devastating effect on many economies in the world, particularly in Africa.

19. When demand dramatically increases for a little-known fashion name because of positive media exposure, this will cause a(n) _____ shift in the demand curve.

    A. upward
    B. downward
    C. leftward
    D. rightward

    D. The demand graph will shift to the right. Product and the supply have not changed, but demand has increased, along with the price.

20. Which of the following would not be counted as a part of India's gross domestic product (GDP)?

    A. an expatriate Indian engineer's wages in New York
    B. a U.S. Embassy employee whose wages are deposited in a local New Delhi bank
    C. a thief's ill-gotten goods from a tourist visiting the Taj Mahal
    D. an Indian peasant trading chickens for rice

    A. An expatriate Indian engineer's wages earned in New York would not be counted a part of India's gross domestic product, because it was not earned in India. However, the sum of all the goods and services produced in a country (even theft) are considered part of its GDP.

21. Studies of Americans clearly indicate that an overwhelming number

    A. see themselves as working-class
    B. do not believe in social classes
    C. see themselves as middle-class
    D. resent the domination of middle-class values

    C. Study after study indicates that Americans see themselves overwhelmingly as middle-class.

22. Despite having sizeable natural resources, only a few countries in Africa have been able to make use of mining as a launching pad for sustained economic development. Which of the following explains this?

    A. lack of legislation governing royalties
    B. a decline in quality and low market prices
    C. a lack of local capital
    D. political instability and government corruption

    D. Political instability and government corruption have prevented most of Africa's countries from making use of abundant natural resources. The lack of local capital does not play a significant role, because sizeable investors do exist in Africa. International investors tend to avoid placing their money where there is political instability and bad governance.

23. Which of the following is consistent with a favorable trade balance?

    A. more goods and services are available for domestic use than are able to be consumed
    B. gold reserves increase
    C. net foreign investment is negative
    D. domestic exports of merchandise exceed imports of merchandise

    D. A favorable trade balance indicates that a country exports more than it imports from another country.

24. During the Middle Ages, international trade flourished as

    A. traders from Venice traded gold for Chinese spices and silks
    B. Arab traders traded salt for gold from Mali
    C. Europeans traded gold for products such as sugar and cloth from the Middle East
    D. all of the above

D. Although many people think of international trade as being a modern phenomena, it in fact has existed as long as mankind itself.

25. Tariffs on _____ imports have raised U.S. prices many times higher than the world average, while helping impoverish many Caribbean nations.

    A. car
    B. sugar
    C. chocolate
    D. coffee

    B. U.S. tariffs on sugar imports from the Caribbean have kept U.S. sugar prices many times higher than the world average and have helped impoverish many Caribbean nations.

26. Despite decades of foreign aid to the third world, many economists are searching for new economic models to explain why most of these economies have failed to improve markedly. The noted Peruvian economist Hernando de Soto argues that the third-world nations have done poorly because of

    A. oppression by the West
    B. lack of capital
    C. lack of property right protection
    D. failures inherent to capitalism

    C. Hernando de Soto argues that many third-world nations have not succeeded economically because of the lack of property rights protection for their citizens. He estimated that some third-world countries have many billions of dollars in capital that are locked away, because the property cannot be securely bought or sold.

27. The German capitalistic model is typified by

    A. cronyism
    B. state-corporate consensus
    C. laissez-faire relationship between the government and the corporate sector
    D. short-term planning

    B. German capitalism is characterized by a consensus between its large corporations and the state.

28. The 1998 collapse of the Long-Term Capital Management, a _____, almost led to the collapse of capital markets around the world, and led to a $3.4 billion bailout.

    A. mutual fund
    B. bond fund
    C. hedge fund
    D. betting pool

    C. Long-Term Capital Management was a hedge fund. A hedge fund uses futures to offset investment risk and is usually only available to the very wealthy.

29. Which is most true?

    A. Economic experts are good at predicting recessions.
    B. Economic experts can usually indicate only that a recession is in progress when firms and consumers suddenly change behavior.
    C. Economic experts often can indicate only that a recession has occurred when firms and consumers resume normal consumption patterns.
    D. none of the above

    B. Despite many years of study, economists can usually indicate only that a recession is in progress when firms and consumers suddenly change behaviors.

30. Economic models are

    A. infallible
    B. never right
    C. a helpful guide
    D. an illusion

C. Economic models are a helpful guide. Marxism is just one example of the damage that can occur when an economic model is taken to an extreme.

31. Which U.S. city has historically been associated with commodity trading?

    A. Los Angeles
    B. New York
    C. Des Moines
    D. Chicago

D. The Chicago Board of Trade (CBOT) was established in 1848 to conduct commodity trading on agricultural commodities such as corn or wheat.

32. The traditional informal channel for transferring funds between various Middle Eastern cities is called

    A. wholesale banking
    B. the Arab Street
    C. the Hawala system
    D. Western Union

C. The Hawala system has come under much scrutiny by international money laundering watchdogs, because it is an informal channel for transferring funds between different parts of the Middle East, thus avoiding traditional bank-oversight institutions.

33. Hyper inflation is relatively rare, but was experienced during

    A. the United States' Great Depression
    B. Weimar Germany
    C. post-World War II England
    D. Mao's China

B. At one point, Weimar Germany's inflation rate was 4 trillion percent (November 15, 1923). In contrast, the United States actually suffered from deflation during the United States' Great Depression, as agricultural prices dropped 51 percent (1929–1933).

34. Which of the following statements about comparative advantage is true?

    A. Comparative advantage usually translates into absolute economic and trade advantages.
    B. When a nation holding a comparative advantage opens itself to international trade, domestic wages usually fall.
    C. Countries gain the most when they specialize in producing products for which they have the greatest relative efficiency.
    D. Protecting domestic production will often increase real wages as inexpensive domestic goods replace imported products.

C. Comparative advantage is the idea that countries gain when they produce those items that they are most efficient at producing. In other words, Saudi Arabia has an advantage in producing high quality oil cheaply, therefore, it should use its export earnings to buy items such as wheat, which it has little ability to produce in comparison with Australia or Argentina.

35. Which of the following is contractionary fiscal policy?

    A. the Federal Reserve sells securities
    B. reductions in personal taxes
    C. decreasing the federal deficit
    D. increasing the federal deficit

C. When government revenues are higher than expenditures with a resulting decrease in the federal deficit, the fiscal policy is said to be contractionary. An expansionary fiscal policy would result in increased deficits and would likely result from the government's attempts to stimulate the economy.

36. Classical economic theory has long argued that low unemployment will result in _____ as workers demand higher wages.

    A. deficits
    B. increased money supply
    C. wage inflation
    D. inflation

C. The Phillips curve represents the relationship between employment and wage inflation and indicates that wages tend to rise as unemployment falls.

37. Despite relatively low unemployment between 1999 and 2004, inflationary pressures have not been evident. Why not?

    A. historically low energy prices
    B. increased efficiencies from high technology investments
    C. downward pricing pressures brought on by cheap offshore manufacturing centers
    D. all of the above

D. Many factors, including historically low energy prices, increased efficiencies due to advances in high technology, and downward pricing pressures from cheap offshore manufacturing centers all have contributed to keeping inflation at bay.

38. If Country A can produce Commodity X and Y while using two output units, and neighboring Country B can produce Commodity X and Y while using three output units, it is most likely that

    A. one country would gain from trade, while the other would not
    B. each country would gain by trading with the other
    C. Country A would produce both commodities, while Country B would produce neither
    D. Country B would produce both commodities, while Country A would produce neither

B. Classical economics suggests that two countries will always mutually benefit by trading with the other.

39. Which of the following would have the same effect as an export on the U.S. balance of payments?

    A. An American buys a computer built in a Chinese factory that was financed by American funds.
    B. An American flies to Brazil via Varig Airlines (a Brazilian carrier).
    C. An American buys preferred stock in Nokia.
    D. An American receives a $25 wire-transfer birthday gift from a relative in Australia.

D. The wire transfer gift would be considered an export, because the funds would be considered a debit in the current account.

40. Importing $10 billion of Chinese goods in 2003, this U.S. company would be China's fifth-largest trading partner if it were a country.

A. IBM
B. P&G
C. Target
D. Wal-Mart

D. Wal-Mart continues to be the largest American importer.

41. The Foreign Corrupt Practices Act makes corrupt payments to foreign officials illegal and extends to

A. large U.S. corporations working outside the United States
B. U.S. citizens working for foreign companies
C. foreign citizens working for U.S. companies
D. all of the above

D. The Foreign Corrupt Practices Act is an important shaper of U.S. business practices overseas. All U.S. citizens, companies, and employees (even if they are not U.S. citizens) fall under the auspices of this act; however, the act applies only to corrupt transactions with foreign government officials.

42. President Bush's economic advisor can

A. set interest rates
B. assist in regulating the stock market
C. provide official economic statistics to the GAO
D. do none of the above

D. The president's economic advisor has no official role in the economy, although his or her comments and views can have a powerful effect.

43. This important sector of the U.S. economy has caused much concern because of its perceived decline.

A. manufacturing
B. mining
C. IT
D. ranching

A. The United States' manufacturing sector's decline has continued to grab headlines. As of January, 2004, the number of such jobs stood at 14.3 million, down by 3.0 million jobs, or 17.5 percent, since July 2000 and about 5.2 million since the historical peak in 1979. Employment in manufacturing was its lowest since July 1950.

44. It was Francis Cabot Lowe's introduction of this machine that helped launch the United States' industrial revolution.

A. steam engine
B. thresher
C. locomotive
D. power loom

D. Francis Cabot Lowe introduced the power loom to New England region in 1813, which eventually led to the industrialization of the United States' economy.

45. After World War II, many economists argued that the developing world should move to

A. the gold standard
B. import substitution policies
C. a tight money supply
D. inflationary policies

B. After World War II, many economists called on developing nations to develop import substitution policies to replace imports with domestically produced goods. Usually this meant using tariff and non-tariff measures to prevent the importation of imported goods in order to protect domestic industries.

46. U.S. producers have requested trade protection in the following trade sectors:

   A. automobiles
   B. steel
   C. textiles
   D. all of the above

   D. U.S. producers from the automobile, steel, and textile industries have all requested trade protection from foreign imports.

47. Which of the following is not true about dumping in the trade context?

   A. Dumping is defined as selling a foreign product on the U.S. market at a below-market rate.
   B. Dumping is remedied by adding a tariff to the foreign product so that its price equals its true value.
   C. While successful dumping claims benefit some companies, they can also raise consumer prices, thus hurting consumers.
   D. U.S. trade law recognizes a difference between competitive pricing and predatory pricing.

   D. In reference to dumping, U.S. law does not make a difference between competitive and predatory (unfair) pricing.

48. If the economy is growing too quickly or too slowly, the _____ will adjust monetary policy by changing the discount rate.

   A. Federal Reserve
   B. U.S. Treasury
   C. commercial banks
   D. President's economic advisor

   A. The Federal Reserve will adjust monetary policy by increasing or decreasing the discount rate or the interest rate the Federal Reserve charges on loans it makes to banks. By increasing or decreasing this rate, the Fed can discourage or encourage banks to borrow the funds it creates and, therefore, make more loans to the public.

49. Consumption + investment + government spending + exports – imports =

   A. inflation
   B. net national product
   C. gross domestic product
   D. balance of payments

   C. Gross domestic product.

50. The largest category included in gross domestic product (GDP) is

   A. military
   B. government
   C. consumption
   D. imports

   C. Personal consumption consistently represents 75 percent of gross national product (GNP), by far the largest category included in calculating a country's GDP.

51. The 1999 _____ meeting in Seattle is best known for the violent anti-globalization protests that occurred.

    A. IMF
    B. WTO
    C. NAFTA
    D. G-7

    B. The 1999 WTO meeting in Seattle became a lighting rod for anti-globalism protesters.

52. Which of the following would not be considered a non-tariff barrier to trade?

    A. increasing the phytosanitary standards for meat imports
    B. limiting Japanese car imports to 10,000 units per year
    C. subsidizing sugar beet production
    D. none of the above

    D. Increasing health standards for meat imports, limiting Japanese car imports, and subsidizing sugar beet production would all amount to non-tariff barriers to trade. A non-tariff barrier is any barrier that does not relate to a direct tariff on an import.

53. In a weak economy, bond yields generally

    A. rise
    B. fall
    C. remain flat
    D. none of the above

    A. In general, in an weak economy, bond yields rise, because the cost of borrowing increases as corporations issue more bonds rather than sell stock to raise capital. Conversely, as the economy improves, borrowing becomes easier, and bond yields fall.

54. An astute foreign observer will often look to this indicator as the first (but not the strongest) indicator of the U.S. economy's strength or weakness.

    A. car sales
    B. GDP growth
    C. Nielson ratings
    D. bankruptcies

    A. Information on automobile sales has two major advantages relative to other economic information. In the first place, they are available early; sales are reported about five business days following the end of the month. Second, unlike other reports, the report's findings are not usually subject to revisions.

55. An important early measure of U.S. business investment plans is this statistic:

    A. bankruptcies
    B. unemployment rates
    C. orders of durable goods
    D. consumer price index

    C. Although it is the smallest of the three areas of consumer spending, the report watched most carefully is spending for durable goods. Purchase of these items could be postponed by consumers so they reflect the consumers' mood toward spending.

Practice Tests

Directions: Following are two mini-practice tests. Select the choice that best answers each question. Fully explained answers follow each test.

Practice Test 1

1. Canada, the United States, and Mexico approved the North American Free Trade Agreement (NAFTA) in December 1992. The agreement provided for

    A. the immediate elimination of all tariffs
    B. opening the Mexican oil industry to foreign investors
    C. the immediate removal of all immigration barriers
    D. none of the above

2. If you are a member of Mercosur, you must be a country located in

    A. Asia
    B. Australia
    C. South America
    D. Europe

3. Despite the general decline of the dollar in 2004 vis-à-vis the euro and the yen, China's currency, the Yuan, closely followed the dollar in its valuation. Many economists said that China had _____ the Yuan to the dollar.

    A. valued
    B. pegged
    C. correlated
    D. rigged

4. Many critics claimed that China's policy of keeping an artificially low Yuan

    A. helped China purchase exports to fuel its export sector at lower than usual prices
    B. hurt other Asian countries by introducing inflation into the region
    C. created an economic nirvana by introducing low-cost goods to the poor
    D. kept Chinese products underpriced, thus undercutting fair competition

5. The G8 was known as the G7 until the introduction of this country:

    A. Russia
    B. Hungary
    C. China
    D. Italy

6. The 1995 conclusion to the General Agreement on Tariffs and Trade (GATT) negotiations, also called the Uruguay Round, resulted in the founding of the

    A. World Trade Organization
    B. North American Free Trade Association
    C. United Nations
    D. South American Free Trade Association

7. Which of these Federal Agencies combats money laundering?

    A. Federal Reserve

    B. Department of Justice

    C. Treasury Department

    D. all of the above

8. The economist John Maynard Keynes was born in 1883 and advocated

    A. that nations let the invisible hand of the market guide economies

    B. a more interventionist government policy, by which the government would use fiscal and monetary measures to mitigate the adverse effects of economic downturns

    C. a return to communal living

    D. for global trade as a means of alleviating the suffering in poorer nations

9. This modern world leader introduced the world to the concept of privatization: the state selling off loss-making state companies

    A. Margaret Thatcher

    B. Ronald Reagan

    C. Franklin Roosevelt

    D. Mikhail Gorbachev

10. Russia has generally maintained a trade surplus with Europe because of

    A. arm sales

    B. Russia's refusal to buy European goods

    C. import restrictions

    D. increasing revenues from energy sales

Answers to Practice Test 1

1. D. The 1992 approval of the North American Free Trade Agreement provided for the gradual elimination of tariffs in many sectors and continued the Mexican oil industry hands-off status from foreign investors. Although NAFTA provided for the loosening of some immigration requirements, it did not provide for the elimination of all immigration barriers.

2. C. Mercosur is the name of a South American free trade association. Members include Argentina, Uruguay, Brazil, and other South American nations.

3. B. Pegged is the economic term used to indicate that a country has stabilized its exchange rate by legislation or market operations.

4. D. Critics of China's policies usually claim that its policy of keeping its currency undervalued underprices goods, making products from more freely traded currencies less competitive.

5. A. Russia was added to the G-7 in 1997 at the behest of President Clinton. The heads of state of the G-8 nations meet to discuss political and economic matters.

6. A. The General Agreement on Tariffs and Trade (GATT) talks resulted in the founding of the World Trade Organization in 1995. The WTO is the only global international organization dealing with the rules for trade between nations.

7. D. The Federal Reserve, the Department of Justice, and the Treasury Department all play a role in combating money laundering.

8. B. Keynes is known for advocating that governments practice a more interventionist economic policy.

9. A. Margaret Thatcher became the first world leader to implement the privatization of loss-making, state-owned enterprises when she sold off 51 percent of British Telecom in 1984. She followed up this sale by selling off British Gas (1986) and British Petroleum (1987).

10. D. Russia maintains an overall trade surplus with Europe because of high revenues from energy sales.

Practice Test 2

1. _____ was legislation enacted in response to the high-profile Enron and WorldCom financial scandals to protect shareholders and the general public from accounting errors and fraudulent accounting practices.

   A. Sarbanes-Oxley Act of 2002

   B. the Taft Act

   C. the Kennedy-Oxely

   D. the Public Accounting Act of 2002

2. The 1951 creation of the European Coal and Steel Community (ECSC) with six members — Belgium, West Germany, Luxembourg, France, Italy, and the Netherlands — is commonly accepted as being the forerunner to the

   A. World Trade Organization

   B. North Atlantic Treaty Organization

   C. European Union

   D. NATO

3. Despite its advanced economy, which of the following countries is not a member of the European Union?

   A. Hungary

   B. Finland

   C. Luxemburg

   D. Switzerland

4. At a price of $5, consumers wish to buy 100 widgets per month, but producers are willing to produce only 50 widgets per month. What best describes what will happen to the price?

   A. The price will double to make up for the deficit of 50 widgets.

   B. The price will reach an equilibrium between supply and demand.

   C. The price will rise upward indefinitely, reflecting the economics of scarcity.

   D. all of the above

5. A decline in the dollar's value would benefit

   A. exporters

   B. tourists

   C. truck drivers

   D. importers

6. Which of the following is true?

   A. A core responsibility of the IMF is to provide loans to countries experiencing payment difficulties.

   B. The International Monetary Fund was created in 1965 to help promote the health of the world economy.

   C. After countries deposit funds in the IMF, they cannot be withdrawn for fear of upsetting the world economy.

   D. all of the above

7. During much of the 19th century, the United States had _____ as Europeans financed the building of canals and railroads.

    A. an unfavorable balance of payments
    B. a favorable balance of payments
    C. a recession
    D. none of the above

8. In 2001, Russia implemented this type of tax system on personal income.

    A. progressive tax
    B. fair tax
    C. flat tax
    D. vice tax

9. The Federal Reserve System was created by Congress in _____ to provide for a safer, more flexible banking and monetary system.

    A. 1847
    B. 1897
    C. 1913
    D. 1946

10. For which of the following products would demand be inelastic?

    A. iceberg lettuce
    B. vegetables
    C. a Ford Explorer
    D. movie tickets

Answers to Practice Test 2

  1. A. Congress enacted the 2002 Sarbanes-Oxley Act to better protect shareholders and the general public from accounting errors and fraudulent company accounting practices such as occurred at Enron and WorldCom.

  2. C. The European Union originated from the European Coal and Steel Community (ECSC), an organization meant to organize the free movement of coal and steel and free access to sources of production. In addition, a common central authority supervised the market, oversaw respect for competition, and ensured price transparency.

  3. D. Despite Switzerland's advanced economy, it continues to remain outside of the European Union.

  4. B. If the quantity demanded is greater than the quantity supplied, the price will rise until the point at which the price reaches the equilibrium price — that is, the intersection of supply and demand.

  5. A. A decline in a currency's value always benefits exporters, while tourists, truck drivers, importers, and other consumers who rely on imported goods or must purchase goods denominated in another currency will generally suffer as their purchasing power diminishes.

  6. B. The IMF was founded in 1965 to help promote the health of the world economy.

  7. A. The United States had an unfavorable balance of payments as European capital financed building projects.

  8. B. In 2001, Russia implemented a flat tax of 13 percent on personal income.

  9. C. The Federal Reserve System was created by Congress in 1913 to help create a safer banking system that could meet the demands of a rapidly growing economy.

10. B. In the event of a large price increase, it would be relatively easy for customers to avoid the price increase by purchasing alternative products, for example, buying carrots rather than lettuce, choosing a Honda Accord rather than a Ford Explorer SUV, or renting a DVD rather than purchasing movie tickets. However, because vegetables comprise an entire category, it would be more difficult for consumers to change their buying habits to avoid the price increases associated with vegetables. Demand (or supply) is elastic if a small change in price results in a large change in demand. Conversely, if a small change in price does not result in a large change in demand, the demand is said to be inelastic.

Mathematics and Statistics

What You Should Know

In both the general and career track sections of the Job Knowledge test, the questions require knowledge of a general understanding of basic mathematics. This includes both general mathematics as well as statistical procedures. The questions encompass word problems and calculations.

The questions in the following section are for your review. Go through each question and try your best to answer it. The explanation of the answer follows immediately afterward so that you can actually learn new material. After you've completed reviewing these questions and answers, three brief practice review tests at the end of the chapter help you determine how much you know. Of course, there is a full-length exam at the end of Part II that also includes math and statistics questions.

Mathematics and Statistics Review Section

Read the following questions and select the choices that best answer the questions.

1. While on a trip to Greece, Janet decides to purchase a pair of shoes that cost 6,274 Drachmas. If each U. S. dollar is worth 200.5 Drachmas, what is the price of the shoes in U. S. dollars?

   A. $12.58
   B. $31.29
   C. $33.45
   D. $125.79

   B. $6{,}274 \text{ Drachmas} \times \dfrac{1 \text{ U.S. dollar}}{200.5 \text{ Drachmas}} = \$31.29$.

2. Dennis ran a race in 2.2 minutes. Kayla ran the same race in 124 seconds. What is the difference between these two times?

   A. 2 seconds
   B. 8 seconds
   C. 14 seconds
   D. 22 seconds

   B. Convert 2.2 minutes to seconds. $2.2 \times 60 = 132$ seconds. The difference in the two times is $132 - 124 = 8$ seconds.

3. The members of the Larchmont Automobile Club were surveyed about their favorite color of car. Each member could only select one color. The survey results are shown in the following table.

Color	Frequency
Red	45
Blue	33
Black	41
White	13
Green	18

What is the relative frequency of the choice "red"?

A. 0.2
B. 0.3
C. 0.45
D. 45

B. Overall, 45 + 33 + 41 + 13 + 18 = 150 people were surveyed. Of these, 45 said red, so the frequency for red is 45, and the relative frequency is 45 ÷ 150 = 0.3.

4. Stanley can type 35 words per minute. If it takes him a half-hour to type a document, about how many words are in the document?

A. 900
B. 1,050
C. 1,500
D. 2,100

B. There are 30 minutes in a half-hour. $30 \times 35 = 1,050$ words.

5. A recipe calls for 3 cups of wheat and white flour combined. If $\frac{3}{8}$ of this is wheat flour, how many cups of white flour are needed?

A. $1\frac{1}{8}$

B. $1\frac{7}{8}$

C. $2\frac{3}{8}$

D. $2\frac{5}{8}$

B. $\frac{3}{8}$ is wheat flour, then $1 - \frac{3}{8}$ or $\frac{5}{8}$ is white flour. So $3 \times \frac{5}{8} = \frac{15}{8} = 1\frac{7}{8}$ cups of white flour are needed.

6. A barrel holds 60 gallons of water. If a crack in the barrel causes $\frac{1}{2}$ a gallon to leak out each day, how many gallons of water remain after 2 weeks?

A. 30
B. 53
C. $56\frac{1}{2}$
D. 59

B. In 2 weeks, or 14 days, $\frac{1}{2} \times 14 = 7$ gallons leak out, leaving 60 − 7 = 53 gallons.

7. Which of the following sets of data is bimodal?

$A = \{2, 3, 3, 3, 4, 4, 5, 7\}$
$B = \{2, 2, 3, 3, 4, 4, 5, 6, 7\}$
$C = \{2, 3, 4, 5, 6, 7\}$
$D = \{2, 3, 3, 4, 5, 5, 7\}$

   A. A
   B. B
   C. C
   D. D

D. A bimodal set is a set that has two modes; in other words, there are two different numbers that appear the most frequently. The set that has this property is D, where the numbers 3 and 5 both occur twice.

8. Jack lives $6\frac{1}{2}$ miles from the library. If he walks $\frac{1}{3}$ of the way and takes a break, what is the remaining distance to the library?

   A. $5\frac{5}{6}$ miles

   B. 4 miles

   C. $4\frac{1}{3}$ miles

   D. $2\frac{1}{6}$ miles

C. $\frac{1}{3}$ of $6\frac{1}{2}$ miles is $\frac{1}{3} \times 6\frac{1}{2} = \frac{1}{3} \times \frac{13}{2} = \frac{13}{6}$ miles walked. The remaining distance is
$6\frac{1}{2} - \frac{13}{6} = \frac{13}{2} - \frac{13}{6} = \frac{39}{6} - \frac{13}{6} = \frac{26}{6} = 4\frac{1}{3}$ miles.

9. A sweater originally priced at $40 is on sale for $30. What percent has the sweater been discounted?

   A. 25%
   B. 33%
   C. 70%
   D. 75%

A. The amount of discount is $40 − $30 = $10. The percent of discount is the amount of discount divided by the original price. $\frac{10}{40} = \frac{1}{4} = 25\%$.

10. Kevin can read 2 pages in 3 minutes. At this rate, how long will it take him to read a 360-page book?

   A. 30 minutes
   B. 2 hours
   C. 6 hours
   D. 9 hours

D. Using the ratio $\frac{\text{pages}}{\text{minutes}}$, the proportion $\frac{2}{3} = \frac{360}{x}$ can be used to find the time. Cross multiply. $2x = 3 \times 360$, so $2x = 1{,}080$ and $x = \frac{1{,}080}{2} = 540$ minutes. Convert minutes to hours. There are 60 minutes in one hour, so $\frac{540}{60} = 9$ hours.

11. Hazel eats $\frac{3}{8}$ of a pizza and divides the rest between her two friends. What percent of the pizza do her friends each receive?

    A. 62.50%
    B. 37.50%
    C. 31.25%
    D. 18.75%

    C. If $\frac{3}{8}$ of the pizza is eaten, then $1 - \frac{3}{8} = \frac{5}{8}$ remains. If that is divided by 2, then each receives $\frac{5}{8} \div 2 = \frac{5}{8} \times \frac{1}{2} = \frac{5}{16} = 0.3125 = 31.25\%$.

12. One-fourth of the cars purchased at a dealership are luxury models. If 360 luxury models were sold last year, how many total cars were purchased?

    A. 90
    B. 250
    C. 1,440
    D. 3,600

    C. If t is the total number of cars sold, and $\frac{1}{4}$ of the total cars sold are luxury, luxury cars sold = 360, so $\frac{1}{4}t = 360$ and $t = 360 \times 4 = 1,440$ total cars sold.

Questions 13–15 are based on the following situation.

The following table shows the number of freshmen and sophomores involved in various sports. Each student participates in only one sport.

Sport	Freshmen	Sophomores
Football	9	13
Soccer	8	19
Basketball	2	5
Baseball	8	6

13. What percent of the students played basketball?

    A. 7%
    B. 10%
    C. 14%
    D. 20%

    B. The total number of students is 70. Of these, $2 + 5 = 7$ play basketball. Finally, $7 \div 70 = 10\%$.

14. Approximately what percent of the freshmen listed played football?

    A. 28.7%
    B. 31.4%
    C. 33.3%
    D. 81.4%

    C. There are 27 freshmen playing sports, and of these, 9 play football. This is about 33.3%.

15. How many more sophomores played these particular sports than freshmen?

    A. 10
    B. 12
    C. 14
    D. 16

    D. A total of 43 sophomores played as opposed to 27 freshmen. The difference is 43 − 27 = 16.

Problems 16–18 are based on the following situation.

    A survey of video-game-playing habits among twelve junior high school students resulted in the following data in hours per week: 9, 2, 2.5, 7, 6.5, 11, 7, 1.5, 1, 4, 12, 8.5

16. What is the average (arithmetic mean) number of hours spent playing video games by the students in the survey?

    A. 5.25 hours
    B. 5.75 hours
    C. 6.0 hours
    D. 6.5 hours

    C. To find the arithmetic mean, add up the twelve scores to get 72. Divide by 12 to get 6.

17. What is the range of the data values for the students given above?

    A. 10 hours
    B. 11 hours
    C. 12 hours
    D. 13 hours

    B. The range is the difference between the largest and smallest values; that is, 12 − 1 = 11.

18. A similar survey among high school students showed that the average number of hours spent a week playing video games per student was 20% less than the same figure for junior high school students. What was the average number of hours per week spent playing video games for high school students?

    A. 4.6 hours
    B. 4.8 hours
    C. 5.2 hours
    D. 7.2 hours

    B. The average number of hours for junior high school students was 6. To reduce 6 by 20%, determine 80% of 6. Thus, 6 × 80% = 4.8 hours.

19. If 400 people can be seated in 8 subway cars, how many people can be seated in 5 subway cars?

    A. 200
    B. 250
    C. 300
    D. 350

    B. If 400 people fit in 8 subway cars, then 400 ÷ 8, or 50, people fit in one subway car. Therefore, 50 × 5, or 250, people fit in 5 subway cars.

20. Rachel ran $\frac{1}{2}$ mile in 4 minutes. At this rate, how many miles can she run in 15 minutes?

   A. $1\frac{7}{8}$

   B. 4

   C. 30

   D. 60

A. The proportion $\dfrac{\frac{1}{2} \text{ mile}}{4 \text{ minutes}} = \dfrac{x \text{ miles}}{15 \text{ minutes}}$ models this situation. Cross multiply.

$$\frac{1}{2} \times 15 = 4x \text{ so } \frac{15}{2} = 4x \text{ and } x = \frac{15}{2} \cdot \frac{1}{4} = \frac{15}{8} = 1\frac{7}{8} \text{ miles.}$$

21. Mr. Scalici earns a weekly salary of $300 plus 10% commission on all sales. If he sold $8,350 last week, what were his total earnings?

   A. $835

   B. $865

   C. $1,135

   D. $1,835

C. The amount of commission is $10\% \times \$8{,}350 = \$835$. Total earnings are $\$300 + \$835$ commission $= \$1{,}135$.

22. Which is the only measure of central tendency that can be used for qualitative data?

   A. the arithmetic mean

   B. the median

   C. the mode

   D. the range

C. The mode, which is simply the most frequently occurring value, is the only measure of central tendency that can be determined with qualitative, non-numerical data.

23. A 10-foot rope is to be cut into equal segments measuring 8 inches each. The total number of segments is

   A. 1

   B. 8

   C. 15

   D. 40

C. The total number of inches in a 10 foot rope is $10 \times 12 = 120$ inches. The number of 8 inch segments that can be cut is $\frac{120}{8} = 15$.

24. A restaurant bill without tax and tip comes to $38.40. If a 15% tip is included after a 6% tax is added to the amount, how much is the tip?

   A. $6.11

   B. $5.76

   C. $5.15

   D. $2.30

A. The tax on the bill is $\$38.40 \times 6\% = \$2.30$. The amount, including tax, is $\$38.40 + \$2.30 = \$40.70$. The tip is $\$40.70 \times 15\% = \$6.11$.

25. Floor tiling costs $13.50 per square yard. What would it cost to tile a room 15 feet long by 18 feet wide?

    A. $20
    B. $405
    C. $1,350
    D. $3,645

    B. The area of a room 15 feet wide by 18 feet long is $15 \times 18 = 270$ square feet. Because there are 3 feet in a yard, there are 3×3 or 9 square feet in a square yard. Convert 270 square feet to square yards. $\frac{270}{9} = 30$ square yards. Because the cost is $13.50 per square yard, the total cost is 13.50×30, or $405.

26. Fencing costs $4.75 per foot. Posts cost $12.50 each. How much will it cost to fence a garden if 10 posts and 34 feet of fencing are needed?

    A. $472.50
    B. $336.50
    C. $315.50
    D. $286.50

    D. The total cost for the posts and fencing is $(10 \times \$12.50) + (34 \times \$4.75) = \$125.00 + \$161.50 = \$286.50$.

27. Brian took an admissions exam. After taking the test, Brian was told that his score was in the 64th percentile. What does this statement mean?

    A. 64 of the students who took the test did better than Brian.
    B. 64 of the students who took the test did worse than Brian.
    C. 64% of the students who took the test did better than Brian.
    D. 64% of the students who took the test did worse than Brian.

    D. If Brian is in the 64th percentile, 64% of the students who took the test did worse than he did.

28. A taxi ride costs $3.00 for the first mile and $1.00 for each additional half-mile. What is the cost of a 10-mile ride?

    A. $10
    B. $12
    C. $13
    D. $21

    D. In a 10-mile trip, after the first mile, there are 9 additional miles. If each additional half-mile is $1, then an additional mile is $2. The cost of the trip is $3 for the first mile + ($2 × 9) for the additional miles. $3 + $18 = $21.

29. Sandy bought $4\frac{1}{2}$ lbs of apples and 6 kiwi fruits. Brandon bought $3\frac{1}{4}$ lbs of apples and 9 kiwi fruits. If apples cost $1.39 per lb and kiwis are 2 for $1.00, how much more money did Sandy spend than Brandon?

    A. $0.24
    B. $0.94
    C. $1.54
    D. $2.32

    A. The cost of Sandy's purchase is $(4\frac{1}{2} \times \$1.39) + (6 \times \$0.50) = \$9.26$. The cost of Brandon's purchase is $(3\frac{1}{4} \times \$1.39) + (9 \times \$0.50) = \$9.02$. Sandy spent $9.26 – $9.02 = $0.24 more.

30. In a standard deck of playing cards, a king of hearts is drawn and not replaced. What is the probability of drawing another king from the deck?

    A. $\frac{1}{4}$

    B. $\frac{1}{13}$

    C. $\frac{1}{17}$

    D. $\frac{3}{52}$

    C. Probability is $\frac{\text{number of successful outcomes}}{\text{number of possible outcomes}}$. Because one king was drawn and not replaced, three kings remain in the deck of 51 cards. So the probability of drawing another king is $\frac{3}{51} = \frac{1}{17}$.

31. A rope is made by linking beads that are $\frac{1}{2}$ inch in diameter. How many feet long is a rope made from 60 beads?

    A. $2\frac{1}{2}$ ft

    B. 10 ft

    C. 30 ft

    D. 120 ft

    A. 60 beads $\times \frac{1}{2}$ inch = 30 inches. Converting this to feet gives 30 inches $\times \frac{1 \text{ foot}}{12 \text{ inches}} = \frac{30}{12} = 2\frac{1}{2}$ feet.

32. A foreign automobile manufacturer has a shipping charge of \$3 per kilogram for all parts sent to the United States. To the nearest dollar, what would be the shipping charges for a motor weighing 200 pounds? Note that there are 0.455 kilograms in a pound.

    A. \$60

    B. \$132

    C. \$152

    D. \$273

    D. Begin by changing the 200 pounds to kilograms.

$$200 \text{ pounds} \times \frac{0.455 \text{ kg}}{1 \text{ pound}} = 91 \text{ kg}$$

Now, at \$3 per kilogram, the shipping charge would be 91 $\times$ \$3 = \$273.

33. While dining out, Chad spent \$25.00. If the bill totaled \$21.00 before the tip was added, approximately what percent tip did Chad leave?

    A. 16%

    B. 19%

    C. 21%

    D. 25%

    B. The percent tip is the amount of tip over the total before tip. The amount of the tip is \$25.00 − \$21.00 = \$4.00. The percent of the tip is $\frac{4}{21} = 0.19 = 19\%$.

34. What is the probability of rolling a sum of 9 using two dice?

    A. $\frac{1}{4}$

    B. $\frac{1}{9}$

    C. $\frac{5}{12}$

    D. $\frac{7}{36}$

    B. There are four possible ways to roll a 9 using 2 dice: 3 and 6, 4 and 5, 5 and 4, and 6 and 3. The total number of possible outcomes when rolling 2 dice is 6^2 or 36. Therefore, the probability of rolling a 9 is $\frac{4}{36} = \frac{1}{9}$.

Problems 35 and 36 are based on the following situation.

In a test of car mileage, 5 cars were tested in both highway and city driving. The following data was recorded for the 5 cars.

			Miles per Gallon		
Car #	*1*	*2*	*3*	*4*	*5*
Highway	20.5	25.3	24.3	27.1	22.9
City	16.9	19.5	17.8	20.2	16.1

35. What is the difference between the average (arithmetic mean) miles per gallon of the 5 cars for highway driving and the average (arithmetic mean) of the 5 cars for city driving?

    A. 3.6 miles per gallon
    B. 5.9 miles per gallon
    C. 6.4 miles per gallon
    D. 6.8 miles per gallon

    B. The highway average is $\frac{20.5 + 25.3 + 24.2 + 27.1 + 22.9}{5} = 24$. The city driving average is $\frac{16.9 + 19.5 + 17.8 + 20.2 + 16.1}{5} = 18.1$. The difference between these two numbers is $24 - 18.1 = 5.9$.

36. What is the range of the data values of the 5 cars for highway driving?

    A. 4.2 miles per gallon
    B. 4.8 miles per gallon
    C. 6.6 miles per gallon
    D. 24 miles per gallon

    C. The range is the difference between the maximum and minimum values. This is equal to $27.1 - 20.5 = 6.6$.

37. When Brett Bayne's flight from Tokyo arrives in Paris, he converts 50,000 yen into francs. If one U.S. dollar is worth 140 yen and one U.S. dollar is also worth 6 francs, approximately how many francs does he receive?

    A. 63
    B. 1,167
    C. 2,143
    D. 4,200

    C. Begin by converting the yen to dollars; after this, we can convert the dollars to francs.

$$50{,}000 \text{ yen} \times \frac{1 \text{ dollar}}{140 \text{ yen}} = \$357.14. \text{ Then,}$$

$$\$357.14 \times \frac{6 \text{ francs}}{1 \text{ dollar}} = 2{,}142.8 \approx 2{,}143 \text{ francs.}$$

38. A savings account earns $2\frac{1}{4}\%$ interest each year. How much interest is earned on a \$1,000 deposit after a 5-year period?

    A. \$22.50
    B. \$100.00
    C. \$112.50
    D. \$150.00

    C. Interest = principle × rate × time. Thus, interest = $\$1{,}000 \times 2\frac{1}{4}\% \times 5 = \$1{,}000 \times 0.0225 \times 5 = \$112.50$

Questions 39–42 are based on the following situation.

A group of claims analysts at Empire Insurance were asked how many years of experience they had in the insurance industry. The results are shown in the following cumulative frequency graph.

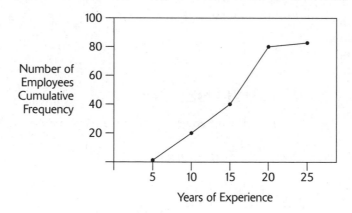

39. According to the graph, approximately how many of the claims analysts surveyed had less than 5 years of experience?

    A. none
    B. 5
    C. 10
    D. 20

    A. Because the graph starts at the point (5, 0), it indicates that no one had less than 5 years of experience.

40. Approximately how many employees took part in the survey?

    A. 25
    B. 83
    C. 100
    D. 225

B. Because the graph depicts the running total of the data collected, look at the point on the graph which is the farthest to the right. It appears to be approximately (25, 83). Because the second coordinate represents the running total of the number of people surveyed, it appears as if 83 people were surveyed.

41. Approximately how many of the employees had 15 years of experience or less?

    A. 20
    B. 30
    C. 40
    D. 50

C. Note that, on the graph, 15 years of experience is associated with 40 employees. Because this graph depicts a running total, you know that 40 employees had 15 years of experience or less.

42. Approximately how many of the employees had more than 20 years of experience?

    A. 3
    B. 40
    C. 80
    D. 140

A. Because 80 employees had 20 years of experience or less and there were a total of 83 people surveyed, only 3 employees had more than 20 years of experience.

Practice Tests

Directions: Following are three mini-practice tests. Select the choice that best answers each question. Fully explained answers follow each test.

Practice Test 1

1. A line on a blueprint measures 1.5 yards. If 1 yard is equivalent to 0.9 meters, approximately what is the length of the line in meters?

    A. 0.6 meters
    B. 1.35 meters
    C. 1.67 meters
    D. 2.4 meters

Problems 2–4 are based on the following graph.

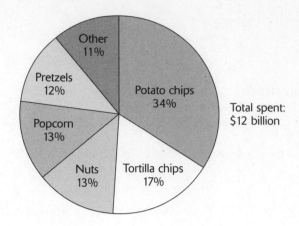

2. What was the total amount spent on nuts and pretzels in 2005?

   A. $1.44 billion
   B. $1.56 billion
   C. $3.0 billion
   D. $3.12 billion

3. What was the ratio of money spent on potato chips to money spent on tortilla chips?

   A. 2 : 1
   B. 3 : 2
   C. 1 : 2
   D. 2 : 3

4. If 30% of the money spent on potato chips was spent on barbecued potato chips, approximately how much money was spent on barbecued potato chips?

   A. $ 1.2 billion
   B. $ 0.6 billion
   C. $ 3.6 billion
   D. $ 2.4 billion

5. Lauren earns $8.40 an hour plus an overtime rate equal to $1\frac{1}{2}$ times her regular pay for each hour worked beyond 40 hours. What are her total earnings for a 45-hour work week?

   A. $336
   B. $370
   C. $399
   D. $567

6. One phone plan charges a $20 monthly fee and $0.08 per minute on every phone call made. Another phone plan charges a $12 monthly fee and $0.12 per minute for each call. After how many minutes would the charge be the same for both plans?

   A. 60 minutes
   B. 90 minutes
   C. 120 minutes
   D. 200 minutes

7. Amelia casts a shadow 5 feet long. Her father, who is 6 feet tall, casts a shadow 8 feet long. How tall is Amelia?

    A. 6 feet 8 inches

    B. 4 feet 10 inches

    C. 4 feet 6 inches

    D. 3 feet 9 inches

8. Paul donates $\frac{4}{13}$ of his paycheck to his favorite charity. If he donates $26.80, what is the amount of his paycheck?

    A. $8.25

    B. $82.50

    C. $87.10

    D. $348.40

9. Tiling costs $2.89 per square foot. What is the cost to tile a kitchen with dimensions of 4 yards by 5 yards?

    A. $57.80

    B. $173.40

    C. $289.00

    D. $520.20

10. The scale on a map shows 500 feet for every $\frac{1}{4}$ inch. If two cities are 6 inches apart on the map, what is the actual distance they are apart?

    A. 125 feet

    B. 750 feet

    C. 2,000 feet

    D. 12,000 feet

Answers to Practice Test 1

1. B. 1.5 yards $\times \dfrac{0.9 \text{ meter}}{1 \text{ yard}} = 1.35$ meters.

2. C. Nuts and pretzels together account for 13% + 12% = 25% of the $12 billion in snack sales. $12 billion $\times$ 25% = $3 billion.

3. A. The quickest way to do this is to work with the percents instead of the numbers. Therefore, the ratio can be expressed as 34 : 17, or 2 : 1.

4. A. Potato chips account for 34% of sales or $12 billion $\times$ 34% = $4.08 billion. Then, 30% of this amount would be the amount spent on barbequed potato chips. Thus, $4.08 billion $\times$ 30% $\approx$ $1.2 billion.

5. C. The overtime rate is $8.40 $\times$ 1.5 = $12.60. Five hours of overtime were completed, so the total earnings are ($8.40 $\times$ 40) + ($12.60 $\times$ 5) = $336 + $63 = $399.

6. D. Let m represent the minutes of the phone calls. The monthly charge for the first plan is $20 + 0.08m$. The monthly charge for the second plan is $12 + 0.12m$. When the monthly charges are the same, $20 + 0.08m = 12 + 0.12m$. Solve for m to find the number of minutes both plans have the same rate.

$$20 + 0.08m - 0.08m = 12 + 0.12m - 0.08m$$

$$20 = 12 + 0.04m$$

$$20 - 12 = 12 + 0.04m - 12$$

$$8 = 0.04m \text{ so } m = \frac{8}{0.04} = \frac{800}{4} = 200 \text{ minutes}$$

7. **D.** Using the ratio $\dfrac{\text{height}}{\text{shadow}}$, the proportion $\dfrac{x \text{ feet}}{5 \text{ feet}} = \dfrac{6 \text{ feet}}{8 \text{ feet}}$ can be used to find the unknown height. Cross multiply. $8x = 5 \times 6$, so $8x = 30$ and $x = \dfrac{30}{8} = 3\dfrac{3}{4}$ feet. Convert $\dfrac{3}{4}$ feet to inches. $\dfrac{3}{4} \times 12 = 9$ inches. The height is, therefore, 3 feet 9 inches.

8. **C.** Let p represent the amount of the paycheck. $\dfrac{4}{13}p = \$26.80$, so $p = \$26.80 \cdot \dfrac{13}{4} = \$87.10$.

9. **D.** There are 3 feet in a yard, so a kitchen 4 yards by 5 yards is equivalent to (4×3) feet by (5×3) feet, or 12 feet by 15 feet. The area of the kitchen is $12 \times 15 = 180$ square feet. The cost to tile is $\$2.89 \times 180 = \$520.20$.

10. **D.** The proportion $\dfrac{500 \text{ ft}}{\frac{1}{4} \text{ in}} = \dfrac{x \text{ ft}}{6 \text{ in}}$ can be used to find the number of actual distance. Cross multiply. $500 \times 6 = \dfrac{1}{4}x$, so $3{,}000 = \dfrac{1}{4}x$ and $x = 3{,}000 \times 4 = 12{,}000$ ft.

Practice Test 2

Problems 1–2 are based on the following situation.

At Erie County Community College, there are seven different classes of students taking Calculus I. The number of students in these classes is 18, 22, 16, 25, 19, 17, and 18.

1. What is the median size of a Calculus I class?

    A. 17
    B. 18
    C. 19
    D. 22

2. Which of the following statements is true?

    A. The modal Calculus I class size is less than the median class size.
    B. The modal Calculus I class size is equal to the median class size.
    C. The modal Calculus I class size is greater than the median class size.
    D. The given data is bimodal.

3. Doug earns 15% commission on all sales over $5,000. Last month, his sales totaled $12,500. What were Doug's earnings?

    A. $750
    B. $1,125
    C. $1,875
    D. $2,625

4. Three boxes are needed to hold 18 reams of paper. How many boxes are needed for 90 reams?

    A. 5
    B. 6
    C. 9
    D. 15

5. Kyle ran 3 miles in $17\frac{1}{2}$ minutes on Saturday, $4\frac{1}{2}$ miles in 22 minutes on Sunday, and 2 miles in 9 minutes on Monday. What was Kyle's average rate of speed while running?

   A. 1.6 minutes per mile
   B. 5.1 minutes per mile
   C. 16.2 minutes per mile
   D. 17.8 minutes per mile

6. On a map, 1 centimeter represents 4 miles. A distance of 10 miles would be how far apart on the map?

   A. $1\frac{3}{4}$ cm

   B. 2 cm

   C. $2\frac{1}{2}$ cm

   D. 4 cm

7. Cards normally sell for $3.00 each. How much is saved if 5 cards are purchased on sale for 2 for $5.00?

   A. $2.50
   B. $5.00
   C. $12.50
   D. $15.00

8. If 3 cans of soup cost $5.00, how much do 10 cans cost?

   A. $15.00
   B. $16.45
   C. $16.67
   D. $17.33

9. Staci earns $9.50 an hour plus 3% commission on all sales made. If her total sales during a 30-hour work week were $500, how much did she earn?

   A. $15
   B. $250
   C. $285
   D. $300

10. The girl's basketball team won three times as many games as they lost. How many games were won if they played a total of 24 games?

   A. 6
   B. 8
   C. 12
   D. 18

Answers to Practice Test 2

1. **B.** Begin by putting the numbers of students in numerical order: 16, 17, 18, 18, 19, 22, 25. Because there are an odd number of numbers, the median will be the number in the middle, which is 18.

2. **B.** The mode is the most frequently occurring number, which is 18. Thus, the mode and the median are the same.

3. B. The amount of commissions over $5,000 is $12,500 – $5,000 = $7,500. Earnings are $7,500 × 15% = $1,125.

4. D. The proportion $\frac{3 \text{ boxes}}{18 \text{ reams}} = \frac{x \text{ boxes}}{90 \text{ reams}}$ can be used to find the number of boxes. Cross multiply. $3 \times 90 = 18x$ so $270 = 18x$ and $x = \frac{270}{18} = 15$ boxes.

5. B. Average is the total time divided by the total miles run. The total time is 17.5 + 22 + 9 = 48.5 minutes. The total number of miles run is 3 + 4.5 + 2 = 9.5. The average is $\frac{48.5}{9.5} = 5.1$ minutes per mile.

6. C. The proportion $\frac{1 \text{ cm}}{4 \text{ miles}} = \frac{x \text{ cm}}{10 \text{ miles}}$ models this situation. Cross multiply. $1 \times 10 = 4x$ so $10 = 4x$ and $x = \frac{10}{4} = 2\frac{1}{2}$ cm.

7. A. Five cards at $3.00 each cost 5 × $3.00 = $15.00. If cards are 2 for $5.00, the cost per cards is $\frac{\$5.00}{2} = \$2.50$, so 5 cards would cost $2.50 × 5 = $12.50. The amount saved is $15.00 – $12.50 = $2.50.

8. C. The proportion $\frac{\$5.00}{3 \text{ cans}} = \frac{\$x}{10 \text{ cans}}$ can be used to find the cost of 10 cans. Cross multiply. $5 \times 10 = 3x$, so $50 = 3x$ and $x = \frac{50}{3} = \$16.67$.

9. D. For a 30-hour week with $500 in sales, total earnings are (30 × $9.50) + (3% × $500) = $285 + $15 = $300.

10. D. Let w represent the games won and l represent the games lost. Then $w = 3 \times l = 3l$. The total number of games played is $w + l = 24$. Substituting $3l$ in for w yields $3l + l = 24$ or $4l = 24$. The number of losses is $\frac{24}{4} = 6$ and the number of wins is 24 – 6 = 18.

Practice Test 3

1. While driving in Canada, Dave sees a sign that says that the distance to the next exit is 80 kilometers. If a mile is approximately equal to 1.6 kilometers, what is the distance to the next exit in miles?

   A. 50 miles

   B. 54 miles

   C. 128 miles

   D. 200 miles

Problems 2–4 are based on the following graph.

The following circle graph shows the distribution of a company's current assets.

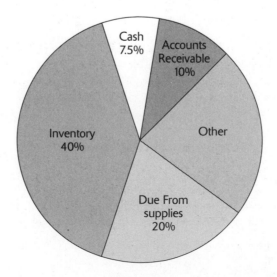

2. If the company has $30 million in cash, what is the total amount of its current assets?

    A. $225 million
    B. $250 million
    C. $380 million
    D. $400 million

3. How much more money does the company have in inventory than in accounts receivable?

    A. $30 million
    B. $60 million
    C. $120 million
    D. $200 million

4. How much money does the company have in other current assets?

    A. $56 million
    B. $85 million
    C. $90 million
    D. $178 million

5. While on a trip to Denmark, Hazel buys a dress that costs 3,500 krones. If there are 7.1 krones in a U.S. dollar, what is the cost of the dress (to the nearest dollar) in U.S. dollars?

    A. $203
    B. $249
    C. $476
    D. $493

6. The quality control department examines a random sample of 450 motors and determines that 9 of them have been assembled incorrectly. At this rate, how many motors would be incorrectly assembled in a shipment of 2,000 motors?

    A. 40
    B. 42
    C. 44
    D. 46

Problems 7–8 are based on the following situation.

Eight employees were asked to contribute to a going-away party for a co-worker. The amounts that were contributed were $15, $5, $20, $20, $25, $40, $35, and $30.

7. What is the difference between the mean contribution and the median contribution?

    A. $0.75
    B. $1.00
    C. $1.25
    D. $1.50

8. If the employee who contributed $5 to the party reconsidered and contributed $10 instead, which of the following would not change?

    A. the range of the contributed amounts

    B. the mean of the contributed amounts

    C. the median of the contributed amounts

    D. the total of the contributed amounts

9. A printer originally priced at $240 is on sale for $180. By what percent has the price been discounted?

    A. 25%

    B. $33\frac{1}{3}\%$

    C. $66\frac{2}{3}\%$

    D. 75%

10. A computer hardware manufacturing company has a shipping charge of $2.75 per kilogram for all parts sent to the United States. If 1 kilogram is approximately equal to 2.2 pounds, what would be the shipping charge, rounded to the nearest dollar, for a part that weighs 44 pounds?

    A. $55

    B. $73

    C. 138

    D. $151

Answers to Practice Test 3

1. A. $80 \text{ km} \times \frac{1 \text{ mile}}{1.6 \text{ km}} = 50 \text{ miles}$

2. D. The $30 million that the company has in cash represents 7.5% of its current assets.

$$\frac{30}{7.5\%} = \frac{30}{0.075} = \$400 \text{ million in current assets}$$

3. C. Of the current assets, 40% are in inventory and 10% are in accounts receivable. The difference between the two, then, is 30%. The total amount of current assets is $400 million. Finally, $30\% \times \$400 = \$120$ million.

4. C. Because the percentages in a circle graph must total 100%, the amount in the "Other" category must represent 22.5% of the total. Then, $22.5\% \times 400 = \$90$ million.

5. D. $3{,}500 \text{ krones} \times \frac{1 \text{ dollar}}{7.1 \text{ krones}} = \$492.9 \approx \$493$.

6. A. This problem can be solved by using a proportion.

$$\frac{\text{incorrect} \rightarrow}{\text{total} \rightarrow} \frac{9}{450} = \frac{x}{2{,}000}. \text{ Cross-multiply.}$$

$$2{,}000 \times 9 = 450x$$

$$18{,}000 = 450x. \text{ Divide by 450.}$$

$$x = 40$$

7. C. To find the median, put the contributed amounts in numerical order: $5, $15, $20, $20, $25, $30, $35, $40. The median of an even number of numbers is the mean of the two numbers in the middle. These two numbers are $20 and $25, so the median is $22.50. To find the mean, add all eight numbers and divide by 8. The mean is $23.75. The difference between the mean and the median, then, is $23.75 – $22.50 = $1.25.

8. C. Changing the $5 to $10 does not change the numbers in the middle, so the median remains the same. The total amount and the mean would be larger, and the range would be smaller.

9. A. The amount of the discount is $240 − $180 = $60. This amount is 25% of the original value of $240.

10. A. 44 pounds $\times \dfrac{1 \text{ kg}}{2.2 \text{ pounds}} = 20$ kg. 20 kg $\times$ $2.75 per kg. = $55.

Management

What You Should Know

In both the general and career track sections of the Job Knowledge test, the questions require knowledge of general basic management operations. This topic covers areas such as basic managerial principles, as well as management techniques and methods. It will require a core understanding of psychology and human behavior, as well as methods to motivate people. The test will also test your knowledge of essential leadership approaches, such as modeling. In addition, it is important to have an understanding of Equal Employment Opportunity policies, as well as regulations and laws.

The questions in the following section are for your review. Go through each question and try your best to answer it. The explanation of the answer follows immediately afterward so that you can actually learn new material. After you've completed reviewing these questions and answers, three brief practice review tests at the end of the chapter help you determine how much you know. Of course, there is a full-length exam at the end of Part II that also includes management questions.

Management Review Section

Read the following questions and select the choices that best answer the questions.

1. What is the most effective method for a firm to improve morale for its employees?

   A. increasing salary
   B. having programs that cater to their emotional, psychological, and domestic needs
   C. having corporate parties all the time
   D. having top management present company directions and strategy

   B. Employees all have emotional, psychological, and domestic problems. Having health plans, child-care facilities, and counseling services are just some examples. Increasing salary is a short-term incentive; employees will quickly adjust to the new salary and morale will drop back down again. The other two choices have smaller effects but not as great as the programs cited in answer B.

2. Which of the two strategies can effectively be used to motivate employees?

   A. behavior modification and job design
   B. overseas posting and self-improvement courses
   C. promotion and holidays
   D. vouchers and gifts

   A. Behavior modification involves changing behavior and encouraging appropriate actions by relating the consequences of behavior to the behavior itself. Job design means to use the job itself to motivate and improve employee motivation. This can be done through job rotation, enlargement, and so on. Answers B, C, and D are all useful but less effective.

3. Which of these strategies cannot be used to motivate the employee?

   A. job rotation
   B. job enlargement
   C. job enrichment
   D. job reduction

D. Job rotation is the movement of employees from one job to another in an effort to relieve the boredom often associated with job specialization. Job enlargement is the addition of more tasks to a job instead of treating each task as separate. Job enrichment is the incorporation of motivational factors, such as opportunity for achievement, recognition, responsibility, and advancement. Job reduction, on the other hand, implies that the employee is not able to take up more responsibilities and is, therefore, bad.

4. This is a program that allows employees to choose their starting and ending times, provided that they are at work during a specified core period. What is it?

   A. double time
   B. flextime
   C. part time
   D. job sharing

   B. Flextime is the program adopted by many U.S. companies as they recognize that making allowances for employees' schedules increases employee morale and productivity. Double time and part time are not correct. Job sharing is not correct, but is a useful management tool that occurs when two people share a job. This allows the employee to keep a job without losing income and yet being able to spend time on personal priorities.

5. With affirmative action programs, legally mandated plans try to increase job opportunities for

   A. professionals
   B. white Caucasian males
   C. highly qualified individuals
   D. women and minorities

   D. Affirmative action programs are legally mandated plans that try to increase job opportunities for minority groups by analyzing the current pool of workers, identifying areas where women and minorities are underrepresented, and establishing specific hiring and promotion goals, with target dates, for addressing the discrepancy.

6. The Equal Pay Act mandates that men and women who do equal work must receive the same wage. Wage differences are acceptable only if they are attributed to seniority or

   A. national origin
   B. religion
   C. performance
   D. location

   C. Performance varies across individuals and as such different wages should be applied. Although people in different locations get different gross wages, that approach is still based on the same base wage with different location allowance. National origin and religion are not relevant.

7. Which of these is not a factor in evaluating employee performance?

   A. productivity
   B. leadership
   C. adaptability
   D. social skills

   D. Productivity, leadership, and adaptability are very important in evaluating employee performance. Productivity is the rate at which work is regularly produced and determines the effectiveness of the firm. A firm needs good leadership to grow. Employees that are potential good leaders should be groomed to top management roles. Adaptability is the ability to be comfortable with change. The only thing that is constant in a firm is usually change. Thus employees need to be able to adapt relatively quickly to changes.

8. In companies, people come and go. Which of these is not a rule for peaceful separation (resignation)?

   A. Prior to leaving, do not disrupt your current employer's business.
   B. Inform everyone that you are leaving the firm.
   C. Sign an agreement with your new employer only after you have left the old position.
   D. Have the recruiting employer indemnify you from judgments, settlements, and attorney fees resulting from litigation initiated by the former employee.

   B. When leaving a company, the decision to leave should only be discussed with those who need to know, such as your immediate supervisor and colleagues. There is no need to let everyone know, because this may dampen morale for the firm and may create more problems later on. There are other rules for peaceful separations, including not disrupting the current employer's workflow and keeping trade secrets of the current employer.

9. The International Monetary Fund (IMF) was established to

   A. promote trade among member nations by eliminating trade barriers and fostering financial cooperation
   B. loan money to underdeveloped developing countries; it was formally known as the International Bank for Reconstruction and Development
   C. ensure that there is no major currency speculation in the world
   D. all of the above

   A. The IMF also makes short-term loans to member countries that have balance-of-payment deficits and provides foreign currencies to member nations. The IMF also avoids financial crises by alerting the international communities about countries that cannot repay their debts. Answer B is what the World Bank does. The World Bank and other multilateral development banks are the largest source of advice and assistance for developing nations.

10. The negotiation process through which management and unions reach an agreement about compensation, working hours, and working conditions is

   A. union labor contract
   B. union Arbitration
   C. union Mediation
   D. collective bargaining

   D. The objective of the collective bargaining is to reach a labor contract. In collective bargaining, each side tries to reach an agreement that meets its demands. Sometimes, if this is not resolved amicably, it will lead to strikes and picketing.

11. In the event that a collective bargaining process fails to go through, what can management do?

   A. strike
   B. boycott
   C. lock out
   D. picket

   C. A lockout is the management's version of a strike, wherein a work site is closed so that employees cannot go to work. A strike is a walkout by employees, one of the most effective weapons employees have for collective bargaining. A boycott is an attempt to keep people from buying the products of the company, while picketing is a public protest against management practices that involves union members marching and carrying anti-management signs at the employer's plant.

12. In marketing management, which of these is not part of the marketing mix?

   A. consumer
   B. place
   C. price
   D. product

A. The marketing mix comprises price, product, promotion, and place. The consumer is never part of the marketing mix. A marketing firm needs to target the consumer and then apply the appropriate marketing mix to that targeted consumer group.

13. The central focus of marketing is to create utility, which refers to a product's ability to satisfy human needs and wants. A McDonald's Big Mac or a two-day vacation at Walt Disney World both satisfy needs or wants. Which of the following is a utility not provided by marketing?

    A. place
    B. possession
    C. form
    D. time

    C. Place is the location where the product or services is provided. Possession is the ability of the consumer to afford and own the product or service. Time is the availability of the product or services to the consumer. These three all can be determined by marketing management. Form utility, on the other hand, is the physical product that gives the consumer the utility level so desired.

14. Why do we need to segment the market before applying the marketing mix?

    A. Because the market is too defragmented, and we need to consolidate.
    B. Because consumers are very heterogeneous, and we need to form similar groups for targeting.
    C. Because it is easier to staff manpower.
    D. Because the marketing mix can be applied only to segments and not masses.

    B. Consumers are very heterogeneous. By segmenting, firms are able to better target the specific groups and then apply a concentrated marketing mix effort on the segment. This way, the consumers have a better product or service that they need and will be more satisfied. Marketing mix for mass marketing is also possible; thus, D is not an answer.

15. Which of these is a multiple target market strategy?

    A. promoting BMW Z4 to a select group of customers
    B. selling generic tires nationwide
    C. combo meals for parents and kids at McDonald's
    D. having product lines with many products

    D. Having a product line caters to the needs of multiple users, because consumers are heterogeneous. Answer A is a single market, but narrow approach, because it is only for a select group of consumers, usually for luxury goods. Answer B is a mass-market approach, while answer C is a combined market approach.

16. Which of these cannot be used as a basis for segmenting consumers?

    A. demographic information, which includes gender and income
    B. geographic information, which includes terrains and population density
    C. psychographic information, which includes personality and motives
    D. medical condition information, which includes health and cancer records

    D. The first three can be used to segment the consumer groups. Psychographic information is particularly interesting, because the study of consumers' behavior reveals that there are certain groups of consumers that a marketing mix will be particularly successful in approaching, if firms understand the lifestyles and personality of the consumers. Medical conditions change with time and location; although it is technically possible to segment based on medical conditions, it will be trivial and a secondary finding compared to the first three answers.

17. What are the 4Ps of the marketing mix?

    A. place, product, people, price
    B. product, people, place, promotion
    C. product, price, people, promotion
    D. product, place, price, promotion

    D. The 4Ps include product, place, price and promotion. People or the consumers are never part of the marketing mix. The consumers need to be segmented and targeted before the marketing mix is applied to the specific market segment. However, a marketing firm cannot control or change the people (consumers) and, hence, they are not part of the marketing mix.

18. In marketing research, what is the difference between primary and secondary data?

    A. The former is used by marketing managers, while the latter is used by consumers.
    B. The former is collected directly from consumers, while the latter is aggregated or compiled information.
    C. The former is collected directly from consumers, while the latter is seldom used by marketing managers.
    D. The former is used by marketing managers, while the latter is aggregated or compiled data.

    B. Primary data is marketing information that is observed, recorded, or collected directly from respondents, while secondary data is market information that is compiled inside or outside an organization for some purpose other than changing the current situation.

19. For consumer buying behavior, which of these is not a psychological variable affecting it?

    A. imagination
    B. perception
    C. attitude
    D. personality

    A. Imagination is the irrelevant answer. Perception is the process by which a person selects, organizes, and interprets information received from his or her senses. Attitude is both knowledge and positive or negative feelings about something. Personality is the organization of an individual's distinguishing character traits, attitudes, or habits. These three psychological factors affect a consumer's buying behavior, so firms need to be aware of them.

20. Which of these is not a social variable of consumer buying behavior?

    A. social roles
    B. reference groups
    C. social learning
    D. social class

    C. Social learning is not a social variable; it is more of a psychological variable. Social roles refer to a set of expectations for individuals based on some position they occupy. Reference groups are groups with whom buyers identify and whose values or attitudes they adopt. Social classes refer to the ranking of people into higher or lower positions of respect. These three are social variables that affect buying behavior.

21. The marketing environment includes the following:

    A. political factors, social factors, competitive factors, technological factors
    B. psychological factors, social factors, competitive factors, technological factors
    C. political factors, social factors, military factors, technological factors
    D. political factors, biological factors, competitive factors, technological factors

    A. The marketing environment includes political factors that cover how laws affect the marketing mix. Social factors include lifestyles and ethics, while competitive factors include economic conditions. Technological factors include technological advances that improve the marketing mix.

22. What is the bottom line for micro marketing?

    A. sales

    B. expense

    C. profit

    D. pricing

C. The bottom line of micro marketing is profit. Profit is the difference between gross sales and expenses. For macro marketing and nonprofit marketing the bottom lines will be different. For macro marketing, the society must benefit as a whole, while for nonprofit marketing, the subjects or goals of the agency has to be fulfilled.

23. Many firms need to develop new products. What do you think is the sequence involved in new product development?

    A. idea development, idea screening, test marketing, product development, commercialization

    B. idea development, idea screening, test marketing, commercialization, product development

    C. test marketing, idea development, idea screening, product development, commercialization

    D. idea development, idea screening, product development, test marketing, commercialization

D. Very few products, out of thousands that are introduced, succeed. It is critical that firms conduct the appropriate steps to ensure the product will be successful. Idea development and screening is the first phase to get feasible ideas on the drawing board. The prototype is then developed before a sample market is tested with that product. When the test market feedback is good, full commercialization is possible.

24. Consumer products are products intended for household or family use. Which of these is not a consumer-convenience product?

    A. furniture

    B. eggs

    C. batteries

    D. newspapers

A. Convenience products are bought frequently, without a lengthy search, and often for immediate consumption. Consumers spend virtually no time planning where to purchase these products and usually accept whatever brand is available. Furniture is a product that requires extensive search.

25. Which of these is not a consumer product?

    A. specialty products

    B. raw materials

    C. shopping products

    D. convenience products

B. Raw materials are natural products taken from the earth, oceans, and recycled solid waste. It is usually the starting phase of any products or business products. Convenience products are frequently purchased products, while shopping products are products in which consumers compare and contrast the benefits and costs. Specialty products are products such as fusion food or designer clothing. Thus, raw materials is the correct answer.

26. In product management, in which stage of the product life cycle is there a negative profit?

    A. introduction

    B. growth

    C. maturity

    D. decline

A. During the introduction phase, the sales volume is low and the cost of product development is high. As such, the profit is negative for the introduction phase. During the growth stage, sales volume picks up, and profit is positive. For maturity and decline, sales volume and profit level drops but are still positive.

27. What is difference between a brand and a trademark?

    A. There is no difference.
    B. Brands are used for consumer goods, while trademarks are for advertising.
    C. A trademark is a brand that is registered and legally protected.
    D. A brand is used for a product or service, while a trademark is used for generic goods.

C. Branding is the process of naming and identifying products. A brand is a name, term, symbol, design, or combination that identifies a product and distinguishes it from other products. A trademark needs to be registered with the U.S. patent and trademark office. It is legally protected.

28. What is price skimming?

    A. temporary price reductions, often employed to boost sales
    B. encouraging purchases based on emotional rather than rational responses to price
    C. a price designed to help a product enter the market and gain market share rapidly
    D. charging the highest possible price that buyers who want the product will pay

D. Answer A is the definition for discounts, answer B is for psychological pricing, answer C is penetration pricing, and answer D is price skimming. Price skimming allows the company to generate much-needed revenue to offset the costs of research and development.

29. Which of these is an example of a marketing direct channel?

    A. IBM selling PCs at a retail store in a mall
    B. IBM selling PCs online on its Web site
    C. IBM selling PCs at Wal-Mart
    D. IBM selling PCs at an IBM authorized retail outlet

B. Direct channel occurs when there is no middleman. Retail stores, including Wal-Mart, have middlemen, as do authorized retail outlets. The IBM Web site is where the manufacturer directly deals with the customer.

30. For a product like the Lamborghini sports car, what kind of distribution should the company use for market coverage?

    A. exclusive distribution
    B. intensive distribution
    C. selective distribution
    D. any; it does not matter

A. The awarding by a manufacturer to an intermediary of the sole right to sell a product in a defined geographic territory is exclusive distribution. Such exclusivity provides an incentive for a dealer to handle a product that has a limited market. The opposite of exclusive distribution is intensive distribution. Selective distribution is market coverage where only a small number of all available outlets are used to expose the product.

31. Which one of these international transportation means is the cheapest?

    A. trains
    B. ships
    C. planes
    D. trucks

B. Transportation means presents a tradeoff between costs, speed, and risk. Although a plane is the fastest and the least risky, it is also the most expensive. Trains are cheaper than trucks but have limited reach with respect to delivery. Ships are the cheapest, which explains why so much global trade occurs through the sea. Ships are used generally for international trade, while trucks are used generally for domestic trade or for trade between neighboring countries, because it offers greater flexibility than ships.

32. For most salespeople, personal selling is a six-step process. Which is the correct sequence?

    A. prospecting, presenting, approaching, handling objections, closing, following up
    B. prospecting, approaching, presenting, closing, handling objections, following up
    C. prospecting, approaching, handling objections, presenting, closing, following up
    D. prospecting, approaching, presenting, handling objections, closing, following up

    D. When a salesperson is trying to make a sale, it is very important that he or she approach the customer after prospecting the right one. A presentation of the product or service is necessary, and the sales person must be able to address objections or questions that follow. After the sale is done, there must always be follow-up. This is to ensure positive word of mouth and repeat purchase.

33. Which of these is not a financial statement?

    A. income statement
    B. balance sheet
    C. inventory sheet
    D. cash flow statement

    C. An income statement is a financial report that shows an organization's profitability over a period of time, while a balance sheet is a snapshot of an organization's financial strength. A cash flow statement reflects the current assets and liquidity of the firm. An inventory sheet keeps track of inventory, which is not part of financial accounting.

34. Which of these is not a profitability ratio?

    A. profit margin
    B. return on assets
    C. return on equity
    D. receivables turnover

    D. Receivables turnover is an asset utilization ratio. The first three answers are all profitability ratios — ratios that measure the amount of operating income or net income an organization is able to generate relative to its assets, owners' equity, and sales.

35. Which of these reflect the three important functions of money?

    A. medium of exchange, measure of value, store of value
    B. medium of exchange, measure of product, store of value
    C. medium of exchange, measure of value, store of deposits
    D. medium of gold, measure of value, store of value

    A. Money, and before it, bartering, has always been used as a medium of exchange. It is also a measure of value, because more of it means one can obtain better goods and services. It also acts as a common denominator in which people can compare the value of the products or services. It also allows people to keep some of their wealth and use it when needed in the future (although this feature is dependent on the health of the economy).

36. What are some of the characteristics of money?

    A. acceptability, divisibility, portability, visibility
    B. acceptability, durability, portability, visibility
    C. acceptability, divisibility, portability, durability
    D. acceptability, divisibility, stability, visibility

    C. Visibility is irrelevant here. Acceptability means that the money can be readily accepted for purchase of goods and services or for debt. Divisibility means there is a wide range of denominations from notes to coins. Portability means that it has to be light and easily moved around. Stability means the money should carry the same worth day to day. Durability means the money must last for a certain period of time and not be defaced or easily damaged.

37. What are the different types of money?

    A. checking accounts, savings accounts, credit cards, counterfeits
    B. checking accounts, money market accounts, credit cards
    C. checking accounts, savings accounts, Certificates of Deposit, counterfeits
    D. checking accounts, savings accounts, credit cards, far money

B. Although counterfeits are used unknowingly, they are not a form of money. Checking accounts, savings accounts, money market, credit cards, and CDs are all forms of money. There is no far money, only near money, which refers to assets that can be turned into cash easily.

38. What is the role of Automated Clearing Houses (ACHs)?

    A. ensure the securities get cleared promptly
    B. ensure that ATM machines of different banks are connected and work in sync
    C. ensure that international funds transfers are in compliance with anti money laundering policies
    D. facilitate payments such as deposits and withdrawals between banks via magnetic tape

D. Most large U.S. employers use ACHs to deposit their employees' paychecks directly to the employees' bank accounts. The advantages of direct deposits to consumers' accounts include convenience, safety, and potential interest earnings.

39. In finance, what are bonds?

    A. loans backed by collateral that the bank can claim if the borrowers do not repay them
    B. loans backed only by the borrowers' good reputation and previous credit rating
    C. an arrangement by which a bank agrees to lend a specified amount of money to an organization upon request
    D. debt instruments that larger companies sell to raise long-term funds

D. Answer A is secured loans, answer B is unsecured loans, and answer C is a line of credit. For bonds, the buyers loan the issuer of the bonds cash in exchange for regular interest payments until the loan is repaid on or before the specified maturity date. A bond is like an IOU.

40. What is the difference between OTC (over-the-counter) markets and organized exchanges?

    A. OTC has no central location, while the latter are organized markets where brokers act as agents to buy and sell.
    B. OTC has no central location, while the latter are organized markets in North America.
    C. OTC has multiple central locations, while the latter are organized markets where brokers act as agents to buy and sell.
    D. OTC has multiple central locations, while the latter are organized markets with only one central market.

A. Organized exchanges are central locations where investors buy and sell securities. Examples include NYSE (New York Stock Exchange) or AMEX (American Stock Exchange). OTC, on the other hand, is a network of dealers all over the country linked by computers, telephones, and Teletype machines. It has no central location.

41. New entrants are newcomers to an existing industry. They typically bring new capacity, a desire to gain market share and substantial resources. Which of these are threats to new entrants?

    A. economies of scale, product differentiation, counterfeiting
    B. economies of scale, product differentiation, switching cost
    C. economies of scale, government policy, counterfeiting
    D. economies of scale, capital requirements, counterfeiting

B. Economies of scale in the production and sale of mainframe computers, for example, gave IBM a significant cost advantage over any new rival. Product differentiation creates high entry barriers through high levels of advertising and promotion. Switching cost is high especially for software familiarity, like Word or Excel, because, after customers are familiar with a product, they often will not try another software product. Government policy can limit entry through license issuance. Huge capital requirements often prevent competitors especially with the cloud of uncertainty of success. Counterfeiting is irrelevant.

42. SWOT analysis is often used to analyze the business situation of a firm. What does SWOT stand for?

   A. situation work operation test
   B. strength weaknesses operation test
   C. strength weaknesses opportunity threats
   D. situation work opportunity threats

   C. The SWOT analysis has proven to be the most widely used and enduring analytical technique in strategic management. It allows the firm to be aware of its internal environment (strengths and weaknesses) and its external environment (opportunity and threats). SWOT presents a systematic way of being aware of the operating environment for a firm.

43. Core competency is something that a firm can do exceedingly well. It is a key strength. To have distinctive competency, a firm must meet three tests. Which of these is not a test?

   A. positive word of mouth
   B. customer value
   C. competitor unique
   D. extendibility

   A. Customer value means that the firm must make a disproportionate contribution to customer perceived value. Competitor unique means the firm has unique and superior features to competitors' capabilities. Extendibility means the firm has a product that can be used to develop new products/services or enter new markets.

44. Reengineering is important to strategy implementation. It breaks away from the old rules and procedures. Which of these is not a principle for reengineering?

   A. organize around outcomes, not tasks
   B. have those who use the output of the process perform the process
   C. treat geographically dispersed resources as though they were centralized
   D. adopt status quo for some areas

   D. Answer A means designing a person's or a department's job around an objective or outcome instead of a single task or a series of tasks. For answer B, with computer based information systems, people who need the result of the reengineering process can do it themselves. For answer C, with modern information systems, companies can provide flexible service locally, while keeping the actual resources in a centralized location for coordination purposes.

Practice Tests

Directions: Following are three mini-practice tests. Select the choice that best answers each question. Fully explained answers follow each test.

Practice Test 1

1. Which of this is not a role of management?

   A. planning
   B. organizing
   C. staffing
   D. customer service

2. Which of the following is not in top management?

    A. Customer Service Officer (CSO)
    B. Chief Executive Officer (CEO)
    C. Chief Financial Officer (CFO)
    D. Chief Operations Officer (COO)

3. First line managers do more

    A. organizing
    B. planning
    C. directing
    D. controlling

4. In every company, there are financial managers. What is the role of a financial manager?

    A. develop and administer activities involved in transforming resources into goods, services, and ideas ready for the market place
    B. focus on obtaining funds for the successful operation of an organization and using those funds to further organizational goals
    C. handle the staffing function and deal with employees in a formalized manner
    D. take responsibility for planning, pricing, and promoting products and making them available to customers

5. What is the role of administrative managers?

    A. develop and administer activities involved in transforming resources into goods, services, and ideas in the market place
    B. focus on obtaining funds for the successful operation of an organization and using those funds to further organizational goals
    C. handle the staffing function and deal with employees in a formalized manner
    D. manage an entire business or a major segment of a business

6. Which is the most important asset for top management?

    A. analytical skills
    B. leadership
    C. human relations skills
    D. technical expertise

7. What is functional departmentalization?

    A. the arrangement of jobs around the needs of various types of customers, such as commercial banking versus consumer banking services
    B. the grouping of jobs according to geographic location such as state, region, country, or continent
    C. the organization of jobs in relation to the products of the firm
    D. the grouping of jobs that perform similar functional activities, such as finance, manufacturing, marketing, and human resources

8. Which of these is not a way to structure a company?

    A. parallel structure
    B. line structure
    C. multidivisional structure
    D. matrix structure

9. Communication is a very important aspect of management structure in an organization. Which of these is not a communication flow?

   A.   diagonal communication
   B.   upward communication
   C.   downward communication
   D.   reverse communication

10. Why do we need to have teams in organizations?

   A.   It allows for the organization to be more cohesive and operate as one for the customer.
   B.   It allows for pooling of skills and creative solutions from a collection of ideas.
   C.   It provides internal rewards in the form of enhanced sense of accomplishment for employees.
   D.   all of the above

Answers to Practice Test 1

1. **D.** Managers plan, organize, staff, and direct. They have to play the strategic roles and have to be free from day-to-day operations. On the other hand, customer service is an operational part of the organization and is for front-line staff.

2. **A.** Customer Service Officer is a front-line staffer. The CSO is the person in contact with the customer and is not involved in any aspect of strategic planning for the company. The CEO, CFO, and COO are involved in strategic planning and provide direction for the company.

3. **D.** First-line managers are directly in contact with the front-line staff and customers. Thus, they need to have more control over daily operations. The other options are roles played by mid-level and higher managers.

4. **B.** Financial managers work with funds that make the company operational and profitable. Option A is the role of production and operations managers, while C is that of a human resource manager, and D is that for a marketing manager.

5. **D.** Administrative managers are generalists, not specialists. They will be trained to manage small or major segments of a business. Answer A is the role of a production and operations manager, answer B is the role for a financial manager, while answer C is that of a human resource manager.

6. **B.** Answer D is for line managers, while answer C is more for managers who manage people instead of products or machines. Although answer A is important, answer B is the most important for top management, because leadership steers the strategic direction of the firm. Other roles can be fulfilled by secondary managers.

7. **D.** Answer A is customer departmentalization, answer B is geographical, and answer C is production departmentalization. Organizing departments via functional roles is a very effective way of assigning tasks and creating effective work structures in an organization.

8. **A.** Answer B is the simplest organizational structure in which direct lines of authority extend from the top managers to the lowest level of the organization. Answer C is a structure that organizes departments into larger groups, called divisions. Answer D is a structure that sets up teams from different departments, thereby creating two or more intersecting lines of authority, also called a project-management structure. Answer A is the answer you want here.

9. **D.** Diagonal communication occurs when managers and co-workers from different departments communicate. Answers B and C are hierarchical levels of communication. In a company structure, there is also horizontal communication. There is no reverse communication.

10. **D.** All of the answers are the benefits of having teams. Although teams bring with them benefits, they sometimes also create problems. Sometimes, personal conflicts can occur and hamper group productivity. Different groups can also refuse to share information and resources. But generally, the benefits outweigh the problems.

Practice Test 2

1. What is not true of being a sole proprietor?

    A.   your personal assets cannot be used to settle debts

    B.   you have more flexibility in management and accounting

    C.   you pay lower tax rates

    D.   the company is easy to set up and dismantle

2. The development and administration of the activities involved in transforming resources into goods and services is known as

    A.   operations management

    B.   marketing management

    C.   financial management

    D.   human resource management

3. The transformation process of operations management involves

    A.   manufacturing, production, outputs

    B.   restructuring, production, inputs

    C.   inputs, conversion, outputs

    D.   inputs, manufacturing, recycling

4. In operations management, manufacturers and service providers differ in several aspects. Which of these is not one of the aspects?

    A.   nature and consumption of output

    B.   uniformity of output

    C.   labor required

    D.   top management

5. Logistics is a very important component in the operations of an organization. What does it entail?

    A.   all activities involved in obtaining and managing raw materials and component parts, managing finished products, packaging them, and getting them to customers

    B.   the logging of activities pertaining to inventory

    C.   the buying of all the materials needed by the organization

    D.   the selling of finished products to retailers with the proper distribution channels

6. What is just-in-time inventory management?

    A.   a model that identifies the optimum number of items to order to minimize the costs of managing (ordering, storing, and using) them

    B.   a technique using smaller quantities of materials that arrive precisely for use in the transformation process and, therefore, require less storage space and other inventory management expense

    C.   a planning system that schedules the precise quantity of materials needed to make the product

    D.   the sequence of operations through which the product must pass

7. When a product is marked as ISO 9000, what does it mean?

    A.   It has International Sales Order of 9000 volume.

    B.   It has been manufactured by an ISO 9000 company, a company known for its computer servers.

    C.   It has met a series of quality standards designed by an international organization.

    D.   It uses replacement cartridges of model ISO 9000.

8. An important goal of product and operations management is reducing cycle time — the time it takes to complete a task or process. Which of these is not a dimension of cycle time?

    A. speed

    B. interactive relationships

    C. responsiveness

    D. management

9. Why is morale an important component of human relations, especially for employees?

    A. High morale contributes to high levels of productivity and high returns to stakeholders.

    B. High morale enables top management to have higher salary.

    C. High morale means the firm will have higher brand loyalty.

    D. High morale helps the firm obtain stock listing.

10. Motivation is very important in ensuring the workforce stays productive. What is the motivation process?

    A. Awareness leads to need and satisfaction.

    B. Satisfaction leads to action and needs.

    C. Need leads to goal-directed behavior, and then to need satisfaction.

    D. Goal-directed behavior leads to action.

Answers to Practice Test 2

1. A. The greatest disadvantage is that one has unlimited liability for damages resulting from the business operations. Answers B, C, and D are all advantages of being a sole proprietor. Other disadvantages include limited sources of funds, skills, and qualified employees. The main advantages are the secrecy of operations and flexibility and control of business, as well as a relative lack of government regulation.

2. A. This is a straightforward definitive style question. Marketing management involves more of the product and marketing mix, financial management relates more to operating funds and cash flow, while human resource management pertains to personnel issues.

3. C. At the heart of operations management is the transformational process through which inputs (resources such as labor, money, and energy) are converted into outputs (goods, services, and ideas). The process combines inputs in predetermined ways using different equipment, administrative procedures, and technology to create a product.

4. D. Nature and consumption of output is very different for manufacturers and service providers. The former handles tangible products, while the latter relates to intangible products. For manufacturers, the tangible products that are produced have to be standardized, while it is very difficult to control service, which is intangible. Labor is more intensive in service industries as compared to manufacturing, which often utilizes automation.

5. A. Answer A is correct because the field of logistics is very broad. It involves procurement, transportation, distribution channels, and packaging. The rest of the answers may be partially true, but do not include all aspects of logistics.

6. B. JIT inventory management is a popular technique that eliminates waste by using smaller quantities of materials that arrive just in time for use in the transformation process and, therefore, require less storage space and other inventory management expense. Answer A is the economic order quantity (EOQ) model, while answer C is Materials Requirement Planning (MRP). Answer D is the definition of routing.

7. C. ISO stands for International Organization for Standardization (ISO), which determines a series of quality standards internationally to ensure consistent product quality under many conditions.

8. D. Management, although is important, is not the dimension of cycle time. Speed determines the delivery of goods and services in the minimum time. Interactive relationships involve a continual dialogue between operations units, service providers, and customers that permits the exchange of feedback on concerns or needs. Responsiveness involves the willingness to make adjustments and be flexible to help customers, and to provide prompt service when a problem develops.

9. A. Motivation affects an employee's attitude toward his or her job, employer, and colleagues. Low morale can contribute to high levels of dissatisfaction, absenteeism, and turnover. That is why firms often invest in programs that ensure that employees are happy.

10. C. Motivation is an inner drive that directs a person's behavior and goals. A goal is the satisfaction of some need, and a need is the difference between a desired state and an actual state. A person who recognizes or feels a need is motivated to take action to satisfy the need and achieve a goal.

Practice Test 3

1. Which of these is not a form of an e-business model?

- **A.** business to business
- **B.** business to consumer
- **C.** consumer to business
- **D.** customer to consumer

2. Which of these is not a characteristic of a board of directors?

- **A.** It is the board's responsibility to ensure that the firm's objectives are achieved on schedule.
- **B.** Board members are legally liable for the mismanagement of the firm.
- **C.** A board's duty involves hiring the CEO and president.
- **D.** They are all employees of the firm.

3. Organizations operate in groups. Which of these are forms of groups in a firm?

- **A.** committees, task forces, self-directed work teams
- **B.** committees, task forces, car-pool groups
- **C.** committees, product-development teams, car-pool groups
- **D.** committees, quality-assurance teams, car-pool groups

4. Understanding customer thinking and needs is very important. When a marketing manager understands that the customers have certain needs to be fulfilled, products and services can be designed to fulfill those wants. What is the highest level of Maslow's hierarchy of needs?

- **A.** esteem needs
- **B.** social needs
- **C.** self actualization needs
- **D.** physiological needs

5. Which of these are ways to compensate the workforce?

- **A.** salary, commission, profit sharing, less work
- **B.** salary, commission, benefits, less work
- **C.** salary, commission, profit sharing, more responsibilities
- **D.** salary, commission, profit sharing, benefits

6. The U.S. workforce is becoming increasingly diverse. What are some primary characteristics of diversity?

- **A.** age, gender, ethnicity, race
- **B.** age, education, ethnicity, race
- **C.** age, gender, work background, race
- **D.** age, gender, ethnicity, marital status

7. What is the difference between a product line depth and product line width?

   A. There is no difference.
   B. Product line depth refers to the different types of products the firm carry, while product line width refers to the different modifications of a product.
   C. Product line width refers to the different types of products the firm carry, while product line depth refers to the different modifications of a product.
   D. The product line depth and width refer to the same product or similar product.

8. When a new cellular phone company enters a new market, it needs to acquire market share rapidly. What kind of pricing strategy should it adopt?

   A. penetration pricing
   B. price skimming
   C. psychological pricing
   D. discounts

9. What is economic expansion?

   A. slowdown of the economy characterized by decline in spending, cutbacks in production, and layoffs
   B. economic situation where the population wants to find work but cannot
   C. a situation that occurs when a nation spends more that it generates in taxes
   D. an economic situation in which people are spending, thus stimulating production of goods and services and employment

10. In the business world, business ethics are very important. It determines the character of the firm and whether there is fraud in the business practice. Social responsibility is an integral part of the management. In the pyramid of social responsibility, which is the highest level?

    A. ethical responsibilities
    B. voluntary responsibilities
    C. legal responsibilities
    D. economic responsibilities

Answers to Practice Test 3

1. **C.** Business to business is called collaborative commerce and involves the use of the Internet for transactions and communications between organizations. Business to consumers involves the delivery of products and services directly to individual consumers through the Internet. Customer to consumer is a market in which consumers market goods and services to each other through the Internet.

2. **D.** The board of directors is a group of individuals elected by the stockholders to oversee the general operation of the corporation and who set the corporation's long range objectives. Directors can be employees of the company or people unaffiliated with the company. Inside directors are usually the officers responsible for running the company. Outside directors are often top executives from other companies, lawyers, bankers, or professors.

3. **A.** Committees are permanent formal groups that performs a specific task. A task force is a temporary group of employees responsible for bringing about a particular change. A self-directed work team is a group of employees responsible for an entire work process or segment that delivers a product to an internal or external customer. A product-development team is a specific type of project team formed to devise, design, and implement a product. Quality-assurance teams are small groups of workers brought together to solve specific quality issues.

4. **C.** Self actualization is at the top of the Maslow's hierarchy and means being the best you can be. Physiological needs means the most basic and first needs to be satisfied, and are the essentials for living: water, food, shelter, and clothing. Esteem needs relate to both self respect and respect for others. Social needs are the needs for love, companionship, and friendship.

5. **D.** Wages are paid to workers based on the number of hours they have worked. Commissions are incentives that are based on a fixed amount or a percentage of the employee's sales. Profit sharing is a form of compensation whereby a percentage of company profits is distributed to the employees whose work helped to generate them. Benefits are non-financial forms of compensation provided to employees, such as pension plans, health insurance, holidays, and so on.

6. **A.** Education, work background, and marital status are secondary characteristics. Diversity involves the participation of different ages, genders, races, ethnicities, nationalities, and abilities in the workplace.

7. **C.** A product line is a group of closely related products that are treated as a unit because of similar marketing strategy, production, or end-use considerations. A product mix refers to all the products offered by an organization. Depth refers to the many modifications of the same product. For example, Honda Civic Si, EX, and DX are part of product line depth. Honda Civic, Honda Accord, and Honda Pilot refer to product line width.

8. **A.** Penetration pricing is a low price designed to help a product enter the market and gain market share rapidly. Price skimming is used to quickly recover high research and development costs. Psychological pricing encourages purchases based on emotional rather than rational responses to the price.

9. **D.** Economies are not stagnant. They expand and contract. Expansion could result in inflation. Contraction, on the other hand, may lead to recession and rising unemployment. A severe recession will lead to a depression.

10. **B.** Voluntary responsibilities are the highest, because they involve being a good corporate citizen, contributing to the community and quality of life. Ethical responsibility is next, because it involves doing what is fair, right, and just. Legal responsibility involves playing by the rules of the game, while economic responsibility means being profitable, and is the lowest form of social responsibility.

Communication

What You Should Know

In both the general and career track sections of the Job Knowledge test, the questions require you to understand the media and media relations, including newspapers, television, radio, the Internet, published documents, and government reports, as well as today's latest technology. In addition, you are required to have a working knowledge of the basic principles of effective communication and the techniques of public speaking.

The questions in the following section are for your review. Go through each question and try your best to answer it. The explanation of the answer follows immediately afterward so that you can actually learn new material. After you've completed reviewing these questions and answers, three brief practice review tests at the end of the chapter help you determine how much you know. Of course, there is a full-length exam at the end of Part II that also includes communications questions.

Communication Review Section

Read the following questions and select the choices that best answer the questions.

1. The journalist may print what he wishes about others, but if that information is wrong and harmful to others' reputation, that writer must suffer the consequences. Such protection for subjects of stories comes under the auspices of which of the following acts?

   A. Freedom of Information
   B. Property Protection
   C. Offending Effrontery
   D. Defamation

   D. The question fits the definition of defamation. Freedom of Information allows press access to public documents. Property Protection Acts don't exist; that is, the choice is bogus. Offending effrontery has to do with obscenity.

2. In some instances, journalists may find that there is a conflict between the 1st Amendment and the 6th Amendment, the latter having to do with

   A. the right to keep and bear arms
   B. the right to a speedy public trial
   C. privacy
   D. copyright

   B. Right to a speedy public trial is the subject of the 6th Amendment and when journalists try to cover trials, there can sometimes be a conflict between freedom of the press and a fair trial. The right to bear arms is in the 2nd Amendment. Privacy is a protection not afforded by the constitution and its amendments. Copyright is not a part of the 6th Amendment.

3. Copyright law protects

   A. literary works
   B. musical works, including any accompanying words
   C. sound recordings
   D. all of the above

   D. All of these are protected by copyright.

4. Johann Gutenberg was known as

- **A.** the person who translated the Bible from German to English
- **B.** a Shakespearean actor who brought styles of proper pronunciation to common people
- **C.** the inventor of moveable type, first producing the Bible
- **D.** editor of the world's first newspaper

C. Gutenberg was the inventor of moveable type, which made possible the printing and multiple copies of written works. The person who translated the Bible from German to English was primarily William Tyndale. Answer B is a bogus choice; there is no such person. The discoverer of the solar system may have been Johannes Keppler or Nicolaus Copernicus, but not Gutenberg.

5. A desktop publisher is

- **A.** a writer who has his/her own small printing press
- **B.** a computer program that allows a writer to lay out, illustrate, and create different typefaces
- **C.** small printers who specialize in niche markets
- **D.** a printer who produces brochures, booklets, and so on, but not books

B. Answer B is the definition of a desktop publisher. Answer A might be termed a private publisher. Answer C might be regarded as specialized publishers. Printers without capability to publish books are just that, but not generally regarded as desktop publishers.

6. Most of the daily newspapers in the United States are:

- **A.** morning papers
- **B.** evening papers
- **C.** all-day dailies
- **D.** weekend editions

A. Morning papers outnumber evening papers 766 to 727. There are fewer evening papers, only 727 compared to 766 morning dailies. All-day dailies are classified as either morning or evening papers, although there may be several editions during the day. Only about 60 percent of morning and evening dailies have Sunday/weekend editions; but a weekend/Sunday paper is not a daily paper, as was asked in the question.

7. The largest circulated daily newspaper in the U.S. is:

- **A.** *USA Today*
- **B.** *The Wall Street Journal*
- **C.** *The New York Times*
- **D.** *The Washington Post*

B. *The Wall Street Journal* has a circulation of nearly 1.8 million. *USA Today* is second with a circulation of 1.67 million. *The New York Times* is third, with 1.08 million. *The Washington Post* is fifth, with 763,000.

8. A joint operating agreement provides for:

- **A.** competing newspapers to combine their circulation and advertising but leave their editorial functions separate
- **B.** advertising in newspapers working with competitors in setting rates
- **C.** legislation that allows for multiple-owner, large newspaper chains
- **D.** an agreement that all newspapers in a chain may be printed from the same press

A. A is the definition of a joint operating agreement. Other choices are bogus and have no specific terms identified with the choice.

9. Muckrakers were

    A. artists who used the media to depict dirty (that is, sexually suggestive) material

    B. American journalists, novelists and critics, who, in the early 1900s attempted to expose the abuses of business and the corruption of politics

    C. journalists who downplay sensationalism

    D. companies that own a number of newspapers around the country

B. B is the definition of muckrakers. Other choices are made up and have no specific bearing on the question of muckrakers.

10. Tabloid newspapers are those that:

    A. are always sensational, with a de-emphasis on current news events

    B. have a printing format that uses pages that are about half the size of a traditional newspaper page

    C. are sold only on newsstands, not by subscription

    D. are published in English, but not generally found in the United States

B. Answer B connotes the origin of the word tabloid, although many tabloid newspapers have come to be associated with sensationalism and include many photographs. Answer A is not necessarily true, because many tabloids carry extensive news of current events. Answers C and D are bogus and have no bearing on the definition of tabloid.

11. Since the middle of the 20th century, the number of cities with more than one daily newspaper has

    A. increased

    B. decreased

    C. stayed the same

    D. cannot be determined

B. The number of cities with dailies has actually decreased since the middle of the 20th century, from 181 to 33. Other choices contradict the right choice and cannot be true.

12. Of all types of magazines, the one with the most rapid growth (1989–2000) is:

    A. health

    B. women's magazines

    C. environment and ecology

    D. comics

D. Comics grew by 299 titles during that time period. While the other choices all had growth, none grew as fast as comics. Health magazines grew by 226 titles. Women's magazines grew by 221 titles. Environment and ecology magazines grew by 260 titles.

13. The top U.S. circulated magazine is:

    A. *Modern Maturity*

    B. *Reader's Digest*

    C. *TV Guide*

    D. *Time*

A. *Modern Maturity* is largest, with a circulation of over 20 million. *Reader's Digest* is second with 12.5 million. *TV Guide* is third with 10 million. *Time* is tenth with just over 4 million.

14. In advertising, CPM is:

    A. creative promotion and marketing
    B. circulation, production, and marketing
    C. cost per thousand
    D. chief promotion manager

    C. Cost per thousand is the basic measurement of advertising efficiency; $m = 1,000$. Other answers were all made up.

15. The basis of the recording industry today, the phonograph was invented by

    A. Lee DeForest
    B. G. Marconi
    C. Thomas A. Edison
    D. Al Jolson

    C. Edison is the inventor of the phonograph. DeForest experimented with both voiced transmissions and the use of various frequencies, including those which are now part of the FM band. Marconi first transmitted signals with successful reception and later conducted successful trans-Atlantic tests. Al Jolson was a vaudeville actor who performed in blackface, eventually appearing in the first sound motion picture.

16. This type of radio transmission broadcasts on the frequency of 550 to 1700 kilohertz:

    A. AM radio
    B. FM radio
    C. short-wave radio
    D. citizens band radio

    A. This is the frequency of AM radio. FM is 88–108 megahertz (MHz). Short wave is 5.0–26.1 MHz. Citizens band (CB) is 29.96–27.41 MHz.

17. This company was a patent trust formed in 1919, which required parties interested in setting up a broadcast operation to pay money for the rights to do so.

    A. General Electric (GE)
    B. Radio Corporation of America (RCA)
    C. Emerson
    D. Columbia Broadcasting System (CBS)

    B. RCA was just such a trust. GE was the manufacturing arm and was broken up by the courts from RCA. Emerson was also an early manufacturer of radios. CBS was a radio network which offered programming to links of radio stations.

18. This act gave the Secretary of Commerce the right to issue licenses to parties interested in radio broadcasting and to decide which radio frequencies should be used for which types of services:

    A. Radio Act of 1912
    B. Radio Act of 1927
    C. Communications Act of 1934
    D. Radio-Telephone Act of 1952

    A. The Radio Act of 1912 is correct. The Radio Act of 1927 set up the Federal Radio Commission. The Communications Act of 1934 set up the Federal Communications Commission. Answer D is bogus — there is no such act.

19. O & O Stations are those

   A. without sanction to operate by the FCC
   B. operated by companies with public stock offerings
   C. interconnected together, coast to coast, with the same network
   D. owned and operated by a network that provides a regular schedule of programming

D. O & O means owned and operated by a network. O & O stations do have sanction by the FCC to operate. Companies with public stock have nothing to do with being O & O. Answer C may be a network, but does not address the question of O & O.

20. Which U.S. president used radio to provide fireside chats to reassure citizens in hard times?

   A. Herbert Hoover
   B. Franklin D. Roosevelt
   C. Harry S. Truman
   D. Dwight D. Eisenhower

B. Franklin D. Roosevelt used radio with what he called fireside chats, reassuring Americans during the great depression and mobilizing them to fight Japan and Germany during World War II. Hoover was president earlier and was the Secretary of Commerce who licensed radio stations before there was a government agency to do so. Harry S. Truman was the president who succeeded Roosevelt. Eisenhower was president after Truman; neither of the latter two were known for fireside chats.

21. This term describes an activity in which promotion personnel pay money to radio DJs in order to ensure that they will devote airtime to artists that their recording companies represent:

   A. networking
   B. conglomerating
   C. payola
   D. musicjacking

C. The term payola is what's defined in the question; it became illegal in the late 1950s. Networking is the stringing of stations together for programming purposes. Conglomerating is the concentration of station ownership. Musicjacking is bogus; there is no such term.

22. Clear Channel and Infinity are the names of two organizations that:

   A. broadcast international shortwave radio
   B. are television networks
   C. are large radio networks-conglomerates
   D. are record companies

C. These two companies are the two largest radio networks, each with several hundred stations. Answer A, international short-wave radio, is false; they are not that. These two companies are radio networks, not television networks or record companies.

23. The radio format most common, or used by the largest number of stations today is

   A. country
   B. news and news talk
   C. adult contemporary
   D. religious

A. Country music format is the most common, with over 2,000 stations using that format. News and talk is used by just under 1,000 stations. Adult contemporary stations number 743. Religious stations number 714.

24. About 80 percent of radio listening occurs where?

    A. individual, portable personal radios

    B. at the office or workplace

    C. in cars and vehicles on the road

    D. in home stereo systems

C. 80 percent of radio listening occurs in cars and on-road vehicles. Choices A, B, and D all have lower percentages of listening.

25. In music technology, the format for compressing a sound sequence into a very small file (about one-twelfth the size of the original file) while preserving the original level of sound quality when it is played is:

    A. CD

    B. MP3

    C. Napster

    D. DVD

B. MP3 fits the definition in the question. A compact disc (CD) is not compressed into a file. Napster is an online site for retrieval of music. DVD (digital video disc) is compressed on a disc for display of video.

26. An example of an agency that exists to make sure that publishers, songwriters and artists are compensated for their artistry is:

    A. FCC

    B. A&R

    C. ASCAP

    D. U.S. Copyright Office

C. ASCAP (American Society of Composers, Authors, and Publishers) is the only licensing agency that compensates artists. The FCC is the Federal Communications Commission. A&R, Artists and Records, is a trade publication. The U.S. Copyright Office does not function as a licensing agency.

27. In the media, as well as other businesses, an organization's control over a product from production through distribution to exhibition is known as:

    A. horizontal integration

    B. vertical integration

    C. conglomeration

    D. networking

B. Vertical integration is defined by the question. Horizontal integration implies many outlets/production at the same level, as do answers C and D.

28. The licensing of mass media material to outlets on a market-to-market basis is known as:

    A. syndication

    B. networking

    C. license lending

    D. outlet rating

A. Syndication is defined in this question. Networking is the stringing together of stations for programming purposes. License lending and outlet rating are bogus terms.

29. The motion picture rating most common with films released today is:

    A.   G
    B.   PG
    C.   PG-13
    D.   R

D. R-rated films are the most frequently released. Over one-half of the thousands of films rated since 1968 have received an R rating. Other choices are of a lower proportion, with G and PG films together accounting for one-third.

30. This person began a television station in Atlanta, but made it a nation-wide superstation by offering it by satellite to cable systems.

    A.   Harold Robbins
    B.   Ted Turner
    C.   Robert Sarnoff
    D.   William Paley

B. Ted Turner fits the description in the question. Harold Robbins is a novelist. Robert Sarnoff began NBC. William Paley began CBS.

31. This person started a fourth TV network to compete with the long-existing three networks of ABC, CBS, and NBC.

    A.   Chris Craft
    B.   Art Linkletter
    C.   Rupert Murdock
    D.   Bill O'Reilly

C. Rupert Murdock started the Fox network. Chris Craft is the name of a group of stations. Art Linkletter is the name of an early TV host. Bill O'Reilly is a network political commentator.

32. Today, ABC Television is owned by:

    A.   Viacom
    B.   General Electric
    C.   AOL Time Warner
    D.   Disney

D. Disney Company owns ABC-TV. Viacom owns CBS. General Electric owns NBC. AOL/Time Warner owns HBO as well as a number of magazines.

33. The Discovery Channel is an example of

    A.   a broadcast station
    B.   a broadcast network
    C.   a cable network
    D.   a superstation

C. The Discovery Channel is a cable network. The Discovery Channel does not broadcast its signal; thus, it is not a broadcast station or a superstation. It is not a broadcast network, but rather uses several cable TV systems to spread its programs.

34. The technology that allows a household to receive one hundred or more television signals is

    A. PBS
    B. DBS
    C. MSO
    D. ARB

B. This household system is DBS, Direct Broadcast Satellite. PBS is Public Broadcast System, a non-commercial broadcast network. MSO, a multi system operator, is a company that owns several cable systems. ARB, the American Research Bureau, became a major institution in developing TV ratings, but does not relate to the question.

35. The television technology that allows the display of picture quality similar to that of 35-millimeter movies with sound quality similar to that of a compact disc:

    A. DBS
    B. PPV
    C. Premium channel
    D. HDTV

D. HDTV, high definition television, is what is described in the question. DBS is direct broadcast satellite. PPV, pay per view, is a premium program system in which the viewer pays for each program ordered. Premium channels are pay cable systems, in which the viewer pays extra for first-run movies and similar programming.

36. The electronic technology that generates, stores and processes data in the form of strings of 0s and 1s:

    A. digital
    B. analog
    C. high fi
    D. pay per view

A. Digital is what is described in the question. Analog is the older system of electronic technology. High fi, or high fidelity, is an enhanced sound reproduction, first developed in the late 1950s. Pay per view is a premium program system where the viewer pays for each program ordered.

37. In television ratings, this is the measure of the percentage of TV sets in the United States that are tuned to a specific show.

    A. reach
    B. household share
    C. national rating point
    D. people rating

C. National rating point is defined in the question. Reach is the percentage of the entire target audience to which a media outlet will circulate. Household share is the percentage of households in which a particular channel was turned on. People rating is the particular demographic category of individuals within each household.

38. Some of the best TV programs can be seen during sweeps, which is

    A. when the networks get rid of, or sweep away, their inventory of their best programs
    B. when there is a nationwide survey of viewing habits, four times a year, as performed by A.C. Nielsen Company
    C. when rating trucks go through neighborhoods, sweeping the frequencies to see how many sets are tuned to each channel
    D. when advertisers sweep their unused revenues to purchase the premium programs of the network

B. Answer B fits the definition of sweeps. Answers A, C and D are all made-up answers.

39. When a TV network wishes to make a program popular, it may do so by having an already established and popular program air just before it, believing that viewers will keep their sets on the same channel. This is known as

    A. hammocking
    B. lead-in
    C. prime time
    D. day-part scheduling

B. Hammocking is the placement of a new program between two popular ones. Prime time is the evening viewing period (8–11 p.m.), when TV has its largest audience. Day-part scheduling is simply the segment of a day as defined by programmers and marketers.

40. Placing the same show at the same time, five days a week, giving it some predictability is known as

    A. syndication
    B. stripping
    C. formatting
    D. piloting

B. Syndication is the licensing of mass media material to outlets on a market-by-market basis. Formatting is putting together the elements that propel a series and give it recognizable personality. Piloting is the trial of a single program to see it its elements are successful.

41. In television ratings, which one is for mature audiences only?

    A. TVY7
    B. TVPG
    C. TV14
    D. TVM

D. TVM is mature audiences only. TVY7 is the rating of programs directed at older children. TVPG is the rating indicating parental guidance suggested. TV14 is the rating where parents are strongly cautioned.

42. The systematic investigation of the reasons people purchase products is known as

    A. subliminal persuasion
    B. public relations
    C. motivational research
    D. advertising globalization

C. Motivational research is defined in this choice. Subliminal persuasion has to do with influencing the unconscious mind. Public relations is the art or science of establishing and promoting a favorable relations with the public through various methods, usually involving the media. Advertising globalization has to do with the advertising on an international basis.

43. Which medium accounts for where the most advertising dollars are spent?

    A. the Internet
    B. broadcast TV
    C. newspapers
    D. radio

B. Broadcast TV, with about $60 billion per year, receives the largest proportion of advertising revenue. The Internet accounts for about $5 billion. Newspapers account for $50 billion. Radio accounts for $20 billion.

44. Generally, an advertising agency

    A. specializes in the creation of ads, but not in their placement in the media

    B. places already produced ads in the media, but does not create them

    C. pays the creator of the ads from media revenues, but neither creates nor places ads

    D. creates advertising and arranges for their placement in media that accept payment for the exhibiting of those ads.

    D. Ad agencies generally both create and place advertising. The other answers do not fit the definition of an advertising agency.

45. Psychographic data are those which are

    A. used for subliminal persuasion; have to do with influencing the unconscious mind

    B. media material surrounding the advertising

    C. information that links demographic categories to personality characteristics of an audience

    D. advertising that uses pictures and visual stimuli to create recognition

    C. This is the definition of psychographic data. Answer A defines subliminal persuasion. Answers B and D are bogus answers and do not fit the definition in the question.

Practice Tests

Directions: Following are three minipractice tests. Select the choice that best answers each question. Fully explained answers follow each test.

Practice Test 1

1. An argument consisting of two premises and a conclusion drawn by deductive inference is

    A. an immediate inference

    B. a syllogism

    C. a true premise

    D. a proposition

2. Filling a story with details to make something seem very real is

    A. induction

    B. fiction

    C. verisimilitude

    D. flashback

3. To determine or test the truth or accuracy of a claim by comparison, investigation, or reference:

    A. verify

    B. belie

    C. recall

    D. disprove

4. In preparing a PowerPoint presentation, you discover some material perfectly suited for your use. However, it is marked with © (the letter C enclosed in a circle). This means that

A. This material is the property of the U.S. government and may be used without reservation.

B. This material has been copied.

C. This material has been created by an organization using this mark as its logo.

D. This material is copyrighted and its reproduction is protected by law.

5. Phatic communication is

A. communication designed to convince the other party

B. dialogue that comes largely from one party

C. communication symbolized by friendly social interest in the people one is with

D. always non-verbal communication

6. The interference in understanding a message, and which can originate externally, be physical in nature, or internally in either the speaker or the listener is

A. feedback

B. noise

C. breakdown

D. encoding corruption

7. Which of these elements contributes to the degree of speech anxiety a person feels?

A. novelty (unfamiliarity)

B. conspicuousness (stands out)

C. audience characteristics

D. all of the above

8. A recognized strategy for dealing with speech anxiety (communication apprehension) is visualization, which is

A. having your speech written out

B. picturing yourself alone in the room as you speak

C. picturing yourself standing/sitting in the room where you're speaking, talking comfortably and confidentially with others

D. using word pictures in your speech, avoiding the abstract convictions

9. One strategy for good listening is empathetic listening, which is

A. trying to understand how the speaker feels and put oneself in his/her position

B. seeing the speaker as having a specific status in your mind's eye

C. touching the speaker as he/she speaks.

D. always looking into the eyes of the speaker

10. This is a theory designed to predict what a person will do to restore harmony under various circumstances when dissonance has been introduced to them in a message.

A. dissonance theory

B. balance theory

C. social judgment theory

D. elaboration likelihood model

Answers to Practice Test 1

1. **B.** Answer B is the definition of syllogism. Immediate inference is the ability to describe the activity between personal experiences, data, facts, region of the referent, and related phenomena. A true premise is the fact that may be a premise of a syllogism. A proposition is a plan, proposal, or scheme suggested for acceptance.

2. **C.** Answer C is correct. Induction is reasoning leading to a conclusion about all the members of a class from examination of only a few members of a class. Fiction comes from the invention of details, rather than a true account. Flashback is a reversion to previously depicted events in a story.

3. **A.** Answer A is correct. Belie is to tell lies or cover up. Recall is to bring back without regard to verifying its truth. Disprove is to show something as not true or actual.

4. **D.** This symbol represents copyright and means that it is protected by copyright law, not that it is copied. Government documents usable to the public are not so marked. Note that this symbol may not be used by a private company as its logo.

5. **C.** Answer C is the definition of phatic communication, which is not exclusively persuasive, one-sided, or non-verbal.

6. **B.** Noise is generally the proper term. Feedback has another definition: communication from the receiver to the sender. Breakdown is too general to be applied here; it is the disintegration of the communication process. Because it may not apply to just the sending of the message, interference is not a matter of encoding.

7. **D.** Answer D is the best possible answer, because all of these are considered the elements that contribute to speech anxiety.

8. **C.** Answer C is the most descriptive element of visualization. Answers A, B, and D do not describe the process of visualization.

9. **A.** Answer A is the definition of empathetic listening. Answers B, C, and D may or may not contain elements of empathetic listening, but the best possible definition with the essential elements is in answer A.

10. **B.** Answer B is the definition of balance theory. Dissonance explains why there is incongruity between ideas of a message and a receiver's beliefs. Social judgment explains elements to consider when trying to change someone's attitude. The elaboration likelihood model explains why people change their attitudes when presented with a persuasive message.

Practice Test 2

1. Ethics in communication have key characteristics. Which of the following is not characteristic of ethical communication?

    A. Ethics have good short-term social consequences.
    B. Ethics are concerned not so much with behavior as it exists, but as it ought to be.
    C. Ethics is the systematic study of the nature of value concepts: good/bad, right/wrong, and so on.
    D. Ethics is the systematic study of the ultimate problems of human conduct, character, and custom.

2. Synesthesia in communication is

    A. forgetting a prepared speech when the speaker is before an audience
    B. making irrelevant analogies in a speech
    C. giving one type of stimulation which evokes the sensation of another
    D. making simple the abstract notions in a message

3. Diphthongs are

    A. voiced sounds in which there is little interference with the outgoing air

    B. Voice modified by the same type of friction or stoppage which, in part, produces the sound

    C. Combinations of vowel sounds produced as one sound, such as "i" in ice

    D. Exaggerations or overstatements used in a message to make a point

4. Connotation refers to

    A. the attitudes, feelings, emotions, and values that we associate with a symbol (for example, a word)

    B. the way words are used in their literal, exact meaning

    C. the indirect, supplemental information that goes with a word

    D. persuading the listener to do something against his/her values

5. The general model of communication takes into account the major aspects of the communication process. This model by Harold Lasswell is as follows: "Who says what to whom by which channel with what effect." What aspect constitutes the major difference between interpersonal communication and mass communication?

    A. the sender

    B. the channel

    C. the message

    D. the effect

6. The placement of prestige onto the sender by virtue of his/her appearance in the media is known as

    A. perception bias

    B. feedback

    C. message amplification

    D. status conferral

7. In mass communication, the group that receives the message in which it is interested and its economic potential constitutes what is known as

    A. a social group

    B. a market

    C. uses and gratification group

    D. the media

8. CNN Headline News is an example of pushing the limits of what aspect of the communication process?

    A. feedback

    B. status conferral

    C. amplification

    D. channel capacity

9. This president can be remembered for having helped shape the 1st Amendment and for keeping its practices while in office:

    A. George Washington

    B. John Adams

    C. Thomas Jefferson

    D. John Quincy Adams

10. This Supreme Court Justice articulated the "clear and present danger doctrine" in his interpretation of the 1st Amendment:

    A. John Jay
    B. John Marshall
    C. Oliver Wendell Holmes
    D. Warren E. Burger

Answers to Practice Test 2

1. **A.** A is not true, because ethics attempts to measure more long-term consequences, not just short-term. All other statements are considered true in the study of ethics.

2. **C.** Answer C is the definition of synesthesia. Forgetting, irrelevant analogies, and abstract notions are not related to synesthesia.

3. **C.** Answer C is the definition of diphthong. Answer A defines the pronunciation of a vowel. Answer B defines the pronunciation of a consonant. Answer D has nothing to do with a diphthong and is a bogus choice.

4. **A.** Answer A is the definition of connotation. Answer B defines denotation. Answers C and D have nothing to do with the term's meaning and are meant to throw you off track.

5. **B.** The channel that is designed to reach many people at one time is mass communication. Answers A, C, and D may be slightly different with mass communication, but the major difference that defines mass is the channel.

6. **D.** Status conferral is the only choice that works here. Perception bias involves seeing only what one wishes in the communication. Feedback is the communication from receiver to sender. Message amplification is the increased importance of the message in the communication process.

7. **B.** The correct answer is the market, which is the audience/receivers with an eye to the potential economic value. Social groups aren't related to mass communication. Uses and gratification groups do not address the question. The media do not relate to the groups of receivers, but rather the channel of communication.

8. **D.** Channel capacity is correct, because of the various displays of different information on CNN Headline News. Feedback does not relate to limits, but rather to communication from receiver to sender. Status conferral does not relate to channel capacity or limits, but rather to the increased importance of the sender in mass communication. Amplification refers to increasing the importance of the message.

9. **C.** Thomas Jefferson both helped shape the 1st Amendment and implement its philosophy during his terms in office. George Washington, the first president, had little to do with shaping the 1st Amendment. John Adams actually worked against some concepts of the 1st Amendment by use of the Alien and Sedition Act. John Quincy Adams also had little to do with the shaping of the 1st Amendment.

10. **C.** Oliver Wendell Holmes brought forth this doctrine in 1919. John Jay was the first Chief Justice. John Marshall was Chief Justice for 35 years during the early part of the 19th century, before this doctrine's use. Warren Burger was Chief Justice during the middle of the 20th century, after this doctrine was articulated.

Practice Test 3

1. What is the first step in developing effective written or oral communication?

    A. Create an outline.
    B. Determine what channel or medium (e-mail, phone, memo, meeting, and so on) to use.
    C. Analyze the audience and the context for the message.
    D. Clarify the message.

2. Most communication starts with a statement of purpose or conclusion, and then presents supporting information or facts. Which of the following is not an acceptable reason to reverse this order and leave the purpose or conclusion to the end of the document or presentation?

    A. The audience is hostile and may resist the main message.

    B. The communicator has done a lot of research and wants to be sure the audience sees all of it.

    C. The culture in which the communication occurs likes the facts first.

    D. The evidence needs to be presented before the audience will understand the conclusion.

3. Of the common mistakes that communicators make in e-mails or memos, what is the most damaging to the credibility of the writer?

    A. poor greetings or no greeting

    B. unnecessary copies

    C. unclear subject lines

    D. careless grammar, spelling, or punctuation

4. Which of the following techniques for opening a presentation should a speaker use with extreme caution?

    A. beginning with a fact or relevant quotation

    B. showing a relevant cartoon or telling a joke

    C. telling a relevant story or anecdote

    D. referring to the occasion or otherwise establishing the context for the presentation

5. What is most important method to establish credibility as a speaker?

    A. creating a positive ethos (sense of authority and trustworthiness)

    B. being very logical and having all of the facts in order

    C. having slides with attractive, complicated graphics

    D. establishing a relaxed rapport with the audience

6. What is the best method for reaching the greatest number of stakeholders with an important message fast?

    A. press conferences

    B. press releases

    C. the Internet

    D. newspaper advertisements

7. When talking to the news media, what should a skilled communicator be careful to avoid completely?

    A. speaking off the record

    B. speaking in personal terms when appropriate

    C. saying, "I don't know, but I will find out for you."

    D. talking from the viewpoint of the public's interest

8. Which of the following techniques for managing crisis communication is most critical?

    A. having a formal, exact, and detailed plan of action

    B. responding quickly to the right people with one consistent message

    C. using the Web as a way to reach reporters, the public, and employees

    D. monitoring the coverage and evaluating effectiveness

9. Which of the following Internet sources provides the most complete and easy-to-find information on traveling or living in specific countries?

   A. www.cnn.com/travel
   B. www.travelocity.com
   C. www.state.gov/travel
   D. www.frommers.com

10. When communicating across cultures, which of the following would help you most to communicate effectively?

   A. Assume all people are the same and like to receive information in the same way.
   B. Be yourself and hope for the best.
   C. Try to adopt the other culture's way of communicating.
   D. Listen and pay attention to context and nonverbal cues.

Answers to Practice Test 3

1. **C.** The first step in developing effective written or oral communication is to analyze the audience and develop an understanding of the context for the message. The more the sender of the message knows about the audience, the more effective the communication will be. The understanding of the audience determines the messages, medium, and timing. Analysis of the audience and the context influences each of the other possible answers. The communicator needs to decide which medium is appropriate for the audience and context and how best to organize the message (the outline). In addition, the communicator needs to ensure the message is clear for this audience and appropriate for the context. Clarifying the message is usually the next step after establishing and understanding the audience and context.

2. **B.** Answers A, C, and D are all good reasons to delay stating the purpose, conclusion, or recommendation until after the presentation of supporting information or facts. A hostile audience will resist a conclusion or recommendation; therefore, the communicator wants to break down the resistance with information to facilitate the audience's support. Another legitimate reason to delay the purpose is that some cultures are more comfortable with an indirect approach. They may even need to build a rapport first. Finally, if a conclusion is complex, the communicator may need to provide some information first to build a foundation for understanding it. The desire to show how much research has been performed is rarely a good reason for delaying the conclusion.

3. **D.** Poor greetings or no greeting, unnecessary copies, or unclear subject lines are all common problems with e-mails. However, credibility is gained or lost when the reader reads the e-mail. In fact, studies of how audiences respond to mistakes in grammar, spelling, or punctuation have found that the audience see the writer as either careless, ignorant, or uneducated, any one of which will cause the reader to see the writer as less credible in what they say.

4. **B.** Any of the techniques listed can be effective when used as an opening in a presentation; however, cartoons and jokes are usually culturally based and can easily offend someone. Few people are comedians, and even those who are should realize that using humor is at the expense of other people and other cultures.

5. **A.** Although being very logical/having all of the facts in order and establishing a relaxed rapport with the audience are both very important for any speaker to be effective, the most important method to establish credibility as a speaker is creating the perception of being honest, trustworthy, and knowledgeable, all part of a positive ethos. Having slides with attractive, complicated graphics can add to a presentation by appealing to the visual side of the audience; however, these elements will not create credibility for the speaker. Only a positive ethos can directly inspire credibility.

6. **C.** The best method for reaching the greatest number of stakeholders with an important message fast is to use today's most ubiquitous technology: the Internet. Press conferences and press releases are useful in delivering information to and through the media, but their reach is often limited. Newspapers or advertisements are even more limited in their reach.

7. **A.** With the news media, nothing is off the record. Anything that an individual tells a reporter can and most probably will make the news, despite the reporter's claiming otherwise.

8. **B.** All of the listed techniques for managing crisis communication are important, but the most important action in a crisis is to respond quickly to the right people with one consistent message.

9. **C.** All of the sites listed contain information on traveling in specific countries, but www.state.gov/travel includes all regions and most countries.

10. **D.** Although the first three items listed are common myths about cultural interaction, when communicating across cultures, they are actually dangerous. All people are not the same and do not like to receive information in the same way; thus, the importance of analyzing the audience.

Computers

What You Should Know

In both the general and career track sections of the Job Knowledge test, the questions require knowledge of general basic computer operations. These questions cover areas such as preparing and using e-mail and using various application programs such as word processing, data processing, and spreadsheets. It is also helpful to know your way around the keyboard and various software and hardware terms. Most of this knowledge can probably be learned through hands-on use of computers in daily functions, whether you are in school or at work. The test will not likely ask many questions about specific programs, such as the differences between World Perfect or MS Word.

The questions in the following section are for your review. Go through each question and try your best to answer it. The explanation of the answer follows immediately afterward so that you can actually learn new material. After you've completed reviewing these questions and answers, three brief practice review tests at the end of the chapter help you determine how much you know. Of course, there is a full-length exam at the end of Part II that also includes computer questions.

Computers Review Section

Read the following questions and select the choices that best answer the questions.

1. Buttons on the _____ let you switch back and forth between open programs.

   A. menu bar
   B. task bar
   C. tool bar
   D. none of the above

   B. Buttons on the task bar will let you switch back and forth between open programs (the bottom bar on the screen). Answer A is what is used to find programs and submenus on the left-hand side of the task bar. Answer C is the bar used within certain programs like Microsoft Word or Excel.

2. Folders can only have _____ within them.

   A. files
   B. other folders
   C. both files and folders
   D. none of the above

   C. Folders can have both other folders and files contained within.

3. Hardware components located outside the system unit are called

   A. printers and modems
   B. telecommunicators
   C. mice
   D. peripherals

   D. Peripherals are defined as being hardware components located outside the system unit. Answer A represents two types of peripherals. Answer B is someone who works within the telecommunication industry. Answer C is the plural of a mouse.

4. Which of the following commands can be used to save a file with a different name?

   A. File⇨ Save
   B. File⇨Save As
   C. File⇨Open
   D. File⇨Close

   B. Answer B is the only option that will allow the user to save a file with a different name. Answer A will save the file with the same name. Answer C will only open the file that the user needs. Answer D will close the file.

5. A megabyte is defined as which of the following:

   A. 1,000 bytes
   B. 1 million bytes
   C. 1 billion bytes
   D. 1 trillion bytes

   B. A megabyte is defined as having approximately 1 million bytes. Answer A is a kilobyte. Answer C is a gigabyte. Answer D is a terabyte.

6. All computers must have

   A. a printer attached
   B. word-processing software
   C. an operating system
   D. a virus-checking program

   C. Every computer needs an operating system in order to function.

7. Which of the following is a popular Web browser?

   A. Internet Explorer
   B. Windows XP
   C. Microsoft Word
   D. Windows 98

   A. Internet Explorer is a popular browser that currently dominates the market. Answers B and D are operating systems. Answer C is Microsoft word-processing software.

8. When you cut and paste within word-processing software, you are accessing the

   A. printer
   B. CD-ROM drive
   C. clipboard
   D. none of the above

   C. The clipboard is where information is stored within word-processing software when the user copies and pastes his or her particular information. Neither answer A nor B has anything to do with cutting and pasting.

9. Memory that can be read-only is known as

   A. RAM
   B. REM
   C. RIP
   D. ROM

   D. ROM is an abbreviation for read only memory. Answer A is an abbreviation for random access memory. Answer B is an abbreviation for rapid eye movement. Answer C is an abbreviation for rest in peace.

10. An individual dot on a computer screen is known as a

    A. pixel
    B. character
    C. point
    D. font

A. A pixel is defined as an individual dot on a computer screen. Answer B is commonly seen in word-processing software to represent one letter or number. Answer D is the style of typeface.

11. Libraries of pictures, images, and photographs that can be used in a document are known as

    A. icons
    B. clipboards
    C. clipart
    D. museums

C. Clipart is defined as a library of images, photographs, and pictures that can be inserted into a document. Answer A is defined as a visual representation of something on your computer. Answer B is defined as the location where information is stored when using the copy and paste functions.

12. A floppy disk stores up to:

    A. 10 MB of data
    B. 1.44 MB of data
    C. 1.44 GB of data
    D. infinite amount of data

B. A floppy disk (3.5") can store up to 1.44MB of data. Its size is displayed on the outside of the disk.

13. Software programs that allow users to legally copy files and give them away at no cost are called what?

    A. timeshares
    B. malware
    C. shareware
    D. world wide web

C. There's commercial software, and then there's shareware. With commercial software, you have to pay for the product before you use it. With shareware, you can use the product for a trial period, and then decide whether you want to keep it and pay for it.

14. What is the function of a disk drive?

    A. to read or write information to a floppy disk
    B. to scan pictures
    C. to calculate numbers
    D. to print

A. A disk drive's function is to read or write information to a floppy disk. Answer B is the function of a scanner. Answer C is the function of the calculator or spreadsheet software. Answer D is the function of the printer.

15. Which of the following would best describe uploading information?

    A. receiving information from a host computer
    B. storing data on the floppy drive
    C. sending information to a host computer
    D. storing data on the hard drive

A. In order to upload information, the user must receive information from a host computer. Answer B describes the process of saving information. Answer C describes downloading. Answer D describes saving data on the computer's hard drive (C:).

16. If you have an address for a Web site:

    A. You can save it as a bookmark for future reference.
    B. You can type it into a web browser and open that location.
    C. It may be invalid as websites often change without notice.
    D. All of the above

    D. All three scenarios in answers A through C occur when using Web site addresses.

17. All of the following are search engines except:

    A. Altavista
    B. Google
    C. Mozilla
    D. Lycos

    C. Mozilla is a Web browser that is similar to Netscape. Answers A, B, and D are all popular search engines.

18. The difference between memory and storage is that memory is _____ and storage is _____.

    A. permanent, temporary
    B. temporary, permanent
    C. dark, light
    D. light, dark

    B. Memory is temporary as it is erased once the computer is restarted or shut off. Storage is a permanent feature. Answer A has the correct terms, but in reverse order.

19. Formatting a disk

    A. erases all data on the disk
    B. makes a backup copy of the data on the disk
    C. moves the data around on the disk to save space
    D. all of the above

    A. Formatting a disk erases all the information that was previously stored on that particular disk.

20. To care for data on disks you should do all of the following except

    A. avoid exposing disks to high temperatures
    B. avoid exposing disks to dust and smoke
    C. avoid bending the disks
    D. keep the disks near magnets to increase the magnetic charge

    D. Keeping the disk near magnets will usually destroy the disk, causing the computer to be unable to read the disk.

21. A CRT is a type of

    A. CPU
    B. RAM
    C. monitor
    D. software program

    C. A CRT is a type of monitor. CRT stands for cathode ray tube.

136

22. A Pentium IV is a

    A. ROM
    B. CPU
    C. hard drive
    D. floppy drive

    B. A Pentium IV is a type of CPU (central processing unit). There are different types of CPUs manufactured by different companies.

23. If you have a document entitled Ronreport.doc and saved it to the MyDocs folder, which is on the C: drive, the path to the document is

    A. C:/Ronreport.doc
    B. C:\MyDocs\Ronreport.doc
    C. C:\MyDocs.Ronreport.doc
    D. C:/MyDocs/Ronreport.doc

    B. The filename path always uses a backslash.

24. Prior to the year 2000, there were many fears that many programs would not work when the year 2000 arrived. The types of problems feared were called

    A. millennium bugs
    B. crazy bugs
    C. Armageddon bugs
    D. all of the above

    A. Millenium bugs were the term used as the year 2000 approached.

25. An online service that connects the user to the Internet is called a(n) _____.

    A. Portal Service Company (PSC)
    B. Gateway Service Insurer (GSI)
    C. Internet Service Provider (ISP)
    D. Guide Web Browser (GBB)

    C. An ISP is the online service that can connect the user to the Internet.

26. A utility that locates resources by hunting for keywords and phrases is called a _____.

    A. Webviewer
    B. Copernicus
    C. search engine
    D. both A and B

    C. A search engine looks for keywords and phrases that are typed into a search box by the user.

27. A word or phrase in a hypertext document that acts as a pointer of information and usually appears underlined and in a different color is called a

    A. modem
    B. server
    C. portal
    D. link

    D. A link is usually a different color and underlined within hypertext. Answer C is a Web site or service that offers a broad array of resources and services, such as e-mail, forums, and search engines.

28. Additional documents included in an e-mail are referred to as

    A. extras
    B. attachments
    C. links
    D. postings

    B. Attachments are additional documents included in an e-mail.

29. In order for your computer to play music, you need which of the following items:

    A. nothing
    B. read only memory (ROM)
    C. network card and speakers
    D. a CD-ROM drive

    C. A network card and speakers are needed in order for sound to be heard by the user.

30. Which of the following file extensions are graphic files?

    A. .bmp and .doc
    B. .txt and .gif
    C. .gif and .bmp
    D. .xls and .ppt

    C. Both .bmp and .gif are types of graphic file extensions. A .doc file extension is a word-processing document from Microsoft Word. An .xls file is a spreadsheet from Microsoft Excel. A .ppt file is a PowerPoint file from Microsoft. A .txt file is a simple text file that can be opened on most computers.

31. Which part is NOT a storage device?

    A. zip disk
    B. 3.5" floppy disk
    C. printer
    D. jump or flash drive

    C. A printer is not a storage device. Answers A, B, and D are all types of storage devices.

32. Acme Corporation sells 1,000 different products to over 15,000 customers. To record the sales and shipments they should use

    A. a word processor
    B. a typewriter
    C. Microsoft PowerPoint
    D. a database

    D. Because much of the information would be alphanumeric, a database is the best choice to use in this instance.

33. Which of the following is not an input device?

    A. keyboard
    B. microphone
    C. monitor
    D. scanner

    C. A monitor is an output device. Answers A, B, and D are all input devices.

34. When a computer prints a report, this output is called a

    A. hard copy
    B. soft copy
    C. DOS
    D. none of the above

    A. The printed report is a hard copy.

35. When choosing a password, the safest choice is:

    A. your last name
    B. a variation of your social security number
    C. the city you live in
    D. a random string of numbers, letters, and characters

    D. The safest choice for a password is a random string of letters, characters, and numbers because it makes it more difficult for others to hack into your account. Answers A, B, and C, while all are easy to remember, are not the safest option.

36. Which of the following is a popular device used to transfer files from one computer to another?

    A. 8 track
    B. floppy disk
    C. CPU
    D. RAM

    B. A floppy disk (3.5") is a popular method for transferring files from one computer to another.

37. To change the layout of a document that you would like to print from Portrait to Landscape, you must go to which of the following:

    A. Edit⇨Copy
    B. File⇨Page Setup
    C. Window⇨New Window
    D. none of the above

    B. To change the page layout from Portrait to Landscape, the user must go to File⇨Page Setup and choose Landscape.

38. Which of the following extensions identifies a file as a Web document?

    A. .doc
    B. .xls
    C. .htm
    D. .gif

    C. The file extension .htm identifies a file that is a Web document. Answer A is a Microsoft Word document. Answer B is a Microsoft Excel file. Answer D is a graphic file.

39. A piece of silicon one-tenth of an inch long that contains miniaturized integrated circuits is known as

    A. a file
    B. a chip
    C. a zip disk
    D. an A and C

    B. A chip is one-tenth of an inch long and contains miniaturized integrated circuits.

40. A potentially damaging computer program that copies itself from computer to computer is known as a

    A. keyboard
    B. Microsoft
    C. virus
    D. DNA

    C. A virus is a potentially dangerous program that can copy itself from computer to computer.

41. Which of the following is an example of anti-virus software?

    A. Ares
    B. Norton Antivirus
    C. Turbo Tax
    D. none of the above

    B. Norton Antivirus is an example of an anti-virus software program. Answer A is a peer-to-peer file-sharing network, similar to Kazaa. Answer C is a popular do-it-yourself tax program.

42. Which of the following is a type of programming language?

    A. C++
    B. Yahoo!
    C. CPU
    D. Access

    A. C++ is a type of programming language; in fact, it is one of the most widely used object-oriented programming languages. Yahoo! is a popular search engine. A CPU is the central processing unit of a computer. Access is a database software.

43. A portable computer is known as which of the following:

    A. PC
    B. laptop
    C. WWW
    D. server

    B. A laptop is a portable computer.

44. Which of the following is not an output device?

    A. pen plotter
    B. floppy disk
    C. inkjet printer
    D. keyboard

    D. A keyboard is an input device. Answer A, B, and C are all output devices.

45. One of the most essential tools on the Internet that can help the user find sites related to a particular topic is known as a(n)

    A. error
    B. Web site
    C. clip art
    D. mouse

    B. A Web site is one of the most essential tools on the Internet that can help users find sites related to a particular topic.

Practice Tests

Directions: Following are three mini-practice tests. Select the choice that best answers each question. Fully explained answers follow each test.

Practice Test 1

1. A .jpg file extension means that the file is a(n)

   A. document
   B. spreadsheet
   C. image, photo, or picture
   D. none of the above

2. To insert a footnote in Microsoft Word you must:

   A. go to File⇨Page Setup
   B. go to Format⇨Paragraph
   C. go to Table⇨Insert
   D. go to Insert⇨Reference

3. A desktop is defined as

   A. a desk made of Brazilian wood
   B. a plastic sheet that is used to cover the top of one's desk
   C. a background that can display several items
   D. none of the above

4. In Windows, a file name cannot contain which of the following:

   A. numbers
   B. spaces
   C. semicolons
   D. asterisks

5. The Save command does which of the following when working on a previously saved file:

   A. creates a new file with the changes made
   B. saves two copies of the file
   C. overwrites the old version with the new version that has just been edited
   D. none of the above

6. An example of system software is

   A. Microsoft Word
   B. Windows XP
   C. Wolfenstein 3-D
   D. Microsoft Excel

7. Newer models of mice use which of the following devices:

    A. laser lights that sense motion

    B. trackballs

    C. rock

    D. none of the above

8. A computer's RAM (random access memory) is erased when

    A. a floppy disk is inserted

    B. the power is switched off or when the system is restarted

    C. you start an application

    D. you access the internet

9. A Trojan horse is which of the following in the computer world:

    A. a type of memory for the computer

    B. a computer fan used to cool the inside components

    C. a computer virus

    D. a modem

10. Two components that most greatly affect the performance of personal computers are:

    A. microprocessors and RAM

    B. RAM and memory

    C. DVD drive and CD-ROM drive

    D. physical size of the personal computer

Answers to Practice Test 1

1. C. A .jpg is a jpeg file, which means the file is a photo, image, or picture. Answer A would have a .doc file extension. Answer B would .xls.

2. D. The footnote option is available through the Insert⇨Reference option. Answer A is the way to set up the margins, layout, and paper size. Answer B is the way to change the indents and spacing and to insert line and page breaks. Answer C is the way to insert a table into Word.

3. C. Answer C is the only answer that matches under the definition.

4. D. The following characters cannot be used in filenames: \ / : * ? " < > |. The other answers can all be used in file names.

5. C. This is the definition of the Save command when working on a previously saved file. Answer A is the definition for the Save As command. Answer B is a fictional answer. No two copies are saved at the same time.

6. B. System software consists of programs that control the operations of computer equipment. Answers A and D are application software that tell the computer how to produce information. Answer C is a popular game.

7. A. Newer models are optical and use laser lights to sense motion. Answer B is the old type of mouse that has been replaced due to its need for regular maintenance.

8. B. The RAM is erased when the computer is turned off or restarted. Answer A allows the user to save his or her work prior to the RAM being erased. Answers C and D do not affect the RAM.

9. C. A Trojan horse is a malicious program that is disguised as legitimate software.

10. A. The microprocessor serves as the brain of the computer. The more RAM one has, the faster the computer can operate. Answer B is only partially correct. Answer C lists two devices that have nothing to do with being the two that greatly affect the performance. Answer D with physical size has nothing to do with performance.

Practice Test 2

1. A keyboard is considered to be what type of component?

 A. software
 B. hardware
 C. malware
 D. virus

2. A gigabyte is approximately how many bytes of data?

 A. 1 million
 B. 8
 C. 1,000
 D. 1 billion

3. Small pictures used to represent programs or data files on your computer are known as

 A. desktop
 B. viruses
 C. icons
 D. software

4. Deleted files automatically go to what location?

 A. the desktop
 B. the recycle bin
 C. the A: drive
 D. the My Computer folder

5. A drive is defined as which of the following:

 A. an electronic location in which you store groups of related files
 B. a collection of computer data that has some common purpose
 C. a physical place in which you store files
 D. none of the above

6. Microsoft Excel files will have which of the following file extensions:

 A. .doc
 B. .ppt
 C. .xls
 D. .gif

7. According to officials within the ergonomics industry, computer users should sit about how many arm lengths away from the monitor?

 A. eight
 B. one
 C. ten
 D. fifteen

8. The RAM on some computers is expandable by adding which of the following?

    A. a new hard drive

    B. more memory

    C. insertion of a floppy disk

    D. none of the above

9. To display special menus with the mouse, the user must do which of the following:

    A. gently tap the left button

    B. gently tap the right button

    C. ALT + CTRL + DEL

    D. hit the ALT key

10. Which of the following techniques is used to move a program window?

    A. maximize the window and drag the title bar

    B. restore the window and drag the title bar

    C. minimize the window and drag the title bar

    D. drag a corner sizing handle

Answers to Practice Test 2

1. B. Physical parts of the computer system like the keyboard, mouse, and monitors are hardware.

2. D. A gigabyte is described as having approximately 1 billion bytes of data. Answer A is the description for a megabyte. Answer B is the description for a byte. Answer C is the description for a kilobyte.

3. C. Small pictures used to represent programs or data files on your computer are called icons.

4. B. Deleted files automatically go to the recycle bin. Files can be restored from the recycle bin to their original location if the recycle bin has not been emptied.

5. C. The definition of a drive is a physical place in which you store files. Answer A is the definition for a folder. Answer B is the definition for a file.

6. C. Microsoft Excel files will have .xls file extensions. Answer A is the file extension for Microsoft Word documents. Answer B is the file extension for Microsoft PowerPoint. Answer D is the file extension for certain images.

7. B. According to experts within the ergonomics industry, computer users should be positioned about one arm's length away from the monitor.

8. B. Answer A would increase the storing capacity of the computer. Answer C would not affect the memory.

9. B. To open special menus, the user must gently tap and immediately release the right mouse button. Answer A is the button used for most commands but does not open a special menu. Answer D is a shortcut to pull up the start menu within Windows.

10. B. In order to move a program window, the user must restore the window and then drag the title bar. Answer A will not move the program window, nor will answer C. Answer D will only change the size of the window, vertically or horizontally.

Practice Test 3

1. The lives of individuals with physical disabilities have greatly improved because of all of the following except:

    A. mouse
    B. touch screen
    C. speech digitizer
    D. software

2. The keyboard function CTRL + P within windows does which of the following?

    A. prints the page
    B. opens another window
    C. saves a file
    D. pulls up the windows task manager

3. What is the function of a disk drive?

    A. to print sheets of paper
    B. to read from or write information to a floppy disk
    C. to calculate numbers
    D. to manage files

4. Which of the following is the most commonly used way to enter text into a word-processing program?

    A. keyboard
    B. mouse
    C. monitor
    D. printer

5. _____ is what you see on your screen after the computer boots up.

    A. a printer
    B. a desktop
    C. nothing
    D. a boot

6. To change the background of your desktop, the user must _____.

    A. press CTRL + C
    B. double click with the left mouse button
    C. single click with the right mouse button
    D. hold down the left mouse button

7. In Microsoft Word, to change the text to bold-faced, the user must _____.

    A. highlight the word and double-click
    B. choose Edit⇨Paste
    C. Both answers A and B
    D. highlight the word and click on the B on the toolbar. The user can also us Format⇨Font to change the text.

8. Excel, SSPS, and Access are examples of what type of programs?

    A. word-processing
    B. virus-writing
    C. databases or statistical entry
    D. image-editing

9. An operating system that rivals, but is less popular than, Windows is which of the following:

   A. Google
   B. Linux
   C. Ad-Aware
   D. Norton

10. A jump drive (or flash drive) is plugged into which of the following?

   A. the 3.5" disk drive
   B. USB port
   C. the mouse port on the back of the computer
   D. both answers A and C

Answers to Practice Test 3

1. **D.** All three choices, mouse, touch screen, and speech digitizer, are technological improvements that greatly alleviate possible problems for those individuals with physical disabilities.

2. **A** The function CTRL + P enables the user to print the screen or document that appears on his or her screen. To save a file, the user can hit CTRL + S. To pull up the Windows task manager, the user must hit CTRL + ALT + DEL.

3. **B.** A disk drive's function is to read from or write information to a floppy disk. The printer is the device to print sheets of paper. To calculate numbers, the computer comes with a calculator, which is found under accessories.

4. **A.** To input text into a word-processing program, the keyboard is the most commonly used device. The mouse controls the programs that you can select. The monitor displays the programs on screen. The printer is used to print a hard copy of your text.

5. **B.** The desktop is what the user sees after the computer boots up. The printer can be accessed through the start button on the desktop.

6. **C.** After users single click the right mouse button, they are able to choose properties and, from there, can change the background. Answer A would copy a document or information if the user were in a program. On the desktop, however, there would be no change. Answer B, double click with left mouse button, does nothing unless moved over an icon and, with that, can open that particular icon. Answer D, drag the mouse, only moves icons to a different location on the screen.

7. **D.** The text can be changed either by selecting the text and clicking on the B on the toolbar or by selecting the text and choosing format, font. Answer A will not change anything. Answer B is what is used to copy text and paste it elsewhere.

8. **C.** Answer B would need examples like Word, WordPerfect, or Notepad. Answer D would need examples like Adobe Photoshop or Paint. Excel, Access, and SSPS are all examples of database/statistical entry programs.

9. **B.** Linux is an operating system that is less popular than Windows. Google is a popular search engine. Norton is a popular type of antivirus software. Ad-Aware is a spyware removal program.

10. **B.** Jump drives or flash drives are plugged into the USB ports in your computer. Answer A is its own drive and only a 3.5" floppy disk can be inserted. Answer C is the port for the mouse.

Answer Sheet for Sample Job Knowledge Test

(Remove This Sheet and Use It to Mark Your Answers)

1 Ⓐ Ⓑ Ⓒ Ⓓ	21 Ⓐ Ⓑ Ⓒ Ⓓ	41 Ⓐ Ⓑ Ⓒ Ⓓ	61 Ⓐ Ⓑ Ⓒ Ⓓ	81 Ⓐ Ⓑ Ⓒ Ⓓ
2 Ⓐ Ⓑ Ⓒ Ⓓ	22 Ⓐ Ⓑ Ⓒ Ⓓ	42 Ⓐ Ⓑ Ⓒ Ⓓ	62 Ⓐ Ⓑ Ⓒ Ⓓ	82 Ⓐ Ⓑ Ⓒ Ⓓ
3 Ⓐ Ⓑ Ⓒ Ⓓ	23 Ⓐ Ⓑ Ⓒ Ⓓ	43 Ⓐ Ⓑ Ⓒ Ⓓ	63 Ⓐ Ⓑ Ⓒ Ⓓ	83 Ⓐ Ⓑ Ⓒ Ⓓ
4 Ⓐ Ⓑ Ⓒ Ⓓ	24 Ⓐ Ⓑ Ⓒ Ⓓ	44 Ⓐ Ⓑ Ⓒ Ⓓ	64 Ⓐ Ⓑ Ⓒ Ⓓ	84 Ⓐ Ⓑ Ⓒ Ⓓ
5 Ⓐ Ⓑ Ⓒ Ⓓ	25 Ⓐ Ⓑ Ⓒ Ⓓ	45 Ⓐ Ⓑ Ⓒ Ⓓ	65 Ⓐ Ⓑ Ⓒ Ⓓ	85 Ⓐ Ⓑ Ⓒ Ⓓ
6 Ⓐ Ⓑ Ⓒ Ⓓ	26 Ⓐ Ⓑ Ⓒ Ⓓ	46 Ⓐ Ⓑ Ⓒ Ⓓ	66 Ⓐ Ⓑ Ⓒ Ⓓ	86 Ⓐ Ⓑ Ⓒ Ⓓ
7 Ⓐ Ⓑ Ⓒ Ⓓ	27 Ⓐ Ⓑ Ⓒ Ⓓ	47 Ⓐ Ⓑ Ⓒ Ⓓ	67 Ⓐ Ⓑ Ⓒ Ⓓ	87 Ⓐ Ⓑ Ⓒ Ⓓ
8 Ⓐ Ⓑ Ⓒ Ⓓ	28 Ⓐ Ⓑ Ⓒ Ⓓ	48 Ⓐ Ⓑ Ⓒ Ⓓ	68 Ⓐ Ⓑ Ⓒ Ⓓ	88 Ⓐ Ⓑ Ⓒ Ⓓ
9 Ⓐ Ⓑ Ⓒ Ⓓ	29 Ⓐ Ⓑ Ⓒ Ⓓ	49 Ⓐ Ⓑ Ⓒ Ⓓ	69 Ⓐ Ⓑ Ⓒ Ⓓ	89 Ⓐ Ⓑ Ⓒ Ⓓ
10 Ⓐ Ⓑ Ⓒ Ⓓ	30 Ⓐ Ⓑ Ⓒ Ⓓ	50 Ⓐ Ⓑ Ⓒ Ⓓ	70 Ⓐ Ⓑ Ⓒ Ⓓ	90 Ⓐ Ⓑ Ⓒ Ⓓ
11 Ⓐ Ⓑ Ⓒ Ⓓ	31 Ⓐ Ⓑ Ⓒ Ⓓ	51 Ⓐ Ⓑ Ⓒ Ⓓ	71 Ⓐ Ⓑ Ⓒ Ⓓ	
12 Ⓐ Ⓑ Ⓒ Ⓓ	32 Ⓐ Ⓑ Ⓒ Ⓓ	52 Ⓐ Ⓑ Ⓒ Ⓓ	72 Ⓐ Ⓑ Ⓒ Ⓓ	
13 Ⓐ Ⓑ Ⓒ Ⓓ	33 Ⓐ Ⓑ Ⓒ Ⓓ	53 Ⓐ Ⓑ Ⓒ Ⓓ	73 Ⓐ Ⓑ Ⓒ Ⓓ	
14 Ⓐ Ⓑ Ⓒ Ⓓ	34 Ⓐ Ⓑ Ⓒ Ⓓ	54 Ⓐ Ⓑ Ⓒ Ⓓ	74 Ⓐ Ⓑ Ⓒ Ⓓ	
15 Ⓐ Ⓑ Ⓒ Ⓓ	35 Ⓐ Ⓑ Ⓒ Ⓓ	55 Ⓐ Ⓑ Ⓒ Ⓓ	75 Ⓐ Ⓑ Ⓒ Ⓓ	
16 Ⓐ Ⓑ Ⓒ Ⓓ	36 Ⓐ Ⓑ Ⓒ Ⓓ	56 Ⓐ Ⓑ Ⓒ Ⓓ	76 Ⓐ Ⓑ Ⓒ Ⓓ	
17 Ⓐ Ⓑ Ⓒ Ⓓ	37 Ⓐ Ⓑ Ⓒ Ⓓ	57 Ⓐ Ⓑ Ⓒ Ⓓ	77 Ⓐ Ⓑ Ⓒ Ⓓ	
18 Ⓐ Ⓑ Ⓒ Ⓓ	38 Ⓐ Ⓑ Ⓒ Ⓓ	58 Ⓐ Ⓑ Ⓒ Ⓓ	78 Ⓐ Ⓑ Ⓒ Ⓓ	
19 Ⓐ Ⓑ Ⓒ Ⓓ	39 Ⓐ Ⓑ Ⓒ Ⓓ	59 Ⓐ Ⓑ Ⓒ Ⓓ	79 Ⓐ Ⓑ Ⓒ Ⓓ	
20 Ⓐ Ⓑ Ⓒ Ⓓ	40 Ⓐ Ⓑ Ⓒ Ⓓ	60 Ⓐ Ⓑ Ⓒ Ⓓ	80 Ⓐ Ⓑ Ⓒ Ⓓ	

CUT HERE

Sample Job Knowledge Test

Time: 60 minutes

90 questions

Directions: The following test consists of questions from each of the eight subject areas that will be on the actual examination. Select the choice that best answers the question. To help you identify your strengths and weaknesses on this test, we've included the subject area at the end of each answer.

1. Treaties must be approved by

   A. a majority of the House and Senate
   B. two-thirds of the Senators voting on the treaty
   C. a majority of the House of Representatives
   D. three-fourths of the Senate

2. A public opinion survey is done and it is reported that the results are not statistically significant. What does this mean?

   A. It means that there are insufficient responses to consider the survey valid.
   B. It means that the results could be due to chance.
   C. It means that different surveys have different results.
   D. It means that the findings of the survey are not substantively important.

3. Concerning the application of rights in the U.S. Constitution's Bill of Rights to the states, which of the following is correct?

   A. All rights in the Bill of Rights have applied to the states since the beginning.
   B. All rights in the Bill of Rights have applied to the states since the passage of the 14th Amendment.
   C. None of the rights in the Bill of Rights applies to the states. The states have their own bills of rights.
   D. Most of rights in the Bill of Rights have been applied to the states based upon Supreme Court decisions. Some still do not apply.

4. Today's Native Americans/American Indians descend from Asiatic ancestors who arrived in North America

   A. on wooden ships
   B. primarily on horseback
   C. across a land bridge now submerged beneath the Bering Sea
   D. under the leadership of a former warlord who would later become known as Chief Powhatan, the founder of the Powhatan Confederacy

5. In 1620, the _____established self-government for the Plymouth Colonists.

   A. the Mayflower Compact
   B. the Fundamental Order of Connecticut
   C. the Articles of Confederation
   D. the Declaration of Rights

6. Which of the following statements is not true?

   A. At the time of the American Revolution, most white residents of the 13 colonies were either of northern or western European descent.
   B. The Naturalization Act of 1790 made citizenship — and all of its accompanying rights — available to free white men of European descent and only to free white men of European descent.
   C. The right to be educated in the language spoken in their homes was first granted during the 1820s to Pennsylvania's German-speaking population.
   D. Less than half of all southern whites belonged to slave-owning families.

7. Yugoslavia was initially established as a kingdom of Serbs, Slovenes, and

   A. Croats
   B. Bosnians
   C. Turks
   D. Hungarians

8. In 1939, the Kingdom of Siam became officially known as

   A. Indonesia
   B. Cambodia
   C. Burma
   D. Thailand

9. Which of the following statements was not a result of the aftermath of communism's 1989 collapse in Eastern Europe?

   A. Industrial production continued relatively unabated.
   B. Living standards immediately rose.
   C. Governments attempted to bring about economic stabilization.
   D. Prices increased dramatically.

10. Mercantilism was an economic policy that attempted to obtain a favorable balance of trade that would result in the maximum inflows of gold and silver. During what century was this economic theory popular?

   A. 16th
   B. 19th
   C. 13th
   D. 21st

11. An examination of 750 circuit boards produced by the AMPEX Corp. revealed that 15 were defective. At this rate, how many defective circuit boards would there be in a lot of 12,750?

   A. 115
   B. 255
   C. 275
   D. 350

12. A television is on sale for 20% off. If the sale price is $800, what was the original price?

   A. $160
   B. $640
   C. $960
   D. $1,000

13. Dan Preston arrives in Toronto, Ontario, Canada, and wishes to convert $300 U.S. dollars to Canadian dollars. If one U.S. dollar is worth $1.47 in Canadian currency, how many Canadian dollars does Dan receive?

   A. $141
   B. $204
   C. $441
   D. $447

14. A blueprint has a scale of 3 feet per $\frac{1}{2}$ inch. If a bathroom is $1\frac{1}{2}$ inches $\times 2$ inches, what are its actual dimensions?

   A. $4\frac{1}{2}$ feet $\times 6$ feet
   B. 6 feet $\times 7\frac{1}{2}$ feet
   C. $7\frac{1}{2}$ feet $\times 9$ feet
   D. 9 feet $\times 12$ feet

15. Top management are compensated more because they are valuable to the organization. These top managers do more

   A. organizing
   B. planning
   C. directing
   D. controlling

16. Why is delegation of authority crucial to the successful execution of company operations?

   A. It gives the top management more time to think and develop strategic business directions.
   B. It makes the entire company more structured and easier to account for financially.
   C. It empowers the employees to make commitments, use resources, and take whatever actions to ensure customer satisfaction.
   D. It provides jobs so that there will be many mid-level and low-level managers.

17. A figure of speech in which a comparison is made by using "as" or "like" is a:

   A. simile
   B. metaphor
   C. synecdoche
   D. cacophony

18. Slander means:

   A. to exaggerate
   B. to reveal only the negative aspects of an idea or person
   C. to use another person's ideas and claim them as your own
   D. to make statements about a person that are injurious to the reputation of a person

19. A new trend has developed in the computer world in which one's work can now be saved using a device that plugs into the USB ports of their computer. This device is known as a

   A. jump drive or flash drive
   B. zip disk
   C. 3.5" floppy disk
   D. DVD-RW

20. Which of the following is considered an output device (produces information from the processing):

   A. mouse
   B. digital camera
   C. printer
   D. zip drive

21. Which of the following describes the Executive Office of the President?

   A. It is the formal name for the Cabinet.
   B. It contains offices such as the Environmental Protection Administration that are cabinet level but not cabinet departments.
   C. It consists of offices that advise the president.
   D. It refers only to those in the White House who write speeches for the president and give political advice.

22. The filibuster has been used to prevent a bill from passing in the Senate. Why hasn't it been as much of a concern in recent years?

   A. It has been eliminated by Senate rules.
   B. The introduction of cloture has allowed the Senate to end the filibusters. Most filibusters are ended today by cloture.
   C. The Senate limits a filibuster today to 30 hours.
   D. The Senate has a track system that allows it to move on to other business if a filibuster stops work on a particular bill or appointment.

23. A state added a constitutional amendment to its state constitution. Can the Congress overturn such an amendment?

   A. yes, only by passing a federal Constitutional Amendment approved by the states
   B. yes, by either passing a law or enacting a federal Constitutional Amendment, approved by the states
   C. no, states can do what they want
   D. yes, by passing a resolution with a two-thirds vote

24. Which of the following amendments to the U.S. Constitution conferred automatic U.S citizenship on all persons born in the United States?

   A. the 13th Amendment
   B. the 14th Amendment
   C. the 15th Amendment
   D. the 16th Amendment

25. Which of the following did not occur during the years of post-Civil War Reconstruction?

   A. The first large-scale attempt by the federal government to bring about racial equality by intervening in political and economic processes and spending large amounts of money to help one group improve its position relative to other groups.
   B. Former Confederate states were placed under martial law.
   C. The passage of the 14th Amendment.
   D. Southern states passing and enforcing laws that effectively denied blacks the right to vote.

GO ON TO THE NEXT PAGE

26. One of the most widely traded agricultural commodities on the planet, coffee grows best in

    A. tropical lowlands
    B. temperate lowlands
    C. tropical highlands
    D. temperate mountain zones

27. Emperor Napoleon III (Louis Napoleon) fell from power

    A. during the Crimean War
    B. during the Paris Commune
    C. during the Franco Prussian War
    D. after being deposed by the Directory

28. From 1895 until the end of the Second World War, Korea was dominated by

    A. China
    B. Russia
    C. Japan
    D. France

29. Price controls (such as fixing the price for gas or renting apartments) are generally opposed by economists because

    A. economists believe that price controls generally cause distorted asset allocation
    B. economists believe that price controls can lead to a shortage of products on the open market
    C. alternative (and often illegal) distribution mechanisms emerge to avoid price controls
    D. all of the above

30. Many trade economists argue that closing off an economy to international market forces creates critical inefficiencies as local producers become _____, expending resources on cornering artificially created markets via specially acquired licenses, legitimate legislation, or personal connections.

    A. corrupt
    B. import-substituting forces
    C. self-reliant
    D. rent-seekers

31. Tanya's bowling scores this week were 112, 156, 179, and 165. Last week, her average score was 140. How many points did her average improve?

    A. 18
    B. 13
    C. 11
    D. 8

Problems 32 and 33 are based on the following graph.

Sales of Video Game X
(Millions of Dollars)

32. Between which two consecutive years was the percent of decrease in sales for video game X the greatest?

    A. year 1 to year 2
    B. year 2 to year 3
    C. year 3 to year 4
    D. year 4 to year 5

33. Sales in Year 3 accounted for approximately what percent of the total sales for the five years shown?

    A. 23%
    B. 43%
    C. 46%
    D. 75%

34. The following table lists the number of points that each of the 7 players on a particular team scored during a basketball tournament.

Player	John	Dean	Kevin	Brett	Steven	Mike	Chris
Points	38	29	36	42	38	42	44

If the number of points that Dean scored is reported incorrectly in the local newspaper as 27, which of the following statements is true?

A. The mean, median, mode, and range of the players' points will change.

B. The median and the mode will remain the same, but the mean and the range will change.

C. The median, mode, and range will remain the same, but the mean will change.

D. The median and the mean will remain the same, but the mode and the range will change.

---

35. Which form of business ownership has restricted liability, lower taxation, and fewer government restrictions?

A. sole proprietorship

B. partnership

C. limited liability corporation

D. cooperatives

36. Customization in operations management is

A. making identical, interchangeable components or products

B. the creation of an item in self-contained units that can be combined or interchanged to create different products

C. making products to meet a particular customer's needs or wants

D. making the best product to clear immigration customs

37. In interpersonal communication, the encoder is

A. the message

B. the listener/receiver

C. the situation in which the message is given

D. the speaker/sender

38. An example of selective perception is:

A. listening only to messages with which you agree

B. selecting only parts of a message in which you are interested

C. remembering only what you wish

D. understanding a message as distorted; trying to make it fit with previously held ideas

39. The First Amendment of the U.S. Constitution provides protection for

A. freedom of speech

B. freedom of the press

C. freedom of religious practices

D. all of the above

40. A bit is defined as:

A. approximately 1 million bytes of data

B. a single character

C. the most basic element of computer data

D. approximately 1 trillion bytes of data

41. The maximize button performs which of the following activities:

A. removes the program window from the desktop but keeps the program running

B. closes a document window or exits a program

C. restores a program window to the size it was set to before it was maximized

D. expands the program window until it covers the entire desktop

GO ON TO THE NEXT PAGE

42. The Social Security system was established based upon a trust fund structure. What has happened to the trust funds?

A. They have eliminated all trust funds that were originally established.

B. They have consolidated the trust funds into a single fund.

C. They have several trust funds (for example, disability, old-age retirement, hospital insurance).

D. They have two trust funds. One must be invested in U.S. government bonds and the other allows individuals to invest in stock index funds.

43. *Amicus Curiae* briefs are filed with the courts. What are they?

A. They are briefs filed by the appellants.

B. They are briefs filed by those who are not participants in the case.

C. They are briefs filed by the government.

D. They are parts of a court's decision that do not act as precedent for future cases.

44. Congressional oversight is a term used to signify

A. when Congress includes preferences for some group in a piece of legislation

B. when Congress exercises review of some activity of the executive branch

C. when Congress leaves out a crucial element in legislation

D. when Congress fails to provide sufficient funds for a program

45. Which of the following was passed during what historians and political scientists have labeled the Progressive Era?

A. the Sherman Anti-Trust Act

B. the Taft-Hartley Act

C. the Emergency Banking Act

D. the Hawley-Smoot Act

46. Which of the following concerning American movies and the American Motion Picture Industry is not true?

A. Thomas Edison was the first American to patent and market a commercial motion-picture camera.

B. During the early years of American movie production, the rate of attendance of non-English-speaking immigrants was lower than the attendance rate of middle class, native-born Americans.

C. During the second decade of the 20th century, the U.S. Supreme Court ruled that movies were a business and not a form of communication and, therefore, their contents were not protected by the 1st Amendment.

D. The first talking movie debuted during the 1920s.

47. The_____ Act gave American workers the right to belong to labor unions and engage in collective bargaining.

A. the Wagner Act

B. the Walsh-Healy Act

C. the Fair Standards Act

D. the Taft-Hartley Act

48. The city of Istanbul's strategic location gives Turkey control of access to

A. the Aegean

B. the Black Sea

C. the Baltic Sea

D. the Red Sea

49. Northern Ireland has what status within the United Kingdom?

A. It is an autonomous member of the commonwealth of former British colonies.

B. It is a crown colony.

C. It is an integral part of the United Kingdom.

D. It is no longer a member of the Commonwealth.

50. While shock therapy is well known for its controversial effect on the Russian and Polish economies, it was first applied to this South American economy:

    A. Chile
    B. Brazil
    C. Argentina
    D. Bolivia

51. Economists view ticket scalping as

    A. an illegitimate enterprise, because the consumer is charged many times over the market price for the tickets
    B. a legitimate and voluntary transaction in which the two parties believe they are exchanging articles of like value
    C. having no consequence or importance
    D. none of the above is true

52. OPEC is an example of this economic phenomenon:

    A. monopoly
    B. cartel
    C. economic community
    D. free trade zone

Problems 53–55 are based on the following situation.

The Beta Company has 9 employees. There are 4 associates, each of whom earns $35,000 a year. There are also 2 managers, each earning $47,000 a year, 1 director earning $52,000, 1 vice president earning $56,000, and 1 owner earning $450,000 a year.

53. What is the average (arithmetic mean) annual income of the employees at the Beta Company?

    A. $88,000
    B. $92,000
    C. $95,000
    D. $128,000

54. What is the median annual income of the employees at the Beta Company?

    A. $35,000
    B. $47,000
    C. $49,500
    D. $52,000

55. What is the modal annual income of the employees at the Beta Company?

    A. $35,000
    B. $47,000
    C. $52,000
    D. $56,000

56. What is the role of the Federal Trade Commission (FTC)?

    A. foster better international trade relations
    B. develop trading product lists
    C. register trading companies and make sure they are legitimate
    D. regulate business practices and curb false advertising, misleading pricing, and deceptive packaging and labeling

57. An Equal Opportunity Employer will not discriminate against an employee based on race, religion, gender, national origin, or color. However in certain circumstances, which one of the following can be a discriminatory factor for employment?

    A. race
    B. religion
    C. color
    D. gender

58. What is the marketing concept?

    A. a group of people who have a need, purchasing power, and the desire and authority to spend money on goods, services, and ideas
    B. a plan of action for developing, pricing, distributing, and promoting products that meet the needs of specific customers
    C. a group of activities designed to expedite transactions by creating, distributing, pricing, and promoting goods, services, and ideas
    D. the idea that an organization should try to satisfy customers' needs through coordinated activities that also allow it to achieve its own goal

GO ON TO THE NEXT PAGE

59. Yellow journalism refers to

    A. newspapers printed on paper stock that quickly deteriorates and turns yellow

    B. alternate or underground newspapers, often anti-institutional

    C. newspapers printed in color

    D. a newspaper characterized by sensational journalism

60. A controlled-circulation magazine is

    A. one sold only to adults at magazine counters

    B. controlled by the desires of its readers who subscribe to it

    C. one whose production and mailing is supported not by charging readers, but usually through advertising revenues, and the publisher decides on its readership

    D. one sent only to certain areas of the country, controlled by Zip code

61. Computer monitors use the same type of technology that television sets do. Which of the following is the technology that they share?

    A. cathode ray tube (CRT)

    B. magnetic resonance imaging (MRI)

    C. computer television rays (CTR)

    D. information technology (IT)

62. The resolution of a printer is measured in:

    A. megabits

    B. dots per inch (DPI)

    C. inches

    D. bytes

63. Dan has created a ten-page essay, but he wants to print only the first three pages. Which of the following printer commands should he use?

    A. page setup

    B. print preview

    C. from _____ to _____

    D. all of the above

64. The Necessary and Proper Clause in the Constitution did what?

    A. allowed states to retain powers not given to the federal government

    B. gave the federal government the power to legislate for the health, safety, and welfare of the people

    C. gave the president the power to act in times of national emergency

    D. allowed the Congress to enact laws that were seen as needed to carry out the powers listed in Article I

65. What is a restricted rule in the House of Representatives?

    A. a rule that permits no amendments to a bill

    B. a rule that permits some specified amendments to a bill

    C. a rule that keeps former members from the floor on issues they had been involved with as legislators

    D. a rule specifying how much legislators can accept from lobbyists for honoraria for speeches

66. Concerning the current balance of trade, which of the following is correct?

    A. It is in balance because of military assistance.

    B. It is in balance because of outsourcing.

    C. It is imbalanced. We buy more from overseas than we sell.

    D. It is imbalanced. We sell more overseas than we buy.

67. The negotiation of treaties and international agreements is the responsibility of

    A. the Senate

    B. the House of Representatives

    C. the Executive Branch

    D. the Judiciary

68. Which amendment gave women the right to vote?

    A. the 16th

    B. the 17th

    C. the 18th

    D. the 19th

69. Which of the following regarding the Marshall Plan is not true?

   A. It aided in the post-World War II European economic recovery.

   B. It contributed to post-World War II American economic prosperity.

   C. It provided procedural guidelines for the integration of racially segregated schools in the American South.

   D. It is so-called because its major goals and intentions were first and most clearly and systematically stated by General George Marshall.

70. Which of the following former U.S. vice-presidents was tried for treason but later acquitted?

   A. John Breckinridge

   B. Aaron Burr

   C. John Calhoun

   D. Garret Hobart

71. According to the recent census, there are more than 34 million foreign-born individuals in the United States. The largest group of this population comes from

   A. Latin America

   B. Asia

   C. Europe

   D. Africa

72. The dominant ethnic group in the Yucatan Peninsula is

   A. Incan

   B. Mayan

   C. Cambodian

   D. Laotian

73. The fundamental goal of Sinn Fein is

   A. to establish a unified Irish Republic without British involvement

   B. to keep Northern Ireland within the United Kingdom

   C. to establish an independent, Protestant state of Ulster

   D. to establish a religious, Catholic government in Northern Ireland

74. The government of the Union of Myanmar, or Burma, responded to the electoral victory of the democratic opposition in 1990 by

   A. handing over power to the newly elected government

   B. forming a coalition government with the opposition

   C. jailing the opposition leadership

   D. none of the above

75. The key U.S. Cabinet-level agency charged with negotiating international trade agreements is

   A. the United States Trade Representative (USTR)

   B. the Department of State

   C. the Department of Commerce

   D. the Department of Treasury

76. In this digital age, instant communication and monetary transfers can have a profound effect on events in other countries. If, in the Tokyo market, the dollar drops sharply against the Japanese yen,

   A. the price of gold on the Zurich Exchange will likely rise

   B. pork belly futures will plummet

   C. American tourists will flock to Tokyo

   D. the dollar will strengthen against the euro

77. Joe plans on buying a 1976 Mini Cooper to tour around England for $6000 or £3000 at a $2:£1 exchange rate. However, shortly before he goes to the bank to change his dollars to pounds, the U.S. dollar goes to $3:£1. How many U.S. dollars will Joe have to change into pounds in order to purchase the Mini Cooper?

   A. $3,000

   B. $6,000

   C. $9,000

   D. Not enough information is provided.

GO ON TO THE NEXT PAGE

78. One-eighth of a bookstore's magazines are sold on a Friday. If $\frac{1}{4}$ of the remaining magazines are sold the next day, what fractional part of the magazines remains at the end of the second day?

A. $\frac{1}{32}$

B. $\frac{1}{8}$

C. $\frac{7}{32}$

D. $\frac{21}{32}$

79. An appliance originally costing $1,000 goes on sale one week for 25 percent off. The following week, it is discounted an additional 10 percent. What is the new sale price of the appliance?

A. $650

B. $675

C. $750

D. $900

80. $\left(\sqrt{2}\right)^4 =$

A. 2

B. 4

C. 8

D. 16

81. What is CRM (customer relationship management)?

A. It is the management and study of customer switching behavior.

B. It is the use of customer information to tie up with other companies.

C. It is the use of information about customers to create marketing strategies that develop and sustain desirable customer relationships.

D. It is the understanding of how customers manage their finances with the company.

82. Manufacturers can use promotion to create consumer demand for a product so that consumers exert pressure on marketing channel members to make it available. This is called a

A. pull strategy

B. push strategy

C. demand strategy

D. supply strategy

83. When analyzing financial statements, we can use ratios to help us analyze an organization's health. Which ratio is not valid?

A. asset utilization ratio

B. cash ratio

C. liquidity ratio

D. debt utilization ratio

84. Which of these is not a responsibility of the Federal Reserve Board?

A. supervise federal deposit insurance programs of banks of the Federal Reserve System

B. regulate banks and other financial institutions

C. ensure checking accounts procedures of NAFTA countries comply

D. control the supply of money

85. The kind of radio transmission that makes possible high fidelity and static-free broadcast of music is:

A. AM radio

B. FM radio

C. short-wave radio

D. citizens band radio

86. Which of the following is the noncommercial radio network, known for its cultural and informational programming?

A. CBS

B. CNN

C. ESPN

D. NPR

87. A television V-Chip is

A. a device that allows parents to block objectionable programming

B. a technology that allows high definition television

C. a device that digitally records shows played on a TV set

D. a technology that automatically displays a TV picture, whether it is broadcast in analog or digital

88. A large computer designed to meet the needs of a large organization is called a

    A. mainframe

    B. notebook computer

    C. personal computer

    D. none of the above

89. A connection between two or more computers so that they can share resources is known as a(n)

    A. icon

    B. bug

    C. network

    D. server

90. What is a URL?

    A. an e-mail address

    B. the title of a Web page

    C. Bill Gates' stock symbol

    D. the address of a page on the World Wide Web

IF YOU FINISH BEFORE TIME IS CALLED, CHECK YOUR WORK ON THIS SECTION ONLY. DO NOT WORK ON ANY OTHER SECTION IN THE TEST.

Answer Key for Job Knowledge Practice Test

1. B	31. B	61. A
2. B	32. D	62. B
3. D	33. B	63. C
4. C	34. B	64. D
5. A	35. C	65. B
6. C	36. C	66. C
7. A	37. D	67. C
8. D	38. D	68. D
9. B	39. D	69. C
10. A	40. C	70. B
11. B	41. D	71. A
12. D	42. C	72. B
13. C	43. B	73. A
14. D	44. B	74. C
15. B	45. A	75. A
16. C	46. B	76. A
17. A	47. A	77. C
18. D	48. B	78. D
19. A	49. C	79. B
20. C	50. D	80. B
21. C	51. B	81. C
22. D	52. B	82. A
23. B	53. A	83. B
24. B	54. B	84. C
25. D	55. A	85. B
26. C	56. D	86. D
27. C	57. B	87. A
28. C	58. D	88. A
29. D	59. D	89. C
30. D	60. C	90. D

Answers to Sample Job Knowledge Test

1. **B.** Article II, Section 2 of the U.S. Constitution specifies that two-thirds of the Senators present must agree to a treaty. This power, along with the power of the Senate to approve the appointment of ambassadors, military officers, and other appointments, gives the Senate the reputation of being the house of Congress that's most concerned with foreign affairs. It should be pointed out, however, that the House is also vital to U.S. foreign affairs, especially its role in the appropriations process. (U.S. government)

2. **B.** In public opinion research, if a finding is not statistically significant, any difference found in the sample could simply be the result of sampling error and may not be a real difference found in the population. In reality, if the full population were surveyed, you may not find that difference. The larger the sample size, the less even a small difference on a question is likely to be statistically significant. If the entire population were surveyed, any difference *is* statistically significant because you are not trying to infer from a sample to a population. Statistical significance is not related to substantive significance. A difference may be statistically significant and of no importance. Answer A is also incorrect because statistical significance has nothing to do with a low response rate, which could reduce the accuracy of a sample. (U.S. government)

3. **D.** The Bill of Rights had been directed at the federal government. However, since the passage of the 14th Amendment, the Supreme Court has applied many of the provisions in the Bill of Rights to the states, beginning with cases in 1897. Especially important was laying out the doctrine of selective incorporation in *Gitlow v. New York* (1925). However, all rights are not applied. One example is the right to be indicted by a grand jury in the 5th Amendment. Many states do not use grand juries to indict people accused of criminal offenses. (U.S. government)

4. **C.** Historical and archaeological evidence indicate that during the last great Ice Age (50,000-1,500 B.C.) migration by foot from Siberia over the Bering Strait land bridge into North America was possible. There is no evidence that the ancestors of today's Native Americans were either sailors or horsemen, thus no evidence that they arrived on horseback or by wooden ships or boats of any sort. Chief Powhatan was the leader of the Powhatan Confederacy during the early 1600s, many centuries after the first of the ancestors of today's Native Americans arrived in North America. Powhatan was also the father of Pocahontas, the Indian princess to whom historians give credit for having saved the life of Captain John Smith, the military commander of the Jamestown, Virginia settlement. (U.S. society)

5. **A.** The Mayflower Compact was the document that established self-government for the Plymouth colonists in 1620. The Fundamental Order of Connecticut was the first American Constitution, written in 1639 by representatives from the Connecticut towns of Hartford, Wethersfield, and Windsor. The Declaration of Rights, written by George Mason, were adopted by the Virginia colonists. It outlined the basic rights and freedoms that were ultimately written into the U.S. Constitution and Bill of Rights. The Articles of Confederation were adopted by the Continental Congress in 1777, thereby uniting the colonies into a loose union of states with a weak central government that had no power to levy taxes. The Quakers were also the descendants of separatists from the Church of England, but they did not begin arriving in America until the 1680s. (U.S. society)

6. **C.** Although during the 1820s a group of Pennsylvanians did indeed petition Congress to make German the official language of their state, the petitioned was denied. The Pennsylvania Germans were never granted the right to be educated in the language spoken in their homes. The Naturalization Act of 1790 made American citizenship available to "free white men of European descent" — and only free white men of European descent. At the time of the American Revolution most white residents of the colonies were of either northern or western European (that is, British, German, French, and Scandinavian) descent. Only approximately one-fourth of all ante-bellum southern whites belonged to slave-owning families. This was because only a minority of southern whites owned sufficient land or other property to profit from slave labor. If the cost of maintaining a slave was not greater than the wealth produced by the slave, rather than being an asset to his/her owner, the slave was a financial liability. (U.S. society)

7. **A.** Formed out of the nationalities that had been part of the old Ottoman and Habsburg empires, Yugoslavia was originally known as the Kingdom of Serbs, Slovenes, and Croats. (World history and geography)

8. **D.** Reflecting the national identity of its people, the ancient kingdom of Siam was renamed Thailand. (World history and geography)

9. **B.** Following the collapse of communism in Eastern Europe, industrial production continued relatively unabated as governments attempted to maintain economic stability. At the same time, prices increased dramatically as products began to be priced at their market rate, hence living standards decreased as otherwise affordable products began to be unaffordable, particularly for those on fixed incomes (such as retirees). (Economics)

10. **A.** Mercantilism was an economic theory that had wide acceptance during the 16th through 18th centuries. This theory stated that colonies existed to benefit the home country, through an exclusive and highly regulated trading relationship. The drive to create colonies resulted in the creation of many European empires. (Economics)

11. **B.** This problem can be solved by setting up a proportion.

$$\frac{\text{Defects} \rightarrow}{\text{Total} \rightarrow} \frac{15}{750} = \frac{x}{12,750}. \text{ Cross-multiply}$$

$$750x = 191,250. \text{ Divide by } 750$$

$$x = 255 \text{ (Mathematics and statistics)}$$

12. **D.** If an item is discounted 20%, the sale price is 80% of the original price. Let p represent the original price. Then $\$800 = 80\% \times p$ and $p = \frac{800}{80\%} = \frac{800}{.80} = \$1,000$. (Mathematics and statistics)

13. **C.** $\$300 \times \frac{1.47 \text{ Canadian}}{1.00 \text{ U.S.}} = \$441$. (Mathematics and statistics)

14. **D.** If the blueprint shows $\frac{1}{2}$ inch for every 3 feet, then 1 inch represents 6 feet. The actual dimensions of a room $1\frac{1}{2}$ inches $\times 2$ inches would be $\left(1\frac{1}{2} \times 6\right)$ by (2×6) or 9 feet by 12 feet. (Mathematics and statistics)

15. **B.** Although top managers do all the listed activities, they are involved in strategic planning most of the time. Staffing and directing are more the responsibility of mid-level managers, while controlling is the primary responsibility of front-line managers. (Management)

16. **C.** C is clearly the answer, because the entire company must work as one to ensure customer satisfaction. That is achieved through empowerment. For answer A, top management is suppose to think and give directions in the first place and should not be involved in day-to-day operations. Answers B and D are not relevant. (Management)

17. **A.** A metaphor fuses the two subjects (generally using "is" instead of "as" or "like"). A synecdoche is a figure of speech in which the part is used for a whole. A cacophony is the frequent use/reuse of the same sounds together. (Communication)

18. **D.** To exaggerate may not be harmful, per se. To reveal only negative aspects is also not injurious, per se. Claiming others' ideas as your own is plagiarism, not slander. (Communication)

19. **A.** Flash drives are becoming more and more popular and easy to use. Storage size varies anywhere from 128mb to 512mb. Answer B is a disk that requires a special drive in the computer for it to fit inside. It has eliminated floppy disks, because it is able to hold many more files. Answer C is a regular floppy disk that is limited in the amount of files it can hold. It has its own drive as well. Answer D is a re-writable DVD used in copying DVD files. (Computers)

20. **C.** The printer is considered an output device. Answer A is an input device; it relays information to the computer. Answer B is an input device, because it relays information to the computer. Answer D is a storage device and allows the user to save larger amounts of data onto it. Zip disk storage amounts range from 100MB and up. (Computers)

21. C. The Executive Office of the President was created under President Franklin Roosevelt by the Executive Reorganization Act of 1939. It was established to provide assistance to the president outside of Cabinet departments. Offices such as the Office of Management and Budget, National Security Council, and the White House Office are within the Executive Office of the President. Typically, these offices are advisory and not line departments or agencies, such as the Cabinet departments and the Environmental Protection Agency. (U.S. government)

22. D. The Senate now operates on a track system, whereby more than one bill can be considered. Although cloture, which cuts off filibusters, has been more successful in recent years, there are still filibusters that have been conducted. Examples are the filibusters by the Democrats on some of President Bush's court appointments. The Senate has simply gone on to other business when the appointments have been filibustered. (U.S. government)

23. B. The supremacy clause in the national Constitution says that national statutes and Constitution are supreme over state statutes and constitutions. (U.S. government)

24. B. The 14th Amendment conferred automatic citizenship on all persons born within the territorial limits of the United States. The 13th Amendment, which abolished slavery, was ratified in 1865. The 15th Amendment was ratified in 1870. It states that U.S. citizens' right to vote "shall not be denied or abridged . . . on account of race, color, or previous condition of servitude." The 16th Amendment was ratified in 1913. It granted the federal government the right to collect taxes based on personal income. (U.S. society)

25. D. Post–Civil War Reconstruction (of the South) was instituted in response to southern states passing and enforcing laws that effectively denied African Americans the right to vote. Up until the years of Post–Civil War Reconstruction (1868–1876), all the major American political parties had adhered to the guiding principles of laissez-faire capitalism — that is, the less government interference in social, political, and economic processes, the better for all concerned. In this view, government should not be in the business of intervening in the process of wealth and opportunity distribution. Its function was merely to ensure that everyone had an opportunity to compete for wealth and opportunity. Thus, Reconstruction was a radical departure from the guiding principles of laissez-faire capitalism, as well as those of the governing Republican Party itself. In an effort to protect the citizenship rights of the former slaves — of which the right to vote is only one — Federal troops were sent to the South, and the region was indeed placed under martial law. (U.S. society)

26. C. Although coffee can be grown in lowland tropical climates, the best grades of Arabica are grown on tropical mountains which enjoy cool, frost-free nights, and warm days. (World history and geography)

27. C. Louis Napoleon was captured by the Germans at the battle of Sedan in the Franco Prussian War. This led to the collapse of the Second Empire and the eventual formation of the Third Republic. (World history and geography)

28. C. Japan won control of Korea from China in 1895 and continued to exploit Korea as a colonial possession until the end of World War II. (World history and geography)

29. D. All the answers are correct, because economists generally oppose price controls as being counter-productive to the stated desire of making products more affordable and available. For example, rent controls on apartments have created situations where either landlords stopped renting apartments due to the lack of financial return (and, thus, the supply of apartments decreased significantly) or suppliers found ways to circumvent the controls and maintain or even increase apartment rents. (Economics)

30. D. Many economists argue that when an economy is closed off to international market forces, many local producers become rent seekers — seeking favorable public policies to bring about the uncompensated transfer of goods or services from another person or persons to themselves. In many cases, these are individuals with a particular license to import or manufacture a particular good that is then sold to the public at many times its market rate. (Economics)

31. B. The average is found by adding up all the scores and dividing by the total number of scores. The average this week is $\frac{112 + 156 + 179 + 165}{4} = \frac{612}{4} = 153$. The amount of improvement is $153 - 140 = 13$. (Mathematics and statistics)

32. D. To begin, quickly note that the answer must be either C or D, because there is an increase between the other pairs of years. Be careful not to jump and pick answer C, however, because the amount of the decrease is bigger. On a percent basis, there is a larger decrease from Year 4 to Year 5.

Percent of decrease Year 3 to Year 4: $\dfrac{\text{decrease}}{\text{original value}} = \dfrac{\$400}{\$600} = 66\dfrac{2}{3}\%$

Percent of decrease Year 4 to Year 5: $\dfrac{\text{decrease}}{\text{original value}} = \dfrac{\$150}{\$200} = 75\%$ (Mathematics and statistics)

33. B. Sales in Year 3 were $600 million out of a total of $50 + $500 + $600 + $200 + $50 = $1,400. Therefore, $600 ÷ $1,400 = 42.9% ≈ 43%. (Mathematics and statistics)

34. B. Changing Dean's score will certainly change the mean. Also, because Dean scored the fewest points, the range will change. The error, however, will not affect the median (the number in the middle) or the mode (the most frequently occurring number). (Mathematics and statistics)

35. C. Answers A and B are similar except that answer B involves another individual. Both have unlimited liability but greater flexibility and less government regulations. Answer C is the correct answer, because it combines both limited liability, as in a corporation, and yet is taxed like a partnership. (Management)

36. C. Answer A is standardization, B is modular design, and C is the best answer. Products are unique and in today's world, customers are very heterogeneous and want to be recognized as individuals. As such, making products to suit individual needs is very important. (Management)

37. D. The encoder is the person designing and sending the message. (Communication)

38. D. Answer A describes selective exposure. Answer B describes selective attention. Answer C describes selective retention. (Communication)

39. D. The First Amendment provides protection for all of these choices. (Communication)

40. C. A bit is the most basic element of computer data. Some examples are 0(off) and 1(on). Answer A is the description of a megabyte. Answer B is the description of a byte. Answer D is the description of a terabyte. (Computers)

41. D. The definition of maximize is to expand the program window until it covers the entire desktop. Answer A is the definition of the minimize button. Answer B is the definition of the close button. Answer C is the definition of the restore button. (Computers)

42. C. Social Security has several trust funds (for example, Old Age Retirement, Disability, Hospital Insurance). The payroll tax is deposited into these funds. All surpluses in these funds must be invested in U.S. government bonds. Each of the trust funds is projected to be in trouble in different years. (U.S. government)

43. B. *Amicus Curiae* briefs are friend-of-the-court briefs. They are written by groups who want to have input; they are not a party to the case, but they have an interest in the outcome. Parts of a decision that don't act as precedent are called *obiter dicta*. (U.S. government)

44. B. Congress's oversight function is to exercise a watchful eye over the executive and judicial branches of government. It is most closely associated with committees, as indicated in the 1946 Reorganization Act. (U.S. government)

45. A. The Progressive Era lasted from approximately the late 1880s to the beginning of World War I. Congress passed the Sherman Anti-Trust Act in 1890. This act made unlawful the formation of trusts, monopolies, and other activities that restrained interstate or foreign trade. Congress passed the Taft-Hartley Act in 1947, which reduced the power of labor unions by, for example, outlawing strikes by government employees and making closed shops illegal. The Hawley-Smoot Act (1930), passed to protect American producers, raised tariffs on products produced in other countries to an all-time high. The Emergency Banking Act, passed in 1935, during the middle of the Great Depression, provided temporary insurance for bank depositors. (U.S. society)

46. B. During the early years of American movie production, most movie-goers were working-class immigrants from or with ancestral ties to countries in Eastern or southern Europe. One reason for the popularity of movies among these immigrants was that movies were cheap. Another reason was that they were silent, which meant moviegoers did not need to know English to enjoy them. Edison was the first American to patent and market a commercial motion-picture camera. In its 1915 *Mutual Film Corporation v. Ohio* decision, the Supreme Court removed movie contents from protection by the 1st Amendment, ruling that movies were a business, not a form of communication, and thus not protected by the 1st Amendment. The first talking movie — *The Jazz Singer,* starring Al Jolson — was released in 1927. (U.S. society)

47. A. The Wagner Act (1935) gave workers the right to join unions and engage in collective bargaining. The Walsh-Healy Act (1936) mandated a minimum wage for workers at companies holding government contracts, as well as an eight-hour day and forty-hour work-week. It also forbade the use of child and convict labor. The Fair Standards Act (1938) mandated a minimum wage, defined a forty-hour week, and forbade the use of child labor by any business engaged in interstate commerce. The Taft-Hartley Act made closed shops and strikes by government employees illegal. (U.S. society)

48. B. Istanbul's location on the Bosphorus Strait has historically given the city control over the only access between the Mediterranean and Black seas, and thus of Russia's access to the Mediterranean. (World history and geography)

49. C. Northern Ireland is an integral part of the United Kingdom. (World history and geography)

50. D. The principles of shock therapy were first applied to Bolivia in 1985, where they were used to successfully combat hyperinflation, open the country to economic trade, and change the governmental role from controlling to regulating the economy. (Economics)

51. B. Economists usually view ticket scalping as a legitimate economic enterprise, because the parties involved are voluntarily exchanging articles of like value. (Economics)

52. B. OPEC is a cartel because its members collude overtly with one another to set prices. (Economics)

53. A. The average must be computed using the weighted average formula. $\frac{4 \times 35 + 2 \times 47 + 52 + 56 + 450}{9} = \frac{792}{9} = 88$, or $88,000. (Mathematics and statistics)

54. B. If the salaries are arranged in numerical order, the salary amount in the middle will be $47,000. (Mathematics and statistics)

55. A. The modal salary is the salary that occurs the most frequently, which is $35,000. (Mathematics and statistics)

56. D. The FTC most influences business activities related to questionable practices that create disputes between businesses and their customers. When it receives a complaint, the FTC issues a complaint stating that the business is in violation. (Management)

57. B. For organizations funded by a church, such as Jesuit universities, only employees consistent with the faith will be associated with the organization. This is because that is a fundamental pillar for the effective operation of the organization. (Management)

58. D. Answer A is the definition for a market, answer B is a marketing strategy, and answer C is the definition of marketing. D, the correct answer, involves the firm. The firm needs to recognize the needs of the consumers and try to achieve its goals through internal coordinated activities. (Management)

59. D. Answer D is what yellow journalism has come to mean. Other choices are bogus and do not relate to the question of yellow journalism per se. (Communication)

60. C. Answer A, sale of adult magazines, does not carry this label. Neither magazines controlled by readers/subscribers nor those limited to specific areas of the country are known as controlled-circulation magazines. (Communication)

61. A. Computer monitors and television sets both use the same CRT (cathode-ray tube) technology. However, computer monitors are built with much better shielding to reduce radiation. IT refers to the entire computer technology industry. MRI is a medical technology. CTR is a made-up answer. (Computers)

62. B. The resolution of a printer is measured in DPI (dots per inch). A dot matrix printer usually has anywhere from 60 to 90 DPI. An inkjet printer, with a DPI of 300 or more, produces far better picture quality. (Computers)

63. C. To print a certain page range, the user must select the from _____ to _____ button from the print menu. Answer A is the way to set up margins, paper, and layout. Answer B displays the file the user will print in order to see if it looks correct. (Computers)

64. D. The Necessary and Proper Clause is also known as the elastic clause. It expanded federal power by liberally interpreting the powers in Article I. The power to regulate interstate commerce was a major power that was used to expand federal powers. (U.S. government)

65. B. A restricted rule allows certain amendments to a bill. For example, it may permit only an amendment that represents the primary alternative to the bill on the floor. A closed rule does not permit any amendments, while an open rule allows any amendments. (U.S. government)

66. C. For many years, U.S. trade balance has been imbalanced. The United States buys more from other countries than they buy from the U.S. This imbalance has increased in recent years. (U.S. government)

67. C. Negotiation of treaties and international agreements is the responsibility of the Executive branch. The U.S. Department of State provides the Foreign Service with detailed instructions for the negotiation and conclusion of treaties and international agreements. The Secretary of State authorizes negotiation. After U.S. representatives negotiate and terms have been agreed upon by the Secretary of State, the treaty is signed and the president submits the treaty to the Senate. The Senate Foreign Relations Committee considers the treaty and reports to the Senate, which must approve the treaty by a two-thirds majority. Finally, the president proclaims the treaty's entry into force. (U.S. government)

68. D. The 19th Amendment (ratified in 1920) gave women the right to vote. The 16th Amendment (1913) gave Congress the authority to levy a federal income tax on wages and other earnings. The 17th Amendment (1913) mandated the direct election of U.S. senators. The 18th Amendment enacted Prohibition, making illegal the sale and manufacture of alcohol within U.S. territorial borders. (U.S. society)

69. C. The Marshall Plan resulted in $13,000,000,000 being made available to Western European countries, and was thereby instrumental in bringing about the relatively rapid Post–World War II Western European economic recovery. Because much of the $13 billion was given in the form of U.S. goods and services, the Marshall Plan also contributed to Post–World War II American economic prosperity. It derived its name from U.S. Secretary of State and former U.S. Army General George Marshall who, during a 1947 speech at Harvard University, proposed that the United States take it upon itself to spearhead a European economic recovery program. The program did not, however, issue guidelines for the integration of racially segregated schools in the south. (U.S. society)

70. B. Aaron Burr (vice-president under Thomas Jefferson) was the only vice-president tried for treason, but he was later acquitted. John C. Calhoun was vice-president under both John Quincy Adams and Andrew Jackson. John C. Breckinridge was vice-president under James Buchanan. Garret A. Hobart was vice-president during President William McKinley's first term. (U.S. society)

71. A. Within the foreign-born population, 53 percent were born in Latin America, 25 percent in Asia, 14 percent in Europe, and the remaining 8 percent in other regions of the world, such as Africa and Oceania (Australia, New Zealand, and all of the island nations in the Pacific). (U.S. society)

72. B. The Yucatan Peninsula of Mexico is predominantly Mayan. (World history and geography)

73. A. Sinn Fein ("We Ourselves") seeks to unite Northern Ireland with the Republic of Ireland, thus ending British rule on the island. (World history and geography)

74. C. Nobel Peace Prize winner Aung San Suu Kyi, whose opposition party won the 1990 election, was repeatedly jailed for her outspoken defense of human rights and calls for democracy. (World history and geography)

75. A. In years past, the State Department was responsible for negotiating all trade agreements. But in 1962, Congress created the Office of the United States Trade Representative to separate the commercial interests of trade from U.S. foreign policy goals. The State Department, the Department of Commerce, and many other agencies still retain roles in trade policy and promotion (Economics)

76. A. When the dollar declines markedly against other currencies, investors tend to gravitate toward gold as a reliable store of value. (Economics)

77. C. In order for Joe to complete his purchase of the Mini Cooper, he will have to purchase British pounds at the rate of $3 to £1. If he is purchasing the Mini Cooper for £3,000, he must then convert 3 × £3,000 =$9,000. He must sell $9,000 to obtain £3,000. (Economics)

78. D. At the end of the first day, $1 - \frac{1}{8} = \frac{7}{8}$ of the magazines remain. $\frac{7}{8} \times \frac{1}{4} = \frac{7}{32}$ sold the next day. So at the end of the second day, $\frac{7}{8} - \frac{7}{32} = \frac{28}{32} - \frac{7}{32} = \frac{21}{32}$ of the magazines remain. (Mathematics and statistics)

79. B. The discounted amount after the first week is $1,000 \times 25\% = \$250$, so the sale price is $1,000 - \$250 = \$750$. The discounted amount after the second week is $750 \times 10\% = \$75$, so the sale price is $750 - \$75 = \$675$. (Mathematics and statistics)

80. B. $\left(\sqrt{2}\right)^4 = \sqrt{2} \cdot \sqrt{2} \cdot \sqrt{2} \cdot \sqrt{2} = \sqrt{16} = 4$ (Mathematics and statistics)

81. C. Relationship marketing is the process of building intimate customer interactions to maximize customer satisfaction. The goal of relationship marketing is to satisfy customers so well that they become loyal and committed to sharing information, and they rely on the company. Thus to build this type of long-term customer relationship, businesses are turning increasingly to information technology, such as customer relationship management (CRM) software. (Management)

82. A. This is called a pull strategy. A push strategy is when manufacturers have to motivate the intermediaries to push the product down to their customers. For example, Mercedes uses a pull strategy. A car is built only when the order is placed. (Management)

83. B. B is the one that is not valid. Asset utilization ratios are ratios that measure how well a firm uses its assets to generate each $1 of sales. Liquidity ratios measure the speed with which a company can turn its assets into cash to meet short-term debt. Debt utilization ratios measure how much debt an organization is using relative to other sources of capital, such as owners' equity. (Management)

84. C. Answers A, B, and D are the responsibilities of the FRB. They also manage regional and national checking account procedures, or check clearing. (Management)

85. B. AM radio is marked with static and has neither high fidelity nor viable stereo capabilities. Short-wave radio is neither static free nor capable of good sound quality. Citizens band radio also has static and not susceptible to quality sound. (Communication)

86. D. NPR, National Public Radio, is the only choice that is non-commercial. CBS, CNN, and ESPN are all commercial networks. (Communication)

87. A. Answers B, C, and D are all made-up choices that do not apply to the question. (Communication)

88. A. A mainframe is a large computer that is designed for handling large amounts of data that are needed within large organizations. (Computers)

89. C. A network requires two or more computers in order to share resources. Answer D is a computer program that provides services to other computer programs (and their users) in the same or other computers. (Computers)

90. D. URL is the abbreviation for Universal Resource Locator, the global address of documents and other resources on the World Wide Web. (Computers)

PART II

WRITTEN EXAM: THE ENGLISH EXPRESSION TEST

About the English Expression Test

What You Should Know

The second part of the FSE is the English Expression test, which covers grammar and usage. Actually it covers not only grammar but also spelling, organization, punctuation, and editing. This portion of the exam takes 70 minutes and consists of 90 questions. You are presented with several long and short passages that may exhibit incorrect grammar, contain spelling errors, or require reorganization of the sentences. You may also be asked to select a sentence that might enhance the paragraph. Some of the questions refer to the passage as a whole, and some about a small section of the passage.

Before taking the full-length sample test at the end of Part III, be sure to read the directions carefully, and then read each passage through before you answer the questions. This gives you an overview of the subject matter, as well as the approach of the passage, including the errors that you may spot. The items are underlined in the paragraph and correspond to the question numbers. Remember that whatever changes you make must make sense in the context of the paragraph.

Before taking these tests, peruse the grammar and usage review in the following chapter. Read through the material and make sure you understand the examples given through the chapter. Depending upon the amount of time you have prior to taking the exam, it would be helpful to spend at least one day per section.

Grammar and Usage Review

Nouns

A noun is a part of speech that names a person, place, or thing. Many different kinds of nouns are used in the English language. Some are specific for people, places, or events, and some represent groups or collections. Some words used as nouns aren't even nouns; they're verbs acting like nouns in sentences.

Nouns can be singular, referring to one thing, or plural, referring to more than one thing. Nouns can be possessive as well; possessive nouns indicate ownership or a close relationship. Regardless of the type, nouns should always agree with their verbs in sentences; use singular verbs with singular nouns and plural verbs with plural nouns. You have to know how a noun works in order to write an effective sentence.

Proper Nouns

If a noun names a specific person or place, or a particular event or group, it is called a **proper noun** and is always capitalized. Some examples are *Eleanor Roosevelt, Niagara Falls, Dracula, the Federal Bureau* of *Investigation, the Great Depression,* and *Desert Storm.* This seems simple enough.

Unfortunately, some writers assign proper-noun status fairly indiscriminately to other words, sprinkling capital letters freely throughout their prose. For example, the *Manhattan Project is* appropriately capitalized because it is a historic project, the name given to the specific wartime effort to design and build the first nuclear weapons. But *project* should not be capitalized when referring to a club's project to clean up the campus. Similarly, the *Great Depression* should be capitalized because it refers to the specific historical period of economic failure that began with the stock market collapse in 1929. When the word *depression* refers to other economic hard times, however, it is not a proper noun but a common noun and should not be capitalized. Some flexibility in capitalizing nouns is acceptable. A writer may have a valid reason for capitalizing a particular term, for example, and some companies use style guides that dictate capital letters for job titles such as manager. But often the use of a capital outside the basic rule is an effort to give a word an air of importance, and you should avoid it.

Verbs Used as Nouns

One special case is when a verb is used as a noun. Here the verb form is altered and it serves the same function as a noun in the sentence. This type of noun is called a **gerund.**

A noun created from the *-ing* form of a verb is called a gerund. Like other nouns, gerunds act as subjects and objects in sentences.

> *Sleeping* sometimes serves as an escape from *studying.*

The gerunds *sleeping* and *studying* are *-ing* forms of the verbs *sleep* and *study. Sleeping* is the noun functioning as the subject of this sentence, and *studying* is an object (in this case, the object of a preposition).

When a noun or pronoun precedes a gerund, use the possessive case of the noun or pronoun.

> *Kelly's sleeping* was sometimes an escape from studying.

Even when you think that the word before the gerund looks like an object, use the possessive case.

> Kelly was annoyed by Bill's questioning
> NOT Kelly was annoyed by Bill *questioning.*

Collective Nouns

A word that stands for a group of things is **called a collective noun.** In fact, the word group itself is a collective noun. Here are a few others: *club, team, committee, furniture, jury, Congress, swarm, herd.*

Usually these nouns are treated as singular, because the emphasis is on a unit rather than its parts.

- The *team is* going on the bus.
- The *committee wants* to find a solution to the problem.
- But when you want to emphasize the individual parts of a group, you may treat a collective noun as plural.
- The *team have* argued about going on the bus.
- The *committee want* different solutions to the problem. If the plural sounds awkward, try rewriting.
- The *team members have* argued about going on the bus.
- *Committee members disagree* about solutions to the problem.

Singular and Plural Nouns

The term **number** refers to whether a noun is singular or plural. Most nouns can be either, depending on whether you are talking about one thing (door), or more than one (dogs). You know the basic rule of adding -s to make the plural of a noun, and you also know that many nouns don't follow that rule — for example, *sheep* (singular), *sheep* (plural); *enemy, enemies; wharf, wharves; hero, heroes; goose, geese,* and so on. You should check your dictionary if you're not sure about a plural. Do not add 's to a singular form to make it plural, even if the noun you are using is a family name: *the Taylors,* not *the Taylor's; donkeys,* not *donkey's; taxis,* not *taxi's.*

The singular and plural forms of some nouns with Latin and Greek endings can cause trouble. The noun *data,* for example, is actually a plural; *datum is* the singular.

> The final *datum is* not consistent with the preceding *data,* which *are* positive.

Although today the plural *data is* widely treated as singular, keep the distinction, particularly in scientific writing.

Here are some other examples of Latin and Greek singular and plural words: *bacterium, bacteria, criterion, criteria, medium, media; alumnus* (masculine singular)/*alumni* (masculine plural), *alumna* (feminine singular)/*alumnae* (feminine plural). If you are writing about one of the *media,* for example, television, use *medium.* The *medium* of television has transformed the functioning of conscious. If you are writing about radio, television, and the press, use *media.* The *media* play a powerful role in influencing purchases.

Possessive Case of Nouns

The **possessive case** of a noun is used to show ownership (Allan's car, my sister's house) or another close relationship (Ingman's friends, the cup's handle, the university's position).

What causes problems with possessive nouns is uncertainty: Do I add an 's or just an apostrophe? Follow this rule: for singular nouns, add 's, even if the noun ends in an -s or -z sound: dog's, house's, Wes's, Keats's. But make an exception when an added -s would lead to three closely bunched s or z sounds (Jesus; Ulysses) or in names of more than one syllable with an unaccented ending pronounced -eez (Empedocles; Socrates; Euripides). Greek names often fall into this category.

For most plural possessive nouns, add an apostrophe alone: *several months' bills, many Rumanians' apartments, the encyclopedias' differences, the Beastie Boys' travel plans.* If a plural noun doesn't end in -s, add -'s, just as you would with a singular noun: *women's issues, mice's tails.*

When a possessive noun sounds awkward, use an of construction instead.

This is a safe and often preferable way to indicate the relationship: *the top of the page* instead of *the page's top; the lawn of the building on the corner* instead of *the building on the corner's lawn, the main characters* of *Pride and Prejudice* instead of *Pride and Prejudice's main characters; the novels* of Dickens instead of *Dickens's novels.*

One last word about possessive nouns: When you are indicating joint ownership, give the possessive form to the final name only, such as *Abbott and Costello's movies; Tom and Dawn's dinner party; Smith, Wilson, and Nelson's* partnership.

Agreement of Nouns and Verbs

Agreement is an important concept in grammar and a source of many writing errors. Verbs must agree with their nouns, which means that a singular noun requires a singular verb, and a plural noun requires a plural verb.

> The dog jumps up and down. (singular)
>
> The dogs jump up and down. (plural)

Remember that a noun ending in -s is often a plural, whereas a verb ending in -s is usually singular: calls on my cell phone (plural noun); he calls (singular verb).

Nouns with Latin or Greek endings and nouns that look plural but sometimes take singular verbs can cause agreement problems.

The **data indicate** that the test samples are more affected by heat than the control group samples. Because data is the plural form of datum, use the plural form of the verb (in this case, indicate). In the following example, criteria is plural. Use the plural form of the verb *(are).*

> The criteria for judging an entry are listed in the brochure.
>
> Rights, which is a plural form, is treated as singular in the following example because human rights is a unit, an issue of concern.
>
> Human rights is an issue that affects everyone.
>
> If you wanted to emphasize the rights individually, you could use the plural verb:
>
> Human rights are ignored in many countries.

In the next example, miles is the plural form, but if fifty miles is used here to name a unit of distance and therefore takes a singular verb:

> Fifty miles is not such a long distance.

Statistics looks plural, and in many situations would be treated as plural: for example, Statistics are being gathered to determine the effect of the new tax plan. But in the next example, statistics refers to a subject of study, so the singular is appropriate. Statistics is the subject I most want to avoid.

Among other frequently used nouns that can take either a singular or plural verb, depending on whether the emphasis is on a single unit or individual items, are *number, majority,* and *minority.*

> The *number* of people coming is surprising. A *number* of people *are* coming. A *number* like five thousand is what he had in mind.

With *number,* use this rule. If it is preceded by *the,* always use the singular. If it is preceded by *a,* use the singular or plural, depending on whether you are thinking of a single unit or individual items.

With *majority* and *minority,* the key is to decide whether you want to emphasize individual people or things or whether you want to emphasize the single unit.

> The *majority is* opposed to the measure (singular = single unit).
>
> A *minority* of the younger people *refuse* to concede the point (plural = individuals).

Verbs

A verb is a part of speech that expresses action or state of being or connects a subject to a complement. Verbs indicate whether the subject performs an action, called active voice, or receives the action, called passive voice. Verbs can be transitive or intransitive. Verb tenses are formed according to person, number, and tense.

Verbs also have moods, which are classifications that indicate the attitude of the speaker. Problems with verbs are often the result of an incorrect tense, or the difficulty many writers have with the past and past participle forms of irregular verbs. Verbs play a key role in constructing sentences.

Action Verbs

An **action verb** animates a sentence, either physically *(swim, jump, drop, whistle)* or mentally *(think, dream, believe, suppose, love)*. Verbs make sentences move, sometimes dramatically, sometimes quietly:

> The gymnast *leaped* high into the air, *twirled*, *landed* on the floor, and *ran* from the room.

> The poet *thought* of beauty, *imagined* a smile, *dreamed* of a flower.

Linking Verbs

Some verbs don't express action but help complete statements about the subject by describing or identifying it. These verbs are called **linking verbs.**

> Diane is happy. Clement feels hot. Maria is a doctor. The music sounds good.

The sentences don't tell you what Diane, Clement, Maria, and the music did but rather what they are. Linking chair verbs "link" their subjects to a classification, state of being, or quality. In the sentences above, **happy hot, doctor,** and good are called **complements** of the linking chair verbs. Here are some common linking verbs:

- appear
- grow
- smell
- be
- look
- sound
- become
- remain
- taste
- feel
- seem

Some of these verbs can be both linking and action verbs.

> Clement *felt* hot (linking verb).
> Clement *felt* along the wall for the light switch (action verb).
> The dog *smelled* bad (linking verb).
> The dog *smelled* the man's boots (action verb).

A quick way to tell whether a verb is functioning as a linking verb is to see whether you can replace it with a form of the verb *to be* and still have a reasonable sentence. For example, test the two sentences above by replacing *smelled* with *was*.

> The dog was bad.
> NOT The dog was the man's boots.

Active and Passive Voice

The term **voice** refers to the form of a verb indicating whether the subject performs an action (**active voice**) or receives the action (**passive voice).**

> Mary *smashed* the ball over the net (active voice).
>
> The ball was *smashed* over the net by Mary (passive voice).

Use the active voice whenever you can; it conveys more energy and emphasis than the passive voice and also results in more concise writing.

Use of the passive voice diminishes the importance of the actor and conveys a sense of diminished responsibility or hedging. Use the passive voice, however, when you want to minimize the role of the actor, or when you want to emphasize the person or thing acted upon rather than the actor. The passive voice is often appropriate in scientific writing because it emphasizes the experiment rather than the researcher.

When we returned, the *car had been towed.* I regret that a *mistake was made. Gold was discovered* there early in the last century. The accident victim *was rushed* to the hospital by the police. *A change* in structure *was found* in the experimental group.

Transitive and Intransitive Verbs

A transitive verb, used with a direct object, transmits action to an object and may also have an indirect object, which indicates to or for whom the action is done. In contrast, an intransitive verb never takes an object. A **transitive verb** takes a **direct object;** that is, the verb transmits action to an object.

> He *sent* the *letter* (*letter* = direct object of *sent).*
>
> She *gave* the *lecture* (*lecture* = direct object of *gave).*

In these sentences, something is being done to an object.

A transitive verb can also have an **indirect object** that precedes the direct object. The indirect object tells to or for whom the action is done, although the words *to* and *for* are not used. In the following examples, notice the difference between the direct and indirect objects.

The direct object *(letter)* receives the action *(sent).* The indirect object *(Robert) is* the person to whom the letter is sent.

> He sent Robert the letter.

The direct object *(lecture)* receives the action *(gave).* The indirect object *(class) is* the group to whom the lecture is given.

> She *gave* her *class* the lecture.

Learn to recognize words that are direct and indirect objects of verbs. When these words are pronouns, they must be in the objective case.

An **intransitive** verb does not take an object. She *sleeps* too much.

> He *complains* frequently.

In these sentences, nothing receives the action of the verbs *sleep* and *complain.*

Many verbs can be either transitive or intransitive.

> She *sings* every day (no object = intransitive).
>
> She *sings arias* (*arias* receives the action of *sings* = transitive).

Verbals: Gerunds, Infinitives, and Participles

In one sense, the three **verbals: gerunds, infinitives, and participles** should not be covered in this section on verbs. Although formed from verbs, verbals are never used alone as the action words in sentences; instead, they function as nouns, adjectives, or adverbs. The gerund ends in -*ing* and functions as a noun.

> Jump*ing* is fun. He liked ski*ing*.

The infinitive is the base form of a verb with *to*. Usually it also functions as a noun, although it can be an adjective or adverb.

> *To jump* is fun (noun; subject of *is*).
>
> I like *to ski* (noun; object of *like*).
>
> She had a suggestion *to offer* (adjective modifying *suggestion*).
>
> He called *to warn* her (adverb modifying *called*).

A participle is a verb that ends in -*ing* (present participle) or -*ed, -d, -t, -en, -n* (past participle). Participles may function as adjectives, describing or modifying nouns.

> The *dancing* bear entertained the crowd. The *beaten* man hobbled into the woods.

But participles have another function. Used with helping verbs such as *to be* and *to have,* they form several verb **tenses.**

> She is *thinking* about the election.
>
> The boat *had been cleaned* before they arrived.

Forming Verb Tenses

To write correctly, you need to know both how to form verb tenses and when to use them. Verb tenses are formed according to person, number, and tense. They are the key to coherent sentence structure.

Person refers to the subject or object of the verb. Number identifies whether a verb is singular or plural. A few terms will help you to understand how verb tenses are formed.

Tense: refers to time; when is the action (or state of being) of the verb taking place?

Person: refers to the person (or thing) that is a subject or object.

- **First person:** *I, we* go; she spoke to *me, us*
- **Second person:** *you, you* (all) go; she spoke to *you, you* (all)
- **Third person:** *he, she, it* goes, *they* go; she spoke to *him, her,* it, *them*

Number: simply refers to whether a verb is singular *(he goes)* or plural *(they go)*. In the sentence "The horse runs in the pasture," "runs" is the third-person singular of the present tense of the verb "run."

Although there are more, six tenses are commonly used in English.

- **Present:** action going on now
- **Past:** action that is over
- **Future:** action that has yet to take place
- **Present perfect:** action in past time in relation to present time
- **Past perfect:** action in past time in relation to another past time
- **Future perfect:** action in a future time in relation to another time farther in the future

Definitions of the perfect tenses are difficult to understand without examples. The following tables show the regular verb *to walk* and the irregular verb *to be* in the six tenses. Regular verbs, like *to walk,* form the past tense and the perfect tenses by adding *-d* or *-ed* to the present tense. But like *to be,* many English verbs are irregular, forming their past tenses in various ways. A list of frequently used irregular verbs is provided in the "Irregular Verbs" section.

Present Tense		
	Singular	*Plural*
First person	I walk	we walk
	I am	we are
Second person	you walk	you walk
	you are	you are
Third person	he, she, it walks	they walk
	he, she, it is	they are

Past Tense		
	Singular	*Plural*
First person	I walked	we walked
	I was	we were
Second person	you walked	you walked
	you were	you were
Third person	he, she, it walked	they walked
	he, she, it was	they were

Future Tense		
	Singular	*Plural*
First person	I will walk	we will walk
	I will be	we will be
Second person	you will walk	you will walk
	you will be	you will be
Third person	he, she, it will walk	they will walk
	he, she, it will be	they will be

Note that in the future tense, traditionally *shall* has been used for will in the first-person singular and plural: I *shall* walk, we *shall* walk. In modern usage, however, *will* has replaced *shall* almost entirely. Although either is correct, *shall* produces an unusually formal effect.

Present Perfect Tense		
	Singular	*Plural*
First person	I have walked	we have walked
	I have been	we have been
Second person	you have walked	you have walked
	you have been	you have been
Third person	he, she, it has walked	they have walked
	he, she, it has been	they have been

Past Perfect Tense		
	Singular	*Plural*
First person	I had walked	we had walked
	I had been	we had been
Second person	you had walked	you had walked
	you had been	you had been
Third person	he, she, it had walked	they had walked
	he, she, it had been	they had been

Future Perfect Tense		
	Singular	*Plural*
First person	I will have walked	we will have walked
	I will have been	we will have been
Second person	you will have walked	you will have walked
	you will have been	you will have been
Third person	he, she, it will have walked	they will have walked
	he, she, it will have been	they will have been

Tense indicates when the action or state of being occurs, and knowing how to use it helps convey your meaning. Forming tenses can be simple or complicated.

Present, Past, and Future

The present, past, and future tenses are part of our everyday language and as writers we are able to use these forms with ease. The present tense indicates action occurring now.

He *beeps* her pager.

Sometimes, the present tense can also be used to indicate future action.

> Her plane *arrives* on Friday.

The past tense indicates action completed in the past.

> He *beeped* her pager.

The future tense is used for action that will occur at a future time.

> He *will beep* her pager.

Present Perfect

The present perfect tense, formed with *has* or *have* and the past participle of the verb, indicates action that occurred in the past and has continued into the present.

> *I have called you* for a year. (And I am still calling you.)

This contrasts with the simple past tense, which suggests an action that both began and ended in the past.

> *I called you* for a year. (But I am no longer calling you.)

The present perfect tense can also be used when you want to emphasize an action that occurred in the past but at no definite time.

> I *have called* many times.

Past Perfect

The past perfect tense, formed with *had* and the past participle of the verb, indicates an action completed in the past *before* another action completed in the past.

> After I *had called you* ten times, I asked the operator to check your number.

Had called is a past action that was completed *before* asking the operator, another completed past action.

In the following example, his being careless for a year *preceded* the accident: past before past.

> He *had been careless* for a year when the accident happened.

Future Perfect

The future perfect tense, formed with *will have* and the past participle of the verb, is used for action that will be completed in the future *before* another future action.

> By next week, I *will have called you* more than a hundred times.

Calling more than a hundred times will take place *before* next week. In the following example, her leaving town will *precede* the future arrival of Henri.

> She *will have left* town before Henri can contact her.

Moods of the Verb

Verb moods are classifications that indicate the attitude of the speaker. Verbs have three moods — the indicative, the imperative, and the subjunctive.

The Indicative and Imperative

The indicative and the imperative moods are easy to understand. You use the **indicative** mood in most statements and questions.

> He *walks* every day after lunch. Does he *believe* in the good effects of exercise?

You use the **imperative** in requests and commands. Imperative statements have an understood subject of you and therefore take second-person verbs.

> Sit down. ([You] sit down.) Please *take* a number. ([You] please take a number.)

The Subjunctive

The tenses of the **subjunctive** mood are formed differently from the indicative tenses, and the subjunctive is used in special kinds of statements. Today, the most common use of the subjunctive mood is in contrary-to-fact or hypothetical statements. In your own writing, you must decide which statements should be in the subjunctive. If something is likely to happen, use the indicative. If something is purely hypothetical, or contrary to fact, use the subjunctive.

Present tense subjunctive:

> If I *were* working, you would be my assistant. (In the subjunctive, *were* is used for all persons.)
> If he worked, he could earn high wages.

Past tense subjunctive:

> If I *had been* working, you would have been my assistant.
> If he *had* worked, he could have earned high wages.

These contrary-to-fact statements have two clauses: the if clause and the consequences clause. The forms of the verbs in these clauses are different from those of verbs used in the indicative mood. In the if clause, use the subjunctive. The following shows how it is formed:

- **Verb "to be," using "were" as an example:** if I were working, if you were working, if she were working.
- **Other verbs, using "worked" as an example:** if I worked, if you worked, if he worked.

Note that the subjunctive present tense is the same as the indicative past tense.

- **Verb "to be," using "had been" as an example:** if I had been working, if you had been working, if she had been working.
- **Other verbs, using "had worked" as an example:** if I had worked, if you had worked, if he had worked.

Note how the subjunctive past tense is the same as the indicative past perfect tense.

In the **consequences clause,** use the conditional, which is formed with could or would.

- **Present conditional:** could, would + base form of verb: You would be my aid; He could earn high wages.
- **Past conditional:** could, would + have + past participle of verb: You would have been my aid; He could have earned high wages.

Not all clauses beginning with if are contrary to fact. When an if clause indicates something that is likely to happen, use the indicative, not the subjunctive.

> If I concentrate, I will solve the problem. If his fever *continues* to fall, he will recover.

Problems with Verbs

Writers sometimes use an incorrect tense or don't know how to use the past participle forms of irregular verbs. Using verb tenses imprecisely or inconsistently can also irritate a reader.

Illogical Time Sequence

Recognize time sequences in your writing and choose verb tenses that logically reflect that sequence. Sometimes the choice of a tense clearly affects your meaning.

> Esther *worked* at the department store for a year.

Use the past tense to indicate a completed action. Esther no longer works at the department store.

> Esther *has worked* at the department store for a year.

Use the present perfect tense to indicate that a past action is continuing in the present. Esther still works at the department store.

> Esther *had worked* at the department store for a year.

Use the past perfect tense to indicate that something else happened after Esther's year. For example, Esther *had worked* at the department store for a year when she was asked to take over sporting goods.

When to Use the Perfect Tense

Learn to use the perfect tenses when they are appropriate to your meaning. Don't limit yourself to the simple past tense when writing about past action. In the following sentences, for example, a perfect tense should have been used to establish time sequence.

> The car wash *stood* where the library was. (no) All the things you *told* me I *heard* before. (no)

In the first sentence, because the library was in the location before the car wash; it would be difficult for them to occupy the same space at the same time. Past perfect should be used for the second verb.

> The car wash *stood* where the library *had been*.

The logic of the second sentence dictates that *heard* should be in the past perfect tense. The word *before* is an obvious clue that the hearing took place before the telling, even though both actions were completed in the past.

> All the things you *told* me, I *had heard* before.

Faulty "If" Clauses

The past perfect tense should also be used in a subjunctive past tense "if" clause.

> If she *had thought* of it, she would have called you.

A common error is to use the conditional would *have* or could *have* in both clauses. Would *have* and could *have* should be used only in the clause that states the consequences.

> If I *had wanted* to, I would *have* made cookies.
> NOT If I would *have wanted* to, I would *have* made cookies.

> If we *had brought* matches, we could *have* made a bonfire.
> NOT If we would *have brought* matches, we could *have* made a bonfire.

Inconsistency in Tenses: Tense Shifts

Another common error is illogically mixing tenses within a sentence or within an entire piece of writing. This error is called a verb tense shift. Choose the tense you want to use in your sentence or in your essay and then make certain that all verbs are consistent with it, either by being in the same tense or by reflecting past and future times in relation to your main tense.

> Robertson *went* into the market, *walks* over to the produce section, and picks through the tomatoes. (tense shifts)

In the preceding sentence there is no logical reason to move from the past tense *(went)* to the present tense *(walks, picks)*. Use the past tense or the present tense, not both: Rewrite the sentence using consistent tenses.

> Robertson *went* into the market, *walked* over to the produce section, and *picked* through the tomatoes. (consistent tenses)

Look at the tenses in this group of sentences.

> Unlike Richardson's, this program will *pay* its own way. It *specified* that anyone who *wanted* to use the service *has to pay* a fee. People who *refused* to do so *won't* receive the benefits. (tense shifts)

Notice that the changes in tense between sentences are not related to a clear time sequence. A rewritten version of this piece shows a more consistent, logical use of tenses.

> Unlike Richardson's, this program will *pay* its own way: It *specifies* that anyone who *wants* to use the service *has to pay* a fee. People who *refuse* to do so *won't* receive the benefits. (consistent tenses)

In this version, all verb tenses except the first (will pay) and last *(won't receive = will not receive)* are in the present tense. The future tense is appropriately used for the first and last verbs because these verbs indicate future consequences.

Irregular Verbs

Even when you understand the correct uses of tenses, you can run into trouble with verbs. The major culprit is the large group of irregular verbs, which form the past tense and past participle in a variety of ways (as in the following table), not by adding *-d* or *-ed* as regular verbs do.

Past and Present Tense of Irregular Verbs		
	Regular Verbs	*Irregular Verbs*
Present	talk, joke	say, bite
Past	talked, joked	said, bit
Past participle	have talked, have joked	have said, have bitten

Irregular verbs cause errors simply because people aren't sure about the correct past and past participle forms: Which is it? "I *drunk* the coffee" or "I *drank* the coffee"? The following table is a list of fifty commonly used irregular verbs with their past tenses and past participles. However, there are many others, so when you aren't sure about a verb, check the dictionary. The entry will include the verb's principal parts: present, past, and past participle.

Common Irregular Verbs		
Present Tense	*Past Tense*	*Past Participle*
be	was, were	(have) been
beat	beat	(have) beaten, beat

Present Tense	Past Tense	Past Participle
begin	began	(have) begun
blow	blew	(have) blown
break	broke	(have) broken
bring	brought	(have) brought
catch	caught	(have) caught
choose	chose	(have) chosen
come	came	(have) come
dig	dug	(have) dug
dive	dived, dove	(have) dived
do	did	(have) done
draw	drew	(have) drawn
dream	dreamed, dreamt	(have) dreamed, dreamt
drink	drank	(have) drunk
drive	drove	(have) driven
eat	ate	(have) eaten
fly	flew	(have) flown
forget	forgot	(have) forgotten
freeze	froze	(have) frozen
get	got	(have) gotten
go	went	(have) gone
grow	grew	(have) grown
hang (an object)	hung	(have) hung
hang (a person)	hanged	(have) hanged
lay	laid	(have) laid
lead	led	(have) led
lend	lent	(have) lent
lie (recline)	lay	(have) lain
light	lighted, lit	(have) lighted, lit
ride	rode	(have) ridden
ring	rang	(have) rung
run	ran	(have) run
see	saw	(have) seen

(continued)

Common Irregular Verbs *(continued)*		
Present Tense	*Past Tense*	*Past Participle*
set	set	(have) set
shake	shook	(have) shaken
shine (emit light)	shone	(have) shone
shine (make shiny)	shone, shined	(have) shone, shined
sing	sang	(have) sung
sink	sank, sunk	(have) sunk
slay	slew	(have) slain
speed	sped	(have) sped
spring	sprang, sprung	(have) sprung
steal	stole	(have) stolen
swear	swore	(have) sworn
swim	swam	(have) swum
take	took	(have) taken
tear	tore	(have) torn
wake	waked, woke	(have) waked, woke, woken
wear	wore	(have) worn

Pronouns

Case is the term describing which pronoun to use in a phrase, clause or sentence, and this can be subjective, objective, or possessive. Choosing between the subjective and objective case can be confusing — for example, the choice of who or whom. Pronouns always clearly refer to their antecedents, the noun they represent, and they also agree with their antecedents in number and gender. Using pronouns with confidence makes writing clearer and easier to read.

A pronoun allows flexibility in writing because it is a word that stands for a noun. Without pronouns, writing and speech would sound clumsy and repetitious. Compare the following two sentences. Obviously, the second sentence is much better.

Charlie left *Charlie's* house, taking *Charlie's* dog with *Charlie.*

Charlie left *his* house, taking *his* dog with *him.*

Dividing pronouns into groups based on what they do is helpful in showing how many purposes they serve.

Personal Pronouns

The **personal pronouns** (*I, me, he, she, it,* and so on) stand for one or more persons or things and differ in form depending on their case — that is, how they are used in a phrase, clause, or sentence. For example, when acting as a subject, the first-person singular pronoun is *I.* When acting as an object, *I* becomes *me.*

Reflexive (Intensive) Pronouns

The **reflexive,** or **intensive, pronouns** combine some of the personal pronouns with *-self* or *-selves (myself, himself, themselves,* and so on). Reflexive pronouns are used to reflect nouns or pronouns, as in *He hurt himself,* or to provide emphasis, as in I *myself don't believe it.* Don't use reflexive pronouns as subjects and objects, however.

The client and I met for lunch.

NOT The client and *myself* met for lunch.

The lunch meeting was between the client and me.

NOT The lunch meeting was between the client and *myself.*

Demonstrative Pronouns

The **demonstrative pronouns** *(this, that, these, those)* single out what you are talking about.

These are the ones we want, but *this is* the most economical choice.

When they stand alone in place of nouns, these words are pronouns. But when they precede nouns, they are adjectives: *this wagon, that dog, these words.*

Relative Pronouns

The **relative pronouns** *(who, whom, which, that)* introduce clauses that describe nouns or pronouns.

The professor *who wrote the textbook is* teaching the class.

The storm *that caused the blackout* has moved east.

The current trend is toward using the relative pronouns *that* and *which* interchangeably, although many teachers and editors prefer that a distinction be made. Use *that* when the clause that follows it is *restrictive,* that is, when it is necessary to define your subject. Use *which* when the clause that follows it is *nonrestrictive,* that is, when it adds information that isn't necessary to define your subject.

The company *that had government contracts* made a profit.

NOT The company *which had government* contracts made profit.

The relative clause *that had government contracts* restricts or limits the subject company. The information in the clause is necessary to the main statement.

The car, *which I bought a week ago,* gets good mileage.

NOT The car, *that I bought a week ago,* gets good mileage.

The clause *which I bought a week ago* adds information about the subject that isn't necessary to our understanding of the main statement that the car gets good mileage.

Use commas with a *which* clause but not with a *that* clause.

Interrogative Pronouns

The **interrogative pronouns** *(who, whom, whose, which, what)* introduce questions.

Which is the best one to choose? *Who* asked the question, "To *whom* does this belong?"

Indefinite Pronouns

Indefinite pronouns don't specify the persons or things they refer to. The most frequently used indefinite pronouns are all, any, anybody, anyone, both, each, either, everybody, everyone, few, many, neither, nobody, none, no one, one, several, some, somebody, someone. There are many others (for example, others here is an indefinite pronoun). Like other pronouns (here, other is an adjective), indefinite pronouns stand in for nouns, even if those nouns aren't specified.

> *Many* are called but few are chosen. *Nobody* likes a bully.

Pronoun Case

Case refers to the way a noun or pronoun is used in a sentence. When it is the subject of a verb, it is in the **subjective case** (the term nominative can also be used for subjective case though we will use subjective case only). When it is the object of a verb or a preposition, it is in the **objective case.**

When a pronoun shows possession of something, it is in the possessive case. With nouns, the subjective and objective cases aren't a problem because nouns have the same form whether they are subjects or objects. The *frog* ate the *bee.* The *bee* stung the *frog.* Regardless of what's happening to the frog or the bee, the nouns *frog* and *bee* don't change form. Some pronouns, however, take different forms depending on whether they are subjects or objects. These pronouns are listed in the following table.

Subjective and Objective Pronouns	
Subjective Case	*Objective Case*
I	me
he	him
she	her
we	us
they	them
who, whoever	whom, whomever

In the sentence *Tension existed between Franklin and Winston,* there is no confusion about what case to use for *Franklin* or *Winston.* But what about in this sentence?

> Tension existed between Franklin and *him.*

Is *him* right? Or should it be *he?* (The pronoun is the object of the preposition *between,* so *him* is correct.)

Subjective Case of Pronouns

Pronouns are used as subjects of verbs. Use the subjective case of pronouns when the pronoun is the subject of a verb.

> I drive to work.
>
> She enjoys math class.
>
> We bought the lodge.
>
> They are fighting over the property line.
>
> The person who won the game was the guest of honor.

When there are **compound subjects,** that is, more than one actor, don't be confused. Pronouns should still be in the subjective case.

> Eileen and he (NOT Eileen and him) enjoy dancing.
>
> The Harrisons and they (NOT The Harrisons and them) are fighting over the property line.

To keep from making pronoun case errors in sentences with compound subjects, drop the subject that is a noun and read the sentence with the pronoun alone. You would never say Him enjoy dancing or Them are fighting over the property line. You'll see immediately that the subjective forms he and they are correct.

You should also use the subjective case of pronouns after forms of the verb to be.

> It is I who chose the location. The person who called the police was he. The real criminals are we ourselves. The winners were they and the Rudermans. The man who phoned was who?

The word after a form of to be is called a **complement.** (It is also sometimes called a predicate nominative or predicate adjective).

Unlike words following action verbs, a complement of a linking verb is not an object, a receiver of action. Instead, the complement identifies or refers to the subject. Compare the following two sentences.

> The president saw Mr. Kahn. The president was Mr. Kahn.

In the first sentence, Mr. Kahn is an object that receives the president's action of seeing. If a pronoun were to be substituted for Mr. Kahn, the pronoun would be in the objective case: him. But in the second sentence, Mr. Kahn isn't receiving any action; Mr. Kahn identities the subject, that is, the president. The correct pronoun to substitute for Mr. Kahn in this sentence would be he.

Pronoun complements can cause case problems. As the rule says, the subjective form of a pronoun is correct after to be, but sometimes it may sound unnatural or awkwardly formal.

> It is I.
>
> I am she. The person I chose was he.
>
> The winners were they.
>
> The best way to handle awkward-sounding constructions is to look for a better way to say the same thing. For example,
>
> They were the winners. OR They won.
>
> He was the person I chose. OR I chose him.

In informal speech and writing, modern usage allows It is me or it's me. Objective pronouns after to be are also gaining some acceptance in other constructions. But when you are writing formally, stay with the established rule.

Objective Case of Pronouns

When a pronoun is the object of the verb or preposition it is in the objective case. Use the objective case of pronouns when the pronoun is a direct or indirect object of a verb.

> Gilbertson *nominated me* for secretary (direct object of *nominated*).
>
> The news *hit them* hard (direct object of *hit*).
>
> Jennifer gave *him* the package and the valise (indirect object of *gave*).
>
> Robert Chang *told us* and *them* the same incredible story (indirect objects of *told*).

You should also use the objective case of pronouns when the pronoun is an object of a preposition.

> The aid pulled a blanket *over* the children and us (object of the preposition *over*).
>
> The person *for whom* they waited never arrived (They waited *for whom*: object of the preposition *for*).

Choosing *between you and me* versus *between you and I* should be easy. Some people incorrectly believe that the subjective forms are more correct, that *I* is superior to *me*. Where this idea comes from is a mystery, perhaps stemming from having *It's me* corrected to *It is I* or from recognizing obvious bad grammar, as in *Me and him really like you*. But don't be influenced by a misguided idea of refinement. The objective case has a clear purpose as the rules show, and not to use it when you should reveals your lack of knowledge. The phrase for *You and I* and *between you and I* are common mistakes that are probably due to over-refinement. The pronouns in these phrases are objects of prepositions, and therefore for you *and me* and *between you and me* are correct.

Watch out for pronoun case when you have a compound object. Remember that when an object is more than one person, it is still an object. Pronouns should be in the objective case.

> The ceremony will be given for Tucker, Martinez, and me. (NOT for Tucker, Martinez, and I)
>
> Without Kate and me (NOT Without Kate and I), the book wouldn't have been published.
>
> The dean nominated Nelson and me (NOT Nelson and I) to serve on the committee.

You can check for pronoun cases in such situations by reading the sentences with the pronoun object alone: *The ceremony will be given for I; Without I, the book wouldn't have been published; The dean nominated I to serve on the committee.* The mistakes show up quickly. *Me* is obviously the right form of the pronoun in these three sentences.

Pronouns as Subjects of Infinitives

When a pronoun is the subject of an infinitive (the basic verb with *to: to swim, to drive,* and so on), use the objective case for the pronoun. This rule shouldn't cause you any problems. Your ear will tell you the objective case is correct.

He wanted *her to drive* the car. Bradford liked *them to leave* early.

Pronoun Case with Appositives

An **appositive** is a word or group of words that restates or identifies the noun or pronoun it is next to: My sister *Hephzibah;* John, *the gardener,* our friend *Carlos,* We, *the people.* The presence of an appositive doesn't change the rule for pronoun case; that is, use the subjective case for subjects and the objective case for objects.

The decision to close the pool was a setback for us *swimmers.* (NOT *we swimmers*)

The best way to make sure you have chosen the correct pronoun case is to read the sentence without the appositive: *The decision to close the pool was a setback for we.* Once again, you can see immediately that us is the right pronoun to use.

Pronoun Case after *As, Than*

Choosing the right pronoun case after *as* or *than* can be difficult.

Look at the following two sentences.

> You respect Professor Morrow more *than I.*
>
> You respect Professor Morrow more *than me.*

Depending on the meaning, either choice could be correct. If the writer means You *respect Professor Morrow more than I (respect Professor Morrow),* then the first sentence is correct. If the writer means You *respect Professor Morrow more than (you respect) me,* then the second sentence is correct.

The key to choosing the right pronoun case is to supply mentally the missing part of the clause.

> Did you work as hard *as they (worked)?*
>
> I like poetry better *than she (likes* poetry).
>
> I like Ed better *than (I like) him.*
>
> They are smarter *than we (are).*

If a sentence sounds awkward to you — for example, *They are smarter than* we — you can avoid the problem by actually supplying the missing word: *They are smarter than we are.*

Who, Whom, Whoever, Whomever

These pronouns cause so much anxiety that they are being treated separately, even though the rules about case are the same as those for *I, he, she, we,* and *they.*

As a subject, choose *who* or *whoever.*

> This is the chef *who won* the award. (subject of *won*)
>
> *Whoever wants* the paper can have it. (subject of *wants*)

As an object, choose whom or whomever.

> Taline was a person *around* whom controversy swirled. (object of the preposition *around*)
>
> *Whomever will* you invite? (You will invite whomever: direct object) In informal speech and writing whom is used infrequently. At the beginning of questions, for example, who is substituted for *whom,* even when *whom* would be grammatically correct.
>
> *Who will you* marry? (You will marry *whom.*)
>
> *Who* did he ask? (He did ask *whom.*)

Even some standardized tests have given up *who/whom* questions. *Who* knows? Maybe *whom* will disappear from the language someday. But at present, especially in formal writing, maintain the distinction between *who* and *whom* — and maintain it correctly.

Possessive Case of Pronouns

The possessive case of nouns is formed with an apostrophe: *Keesha's* costume, *the wolf's fangs.* But personal pronouns and the relative pronoun *who* change form to indicate possession.

> My house is bigger than your house.
>
> His anger evaporated in the face of her explanation.
>
> The bulldog bared its teeth at us.
>
> Our decision affected their plans.
>
> The economist, whose book had received good reviews, agreed to speak.
>
> No coach tried harder to help than hers. Your plans are more definite than ours.

Remember that possessive-case nouns and pronouns are different; possessive pronouns do not have apostrophes. You have to distinguish between *its, it's,* and *whose, who's.* The possessive of *it* is *its,* NOT *it's;* the possessive of *who* is *whose,* NOT *who's.* It's and *who's* are contractions *(it's = it is; who's = who is).* The cat lost its *whiskers.* (Note that it's not *it's whiskers*)

> It's (it is) Friday!
>
> The technician *whose supervisor* (note that it's not *who's supervisor*) called left the meeting. *Who's (who is)* the author of the book?

Use a possessive pronoun with a gerund, the verb form that functions as a noun. This rule is broken frequently, with many writers using the objective rather than the possessive case.

> I didn't like *his going* (NOT *him going*) to New York without me. *Their smiling* (NOT *Them smiling*) irritated her. Please forgive our *intruding.* (NOT *us intruding*)

Pronoun Reference

Pronouns always refer to the noun they represent, their antecedent. If you understand how pronouns relate to nouns, you can avoid confusion in your writing.

Finding the Antecedent

Remember that pronouns stand in for nouns. An **antecedent** is the noun or group of words acting as a noun that a pronoun refers to. Notice the antecedents in the following example.

> Kelly lifted *Mickey* into the air and then set *him* down.
> The *debt* plagued *John and Sandy*. *It* ruined any chance *they* had for a peaceful relationship.

Neither of these examples would make a reader wonder who or what is being talked about. *Him* in the first example is *Mickey, It* and *they* in the second example are *debt* and *John and Sandy*.

Unclear Antecedents

In the following sentences, locate the antecedents of the pronouns.

> The counselor was speaking to Dave, and *he* looked unhappy.

Who looked unhappy in this sentence — the counselor or Dave? In the following sentence, did the housekeepers clean the guests or the rooms?

> After the guests left the hotel rooms, the housekeepers cleaned *them*.

In the second example, your good sense tells you the housekeepers cleaned the rooms and didn't clean the guests. But although sometimes you can count on context or good sense to help you figure out which pronoun goes with which antecedent, you shouldn't have to. And what about in the first sentence? No clue exists as to whether the counselor or Dave looked unhappy. These are examples of ambiguous pronoun references, and you should avoid them in your writing.

You can solve the problem in various ways, including changing the sentence structure or eliminating the pronoun, as in the following sentences.

> The counselor was speaking to Dave, who looked unhappy. After the guests left, the housekeepers cleaned the hotel rooms.

Be sure to read your sentences carefully to make sure that you have avoided unclear pronoun references.

Indefinite Antecedents

More subtle errors occur when you use a pronoun reference that is too general or indefinite or one that exists only in your mind.

> I told Uncle Richard, Aunt Gretchen, and then Father, *which* infuriated Gary.

Did telling all three people infuriate Gary, or was it only telling Father? Rewrite the sentence to make your meaning clear.

> First I told Uncle Richard and Aunt Gretchen. Then I told Father, which infuriated Gary.
> OR My telling Uncle Richard, Aunt Gretchen, and then Father infuriated Gary.

In the following sentence, no antecedent exists for *them*. The writer is thinking "bagels" but not specifying them. *Bagel* shop is not a correct antecedent for *them*. To solve the problem, substitute *bagels* for *them*.

> Although Mark likes working at the bagel shop, he never eats *them* himself.

In the next sentence, the antecedent for *it* is vague. Was it just the sky that filled the observer with hope and joy? A hint in rewriting: Substitute *The scene* for *It*.

> The hills were lush green, the trees in full bloom, the sky a brilliant blue. It filled me with hope and joy.

What is the exact antecedent for *this* in the following sentence?

> The paper was too long, too general, and too filled with pretentious language. *This* meant Joe had to rewrite it.

A possible rewrite might be as follows:

> The paper was too long, too general, and too filled with pretentious language. *These problems* meant that Joe had to rewrite it.

Don't try to remedy a vague pronoun reference by changing the pronoun, as in the following example.

> The paper was too long, too general, and too filled with pretentious language, *which* meant Joe had to rewrite it.

The reference for *which* is as indefinite as was the reference for *this,* and so the problem has not been solved.

The vague *this* and the indefinite *it* are so common in writing that they often go unnoticed. *It* can be used as an indefinite indicator occasionally: It's *true,* It is *raining,* It is *a ten-minute drive to the school.* But don't overdo this construction. For vivid writing, provide clear antecedents for pronouns.

Pronoun Agreement

A pronoun must agree with its antecedent in number (singular or plural) and gender (masculine or feminine). In the following sentence, Harold is the antecedent of his, he'd, and his.

> *Harold,* after saying goodbye to *his* family, discovered *he'd* lost his wallet.

In the following sentence, *Garcias is* the antecedent of *they,* even though it follows the pronoun.

> Until *they* buy the house, the *Garcias* are staying in a hotel.

Look at the next example. Here, *Peterson and Mancini* is a compound antecedent, which requires the plural pronoun *their.*

> Peterson and Mancini took their cue from the senator.

Agreement Problems with Indefinite Pronouns

Indefinite pronouns cause many agreement problems. Some pronouns (*several, few, both,* and *many*) are clearly plural and take both plural verbs and plural pronouns.

> *Several are* expected to give up *their* rooms.
> *Both tell their* parents the truth.

Some pronouns may feel as though they should be plural, but they are singular and take singular verbs and pronouns. In this group are *each, either, neither, everyone, everybody, no one, nobody, anyone, anybody, someone,* and *somebody.*

> *Each is* responsible for *his or her* (NOT *their)* own ticket.
> *Everyone wants* to get *his or her* (NOT *their)* name on the winner's list.

When the use of a singular form would lead to a statement that doesn't make sense, you should use a plural form. For example, in the sentence *Everyone left the lecture because he thought it was boring, they* would be a better choice than *he* for the pronoun. However, the general rule is to use singular forms of verbs and pronouns with these indefinite pronouns.

Some indefinite pronouns (*none, any some, almost*) fall into an "either/or" category; they may take singular or plural verbs and pronouns, depending on meaning. Sometimes the distinction is subtle. *None (not one = singular)* of the survivors *was* hurt. *None (no survivors = plural)* of the survivors *were* hurt.

> *Some is* better than none. *(some = a* quantity = singular)
> *Some are* delicious. *(some = a* number of things = plural)

All is well. (*all* = the sum of all things singular)

All *are* well. (*all* = *a* number of people plural)

If a plural meaning is not clear from the context, use singular verbs and pronouns.

Pronouns with Collective Nouns

Collective nouns can also require either singular or plural verbs and singular or plural pronouns, depending on meaning.

The *team* plays according to its schedule. (emphasize unit = singular)

The *team* couldn't agree on *their* goals. (emphasize individuals = plural)

However, if you are uncertain, choose a singular verb and a singular pronoun, or rewrite the sentence to make it clearly plural.

The team *members* couldn't agree on *their* goals.

Sexism in Pronouns: He or She?

Traditionally, *he* had been the automatic gender choice when the gender of a pronoun's antecedent is unknown, or when the antecedent represents both sexes. The tactful *person* keeps *his* opinion to *himself*.

The *reader himself will* decide whether *he* wants to accept Smith's premise.

This usage is outdate and is considered to be sexist and offensive. There are two good ways to rewrite such sentences.

When possible, rewrite sentences using third-person plural forms.

Tactful *people* keep *their* opinions to *themselves*.

Also when possible, use *he* or *she*.

The *reader will* decide whether *he or she* wishes to accept Smith's premise.

A third possibility is to use *their* even when the antecedent is singular.

A ticket holder must check their number.

However, this creates a grammatical blunder because it is an agreement error that is unacceptable in formal writing.

Use third-person plural whenever that solution is possible and *he or she* when the plural form is awkward or inappropriate. However, constant repetition of *he or she* slows the flow of a sentence, and you risk annoying your reader if you use the phrase too often.

Modifiers: Adjectives and Adverbs

Adjectives and adverbs are parts of speech called modifiers. An adjective modifies a noun or pronoun and an adverb modifies a verb, adjective, or another adverb.

Some adjectives and adverbs require memorizing a few rules. For example, *bad* is always used as an adjective, while *badly* is an adverb. Adjectives and adverbs can also be used to show comparative or superlative degree. By adding *-er* you can compare two peoples, things, or an action, or by adding *-est* you can compare more than two things. You can make your sentences more precise and interesting by using appropriate adjectives and adverbs.

The Modifier

A **modifier** describes or limits another word or group of words. To correctly identify the modifier as an adjective or adverb, it is important to identify the word the adjective or adverb is modifying.

An **adjective modifies** a noun or pronoun. In the following sentence, *orange* is an adjective modifying the noun *curtains,* and *cool* is an adjective modifying the noun *breeze.*

> The *orange* curtains billowed in the *cool* breeze.

In the next example, *happy is* an adjective modifying the pronoun I; this kind of adjective, one following a linking chair verb, is called a predicate adjective. *Thoughtful is* an adjective modifying the noun *gesture.*

> I am *happy* because of the *thoughtful* gesture.

An **adverb modifies** a verb, an adjective, or another adverb. Adverbs answer questions such as *how, how much, when, where,* and *why.* In the following sentence, *sadly* modifies the verb *smiled* and answers the question "How did he smile?"

> He smiled *sadly.*

In the next example, *immediately* answers the question "When did they come?"

> They came *immediately.*

Here answers the question "Where did she walk?"

> She walked *here.*

Very modifies the adjective *bright:* "How bright were the curtains?"

> The orange curtains were *very* bright.

Remarkably modifies the adverb *quickly:* "How quickly did the baby crawl?

> The baby crawled *remarkably* quickly.

Adjectives and adverbs don't form the core of sentences as nouns and verbs do, but they give sentences texture and precision. Without adjectives and adverbs, you wouldn't know what color the curtains were or how the baby crawled. Use adjectives and adverbs to contribute to what you are saying. For example, in "Jan smiled *sadly,*" you know Jan's smile is not the usual happy smile. *Sadly* performs a function. On the other hand, in "I ranted *angrily,*" does the adverb add anything to the verb? To rant means to express anger; thus *angrily* is unnecessary. Avoid using adjectives and adverbs that don't tell anything or that state the obvious.

Recognizing Adjectives and Adverbs

Adverbs often end in *-ly (remarkably, sadly, quickly),* but not always *(here, there, fast, late, hard, not, never).* And some adjectives end in *-ly* (a *lively* child, *friendly* dog, *hilly* area). The lesson to be learned from these examples is that to decide whether a word is an adjective or an adverb, look not at the word itself but at what the word modifies: Adjectives will always modify nouns and pronouns, while adverbs modify verbs, adjectives, and other adverbs. In the following example, old and red are adjectives modifying the noun barn.

> The old *red* truck needs repairs.

In the next sentence, *very* is an adverb modifying the adjective *old,* not the noun *truck.*

> The *very* old red truck needs repairs.

Hard is an adverb modifying the verb *worked.*

> They worked *hard* all afternoon.

Here, *hard* is an adjective modifying the noun *work*.

> The *hard* work took all afternoon.

Using Adjectives after Linking Verbs

It's natural to associate adverbs rather than adjectives with verbs; adverbs modify verbs. But with linking verbs such as *be, become, smell, taste, seem,* and *look* use adjectives (called predicate adjectives).

> The substance tastes *sweet* (not *sweetly*).
>
> They were joyful (not *joyfully*).

Notice the use of adjectives or adverbs in the following sentences, depending on whether a verb is functioning as a linking verb or an action verb.

In the following example, grow is an action verb meaning *to develop, increase in size,* and its modifier should be an adverb *(beautifully).*

> Flowers grow *beautifully* in that climate.

Here, grow is a linking verb meaning to *become,* so the complement should be an adjective *(beautiful).*

> Bronze grows *beautiful* as it ages. This is logical as well as correct because bronze does not increase in size as it ages.

In the next example, *smells* is a linking verb and takes an adjective; that is, the dog's odor is unpleasant.

> The dog smells bad.

Here, *smells* is an action verb and takes an adverb; that is, something is wrong with the dog's sense of smell.

> The dog smells *badly*.

Problem Adjectives and Adverbs

Some adjectives and adverbs seem interchangeable but are not. You will need to remember a few rules to distinguish how they are used.

Good, Well

Good is always an adjective: *good* bread; *good options*; dinner was *good*. Don't use *good* as an adverb. Use *well,* an adverb meaning to perform capably.

> She sings *well*.
>
> NOT She sings *good!*
>
> He listens *well*.
>
> NOT He listens *good*.

Some confusion arises between *good* and *well* because well can also be used as an adjective meaning in *good health*.

> The actor was *well* in time for the play's opening.
>
> Not The actor was *good* in time for the play's opening.

To see the distinction between *well* used as an adjective and *good* used as an adjective, look at the following sentences, both with the linking verb *looked.*

The actor looked *good* at the opening night party. (The actor looked attractive.) The actor looked *well* at the opening nigh party tonight. (The actor looked to be in good health.)

Bad, Badly

Bad is an adjective and *badly* is an adverb. They are often used incorrectly for each other.

> I feel *bad* about the mayor's losing the election.
>
> NOT I feel *badly* about the mayor's losing the election.

Here, *feel* is a linking verb and should be followed by an adjective, not an adverb. In the next examples, *badly is* an adverb describing how the team played.

> The soccer team played *badly* in the last game.
>
> Not The soccer team played *bad* in the last game.

In the following sentence, the adjective *bad* follows a linking verb, so the appearance of the faucet is being discussed. The faucet looked *bad*. When the adverb *badly* follows the action verb, it explains how seriously the faucet leaked. The faucet leaked *badly*.

Most, Almost

Most is an adjective meaning *the greatest in number, amount. Most* people agree that exercise is good for you. *Most* crimes go unpunished. But *most* is an adverb when it is used to form the superlative of an adjective: She is the *most* intelligent woman in the group. He is the *most* appealing when he first wakes up. *Almost* is always an adverb. It means *nearly. Almost* modifies the adjectives *every* and *all. Most* cannot be used to modify *every* or *all.*

> *Almost* every person agreed.
>
> NOT *Most* every person agreed.

> *Almost* all the people came.
>
> NOT *Most* all the people came.

Forming the Comparative and Superlative Degrees

As shown in the following table, adjectives and adverbs change to show the **comparative degree** and **superlative degree.**

Comparative Versus Superlative Degree		
Positive Degree	*Comparative Degree*	*Superlative Degree*
sweet (adjective)	sweeter	sweetest
sweetly (adverb)	more sweetly	most sweetly

Follow these simple rules in forming comparative and superlative degrees with adverbs and adjectives.

- Use the comparative degree when you are comparing two people, things, or actions: Apples are *sweeter* than lemons. A wren sings *more sweetly* than a robin.

- Use the superlative degree when you are comparing more than two. The superlative degree puts the modified word over all the others in its group: The apples are *sweeter* than the lemons, but the strawberries are the *sweetest of* all. Of all birds, the lark sings *most sweetly.*

Most one-syllable and some two-syllable adjectives form the comparative and superlative degrees by adding *-er* or *-est*. Notice that the adjective's final consonant is sometimes doubled and that a *y* is changed to *-i*: *tall, taller, tallest; smart,* *smarter, smartest; big, bigger, biggest; dry, drier, driest; happy, happier, happiest.* There are a few exceptions to the rule: *good, better, best; bad, worse, worst.* If an adjective has two or more syllables, it usually forms the comparative and superlative degrees with *more* and *most: more intelligent, most intelligent; more difficult, most difficult.*

Most adverbs form the comparative and superlative forms with more and most: *more slowly, most lowly, more gracefully, most gracefully, more quickly, most quickly.* A few exceptions exist: *hard, harder, hardest; fast, faster, fastest; soon, sooner, soonest.*

Be careful not to double comparisons when you form degrees of adjectives: *funny, funnier* (not *more funnier*), *funniest* (not *most funniest*). To use the *-er, -est* forms with *more, most* is redundant and incorrect.

Whenever you aren't sure about how to form the comparative and superlative of a particular adjective or adverb, check your dictionary.

Be aware that there are some adjectives and adverbs that should not be compared because of their meanings. One of the most frequently miscompared adjectives is *unique,* meaning *one of a kind.* Something cannot be *more unique* or *most unique.* Something is either *one of a kind* or it isn't. Adjectives like this (and their adverbial forms) are absolute; *absolute* itself is an absolute adjective. Among others to watch out for are *essential,* meaning *absolutely necessary; universal,* meaning *present everywhere;* and *immortal,* meaning *living forever.* With these adjectives and adverbs, something either is or it isn't, and therefore comparative degrees are meaningless. Advertisements freely use the superlative *best* when referring to a product. Because *best* means surpassing all others in quality, a claim such as "the orange juice toothpaste for you" cannot be substantiated.

Although in informal usage people may use phrases such as *less perfect, more straight,* or *very round,* in formal, objective and scientific contexts, these adjectives cannot be given comparative or superlative degrees.

Prepositions, Conjunctions, and Interjections

Prepositions, conjunctions and interjections are the connecting elements in sentences. Finding the link between words is how to identify prepositions. The important rules about using prepositions are avoid using excess prepositions and use prepositional idioms correctly. A sentence may end with a preposition; however, you may wish to avoid doing so in very formal contexts.

Conjunctions are parts of speech that connect words, phrases, or clauses. There are three types of conjunctions: coordinating, correlative, and subordinating. They are the key to logically constructed sentences.

Interjections are used to express powerful or sudden emotion and are usually not grammatically connected to any other sentence. While there are no formal rules for interjections, they are most effective if used sparingly. They occur in dialogue and narration more frequently than in analytical or critical writing, and they may be inappropriate in formal writing.

The Preposition

A **preposition** shows the relationship between a noun or pronoun and another noun or pronoun.

The map *over* the <u>desk</u>. The map *between* the <u>preface</u> and the <u>title page</u>. Everyone *except* the aide *in* the blue suit. A letter *about* <u>them</u>.

The italicized words in the preceding phrases are prepositions; the underlined words are **objects of the prepositions.** When the object is a pronoun, remember that the pronoun should be in the objective case.

Recognizing Prepositions

How do you recognize a preposition? Prepositions aren't as obvious as nouns and verbs. Look for a word that establishes a certain kind of relationship with another word. For example, in the previous phrases, how is *map* related to *desk?* The map is *over* the fence. How is *Everyone* related to the aide? The aide is left out of the group *Everyone.* How is aid related to *suit?* The aide is *in* it. The following shows several words commonly used as prepositions.

- about
- above
- across
- after
- against
- along
- among
- around
- at
- before
- behind
- below
- beneath
- beside
- between

- beyond
- by
- concerning
- down
- during
- except
- for
- from
- in
- into
- like
- of
- off
- on
- out

- over
- past
- since
- through
- to
- toward
- under
- underneath
- until
- unto
- up
- upon
- with
- within
- without

Some prepositions, called **compound prepositions,** are made up of more than one word, such as *according to, because of, in front of, instead of, in spite of,* and *next to.*

Confusing Use of Prepositions

The unnecessary use of prepositions is a common error. Be careful not to use a preposition where it isn't needed.

> Where have you been?
> NOT Where have you been *at?*

> Where is Celine going?
> NOT Where is Celine going *to?*

Also, don't use two prepositions when you need only one.

> Don't go *near* the water
> NOT Don't go *near to* the water.

> The book fell *off* the table.
> NOT The book fell *off of* the table.

Prepositions at the End of a Sentence

It is not correct to state that a sentence should not end with a proposition. The sound and context of the sentence determine the appropriate word order. Ending sentences with preposition is natural in most contexts. Not to do so may sound artificial and stilted.

> It is a situation up with which I will not put.
> COMPARE TO It is a situation which I will not put up with.

> My friend would not tell me from whom the hint about my appearance came.
> COMPARE TO My friend would not tell me whom the hint about my appearance came from.

However, avoiding a preposition at the end of a sentence creates a formal effect which may be appropriate in some written and spoken contexts.

> The terms of the new treaty present complex situations to think about.
>
> COMPARE TO Complex situations to think about arise from the new treaty.

Defining Conjunctions

Conjunctions are words that join or link elements. Like prepositions, they get a job done rather than adding excitement to your writing. But choosing the right conjunction makes the logic of your thought clear. For example, which of the following two sentences creates the more logical connection?

> They wanted to see a performance by the new band, *and* tickets were not available.
>
> They wanted to see a performance by the new band, *but* tickets were not available.

Because the two clauses suggest contradictory ideas, *but* provides a more logical connection than *and*.

Coordinating Conjunctions

The **coordinating conjunctions** are *and, but, for, nor, or, so,* and *yet*. These conjunctions join words, phrases, or clauses that are grammatically equal in rank.

- **Words:** bacon and eggs, fax and pager, ideas nor dreams
- **Phrases:** We discovered dust balls under the couch and in the closet.
- **Clauses:** Art is long, but life is short.

Each clause ("Art is long" and "life is short") can stand alone. The two clauses are grammatically equal, and, because their word order is the same, they are parallel.

Correlative Conjunctions

Correlative conjunctions are like coordinating conjunctions except that they come in matched pairs: *either/or, neither/nor, both/and, not only/but also,* and *whether/or*.

- **Words:** Neither ideas nor dreams
- **Phrases:** We discovered dust balls not only under the couch but also in the closet.
- **Clauses:** Either the mouse was tired, or the maze was too difficult.

Subordinating Conjunctions

Subordinating conjunctions join unequal elements. A subordinating conjunction joins a clause that can't stand alone (called a **subordinate or dependent clause**) to a clause that can (called an **independent clause**).

> We will discontinue research in this area *unless* the results of the experiment are promising.

The clause beginning with *unless* cannot stand alone; it is subordinate to, or dependent on, the independent clause *We will discontinue research in this area. Unless* is the subordinating conjunction that links the two clauses.

> The plane arrived *before* we did.

Before we did is a dependent clause; it cannot stand alone. It depends on the independent clause *The plane arrived. Before* is the subordinating conjunction that links the clauses.

The following are some words that can act as subordinating conjunctions.

- after
- although
- as
- as if
- as long as
- as though
- because
- before than

- even if that
- if
- in order that
- provided (that)
- since
- so (that)
- though
- till

- unless
- until
- when
- whenever
- where
- wherever
- while

Some of these words were also on the list of prepositions. Once again, remember that a word's part of speech depends on its function, not on the word itself. A preposition shows a relationship between words and has an object, whereas a subordinating conjunction joins a dependent clause to an independent one.

The puppy stood hesitantly *before* the door.

In the preceding sentence, *before* is a preposition; its object is *door*. The preposition shows the relationship between the puppy and the door.

Before the expedition can begin, the details must be addressed.

Here, *before* is a subordinating conjunction, linking the dependent clause *Before the expedition can begin* to the independent clause *the details must be addressed*.

Using Interjections

Interjections are words used to express a burst of emotion or surprise. They are not grammatically related to other elements in a sentence.

Hey! Wow! Oh, no! Bravo!

Curses and obscenities are also often used as interjections: *Damn!* Avoid these uses of interjections unless you are writing fiction or for some other special purpose.

Interjections can add a sudden and emotional tone to your writing if they are used judiciously. They are more common in narration and dialogue than in other forms of prose, and they may sometimes appear in speeches to create special effects. Limit your use of them, particularly in formal writing. Even in informal writing the power of interjections will be diluted if they are used too often. Generally, although not always, exclamation points immediately follow interjections. Never use more than one exclamation point after an interjection. Doing so suggests you are unable to convey ideas in words and must rely on a punctuation trick.

Ouch! Hurrah! Mercy! Ah, to be in Paris in the spring!

Phrases, Clauses, and Sentences

Clauses and phrases are the building blocks of sentences. A phrase is a group of words that act as a part of speech but cannot stand alone as a sentence. Clauses are groups of words that have a subject and a predicate. Independent clauses express a complete thought and can stand alone as a sentence, but subordinate clauses depend on other parts of the sentence to express a complete thought.

A sentence expresses a complete thought and contains a subject, a noun or pronoun, and a predicate, a verb or verb phrase. The four basic types of sentences — simple, compound, complex, and compound-complex — use phrases and clauses in varying degrees of complexity.

The Phrase

A **phrase** is any group of related words that, unlike a sentence, has no subject-predicate combination. The words in a phrase act together so that the phrase itself functions as a single part of speech. For example, some phrases act as nouns, some as verbs, some as adjectives or adverbs. Phrases can't stand alone as sentences.

The chance that you'll ever be asked to differentiate between a gerund phrase and an infinitive phrase or a participial phrase and a prepositional phrase is small. Then why learn about these phrases? First, if you understand how they work and can recognize them, you can avoid mistaking them for sentences. Second, you can avoid misplacing them or leaving them dangling in sentences. Third, you can learn to use them effectively in combining sentences. A series of short, choppy sentences can be turned into a more mature, effective sentence by using phrases and clauses.

The Prepositional Phrase

The most common phrase is the **prepositional phrase.** You'll find these phrases everywhere — in sentences, clauses, and even in other phrases. Each prepositional phrase begins with a preposition *(in, of, by, from, for)*. and includes a noun or pronoun that is the object of the preposition.

> *in* the *room*
>
> *of* the *people*
>
> *by* the *river*
>
> *from* the *teacher*
>
> *for* the *party*

The object of a preposition can have its own modifiers, which also are part of the prepositional phrase.

> in *the hot, crowded* room
>
> of *the remaining few* people
>
> by *the rushing* river
>
> from *the tired and frustrated* teacher
>
> for *the midnight victory* party

Prepositional phrases function as either adjectives or adverbs.

> The technician *in the lab coat* pulled out a cellular phone.

The prepositional phrase here acts as an adjective describing the noun technician.

> Most of the audience snoozed *during the tedious performance.*

The prepositional phrase here acts as an adverb modifying the verb *snoozed.*

Phrases Containing Verbals

Verbals act as nouns, adjectives, and adverbs in sentences.

The Participial Phrase

A **participial phrase** begins with a past or present participle and is followed by its objects and modifiers. Like participles alone, participial phrases are used as adjectives.

> *Seeing the clear air,* Sal realized he was finally out of Los Angeles.

In the preceding sentence, the present participle *seeing* introduces the participial phrase, which includes the participle's object *(air)* and its modifiers *(the, clear)*. This participial phrase acts as an adjective modifying the subject of the sentence *(Sal)*.

> The soldiers, *trapped by the enemy,* threw down their guns.

Here, the past participle *trapped* introduces the participial phrase *trapped by the enemy.* The entire phrase acts as an adjective modifying the subject of the sentence *(soldiers)*. Notice the phrase-within-a-phrase here. By *the enemy* is a prepositional phrase modifying the participle *trapped.* Remember that phrases can act as modifiers in other phrases.

The Gerund Phrase

At first, a **gerund phrase** may look like a participial phrase because gerund phrases begin with the *-ing* form of a verb *(riding, seeing, talking chair)* and have objects and modifiers. But a gerund phrase always acts as a noun in a sentence, not as an adjective. Like other nouns, a gerund phrase can serve as the subject of a sentence, the object of a verb or preposition, or the complement of a linking verb.

In the following example, the gerund phrase *Reading sociological novels* acts as a noun and is the subject of the verb interested.

> *Reading sociological novels* interested Latoya.

In the next sentence, the gerund phrase *seeing the suspect* is the direct object of the verb reported. Notice that the entire phrase, not just the word *suspect,* is the direct object.

> The police officer reported *seeing the suspect.*
>
> Here, the gerund phrase *talking often and loudly* is the object of the preposition *by.*
>
> The senator made a reputation by *talking often and loudly.*

In the final example, *Losing a credit card* is a gerund phrase acting as the subject of the sentence. *Asking for identity theft* is a gerund phrase acting as a complement of the linking verb *is.*

> *Losing a credit card* is *asking for identity theft.*

The Infinitive Phrase

An **infinitive phrase** contains an infinitive (for example, *to sleep, to have slept, to consider, to throw*) and its objects and modifiers. Infinitive phrases usually function as nouns, though they can be used as adjectives and adverbs.

In this sentence, *To sleep all* night is an infinitive phrase acting as a noun. It is the subject of this sentence.

> *To sleep all night* was my only wish.

Here, *To take an unpopular stand* is an infinitive phrase acting **as a noun**. It is the direct object of the predicate *didn't want.*

> The representatives didn't want *to take an unpopular stand.*
>
> Next, the infinitive phrase *to spend foolishly* acts as an adjective modifying the noun *money.*
>
> Midas had plenty of gold *to spend foolishly.*

In the following sentence, the infinitive phrase to *clear her mind* acts as an adverb modifying *drove.* It answers the question "Why did she drive?"

> After the confrontation, she drove miles to *clear her mind.*

Breaking up an infinitive with one or more adverbs between the *to* and the base verb is called **splitting an infinitive.** Careful writers still split infinitives.

They taught her to *spend* money *wisely.*

NOT They taught her to *wisely spend* money.

Sometimes, however, not splitting an infinitive is almost impossible.

We expect the population to *more than double* over the next twenty years.

Other times, not splitting an infinitive causes ambiguity or sounds unnatural. In these cases, clarity and smoothness take precedence over unsplit infinitives. In the following sentence, does *further* modify *corporate efforts* or *discuss?*

We wanted to *discuss further corporate efforts* to modernize.

Splitting the infinitive makes the sentence clearer.

BETTER We wanted to *further discuss corporate efforts* to modernize.

Splitting the infinitive in the following sentence makes it less stilted, more natural.

The glutton planned *to grab quickly* the food from the buffet.

BETTER The glutton planned *to quickly grab* the food from the buffet.

Types of Clauses

Like a phrase, a **clause** is a group of related words, but unlike a phrase, a clause has a subject and predicate. An **independent clause,** along with having a subject and predicate, expresses a complete thought and can stand alone as a sentence. On the contrary, a **subordinate** or **dependent clause** does not express a complete thought and therefore is *not* a sentence. A subordinate clause standing alone is the most common type of sentence fragment.

Independent Clauses

He saw her; The Washingtons hurried home, Free speech has a price. Grammatically complete statements like these are sentences and can stand alone. When they are part of longer sentences, they are referred to as **independent (or main) clauses.**

Two or more independent clauses can be joined by using coordinating conjunctions *(and, but, for, nor, or, so,* and *yet)* or by using semicolons. The most important thing to remember is that an independent clause *can* stand alone as a complete sentence.

In the following example the independent clause is a simple sentence.

Jacques cleaned the messy kitchen.

Here, the coordinating conjunction *and* joins two independent clauses:

Julia left left, and Jacques cleaned the messy kitchen.

Here, a semicolon joins two independent clauses:

Julia left; Jacques cleaned the messy kitchen.

All sentences must include at least one independent clause.

After he told Julia to leave, Jacques *cleaned the messy kitchen.*

The independent clause is preceded by a clause that can't stand alone.

Jacques cleaned the messy kitchen while he waited for Julia to leave.

The independent clause is followed by a clause that can't stand alone.

Beginning sentences with coordinating conjunctions

Any of the coordinating conjunctions *(and, but, or, nor, for, so, yet)* can be used to join an independent clause to another independent clause. And a coordinating conjunction can be used to begin a sentence. (Notice the preceding sentence, for example.) Sometimes beginning a sentence this way creates exactly the effect you want; it separates the clause and yet draws attention to its relationship with the previous clause. Use this technique when it works for you.

Subordinate Clauses

A **subordinate clause** has a subject and predicate but, unlike an independent clause, cannot stand by itself. It *depends* on something else to express a complete thought, which is why it is also called a **dependent clause.** Some subordinate clauses are introduced by relative pronouns *(who, whom, that, which, what, whose)* and some by subordinating conjunctions *(although, because, if, unless, when).* Subordinate clauses function in sentences as adjectives, nouns, and adverbs.

Relative Clauses

A **relative clause** begins with a relative pronoun and functions as an adjective.

In the following sentence, the relative pronoun *that* is the subject of its clause and *won* is the predicate. This clause couldn't stand by itself. Its role in the complete sentence is to modify *novel,* the subject of the independent clause.

> The novel *that won the Pulitzer Prize* didn't sell well when it was first published.

In the next example, *which* is the relative pronoun that begins the subordinate clause. *Celebrities* is the subject of the clause and *attended* is the predicate. In the complete sentence, this clause functions as an adjective describing *ceremony.*

> The ceremony, *which several celebrities attended,* received intense coverage.

Note that in a relative clause the relative pronoun is sometimes the subject of the clause, as in the following sentence, and sometimes the object, as in the next sentence.

> Arthur, who comes to the games every week, offered to be scorekeeper.

Who is the subject of the clause and *comes* is the predicate. The clause modifies *Arthur.* In the following sentence, *coach* is the subject of the clause, *trusted* is the predicate, and *whom* is the direct object of *trusted.* Again, the clause modifies *Arthur.*

> Arthur, *whom* the coach trusted, was asked to be scorekeeper.

Noun Clauses

A **noun clause** serves as a noun in a sentence.

> *What I want for dinner* is a hamburger (subject of the predicate *is*).
>
> The host told us *how he planned the party* (object of the predicate *told*).
>
> The vacation is *what I need most* (complement of the linking chair verb *is*).
>
> Give it to *whoever arrives first* (object of the preposition *to*).

Adverbial Clauses

Many subordinate clauses begin with subordinating conjunctions **called adverbial clauses.** Examples of these conjunctions are *because, unless, if, when,* and *although.* What these conjunctions have in common is that they make the clauses that follow them unable to stand alone. The clauses act as adverbs, answering questions like *how, when, where, why, to what extent,* and *under what conditions.*

> While Mount Saint Helens was erupting and spewing fountains of lava into the air, we drove away as quickly as we could.

In the preceding sentence, *while* is a subordinating conjunction introducing the adverbial clause; the subject of the clause is *Mount Saint Helens* and the predicate is *was erupting* and *[was] spewing*. This clause is dependent because it is an incomplete thought. What *happened* while the volcano was erupting? The independent clause *we drove away as quickly as we could* completes the thought. The adverbial clause answers the question "When did we drive?"

In the following sentence, *because* introduces the adverbial clause in which *van* is the subject and *needed,* the predicate. This clause is an incomplete thought. What *happened* because the van needed repairs? The independent clause *The group of tourists decided to have lunch in the village* is necessary to complete the thought. Again, the subordinate clause as a whole acts as an adverb, telling why the tourists decided to have lunch in the village.

> The group of tourists decided to have lunch in the village *because the van needed repairs.*

The Sentence

The standard definition of a **sentence** is that it is a group of words containing a subject and a predicate and expressing a complete thought. But for this definition to be helpful, you must be able to recognize a subject and a predicate and understand what is meant by "a complete thought."

Subject and Predicate

A sentence has a **subject** (what or whom the sentence is about) and a predicate. The **predicate** tells what the subject does or is or what is done to the subject (for example, the books *were left* outside). The **simple subject** is a noun or pronoun. The **complete subject** is this noun or pronoun and the words that modify it. The **simple predicate** is a verb or verb phrase (for example, *has walked, will have walked*). The **complete predicate** is the verb or verb phrase and the words that modify or complete it.

In the following example, *Stan* is both the simple and the complete subject of the sentence. *Bought* is the simple predicate. *Bought food* is the complete predicate: the verb is *bought* and its direct object is *food.*

> Stan bought food.

In the following example, *dog* is the simple subject. *The angry old dog growling loudly* is the complete subject. *Stood* is the verb; *stood on the porch* is the complete predicate.

> The angry old dog growling loudly stood on the porch.

In this sentence, *The argument that money is a burden* is the complete subject. *Argument* is the simple subject modified by the adjective clause *that money is a burden.* The rest of the sentence is the complete predicate. The simple predicate is the verb *originated.*

> The argument that money is a burden probably originated with a rich man who was trying to counter the envy of a poor man.

In the first sentence, subject and predicate are easy to identify. In the second sentence, you can still pick out the simple subject and verb fairly easily, despite the modifiers. But the third sentence is more complicated. As you begin to write more sophisticated sentences, the simple subject and simple predicate may seem to get lost in a web of modifying words, phrases, and clauses. To ensure that you have a complete sentence, however, you still should be able to identify the core noun or pronoun and the core verb or verb phrase.

Expressing a Complete Thought

In addition to having a subject and predicate, a sentence must be able to stand on its own. It can't depend on something else to express a complete thought. Look at the following examples.

> The gymnast jumped.

This is a grammatically complete sentence, though perhaps not an interesting one. It has a subject *(gymnnast)* and a predicate *(jumped).* It expresses a complete thought — you know what happened. You might want to know more about the person — who is this gymnast and why he or she jumped, for example. You might want to know more about the jump itself — when it occurred, how high it was, and so on. But the basic action is complete: *The gymnast jumped.*

The next example is an incomplete sentence. It still has a subject *(gymnast)* and a predicate *(jumped),* but the presence of "when" keeps this group of words from being a complete thought: What happened during the jump?

> When the gymnast jumped.

The following sentence is still an incomplete sentence. Now, you know something about where the gymnast jumped, but the thought is still incomplete: What *happened* when the gymnast jumped high into the air?

> When the gymnast jumped high into the air.

The next example is a complete sentence again. The question "What happened when he jumped?" has been answered: *the crowd roared approval.* Even if the phrase *high into the air* were to be deleted, the thought would be complete.

> When the gymnast jumped high into the air, the crowd roared approval.

Sentence Types: Simple, Compound, and Complex

The ability to vary sentence types in your writing will allow you to control the pacing and clarity of your paragraphs. Using a variety of sentence types also makes for more interesting reading.

A **simple sentence** has one independent clause and no subordinate clauses.

> Old-growth forests in the United States are disappearing. Citizens must act.

A **compound sentence** has two or more independent clauses, joined by coordinating conjunctions, and no subordinate clauses.

> Old-growth forests in the United States are disappearing, and citizens must act (two independent clauses joined by and).

A **complex sentence** contains one independent clause and one or more subordinate clauses.

> Because old-growth forests in the United States are fast disappearing (subordinate clause beginning with subordinating conjunction), citizens must act now (independent clause).

> Forests that have existed for thousands of years are in danger. "That have existed for thousands of years" is a subordinate clause beginning with a relative pronoun; "Forests . . . are in danger" is an independent clause.)

A **compound-complex sentence** joins two or more independent clauses with one or more subordinate clauses.

> Forests that have existed for thousands of years are in danger, and citizens must take action. ("Forests are in danger" and "citizens must take action" are independent clauses; "that have existed for thousands of years" is a subordinate clause.)

Make use of all these types of sentences. Don't string together a long series of simple sentences, but, on the other hand, don't always write compound and complex sentences. Begin with a simple sentence, or follow several long compound and complex sentences with a simple one. It can have a surprisingly forceful effect.

Because America seemed to provide limitless natural resources, until the second half of the twentieth century we spent them freely. We mined for minerals, diverted rivers, and cut down trees, many of which had been growing for thousands of years before the first settlers arrived. Over the years, America's wilderness has given way to prosperous cities, and skyscrapers have replaced giant old trees. *America has succeeded. But now we are paying the price.*

Common Sentence Errors

Once you understand what a sentence is, you'll be able to tell what works and what doesn't work. To avoid errors like run-on sentences and fragments, you should learn to recognize how complete sentences are put together. Other errors, such as lack of subject-predicate agreement, misplaced modifiers, faulty parallelism, and style problems like wordiness, require careful attention to the way words function within a sentence. As a critical reviewer of your own writing, you'll be able to avoid these mistakes.

Run-On Sentences

One of the most common mistakes with independent clauses is joining them without the proper punctuation. This error is called a **run-on sentence** or **comma splice.** An independent clause standing alone should end in a period, question mark, or exclamation point.

Joining Independent Clauses

If you want to join independent clauses, however, you should use a semicolon or one of the seven coordinating conjunctions between them. A comma should precede the coordinating conjunction, but a comma without a conjunction is not sufficient.

This is a run-on sentence, or comma splice. A comma alone cannot join independent clauses.

> I went to the *database. I* found the information I needed.
>
> NOT I went to the *database, I* found the information I needed.

Here, the independent clauses are separate sentences. Each ends correctly with a period.

> I went to the *database; I* found the information I needed.

The two independent clauses are correctly joined with a semicolon.

> I went to the *database, and I* found the information I needed.

The two independent clauses are correctly joined with a coordinating conjunction *(and)* preceded by a comma.

Run-ons with Conjunctive (Sentence) Adverbs

Watch out for another kind of run-on sentence. Some words look like coordinating conjunctions but aren't. These words cannot be used to join independent clauses with a comma. Remember that the only time you can join independent clauses with a comma and not create a run-on sentence is when one of the seven coordinating conjunctions *(and, but, for, nor, or, so, yet)* follows the comma.

The words that look suspiciously like coordinating conjunctions but are actually adverbs are called conjunctive adverbs or sentence adverbs. The use of a comma to join a clause beginning with one of these words is frequent, but no matter how common the practice, it still creates a run-on, and it is not acceptable. The following shows common conjunctive adverbs.

- also
- besides
- consequently
- further, furthermore
- hence
- however
- indeed
- likewise
- moreover
- nevertheless
- otherwise
- similarly
- then
- therefore
- thus

Some transitional phrases pose the same problem — for example, *as a result, even so, for example, in other words, on the contrary.* If you keep in mind the rule that independent clauses can be joined with a comma only when the comma is followed by one of the seven coordinating conjunctions, you should be able to avoid these tricky run-ons.

Scientists were convinced by the *evidence; however,* the Food and Drug Administration was slow to respond.

NOT Scientists were convinced by the *evidence, however,* the Food and Drug Administration was slow to respond.

The hurricane damaged the *arena. Nevertheless,* the game was played on schedule.

NOT The hurricane damaged the *arena, nevertheless,* the game was played on schedule.

Folic acid appears to exert a protective *effect. For example,* one study showed that it cut the rate of neural tube defects by two thirds.

NOT Folic acid appears to exert a protective *effect, for example,* one study showed that it cut the rate of neural tube defects by two thirds.

Run-on sentences such as the ones described above are basic errors. Occasionally, however, joining independent clauses with only a comma may be acceptable — for example, when the clauses are very short and have the same form, when the tone is informal and conversational, or when the rhythm of a sentence calls for it.

Some people eat to live, gourmets live to eat.

I hardly recognized her, she was so thin. (A "because" is understood here.)

They smiled, they touched, they kissed.

Sentence Fragments

Most **sentence fragments** are phrases, or subordinate clauses, or combinations of the two. Don't ever let length be your guide, for a sentence can be two words *(He jumps)* and a fragment fifty.

Recognizing Fragments

At first glance, a sentence fragment may look like a sentence because it begins with a capital letter and ends with a period. When you look more closely, however, you'll see that the group of words is missing one or more of the three elements required to make it a sentence: a subject, a predicate, and a grammatically complete thought.

If you want more coverage than the newspaper story.

This is a subordinate clause. It is missing an independent clause that would complete the thought.

If you want more coverage than the newspaper story, *we will check primary sources.*

When you write sentences beginning with subordinating conjunctions, make sure that you have an independent clause following the subordinate clause.

We saw the dolphins leaping behind the boat. *Splashing and arcing in the spray.*

A sentence here is followed by a fragment, a participial phrase that cannot stand alone. The problem could be solved if the period after *boat* were changed to a comma.

He pointed at Ms. Wolfe. The woman who appeared to be in charge.

The pronoun *who* makes this a relative clause that can't stand alone. It acts as an appositive identifying Ms. Wolfe, and it should be joined to the main clause with a comma.

The chairman of the committee, whose term was dependent on his party's being in power, which was, according to most of the polls, unlikely to be the case after the next general election. (fragment)

This is a more complicated fragment, consisting of a subject and two subordinate clauses, each containing phrases. You don't need to identify all the elements in this fragment, but realize that a predicate for the subject of the sentence *(chair)* is missing. To make a complete sentence, add a predicate — for example, *insisted on bringing the motion to a vote.*

The last example is typical of the sophisticated fragments that might escape your notice. Keep your eye on the three key requirements: subject, predicate, complete thought. It's particularly important to check a complicated sentence you've written just to make sure it isn't a complicated fragment instead.

Acceptable Fragments

Some sentence fragments are acceptable for a specific effect. Intentional fragments can be found throughout good writing.

In dialogue, to use an obvious example, fragments are appropriately conversational.

> "Where are you going?" I asked. *"Out for a walk."*

Experienced writers also use fragments occasionally to emphasis a point, answer a question, or create a transition.

> Many of the people who drove by refused to stop and help. *But not* all *of them.*

> Why should you consider a gas-electric hybrid car rather than one with a conventional engine? *For* many reasons.

> And now the contrary view.

Before you consider using an intentional fragment, be sure this use a fragment is warranted: Could you achieve the effect you're after without it? In the first example above, a dash after movie would achieve the same effect that the fragment does.

> Many of the people who drove by refused to stop and help — but not all of them.

Placement of Modifiers

Keep related parts of a sentence together to avoid the common mistake of a misplaced modifier. If it isn't clear in a sentence exactly which term a modifier applies to, it is a misplaced modifier.

Misplaced Modifiers

Any kind of modifier can be misplaced: an adjective, an adverb, a phrase or clause acting as an adjective or adverb. If you put a modifier in a place it doesn't belong, you risk confusion, awkwardness, and even unintentional humor.

> The man *with a beard weighing 180 pounds* stood on the corner (misplaced modifier).
> The man, not the beard, weighs 180 pounds. Rewrite the sentence so that the meaning is clear.
> The man weighing 180 pounds and wearing a beard stood on the corner.

In the next sentence, it's doubtful that Anna wanted to be cremated before she died, but the placement of the adverbial phrase suggests that's just what she wanted.

> Perhaps anticipating what modern science would discover, Anna Anderson, who claimed to be the missing Anastasia, requested she be cremated *before her death* (misplaced modifier).
> Rewrite the sentence to make it clear that the phrase *before her death* modifies *requested,* not *cremated.*

Perhaps anticipating what modern science would discover, Anna Anderson, who claimed to be the missing Anastasia, *requested before her death* that she be cremated.

In the following sentence, the placement of the modifier *by Friday* leaves us with a question: Did we know by Friday, or would we call for a strike by Friday?

> We knew *by Friday* we would call for a strike (unclear modifier).
> To avoid any possible confusion, add *that.*
> We knew that by Friday we would call for a strike.
> OR We knew by Friday that we would call for a strike (depending on your meaning).

In these examples, the suggested rewritten versions are not the only possible ways to correct the problem. Revise with your own sentences when you find confusing modifiers; you may not only correct the problem but also improve the sentence by making it more concise or changing its emphasis.

Remember that the placement of even a simple modifier can change the meaning of a sentence. Watch the effect of the placement of *not* below.

> *Not all* the first-team players were available. All the first-team players were *not available.*

In the first sentence, maybe the team could still limp along through a game with first-team players and subs. In the second, the game would probably be canceled.

Misplaced Participial Phrases

Among the most common misplaced modifiers are participial phrases. Beginning writers often overlook whether the subject of the participial phrase is clear to the reader.

> Advancing across the desolate plains, the hot sun burned the pioneers. (misplaced modifier)

If not the sun but the pioneers are advancing, make this clear.

> Advancing across the desolate plains, the pioneers were burned by the hot sun.
> BETTER The hot sun burned the pioneers advancing across the desolate plains. (if you want to avoid the passive voice)

No matter how you decide to rewrite the sentence, you must make sure the modifier is modifying the right word.

In the following example, the placement of *on the hillside* between *buildings* and the participial phrase *constructed of highly flammable materials* may not cause serious confusion; because we read carefully, we probably figure out that it is the buildings that are constructed of highly flammable materials, not the hillside.

> The buildings on the hillside constructed of highly flammable materials were destroyed first. (misplaced modifier)

But improve the sentence by placing the modifier next to the word that it modifies:

> On the hillside, the buildings constructed of highly flammable materials were destroyed first.

In the next example, the question is: In the glass case, was the collector preserving the ancient specimen or only the teeth?

> The *teeth* of *the ancient specimen preserved in a glass case* were the pride of the collection. (unclear modifier)

If the answer is the teeth, then rewrite the sentence to place the participial phrase *preserved in a glass case* after the word it modifies.

> The ancient specimen's *teeth, preserved in a glass case,* were the pride of the collection.
> OR *Preserved in a glass case, the teeth* of the ancient specimen were the pride of the collection.

Dangling Modifiers

Dangling modifiers are similar to misplaced modifiers except that the modifier isn't just separated from the word it modifies; it is *missing* the word it modifies. The writer has the term being modified in mind — but not on paper.

> *Having eaten dinner,* the idea of a cheeseburger was unappealing. (dangling modifier)

The dangling participle is the most notorious of the dangling modifiers. In this example, the participial phrase *Having eaten dinner* has nothing to modify; it certainly is not modifying *idea* or *cheeseburger.* One way to correct the problem is simply to add the missing word.

> Having eaten dinner, I found the idea of a cheeseburger unappealing.

In the following example, the participial phrase *Studying the lecture notes* dangles in this sentence.

> *Studying the lecture notes,* the ecosystem became clear (dangling modifier). *Studying the lecture notes* doesn't modify *ecosystem.* Rewrite the sentence.

> The ecosystem became clear when I studied the lecture notes.

In the next sentence, the infinitive phrase *To win the election* is lacking a word to modify; it cannot modify *money.*

> *To win the election, money is* essential (dangling modifier). Rewrite the sentence to add an appropriate subject.

> To win the election, a candidate needs money.

In the following sentence, *When upset and sad* is an **elliptical clause,** meaning that a word or words have been omitted. In this clause, a subject and verb are missing; they are implied but not stated: *When (she was) upset and sad.*

> *When upset and sad, her room* was her refuge (dangling modifier).

Elliptical clauses are acceptable, but a subject must follow one or the clause will dangle.

> When upset and sad, she used her room as a refuge.

Parallel Structure

Parallelism in sentences refers to matching grammatical structures. Elements in a sentence that have the same function or express similar ideas should be grammatically parallel, or grammatically matched. Parallelism is used effectively as a rhetorical device throughout literature and in speeches, advertising copy, and popular songs.

> Roses are red/violets are blue/sugar is sweet/and so are you. —Nursery rhyme

> Reading is to the mind what exercise is to the body. —Joseph Addison

> Ask not what your country can do for you; ask what you can do for your country. —John F. Kennedy

Skillful parallelism lends balance and grace to writing. It can make a sentence memorable. But even in ordinary prose, parallelism is important for clarity and smooth sentences.

Faulty Parallelism

A failure to create grammatically parallel structures when they are appropriate is referred to as **faulty parallelism.** Notice the difference between correct parallel structure and faulty parallelism.

> What counts isn't how you look but how you behave.
> NOT What counts isn't how you look but your behavior.
> The president promises to *reform* health care, *preserve* social security, and *balance* the budget.
> NOT The president promises to *reform* health care, *preserve* social security, and *a balanced budget.*

Check for faulty parallelism in your own writing. Nouns should be parallel with nouns, participles with participles, gerunds with gerunds, infinitives with infinitives, clauses with clauses, and so on. Be particularly vigilant in the following situations.

Parallel Structure in a Series

When your sentence includes a series, make sure you have not used different grammatical structures for the items.

> The tour included *skiing* in the Alps, *swimming* in the Adriatic, and *the drive* across the Simplon Pass. (faulty parallelism)
> The tour included *skiing, swimming* in the Adriatic, and *the driving* across the pass. (faulty parallelism)
> The tour included *skiing* in the Alps, *swimming* in the Adriatic, and *driving* across the Simplon Pass. (parallel)

In the parallel version, all the elements in the series begin with gerunds: *skiing, swimming, driving*. In the nonparallel version, the final element is a noun but not a gerund.

The elements would remain parallel in the correct version even if the phrases following the gerunds were changed or omitted. The length of the items in the series does not affect the parallel structure.

It doesn't matter what grammatical structure you choose for your series as long as you remain with it consistently.

> She liked to *gather* data, *to analyze* it, and *to reach* logical conclusions (parallel).
>
> She liked *gathering* data, *analyzing* it, and *reaching* logical conclusions (parallel).

When you use words such as *to, a, an, his, her;* or *their* with items in a series, you can use the word with the first item, thus having it apply to all the items, or you can repeat it with each item. However, if you repeat it, you must do so with all the items, not just some of them.

> She liked to *gather* data, *to analyze* it, and *to reach* logical conclusions (parallel).
>
> She liked to *gather* data, *analyze* it, and *to reach* logical conclusions (not parallel).

> He liked *their* courage, stamina, and style (parallel).
>
> He liked *their* courage, *their* stamina, and *their* style (parallel).
>
> He liked *their* courage, stamina, and *their* style (not parallel).

> She saw *a* van, car, and pick-up collide (parallel).
>
> She saw *a* van, *a* car, and *a* pick-up collide (parallel).
>
> She saw *a* van, *a* car, and pick-up collide (not parallel).

Parallel Structure in Comparisons and Antithetical Constructions

When you are comparing things in a sentence, obviously parallelism will be important. Make sure that the elements you are comparing or contrasting are grammatically parallel:

> Clinton spoke more *of being governor* than *of being president*.
> NOT He spoke more of his *term as governor* than *being* president.

> The climate at the beach is damper than *the climate in the valley*.
> NOT *The climate at the each is damper* than *the valley*.

In the second sentence, *climate* is being contrasted to the *valley*. What the writer wants to contrast are the climate at the beach and the climate in the valley.

In antithetical constructions, something is true of one thing but not another. *But not* and *rather than* are used to set up these constructions, and, as with comparisons, both parts of an antithetical construction should be parallel.

> The administration approved the student's right *to drop* the class but not *to meet* with the professor.
> NOT The administration approved the student's right *to drop* the class but not *meeting* with the professor.

> The committee chose *to table* the motion rather than *to vote* on it.
> NOT The committee chose *to table* the motion rather than *voting* on it.

Parallel Structure with Correlative Conjunctions

Errors in parallel structure often occur with correlative conjunctions: *either . . . or; neither . . . nor; both . . . and; not only . . . but also; whether . . . or.* The grammatical structure following the second half of the correlative should mirror the grammatical structure following the first half.

The experts disputed <u>not only</u> *the newspaper article* <u>but also</u> *the university's official statement.* (parallel: phrase with phrase).

The experts disputed <u>not only</u> *the newspaper article* <u>but also</u> *they disputed the university's official statement.* (faulty parallelism: phrase with clause).

<u>Either</u> I *like the job* or I *don't like it* (parallel: clause matched with clause).

<u>Either</u> I *like the job* or I *don't* (parallel: clause matched with clause).

<u>Either</u> I *like the job* or *not* (faulty parallelism: clause matched with adverb).

I have <u>neither</u> *the patience to complete it* nor *the desire to complete it* (parallel: noun phrase with noun phrase).

I have <u>neither</u> *the patience to complete it* nor *do I desire to complete it* (faulty parallelism: phrase matched with clause).

You can improve this sentence even more:

I have <u>neither</u> *the patience* nor *the desire* to complete it.

Patience and *desire* are both nouns, and the phrase *to complete it* can serve both of them.

Be sure that any element you want to repeat appears *after* the first half of the correlative conjunction. Look at the position of *as* in the following examples. In the second sentence, *as* appears before *either* and is repeated after *or,* which makes the construction not parallel.

They acted *either as* individual citizens *or as* members of the committee.

NOT They acted *as either* individual citizens *or as* members of the committee.

In the following example, the last sentence, *we expected* appears *before* the first half of the correlative conjunction and should not be repeated after the second half.

We expected <u>not only</u> to be late <u>but also</u> to be exhausted.

OR *We expected to be* <u>not only</u> late <u>but also</u> exhausted (better).

BUT NOT *We expected* <u>not only</u> to be late <u>but also</u> we *expected* to be exhausted.

Parallel Structure with verbs

When you have more than one verb in a sentence, be sure to make the verbs parallel by not shifting tenses unnecessarily. Also, don't shift from an active to a passive verb.

Kate *prepared* the speech on the plane and *delivered* it at the conference (parallel: both verbs are active).

Kate *prepared* the speech on the plane, and it *was delivered* by her at the conference (faulty parallelism: active and passive verb).

Sometimes sentences use a single verb form with two helping verbs. Look at the following example.

We *can,* and I promise we will, *ensure* that this does not occur (correct).

This sentence is correct because both *can* and *will* are correct with the base verb *ensure*. But look at this example.

The governor has in the past and will in the future *continue to support* the measure (incorrect).

To support belongs with *will continue,* but not with *has*. If you read the sentence without *and will in the future continue,* you will see this immediately: *Governor has in the past to support the measure*. Rewrite the sentence to include a participial form for *has*.

The governor *has* in the past *supported,* and will in the future *continue to support,* the measure.

OR Just as Robert *has supported* this measure in the past, he will *continue to support* it in the future.

Combining Sentences

When writing paragraphs, vary your sentences in type and length. Either a series of choppy sentences or a string of long sentences can bore or frustrate a reader. Experiment too with different word order within your sentences.

Writers, particularly inexperienced ones, sometimes create a series of short sentences that sound choppy and lack good connections. If you can vary the length and complexity of your sentences, you will increase your reader's interest in your ideas.

Combining Simple Sentences

If you have written a series of simple sentences, try alternate methods of combining them to vary the pacing of the paragraph. Look at the following example:

> Old-growth forests are disappearing. Citizens should take action. For example, wood substitutes are becoming more available. People can ask their contractors to use these substitutes.

These simple sentences can be combined to make compound and complex sentences.

> Old-growth forests are disappearing, and citizens should take action. For example, people can ask their contractors to use wood substitutes, which are becoming more available.

Be sure when you combine simple sentences that you let meaning be your guide. For example, use a complex sentence if you want to make one idea subordinate to another and a compound sentence if you want to join ideas of equal weight. In the example above, the first two clauses are of equal weight: the forests are disappearing, and people should do something about it. In the second sentence, the main idea is that people should ask their contractors to use wood substitutes; the subordinate point is that these substitutes are becoming more available.

Combining Sentences using Phrases

You can combine short sentences by using phrases as well as clauses. Look at the following example.

> Scientists first identify the defective gene. Then they can create a screening test. Physicians can use this screening test to diagnose the condition early.
>
> BETTER After identifying the defective gene, scientists can develop a screening test to help physicians diagnose the condition early.

Notice that in the second version the participial phrase *After identifying the defective gene* and the infinitive phrase *to help physicians diagnose the condition early* turn three choppy sentences into one smooth one.

Varying Word Order in Sentences

Instead of beginning every sentence with the simple subject, try beginning with a modifier, an appositive, or the main verb. You can also try delaying completion of your main statement or interrupting sentences with parenthetical elements. Look at the following examples.

Begin with a single-word modifier.

> *Suddenly* the wind rushed into the room.
>
> INSTEAD OF The wind *suddenly* rushed into the room.

Begin with a modifying phrase or clause.

> *Unregulated and easily accessible,* the Internet presents dangers as well as opportunities.
>
> INSTEAD OF The Internet, *unregulated and easily accessible,* presents dangers as well as opportunities.

In front of an audience, she was a star.

INSTEAD OF She was a star *in front of an audience.*

When the manager told me what the apartment cost, I decided living at home with Mom and Dad wasn't so bad.

INSTEAD OF I decided living at home with Mom and Dad wasn't so bad *when the manager told me what the apartment cost.*

Begin with an appositive.

A frequently misdiagnosed condition, iron overload can lead to serious diseases.

INSTEAD OF Iron overload, *a frequently misdiagnosed condition,* can lead to serious diseases.

Put the verb before the subject.

Directly in front of the building *stood a statue.*

INSTEAD OF *A statue stood* directly in front of the building.

Greater than the novel's shortcomings *are* its *strengths.*

INSTEAD OF *The novel's strengths* are greater than its shortcomings.

Delay completing your main statement.

We saw the ballot measure, so important to the students, the faculty, and indeed everyone in the community, *lose by a one-percent margin.*

INSTEAD OF *We saw the ballot measure lose by a one-percent margin* even though it was so important to the students, the faculty, and indeed everyone in the community.

Insert an interruption — a surprise element — in a sentence; use parentheses or dashes.

My home town — it is closer to being a junction than a town — recently acquired its first traffic light.

Never sacrifice meaning or clarity for variety, however. And remember that any technique you use for sentence variety will be self-defeating if you use it too often in a short piece of writing.

Periods, Question Marks, and Exclamation Points

As you write, you use periods, question marks, or exclamation points to end your sentences. Periods are used to complete most sentences. Question marks end sentences that ask questions. Exclamation marks indicate statements of strong emphasis or emotion either in a command, an interjection, or a strongly worded sentence. Exclamation points, like dashes and parentheses, should be used sparingly for the greatest impact. Basic rules exist for using these punctuation marks correctly.

Uses of the Period

Use **periods** to end complete sentences that are statements, commands and requests, or mild exclamations.

On the east coast of the United States, retirees may spend winters in Florida and summers on Cape Cod.

Please open your books to the third chapter.

How odd it was to see clouds when the forecast had been for sunshine.

Don't use periods at the end of phrases or dependent clauses. If you do, you create sentence fragments.

When he visits Seattle, Mr. Kleiman expects rain.

NOT *When he visits Seattle.* Mr. Kleiman expects rain.

Abbreviations

Most common abbreviations end in a period: *Mr., Mrs., a.m., etc., Tues., Sept.* But other abbreviations are written without a period, and contemporary usages tends in that direction. In general, you can omit periods for abbreviations written in capital letters *(FBI, IBM, NBC)* if the abbreviation doesn't appear to spell out another word. For example, USA is acceptable, but *MA.* should include periods, because it could be mistaken for a capitalization of the slang word *ma.* Most abbreviations that end in a lowercase letter should still be written with periods: *i.e., Dr., yr., mo.* Exceptions to this rule include *mph, rpm,* and metric measurement abbreviations such as *ml, cm, gm.* Do not use periods with Zip code abbreviations for states: *AL, AZ, CA, NY, WY,* and so on. If you are uncertain about using periods with a particular abbreviation, check a dictionary or style guide.

Periods with Quotation Marks

Always keep periods inside quotation marks, whether or not they are part of the quotation

> The technician said, "a replacement part will be shipped on Monday."
>
> The technophobe insisted on referring to every part of the machine as "*a gidget*."

In the first sentence, the period is part of the quoted sentence. In the second sentence the phrase *"a gidget"* does not end in a period, but the period for the complete sentence still correctly appears within the quotation marks.

Punctuation with Abbreviations

If a sentence ends with an abbreviation, use only one period.

> He introduced his friend as Harold *Ruiz, MD.*
>
> She told her mother, "I won't be satisfied until I earn my *Ph.D.*"

Use of the Question Mark

Obviously, the role of the **question mark** is to end a question. The question mark immediately follows the question, even when one question interrupts or comes after a statement.

> *Who knows?*
>
> No doubt she thought she was doing the right thing, but can't *we agree she was wrong?*

An exception to this rule occurs when the question is followed by a phrase or clause that modifies it. Then, put the question mark at the end of the statement.

> How could the mother be so certain of the driver's identity, *considering the shock she* must *have* felt at *seeing her own daughter lying in the road?*

Courtesy Questions

If a question is asked as a polite request or as a courtesy, you can use either a question mark or a period. Although the difference in tone is slight, the period makes the question more routine and general, the question mark more directed and personal.

Would you please send me your catalog of printers. Would you please send me your catalog of printers?

Commas and Periods with Question Marks

After a question mark, don't use a period or comma, even if your sentence would normally call for one.

> The audience shouted "yes" when the speaker asked "is the time for action now?"
>
> NOT The audience shouted "yes" when the speaker asked "is the time for action now?" .

"Do you want to leave?" Patty asked.

NOT "Do you want to leave?", Patty asked.

Questions that end with abbreviations are an exception.

Was it at precisely 4 *a.m.*?

Question Marks with Quotation Marks

If the material being quoted is a question, put the question mark within the quotation marks.

"Do you think I'll get the job?" Susannah asked.

David looked around and said, "Who can speak for the opposing points of view?"

If the quotation is not a question, put the question mark outside the quotation marks. If the quoted material would normally end with a period, drop the period.

Who was it that said, "All that glitters is not gold"?

NOT *Who was it that said, "All* that glitters is not gold."?

Indirect Questions

When a question is being reported rather than directly asked, it ends with a period rather than a question mark. Compare the following sentences.

Ethan asked, "What made the sky so brilliant tonight?" (direct question)

Ethan asked what made the sky so brilliant tonight (indirect question).

We asked if the speaker would entertain questions after the talk (indirect question).

Would the speaker entertain questions after the talk? (direct question)

Use of the Exclamation Point

Exclamation points follow interjections and other expressions of strong feeling. They may also be used to lend force to a command.

What a mess! The lights! The music! The dazzling costumes! My eyes and ears couldn't get enough of the spectacle. Sit down and shut your mouth! Now!

An exclamation point is particularly useful if you're writing dialogue because it shows the feeling behind a statement.

Exclamation Points with Quotation Marks

If the material being quoted is an exclamation, put the exclamation mark within the quotation marks.

"I hate you!" she screamed.

"What rubbish!" he said, leaving the room.

If an exclamation includes a quotation that is not an exclamation, put the mark outside the quotation marks.

For the last time, *stop calling me your "baby doll"!*

Exclamation Points with Commas and Periods

After an exclamation point, omit a comma or a period.

"We prevailed!" he exulted.

NOT "We prevailed!," he exulted.

What a terrible way to end our trip!

NOT What a terrible way to end our trip!.

Problems with Exclamation Points

In formal writing, use exclamation points infrequently. Overuse of exclamation points not only dulls their effect, but also characterizes an immature style.

The film's last scene poignantly showed that the battle had been for nothing, that he had lost his country and his dream forever.

NOT The film's last scene was so *poignant! A viewer* knew he'd lost his country. His dream was dead!

Commas, Semicolons, and Colons

Commas add pacing to your sentences and make them clearer. Careless writers either neglect to use or overuse commas, which complicates their sentences or obscures their meaning. The rules for commas are simple and easy to learn.

The semicolon and colon are often confused and sometimes overused. The main rule for these punctuation marks is to use them sparingly. Semicolons join independent clauses and items in a series. Colons are used to introduce a list, a quote, or formal statement, and they are used to introduce a restatement or explanation. Once you master the rules for effective punctuation, your writing will improve.

Uses of the Comma

Commas are always used to join independent clauses, after introductory clauses and phrases, to set off interruptions within the sentence, with nonrestrictive phrases and clauses, and between items or modifiers in a series. There are some special situations in which commas should also be used. For example, use commas with quotations, dates, addresses, locations, and numbers with four or more digits. Commas should never be used around restrictive clauses or to separate a subject and verb, or a verb and its direct object.

The best way to approach commas is, first, to recognize that they signal a pause, and, second, to know which rules can be bent without jarring or misleading your reader and which ones cannot. The comma is the most frequently used internal punctuation in sentences, and people have more questions about it than about any other punctuation mark. Editors have varied opinions about when a comma is needed. You're likely to read one book in which commas abound and another in which they are scarce. Circumstances may change depending on the context or the writing. Generally, the trend has been towards lighter punctuation, but careful writers follow the traditional rules for uses of the comma.

Sometimes a comma is absolutely necessary to ensure the meaning of a sentence, as in the following examples.

Because I wanted to *help, Dr. Hodges,* I pulled the car over to the side of the road.

Because I wanted to *help Dr. Hodges,* I pulled the car over to the side of the road.

In the first sentence, the pair of commas indicates that Dr. Hodges is being addressed. In the second sentence, Dr. Hodges is the object of the help.

Do not omit a comma if it will lead your reader to a momentary misunderstanding. Look at the example below.

When we are cooking, children cannot come into the kitchen.

NOT *When we are cooking children* cannot come into the kitchen.

Without a comma, the reader may suspect you of cannibalism.

Joining Independent Clauses

When you join independent clauses with a coordinating conjunction, precede the conjunction with a comma.

Lenin never answered these charges, *but* soon afterward he was compelled to give up part of the money.

The novel lacks fully developed characters, *and* the plot is filled with unlikely coincidences.

If you are using an informal style, when the independent clauses are short and closely related, you may use a comma or omit it, depending on whether or not you want to indicate a pause.

It was an admirable *scheme and* it would work.

OR It was an admirable *scheme, and* it would work.

When you use a comma between independent clauses, it *must* be accompanied by one of the coordinating conjunctions. If it isn't, you create a run-on sentence.

It had been a tumultuous year that had taken everybody by *surprise, and* it left the revolutionaries worse off than they had been before.

NOT It had been a tumultuous year that had taken everybody by *surprise, it* left the revolutionaries worse off than they had been before.

After Introductory Clauses

Use a comma after an introductory adverbial clause. With a lengthy clause, the comma is essential.

After the boxer entered the ring, the audience stomped and cheered.

If you receive a manuscript inappropriate for your publication, acknowledge it by explaining to the correspondent why the material won't see print.

After Introductory Phrases

Unlike a clause, a phrase is a group of words without a subject and a predicate. If an introductory phrase is more than a few words, it's a good idea to follow it with a comma. And always use a comma if there is any possibility of misunderstanding a sentence without one.

By taking the initiative to seek out story leads, a reporter will make a good impression on the editor.

At the beginning of the visiting professor's lecture, most of the students were wide awake.

Unlike so many performances of the symphony, this one was spirited and lively.

Before eating, Jack always runs on the beach.

Note that the introductory phrase in the last example, although short, would lead to a momentary misunderstanding if the comma were omitted.

A participial phrase at the beginning of a sentence is *always* followed by a comma.

Smiling and shaking hands, the senator worked her way through the crowd.

Do not confuse a participial phrase with a gerund phrase, however. A gerund phrase that begins a sentence would not be followed by a comma. Compare the following two sentences.

Thinking of the consequences, she agreed not to release the memo to the press (introductory participial phrase, modifying *she:* use a comma).

Thinking of *the consequences* caused her to worry (gerund phrase, functioning as the subject of the sentence: do *not* use a comma).

In informal contexts, use of a comma after most short introductory phrases is optional.

> *Later that day* Jack and Linda drove to the ocean. *After the main course I* was too full for dessert. *For some unknown reason* the car wouldn't start.

To Set Off Interrupting Elements

Some phrases, clauses, and terms interrupt the flow of a sentence and should be enclosed in commas. Examples of these interrupters are conjunctive adverbs, transitional phrases, and names in direct address.

Conjunctive adverbs and transitional phrases — *such as consequently, as a matter of fact, of course, therefore, on the other hand, for example, however, to tell the truth, moreover* — are usually followed by commas when they begin sentences.

> *For example, you* shouldn't use the solution on soft surfaces. *Therefore,* he refused to go with us.

When they interrupt a sentence, they are usually enclosed in commas.

> As the project moves along, of course, you will be given greater independence.
> One who is strong at research, for example, might be assigned to search the Web.

Know what your intention is. If you want the reader to pause, use the commas. If you don't, omit them. Look at the following two examples.

> The committee, therefore, agreed to hear the students.
> The committee therefore agreed to hear the students.

Both sentences are correct. In the second sentence the expression would be read as part of the flow of the sentence, not as an interrupter.

A name or expression used in direct address, in a written speech for example, is always followed by a comma, or enclosed in commas when it interrupts the sentence.

Sometimes a reader or readers are addressed directly by a text, and when this occurs, use commas.

> Friends, I am here to ask for your support.
> I insist, Senator McCarthy, that my readers will learn the truth about your charges.

Other interrupters may also require commas. Check your sentence for elements outside the main flow of the sentence and enclose them in commas.

> It is too early, I believe, to call for a pizza delivery.
> The tour, we were told, was organized by archeologists.

Dashes and parentheses can also be used to set off some kinds of interrupting elements, but commas are better when you want to draw less attention to an interruption.

With Restrictive and Nonrestrictive Elements

Look at the following two sentences. In the first sentence, *who* arrived yesterday is a restrictive clause, that is, one that restricts, limits, or defines the subject of the sentence. In the second sentence, the same clause is nonrestrictive, that is, it doesn't restrict or narrow the meaning but instead adds information. In the simplest terms, a restrictive element is essential to the reader's understanding; a nonrestrictive element is not.

> The women who arrived yesterday toured the site this afternoon.
> The women, *who* arrived yesterday, toured the site this afternoon.

In the first sentence, *who* arrived yesterday defines exactly which women are the subject of the sentence, separating them from all other women. In the second sentence, however, the information *who* arrived yesterday is not necessary to the sentence. It does not separate the women from all other women. The clause adds information, but the information isn't essential to our knowing which women are being discussed. As writer, you must decide which kind of information you intend to give.

Commas make all the difference in meaning here. Restrictive (or essential) elements shouldn't be enclosed in commas, while nonrestrictive (or nonessential) elements should be. Review the following sentences.

> The workers *who went on strike* were replaced (restrictive).
>
> The workers, *who went on strike,* were replaced (nonrestrictive).

In the first sentence, only some workers were replaced. The absence of commas restricts the subject to only those workers who went on strike. In the second sentence, all the workers were replaced. The information that they went on strike is not essential; it doesn't define exactly which workers were replaced.

In the following sentence, the phrase *who are over* fifty is essential in limiting the subject *workers* and therefore should not be enclosed in commas. The second sentence means that all workers are over fifty, which is absurd.

> Workers *who are over* fifty have difficulty finding a new job.
>
> NOT Workers, *who are over* fifty, have difficulty finding a new job.

Whether to use commas around modifying elements is based entirely on whether the element is restrictive (essential or limiting) or nonrestrictive (added information).

> My brother, *who is thirteen,* plays video games more than he reads (added information).
>
> The photographer *who took the pictures is* being sued for invasion of privacy (essential).
>
> Cats, *more independent than dogs,* are good pets for people who work all day (added information).
>
> Cats *who are fussy eaters* are a trial to their owners (essential).
>
> My brother, *swimming in the ocean,* saw a shark (added information).
>
> People *swimming in the ocean* should watch for sharks (essential).

With Appositives

Appositives are words that restate or identify a noun or pronoun. When appositives are nonrestrictive, they are enclosed in commas.

> Kublai Khan, *grandson of Genghis,* was the first Mongol emperor of all China.
>
> Brent Easton Ellis, *author of "Bright Lights, Big City,"* is well known for writing explicit descriptions of bizarre experiences.
>
> Blogs, diary-like real-time Web sites, contribute to the political dialogue.

Sometimes, however, an appositive is essential because it limits the subject. It must *not,* therefore, be enclosed in commas. Look at the following examples.

> Shakespeare's play *Hamlet* was probably written about 1600. NOT Shakespeare's play, *Hamlet,* was probably written about 1600.

In this example, if you enclose *Hamlet* in commas, you suggest that Shakespeare wrote only one play. Obviously, the appositive *Hamlet* is restrictive; it limits the subject *play.*

Between Items in a Series

Use commas to separate items in a series. Although some editors feel that it is acceptable to omit the final comma in a series — journalists and business writers sometimes do — it usually should be included.

He bought a dishwasher, microwave, refrigerator, and washer from the outlet.

Her play is filled with coincidences, false anticipations, and nonresponsive dialogue.

Omitting a final comma may create ambiguity. Because writing should be consistent throughout a piece of writing, consistently use the final comma and avoid possible problems.

Hair, clothing and jewelry all send messages to a prospective employer (acceptable).

Hair, clothing, and jewelry all send messages to a prospective employer (better).

She told us about the *subway, the elevators at Bloomingdale's and the Metropolitan Museum of Art* (ambiguous: the elevators at both Bloomingdale's and the Metropolitan Museum or just at Bloomingdale's?).

She told us about the subway, *the elevators at Bloomingdale's, and the Metropolitan Museum of Art* (better).

Don't use commas if all items in a series are joined by *and* or *or.*

He asked to see *Martha and Helen and Eileen.*

NOT He asked to see *Martha, and Helen, and Eileen.*

Between Modifiers in a Series

Modifiers in a series are usually separated with commas. But don't put a comma between the final modifier and the word it modifies.

It was a dark, gloomy, *forbidding house.* NOT It was a dark, gloomy, *forbidding,* house. In this example, all three modifiers — dark, gloomy, and *forbidding* — modify *house.*

Sometimes, however, what seems to be a modifier is actually part of the element being modified. Look at the following examples.

Buckingham is a tall, *good-looking, speedy* horse.

Speedy horse, not just horse, is the element being modified. Therefore, don't use a comma after *speedy.*

They bought a beautiful, spacious summer *home.*

Summer *home, not* just *home,* is being modified. Don't use a comma after spacious.

To test whether you should use a comma before the last adjective in a series, see if it makes sense to reverse the order of the adjectives. If you can reverse them without changing the meaning or eliminating sense, then use commas between them. If you can't, don't.

It was a dark, gloomy, *forbidding house.*

It was a *forbidding,* dark, gloomy house (no change in meaning).

The order of the adjectives can change; therefore, use commas between them.

They bought a *beautiful, spacious summer* home.

They bought a summer, *beautiful, spacious* home (does not make sense). By changing the order of the adjectives, the sentence becomes nonsensical. Therefore, you would not use a comma between spacious and summer.

Commas with Quotation Marks

Commas go inside quotation marks, whether or not they are part of the quotation.

Tom's line "Blow out your candles, Laura — and so good-bye," ends the play.

"I can't believe you ate the entire *watermelon,*" she said.

Problems with Commas

A common mistake people make with commas is putting them where they don't belong.

Don't use commas around restrictive elements.

> The novel *The Davinci Code* quickly became a best seller.
> NOT The novel, *The Davinci Code,* quickly became a best seller.

Don't separate subject from verb with a comma.

> The girl *in the window is* not my sister.
> NOT The girl *in the window, is* not my sister.

Don't separate a verb and a direct object or complement with a comma.

> *I saw immediately the mistake I* had made.
> NOT *I saw immediately, the mistake I* had made.

When your sentence includes paired elements — for example, with correlative conjunctions — don't use a comma to separate them.

> I wanted *either a trip to Thailand or a new Mercedes.*
> NOT I wanted *either a trip to Thailand, or a new Mercedes.*

In other situations when you are unsure about using a comma, don't add one out of insecurity. Check grammar handbook, and if the answer isn't there, count on your own ear to tell you when a pause is important.

Uses of the Semicolon

Some writers often mistakenly use semicolons to connect fragments or sentences that really should have been two separate sentences. Use the **semicolon** to connect two independent clauses when their meanings are closely related, or use it to connect a series of items if the items themselves are long or contain commas.

Joining Independent Clauses

A semicolon is much like a period, but whereas a period keeps two independent clauses apart and turns them into separate sentences, a semicolon joins them to show a close connection. Compare the following examples.

> I helped the committee all I could. I even searched the back issues of the paper to find evidence.
> I helped the committee all I could; I even searched the back issues of the paper to find evidence.
> I helped the committee all I *could, and I* even searched the back issues of the paper to find evidence.

All three examples are correct. The semicolon emphasizes a close relationship between the two independent clauses.

Often, you'll find a conjunctive adverb or transitional phrase in the clause following a semicolon, because those words point out the relationship between the clauses.

> The results of the inquiry were *unclear; however,* the head of the project resigned.
> Some people continued to support us; others, *on the other hand,* refused to speak to us.

Indicators like these aren't required. But don't use a semicolon unless you want to emphasize the close connection between clauses.

> It was time to vote; we were sick of the endless wrangling. (Yes, use the semicolon.)
> It was time to vote; the vice-chair brought in the brown-bag lunches and put them on the table. (No, don't use the semicolon, unless the vote concerns lunch.)

You may follow a semicolon that divides independent clauses with one of the seven coordinating conjunctions, although it is not necessary to do so as it is when you separate independent clauses with a comma.

> That night the timber wolf appeared to *revive; but* when we woke in the morning, full of hope that we had saved it, we were saddened to find its body at the edge of the clearing.

It would be perfectly correct to use a comma before *but* in this example; the semicolon, however, creates a stronger pause. Also, because there are already two commas in the second clause, a semicolon is desirable, because it indicates the main break in the sentence.

Between Items in a Series

In a series, use a semicolon between items if the items are particularly long, or if they themselves contain commas.

> The planning committee included David H. Takahashi, president of the Kiwanis *Club;* Leroy Carter, head of the local merchants group; Maria Gilbert, editor of the local *paper,* and Ivy Quinn, Spanish department chair at the college.

> Chancellor Stone's report states that the college, plagued by financial worries, cannot fulfill these *needs;* that the community response, while positive, has not resulted in substantial *donations;* and that charitable organizations, service clubs, and private donors have been overwhelmed with similar requests.

Notice that when semicolons are used in series, the series' items do not have to be independent clauses.

Semicolons with Quotation Marks

Follow this rule when dealing with quotation marks: always place semicolons outside the quotation mark.

> He asked me to be quiet and mind my *"atrocious manners"; I* told him I'd say what I pleased.

> Theologians categorize superstitions as "vain observances, idolatry, divination, and improper worship"; all are intended to help determine the future.

Problems with Semicolons

Except when used to separate items in a series, a semicolon must be followed by an independent clause or you create a sentence fragment.

> I expected to win the debate; *even if my opponent had more experience* (sentence fragment).

> I had studied the subject thoroughly; *and researched even the minor point.* (sentence fragment).

These sentences could be corrected either by changing punctuation or by making the second clause independent.

> I expected to win the *debate, even* if my opponent had more experience.

> I had studied the subject *thoroughly; I* had researched even the minor points.

Uses of the Colon

A **colon** is used to introduce a list. It can be a formal introduction using *as follows,* or less formal.

> The ceremony to honor Dr. Mills included *everything:* a moving introduction, a recitation of her achievements, a series of testimonials, and a stirring forecast of her future in the new position.

> The questions were as *follows:* Where did you last work? For how long? What was your job title? What were your primary achievements?

As follows and *following* are clear indications that a colon is appropriate, but as the first example shows, these formal introductory elements aren't required. Also, use a lowercase letter after the colon unless your list is made up of complete statements, as in the second example.

Introducing a Quotation or Formal Statement

The colon is used to introduce a quotation or formal statement. An independent clause must precede the colon. The statement following the colon begins with a capital letter.

> *Remember this:* A first draft of a piece of writing is only preliminary and it will need to undergo several revision cycles.

> *Joan Didion made the following observation:* "The impulse to write things down is a peculiarly compulsive one, inexplicable to those who do not share it."

Introducing a Restatement or Explanation

A colon may be used between two independent clauses when the second clause explains or restates the first clause.

> The program was an unqualified success: hundreds of people attended.

> These shoes are the best: they are durable, inexpensive, and stylish.

Notice that when the colon is used in this way, it may be followed by a lowercase letter, just as a semicolon would be.

To test whether you should use a semicolon or a colon between clauses, ask yourself whether you could insert the phrase *that is* after the mark. If you can, use a colon; if you can't, use a semicolon.

> These shoes are the best: *that is,* they are durable, inexpensive, and stylish.

A colon is appropriate in the previous example. The phrase can be inserted here. The second clause explains the first clause. The phrase *that is* doesn't work in the next sentence. A semicolon is appropriate.

> He struggled for years; success finally arrived.

> NOT He struggled for years; *that is,* success finally arrived.

Colons with Quotation Marks

Follow this rule when using quotes in a sentence: always place colons outside quotation marks.

> The article was called "Further Thoughts on Steroids and Sports": it was a reaction to Senate hearings on the subject.

> This statement is from "Dear Abby": "If your friend is too picky, pick another friend."

Problems with Colons

Don't use a colon to separate sentence elements that belong together, such as an action verb from its objects or a linking verb from its complements.

> The university sent us *catalogues,* maps, housing applications, and transportation information.

> NOT The university sent us: *catalogues,* maps, housing applications, and transportation information.

> The four things I want are success in business, a happy marriage, creative fulfillment, and peace of mind.

> NOT The four things I want are: success in business, a happy marriage, creative fulfillment, and peace of mind.

Dashes, Parentheses, and Quotation Marks

Dashes and parentheses are interruptions within the sentence that can provide extra information. In many cases they may be necessary and valuable additions. Brackets are used to add a word or phrase of your own to a quotation. An ellipsis is used to indicate a word or phrase has been omitted from a quotation.

Writers are sometimes tempted to overuse dashes and parentheses. Your writing should be direct and well organized, which means you will use them sparingly.

Uses of the Dash

Think of the **dash** as indicating an interruption you want to draw attention to. Other punctuation marks — commas and parentheses — serve similar purposes. Commas are more neutral, and parentheses are usually used with information that is clearly incidental.

Introducing a List, Restatement, or Explanation

Like a colon, a dash can be used to introduce a list or to restate/explain. Begin the clause after the dash with a lowercase letter.

The dash introduces a list.

> The exhibition featured surrealist artists — *Dali, Magritte and Chirico.*

The dash introduces a restatement and explanation.

> She was extraordinarily *tall — the tallest woman I'd ever seen — and took a seat at the counter.*

The dash adds explanation.

> The investigator relentlessly questioned the *suspect — he was* determined to get *him* to *respond.*

Although the colon and dash are frequently interchangeable in this function, the dash is less formal.

Dashes with Appositive that Contain Commas

When an appositive contains commas, dashes help readers see the importance of the pauses.

> In some languages — French, the Nigerian language Edo, English — every clause in which a verb has a tense must have an overt subject.

Uses of Parentheses

Parentheses are a pair of signs ( ) helpful in setting off text. You use parentheses in specific situations.

Setting off Incidental Information

Parentheses are used to enclose incidental information, such as a passing comment, a minor example or addition, or a brief explanation. As with the dash, the decision to use parentheses is a judgment. Sometimes commas or dashes might be a better choice.

> Some of the local store owners (*Mr.* Kwan *and Ms. Lawson,* for example) insisted that the street be widened.
> NOT AS EFFECTIVE Some of the local store owners, *Mr. Kwan and Ms. Lawson,* for example — insisted that the street be widened.

The sentence's emphasis is on widening the street, so the names of the store owners can be deemphasized by placing them in parentheses.

> Roger Worthington (a poorly drawn character in *the novel*) reveals the secret in the last chapter.
> BETTER Roger Worthington, a poorly *drawn character in the novel,* reveals the secret in the last chapter.

Because the sentence appears to come from a review, including the information about the character without parentheses is stronger.

Other Punctuation Marks with Parentheses

Don't put any punctuation mark before parentheses, and put a comma after the closing parenthesis only if your sentence would call for the comma anyway.

> Use a pointed stick (a *pencil with the lead point broken off* works *well)* or a similar tool.

No comma appears before or after the parentheses. If you were to remove the parenthetical remark, the remaining sentence would not need a comma: *Use* a pointed *stick or* a similar tool.

> Banging the wall and screaming (*unrestrained by* his *parents,* I might add), Sam was acting like a brat.

In the preceding sentence, no comma appears before the parentheses. A comma follows the parentheses because if you were to remove the parenthetical comment, the remaining sentence would require a comma: *Bang*ing *the wall* and screaming, Sam was acting *like* a brat.

Miscellaneous Uses of Parentheses

Sometime parentheses are used in special situations. For example, use parentheses to enclose a date or a citation.

> Sir William Walton (1902–1983) composed the oratorio *Belshazzar's Feast.*

In some scientific, business, or legal writing, parentheses may be used to restate a number. Be sure this use is justified. In most prose, it is not; it creates an inappropriately official tone.

> The bill is due and payable in *thirty (30)* days (acceptable).

> My grandfather knew my grandmother for sixty (60) years (not appropriate).

Problems with Parentheses

Like dashes, parentheses are punctuation marks with high visibility, so don't overuse them. If you find yourself putting much information in parentheses, check the way you have organized your material. Your writing should be straight-forward, not filled with asides or passing comments.

Uses of Quotation Marks

Quotation marks are used to indicate the beginning and end of a quote. They tell the reader when you've used written material from other sources or direct speech.

Direct Quotations

Direct quotation occurs when you report dialogue or when you use an item verbatim from another text. Use quotation marks at the beginning and end of a direct quotation.

> *"Nanette is my best friend,"* Tanya told Louise.

When you are incorporating a short quotation into a paper, use quotation marks and quote the material exactly.

> As film critic Pauline Kael writes, *"At his greatest, Jean Renoir expresses the beauty in our common humanity — the desires and hopes, the absurdities and follies, that we all, to one degree or another, share."*

In a double-spaced paper, indent and single space quotations longer than five typed lines.

Quotations within Quotations

Use single quotation marks within double ones to indicate a quotation within a quotation.

> "My father began by saying, 'I refuse to listen to any excuses,'" he told the psychiatrist.

If you are indenting and single spacing a quoted passage, however, use the same marks that appear in the passage. In the following example, the writer is quoting a passage by the historian of philosophy W. T. Jones who in turn is quoting George Berkeley.

> W. T. Jones describes Berkeley's problem with abstract ideas: The trouble, Berkeley believed, stems from our tendency to think in words instead of about things the words signify. *"We need only to draw the curtain of words, to behold the fairest tree of knowledge, whose fruit is excellent, and within the reach or our hand."* Berkeley therefore devoted the opening ages of his "Principles" to the study of the nature and abuse of language.

A Summary of the Rules

One of the biggest problems with quotation marks is knowing whether another mark, such as a period or comma, goes inside or outside the quotation marks. Following is a summary of the correct placement of punctuation with quotation marks:

- Put periods and commas inside quotation marks, whether or not they are part of the quotation.
- Put question marks, exclamation points, and dashes inside quotation marks if they are part of the quotation, outside the quotation marks if they are not.
- Put colons and semicolons outside quotation marks.

For examples, look under the individual punctuation marks covered in this section.

Problems with Quotation Marks

Aside from understanding how to use other punctuation marks with quotation marks, you shouldn't have much difficulty — if you keep one thing in mind. Reserve quotation marks for direct quotations and for the other uses indicated above. Don't use quotation marks around the title of your paper. Don't use them to signal — and somehow justify — the use of clichés or slang expressions. Don't use them to indicate that you are being clever or cute. In fact, don't use them to call attention to your tone at all. A piece of writing peppered with questionable quotation marks indicates an amateurish style.

Brackets and Ellipsis

Brackets and ellipsis are specialized marks used with quotations. They appear most frequently in writing which is based on research sources of information. However, they sometimes occur in other contexts. When writing a paper based on research, consult a handbook of the academic or professional discipline you are writing for to learn the appropriate format.

Using Brackets

Brackets indicate a word or phrase has been added to or inserted in a direct quotation for purposes of explanation or additional information.

After the Superior Court ruling, the attorney said "Our work in addressing the First Amendment issue in this case [on appeal] begins now." The words *on appeal* explain when the work will occur.

> According to *American Educator,* the three subtypes of Attention Deficit Hyperactivity Disorder are predominantly hyperactive, predominantly inattentive, and combined [each of which produces different behavioral problems]. The material in brackets provides added information.

Using an Ellipsis

An **ellipsis** indicates an omission from a quotation. This mark consists of spaced periods. A three-period ellipsis indicates that you are omitting something from a sentence that continues after the ellipsis.

> Arnold Rampersad writes of Langston Hughes that he "composed with relative casualness, unlike other major black points of his day. . . with their highly wrought stanzas."

The phrase *such as Countee Cullen and Claude McKay* has been omitted from the quotation.

Use four periods if you are omitting the last part of a quoted sentence that ends in a period but what remains is still a complete thought. The first period comes immediately after the sentence and has no space before it. It functions as a period. The following three periods are spaced and indicate that material has been omitted. If the original sentence ended in a question mark or exclamation point, substitute that mark for the first dot.

> Rampersad adds, *"He seemed to prefer, as Whitman and Sandburg had preferred, to write lines that captured the cadences of common American speech. . . ."*

The phrase "with his ear always especially attuned to the variety if black American language," which ended the sentence, has been omitted from this quotation.

Compound Words and Wordiness

Effective writing requires more than just correct vocabulary. You must also spell words correctly. Most word-processing software has a spelling correction feature, but you also need a good dictionary to reduce spelling mistakes and find word definitions. Spelling checkers do not distinguish homonyms (*too/to*); nor do they determine if the word is the one you intended or a similar sounding words (*petal* for *peddle*).

Be aware of the impact of the words you choose. Words have specific meanings and should not be repeated without a good reason. Unnecessary or repeated words and phrases make writing seem cluttered. You can avoid wordiness by using the active voice, which is more direct than the passive voice. Proper spelling and careful word choice are essential ingredients for good writing.

Spelling of Compound Words

Compound words are a spelling problem, not a vocabulary problem; to hyphenate or not to hyphenate is usually the issue. Unfortunately, there's no simple answer. Compound words are sometimes spelled as one word (*halfback, oversight ,waterproof, halfhearted, midweek),* sometimes written as separate words (*water repellent, decision maker, reddish orange),* and sometimes hyphenated (*half-moon, self-knowledge, one-half, able-bodied).* Some words lose their hyphens and are spelled as one word. Some rules apply, but there are too many to memorize, with too many exceptions. For example, while *wagon train* and *pool table* are each written as two words, *wagonload* and *poolroom* are each written as one, with no rule to explain the difference.

The best thing to do when you aren't sure is to consult an unabridged dictionary. If the compound is a noun, you have a good chance of finding it. If it's an adjective, your chances are fair. If you can't find the word you're looking for, you can try applying some general principles.

Current Trends in Spelling Compound Words

The current trend is away from hyphens, as in *handshake, notebook, taxpayer, poolroom, crosswalk.* When a compound is temporary (that is, used for a particular purpose or not in the dictionary), you can either hyphenate it or spell it as two words: *quasi-normal, pool cover.*

Compound Adjectives

Many, but not all, **compound adjectives** are hyphenated when they appear before nouns (*cross-country trip, full-length mirror, half-baked scheme* but *midweek meeting, worldwide circulation, halfhearted support*). Again, check your dictionary. When a compound adjective is created for your sentence and not in the dictionary, hyphenate it: *horseshoe-shaped driveway, velvet-trimmed coat.* Using a hyphen is especially important if the compound adjective could mislead a reader. For example, *fast-moving van* means a van that is going fast, whereas *fast moving van* means a moving van that is going fast.

When a compound adjective follows a noun, the hyphen is omitted: The athlete was *top ranked;* the driveway was *horseshoe shaped;* the coat was *velvet trimmed;* the van was *fast moving.*

Compound Adverbs

While most **compound adverbs** are written as two words (*distributed all over, going full speed),* those adverbial compounds beginning with *over* or *under* are spelled solid (*overeagerly, underhandedly).* Adverbial compounds consisting of spelled-out fractions are hyphenated: *two-thirds completed.*

Words with Prefixes and Suffixes

Words with prefixes and suffixes, with a few exceptions, are spelled as one word whether they are nouns, verbs, adjectives, or adverbs. Among the most common prefixes and suffixes are

- anti (antiwar)
- bi (bilingual)
- co (coauthor)
- counter (counterclockwise)
- extra (extrasensory)
- inter (internecine)
- intra (intramural)
- mid (midlevel)
- mini (minivan)
- multi (multimedia)
- neo (neoconservatism)
- non (nonbeliever)
- over (override)
- post (postwar)
- pre (prefabricated)
- pseudo (pseudoscientific)
- re (reexamine)
- semi (semiconductor)
- sub (substandard)
- trans (transatlantic)
- un (unexamined)
- under (undervalued)

Exceptions exist. Check a dictionary first, and, if the word is not there, it is customary to use a hyphen in the following situations.

- The second element is capitalized: anti-British, mid-Victorian (BUT transatlantic).
- There might be confusion with another word: recover versus re-cover.
- The second element consists of more than one word: non-church attending.
- The prefix ends with the same letter that begins the root word: anti-intellectual (but reenter, reexamine).

Wordy Expressions

A redundant expression says the same thing twice, and doubletalk avoids getting directly to the point. Both are examples of wordy expressions. Other such expressions use more than one word when one will do — for example, *in the vicinity of* instead of *near* — not necessarily to mislead or cover up but because a writer is careless, afraid to write simply, or mistakenly thinks longer phrases are more impressive than shorter ones.

Redundant Expressions

In writing, **redundancy** means conveying the same meaning twice. Like other kinds of wordiness, redundancy makes writing fat. Sometimes people use redundant expressions because they don't recognize the precise definition of a word.

For example, close proximity is redundant because proximity by itself means nearness. Can there be any other kind of nearness than close nearness? Other times people fall into redundant expressions because they don't pay enough attention to what they are writing — for example, small in size, few in number, or red in color.

Look for redundant expressions and you'll find them easily. Use the following short lists to get started. When you write, check your drafts to make sure you are getting the full value of the words you choose and not adding unnecessary ones.

Adjectives, adverbs, and nouns:

- advance planning
- advance warning
- close intimates
- close scrutiny
- consensus of opinion
- currently at this time
- empty void
- end result
- exact same
- famous celebrity

- free gift
- fundamental basis
- future ahead
- human artifact
- more better
- new innovation
- now pending
- past history
- present incumbent
- rejected outcast

- sad lament
- same identical
- sudden impulse
- true fact
- two opposites
- unexpected surprise
- unimportant triviality
- wealthy millionaire
- yearly annual

Verbs:

- advance forward
- continue on
- cooperate together
- enter into (buildings)
- join together

- leave from
- lower down
- proceed forward
- raise up
- retract back

- retreat back
- return back
- share in common
- share together

Expressions with Expletives

Many wordy expressions make use of expletives: *there is, there are,* or *it is.* These constructions can often be eliminated.

There is a famous author who lives on my block.
BETTER A famous author lives on my block.

There are many people who like reading magazines.
BETTER Many people like reading magazines.

There are some animals that thrive in arctic temperatures.
BETTER Some animals thrive in arctic temperatures.

It is rarely *the case that* people refuse to help.
BETTER People rarely refuse to help.

It is a fact that most of us like to be praised.
BETTER Most of us like to be praised.

Overused Intensifiers

Intensifiers are words intended to add force to what you say: *very, absolutely, positively, really, quite,* and so on. Sometimes you need them, but more often you can prune them without affecting your tone or meaning. Review the following examples.

Roosevelt, *certainly a quite active president,* refused to give in to his handicap.

BETTER Roosevelt, *an active president,* refused to give in to his handicap.

She *positively expects* to win this election.

BETTER She *expects* to win this election.

The results were *very surprising.*

BETTER The results were *surprising.*

Selected List of Wordy Expressions

Thousands of wordy expressions exist, and new ones are created every day. Following are a few examples. Check your writing for similar roundabout ways of saying something.

- **after the conclusion of = after:** After the concert we left NOT After the conclusion of the concert we left.
- **all of = all:** All the boys came NOT All of the boys came.
- **any and all = any** or **all:** We appreciate any suggestions NOT We appreciate any and all suggestions.
- **at the present moment, at this point in time = now:** We are looking for a solution now NOT We are looking for a solution at the present moment.
- **by means of = by:** He came by car NOT He came by means of a car.
- **due to the fact that = because:** Because he called, we waited NOT Due to the fact that he called, we waited.
- **for the purpose of** (+ gerund) **= to:** The meeting is to discuss plans NOT The meeting is for the purpose of discussing plans.
- **for the simple reason that = because:** She won because she was best NOT She won for the simple reason that she was best.
- **he/she is the person/who = he is/she is:** She is admired NOT She is a person who is admired.
- **in a place where = where:** They lived where no trees grew NOT They lived in a place where no trees grew.
- **in connection with = about:** He telephoned about the rally NOT He telephoned in connection with the rally.
- **in order to = to:** He said this to help you NOT He said this in order to help you.
- **in spite of the fact that = although or though:** Although she agreed, she was sad NOT In spite of the fact that she agreed, she was sad.
- **in the near future = soon:** We'll see you soon NOT We'll see you in the near future.
- **in view of the fact that = because:** Because she helped us, we won NOT In view of the fact that she helped us, we won.
- **is located in = is in:** Ventura County is in California NOT Ventura County is located in California.
- **it often happens that = often:** Often he is invited to attend NOT It often happens that he is invited to attend.
- **on the part of = by:** A suggestion by the consultant helped NOT A suggestion on the part of the consultant helped.
- **owing to the fact that = because:** Because he was here, we stayed NOT Owing to the fact that he was here, we stayed.
- **practice in the field of = practice:** She practices medicine NOT She practices in the field of medicine.
- **rarely ever = rarely:** She rarely speaks to a large group NOT She rarely ever speaks to a large group.
- **the fact is that, the truth is that = often omit altogether:** You are the right candidate NOT The fact is that you are the right candidate.
- **which was when = when:** I spoke with him yesterday when he called NOT I spoke with him yesterday, which was when he called.
- **with the exception of = except:** I like all sports except boxing NOT I like all sports with the exception of boxing.

Active Voice versus Passive Voice

Reduce wordiness by using the active voice rather than the passive voice of the verb whenever you can. The active voice is not only more energetic but also more concise. Look at the following examples of weak passives:

The windows *had been smashed by* the wind sometime during the night.

BETTER The wind *smashed* the windows sometime during the night.

A speech was *given* by the delegate from Michigan, and a challenge was issued by him to everyone attending.

BETTER The delegate from Michigan gave a speech and *issued* a challenge to everyone attending.

After the town *was hit* by a tornado, a call to the Red Cross was *made* by our mayor.

BETTER After a tornado *hit* the town, our mayor called the Red Cross.

Answer Sheet for Sample English Expression Test

(Remove This Sheet and Use It to Mark Your Answers)

CUT HERE

1 Ⓐ Ⓑ Ⓒ Ⓓ	21 Ⓐ Ⓑ Ⓒ Ⓓ	41 Ⓐ Ⓑ Ⓒ Ⓓ	61 Ⓐ Ⓑ Ⓒ Ⓓ	81 Ⓐ Ⓑ Ⓒ Ⓓ
2 Ⓐ Ⓑ Ⓒ Ⓓ	22 Ⓐ Ⓑ Ⓒ Ⓓ	42 Ⓐ Ⓑ Ⓒ Ⓓ	62 Ⓐ Ⓑ Ⓒ Ⓓ	82 Ⓐ Ⓑ Ⓒ Ⓓ
3 Ⓐ Ⓑ Ⓒ Ⓓ	23 Ⓐ Ⓑ Ⓒ Ⓓ	43 Ⓐ Ⓑ Ⓒ Ⓓ	63 Ⓐ Ⓑ Ⓒ Ⓓ	83 Ⓐ Ⓑ Ⓒ Ⓓ
4 Ⓐ Ⓑ Ⓒ Ⓓ	24 Ⓐ Ⓑ Ⓒ Ⓓ	44 Ⓐ Ⓑ Ⓒ Ⓓ	64 Ⓐ Ⓑ Ⓒ Ⓓ	84 Ⓐ Ⓑ Ⓒ Ⓓ
5 Ⓐ Ⓑ Ⓒ Ⓓ	25 Ⓐ Ⓑ Ⓒ Ⓓ	45 Ⓐ Ⓑ Ⓒ Ⓓ	65 Ⓐ Ⓑ Ⓒ Ⓓ	85 Ⓐ Ⓑ Ⓒ Ⓓ
6 Ⓐ Ⓑ Ⓒ Ⓓ	26 Ⓐ Ⓑ Ⓒ Ⓓ	46 Ⓐ Ⓑ Ⓒ Ⓓ	66 Ⓐ Ⓑ Ⓒ Ⓓ	86 Ⓐ Ⓑ Ⓒ Ⓓ
7 Ⓐ Ⓑ Ⓒ Ⓓ	27 Ⓐ Ⓑ Ⓒ Ⓓ	47 Ⓐ Ⓑ Ⓒ Ⓓ	67 Ⓐ Ⓑ Ⓒ Ⓓ	87 Ⓐ Ⓑ Ⓒ Ⓓ
8 Ⓐ Ⓑ Ⓒ Ⓓ	28 Ⓐ Ⓑ Ⓒ Ⓓ	48 Ⓐ Ⓑ Ⓒ Ⓓ	68 Ⓐ Ⓑ Ⓒ Ⓓ	88 Ⓐ Ⓑ Ⓒ Ⓓ
9 Ⓐ Ⓑ Ⓒ Ⓓ	29 Ⓐ Ⓑ Ⓒ Ⓓ	49 Ⓐ Ⓑ Ⓒ Ⓓ	69 Ⓐ Ⓑ Ⓒ Ⓓ	89 Ⓐ Ⓑ Ⓒ Ⓓ
10 Ⓐ Ⓑ Ⓒ Ⓓ	30 Ⓐ Ⓑ Ⓒ Ⓓ	50 Ⓐ Ⓑ Ⓒ Ⓓ	70 Ⓐ Ⓑ Ⓒ Ⓓ	90 Ⓐ Ⓑ Ⓒ Ⓓ
11 Ⓐ Ⓑ Ⓒ Ⓓ	31 Ⓐ Ⓑ Ⓒ Ⓓ	51 Ⓐ Ⓑ Ⓒ Ⓓ	71 Ⓐ Ⓑ Ⓒ Ⓓ	
12 Ⓐ Ⓑ Ⓒ Ⓓ	32 Ⓐ Ⓑ Ⓒ Ⓓ	52 Ⓐ Ⓑ Ⓒ Ⓓ	72 Ⓐ Ⓑ Ⓒ Ⓓ	
13 Ⓐ Ⓑ Ⓒ Ⓓ	33 Ⓐ Ⓑ Ⓒ Ⓓ	53 Ⓐ Ⓑ Ⓒ Ⓓ	73 Ⓐ Ⓑ Ⓒ Ⓓ	
14 Ⓐ Ⓑ Ⓒ Ⓓ	34 Ⓐ Ⓑ Ⓒ Ⓓ	54 Ⓐ Ⓑ Ⓒ Ⓓ	74 Ⓐ Ⓑ Ⓒ Ⓓ	
15 Ⓐ Ⓑ Ⓒ Ⓓ	35 Ⓐ Ⓑ Ⓒ Ⓓ	55 Ⓐ Ⓑ Ⓒ Ⓓ	75 Ⓐ Ⓑ Ⓒ Ⓓ	
16 Ⓐ Ⓑ Ⓒ Ⓓ	36 Ⓐ Ⓑ Ⓒ Ⓓ	56 Ⓐ Ⓑ Ⓒ Ⓓ	76 Ⓐ Ⓑ Ⓒ Ⓓ	
17 Ⓐ Ⓑ Ⓒ Ⓓ	37 Ⓐ Ⓑ Ⓒ Ⓓ	57 Ⓐ Ⓑ Ⓒ Ⓓ	77 Ⓐ Ⓑ Ⓒ Ⓓ	
18 Ⓐ Ⓑ Ⓒ Ⓓ	38 Ⓐ Ⓑ Ⓒ Ⓓ	58 Ⓐ Ⓑ Ⓒ Ⓓ	78 Ⓐ Ⓑ Ⓒ Ⓓ	
19 Ⓐ Ⓑ Ⓒ Ⓓ	39 Ⓐ Ⓑ Ⓒ Ⓓ	59 Ⓐ Ⓑ Ⓒ Ⓓ	79 Ⓐ Ⓑ Ⓒ Ⓓ	
20 Ⓐ Ⓑ Ⓒ Ⓓ	40 Ⓐ Ⓑ Ⓒ Ⓓ	60 Ⓐ Ⓑ Ⓒ Ⓓ	80 Ⓐ Ⓑ Ⓒ Ⓓ	

Sample English Expression Test

Time: 70 minutes

90 questions

Directions: In the passages that follow, certain words and phrases are underlined and numbered. Following each passage, you find alternatives for each underlined part. Choose the one that best expresses the idea, makes the statement appropriate for standard written English, or is worded most consistently with the style and tone of the passage as a whole. If you think the original version is best, you can often choose answer A, which is usually the same as the original version. You may also find questions about a section of the passage, or about the passage as a whole. These questions do not refer to an underlined portion of the passage, but rather are identified by a number in brackets, like this: [2].

For each question, choose the answer you consider best and circle the letter of that choice. Read each passage through once before you begin to answer the questions that accompany it. You cannot determine most answers without reading several sentences beyond the question. Be sure that you have read ahead before choosing a final answer.

Frederick Douglass (1817–1895), [1]is regarded as being one of the most famous men in America because of his [2]vigorous battle, fought in the cause of freedom for both blacks and women. [3]Due to the Civil War, Frederick Douglass acted as advisor to President Abraham Lincoln. He recruited black soldiers for the Union and successfully lobbied for their equal pay.

1. Choose the correct phrase.

    A. is regarded as being

    B. *Omit "is regarded as being."*

    C. is regarded as

    D. *Omit "is regarded as."*

2. Choose the word that most accurately fits the sentence.

    A. vigorous

    B. heartfelt

    C. serious

    D. profound

3. What is the best way to introduce this sentence?

    A. Due to

    B. Because of

    C. During

    D. In

Harriet Beecher Stowe's novel *Uncle Tom's Cabin* was both important and controversial in its time [4]in that the eyes of the public were opened. People were able to understand the profound suffering caused by slavery. Those who espoused slavery were critical of and offended by Stowe's portrayal of the [5]situation. In response to the criticism expressed by those [6]outraged Southerners Stowe wrote *A Key to Uncle Tom's Cabin,* which provided proof of the veracity of events written in the novel.

4. What is the correct phrase to use?

    A. in that

    B. because of

    C. that

    D. because

5. Choose the best word.

    A. situation

    B. conditions of slavery

    C. livelihood

    D. tradition

6. What is the accurate way to write these words?

    A. outraged Southerners

    B. outraged southerners

    C. outraged Southerners,

    D. outraged Southerners;

GO ON TO THE NEXT PAGE

[7]The fact that George Washington had false teeth is fairly common knowledge. [8]However what we aren't aware of is the story behind these unusual objects.

[9]As a young man [10]in his early 20s George had a multitude of dental problems that often required extractions. [11]If memory serves, history books tell us that the false teeth were carved of [12]wood which may have been true. George had several pairs of awkward, poorly fitted false teeth. He was in pain much of the time because of this [13]condition. [14]After trying six dentists, he finally met Dr. John Greenwood, who was able to design more realistic dentures, using hippopotamus teeth that he shaped and polished. Springs connected the upper and lower plates. Although these dentures appeared more natural than the former ones, Washington's mouth was [15]distorted, creating the familiar profile. In addition he had difficulty speaking and eating, and he was in excruciating pain. Just before his presidential inauguration ,Washington decided to have the lower plate [16]reworked. Supposedly, teeth from several fresh cadavers were used as replacements for the hippopotamus teeth.

Throughout his adult life, George Washington was self-conscious about his appearance, rarely smiling.

7. What is the best way to begin this sentence?

   A. The fact that
   B. In fact
   C. *Omit this phrase.*
   D. It's a fact that

8. What is the best way to punctuate this word?

   A. However
   B. However,
   C. *Omit "however."*
   D. It seems that

9. What is the clearest way to express this thought?

   A. As a young man
   B. As a young man,
   C. As a young man;
   D. *Omit this phrase.*

10. What is the clearest way to express this thought?

   A. in his early 20s
   B. in his early 20s,
   C. in his early 20s;
   D. *Omit this phrase.*

11. What is the best way to punctuate this phrase?

   A. If memory serves
   B. *Omit this phrase.*
   C. If memory serves:
   D. If memory serves;

12. What is the clearest way to express this thought?

   A. wood which may have been true.
   B. wood, which may have been true.
   C. wood; which may have been true.
   D. wood: which may have been true.

13. Choose the best word.

   A. condition
   B. situation
   C. *Omit "because of this condition."*
   D. circumstance

14. What is the clearest way to express this thought?

   A. After trying six dentists,
   B. *Omit this phrase.*
   C. After meeting with six dentists,
   D. After seeking help from six dentists,

15. Which word best expresses the meaning of the sentence?

   A. distorted
   B. pushed out
   C. misshapen
   D. abnormal

16. Which word best expresses the meaning of the sentence?

   A. reworked
   B. repaired
   C. remade
   D. adjusted

Let's think about [17]horrible menacing blood-sucking creatures. Vampires come to mind, along with mosquitoes and ticks. Because the latter two are more common and, therefore, more familiar, we'll consider the vampire — vampire bat, that is.

There is plenty of evidence to be found in ancient cultures to support the [18]idea of vampire bats. The ancient Mayans sculpted [19]man-shaped figures having heads of bats and fangs. Latin American cultures relate vampire bats and witchcraft. Last, but not least, fiction records the [20]exploits in the life of Count Dracula.

In fact, vampire bats are an [21]actuality. They can be found [22]exclusively in Central and South America. They prey primarily on farm animals, unless the bats are rabid, in which case humans need to beware. Of approximately 1,000 species of bats, only three are vampire, living entirely on a diet of blood. Each evening, these tiny creatures emerge, follow their heat-sensitive noses, and land close to their sleeping prey. They then crawl across the ground, cut a slice of skin from the nose, hoof, or ear tip of the victim, and lap up their meal with a grooved tongue. At each feeding, they consume half their body weight, about two tablespoons, or half an ounce. [23]If one didn't consider the fact that these bats carry [24]diseases; [25]they might even be considered appealing. These bats greet each other with a hug, suckle orphans, share food with less well-fed cave mates, and rest 80% of the time. Even though the thought of these blood suckers causes horror, they are able to provide mankind with one benefit. Researchers have been able to use the vampire bats' anti-clotting serum to produce a drug that can benefit those suffering from heart attack.

17. Choose the phrase that is correctly punctuated.

    A. horrible menacing blood-sucking

    B. horrible menacing, blood-sucking

    C. horrible, menacing blood-sucking

    D. horrible, menacing, blood-sucking

18. Choose the most appropriate word.

    A. idea

    B. concept

    C. thought

    D. circumstance

19. Choose the phrase that provides the clearest description.

    A. man-shaped figures having heads shaped like bats and fangs.

    B. figures shaped like men, but having bat-shaped heads and fangs.

    C. human figures with heads like bats and fangs.

    D. figures shaped like humans but having fangs and bat-shaped heads.

20. Choose the best word.

    A. exploits

    B. antics

    C. behavior

    D. habits

21. Choose the word that best completes the sentence.

    A. actuality

    B. reality

    C. real creature

    D. real

22. Choose the word that best fits the sentence.

    A. exclusively

    B. primarily

    C. merely

    D. mainly

23. Choose the phrase that best fits the sentence.

    A. If one didn't consider the fact . . .

    B. If one considered the fact . . .

    C. Thinking about the fact . . .

    D. If you think about the fact . . .

24. Choose the answer that is punctuated correctly.

    A. diseases; they

    B. diseases they

    C. diseases, they

    D. diseases — they

25. Choose the phrase that is correctly stated.

    A. they might even be . . .

    B. the bats might even be . . .

    C. it might even be . . .

    D. he/she would even be

GO ON TO THE NEXT PAGE

In the spring of 2005, astronomers discovered that, in addition to [26]its glimmering rings and a huge fog-shrouded moon, the planet Saturn has a very unusual hot spot at the tip of its pole. Infrared images showed that the warmest area on the planet is at the [27]very southernmost tip [28]of the planet. [29]Astronomers aren't surprised and think that because of the tilt of the planet as it orbits the sun has exposed the southern polar region to the sun for nine years. No wonder it is hot!

26. Choose the answer that correctly expresses the possessive form.

   A.   its
   B.   it's
   C.   its'
   D.   it has

27. Choose the answer that best completes the sentence.

   A.   Leave this word where it is.
   B.   Place this word somewhere else in the sentence.
   C.   Place this word before warmest.
   D.   *Omit this word.*

28. Choose the answer that best completes the sentence.

   A.   Leave this phrase at the end of the sentence.
   B.   Place this phrase in the center of the sentence.
   C.   Place this phrase at the beginning of the sentence.
   D.   *Omit this phrase.*

29. Choose the sentence grouping that gives the clearest expression of ideas.

   A.   *Keep the sentence as is.*
   B.   Astronomers . . . surprised. Their theory is that because of the tilt of the planet it its orbit the sun's rays have focused on the Southern region for nine years.
   C.   Astronomers aren't surprised because of the tilt . . .years.
   D.   Astronomers aren't surprised. The tilt of the planet in its orbit has exposed the southern polar region to the sun for nine years.

[30]Those people searching for the [31]ultimate of winter thrills are now going into restricted wilderness areas, often at their own peril. This is especially true of those who ski in western areas of the United States, where the danger of avalanche is very real. [32]Currently several companies that produce outdoor gear are expanding their product lines with a potentially life-saving piece of ski equipment, the avalanche rescue beacon. Originally produced for ski patrols and search-and-rescue teams, the beacon is now available to all. Units can be purchased or rented at many ski resorts. When worn by a skier, the device transmits a signal that can be read by other rescue beacons. [33]A switch on the beacon allows the wearer to change it from a transmitter to a receiver. Thus, friends who are wearing beacons are able to begin a search for a buried skier immediately after an avalanche. Traditional avalanche rescue methods involve teams of people [34]working on a grid, using poles to probe the snow, advancing across the avalanche field, and hoping to find the victim in time. If the victim isn't located in approximately 15 [35]minutes suffocation will occur. There has been times when a ski or body part is visible [36]at the surface, making a rescue successful. Without a beacon, however, there often is little chance of recovering an avalanche victim alive.

30. Choose the wording that best fits the sentence.

   A.   Those people
   B.   *Omit "people."*
   C.   *Omit "Those."*
   D.   *Omit "Those people," and insert "skiers" after "thrills"*

31. Choose the wording that best fits the sentence.

   A.   ultimate of winter thrills
   B.   ultimate winter thrill of thrills
   C.   penultimate winter thrill
   D.   penultimate thrill of winter

32. Choose the wording that best fits the sentence.

   A.   Currently several companies that produce outdoor gear
   B.   Currently, those companies that produce outdoor gear
   C.   Currently, several companies that produce outdoor gear
   D.   At this time outdoor gear production companies

33. Choose the best sentence placement.

    A. *Leave the sentence where it is.*

    B. *Place this sentence before the previous sentence.*

    C. *Place this sentence after the following sentence.*

    D. *Remove this sentence.*

34. Choose the wording that best fits the sentence.

    A. working on a grid

    B. establishing a grid

    C. making a grid

    D. using a grid

35. Choose the best punctuation.

    A. none

    B. ;

    C. ,

    D. .

36. Choose the wording that best fits the sentence.

    A. on the surface

    B. near the surface

    C. under the surface

    D. *Remove this phrase.*

[37][1]Because American Sign Language (ASL) is a visual language, it will always be the language of the deaf or hard-of-hearing community. [2]As with traditional foreign languages, colleges are now offering courses in ASL. [3]More and more frequently, however, those studying ASL are of the hearing world. Some people [38]take ASL because of family or friends who are deaf or hard of hearing. Others have a curiosity about or fascination with the language or [39]may wish to become an ASL interpreter or Signed English transliterator.

ASL isn't mime, but is a complete language with [40]its own grammatical structure. Hand and body position and orientation [41]as well as facial and body expression comprise the grammatical structure. There is no one-to-one relationship with English, [42]although ASL is distantly related to French Sign Language.

[43]Fingerspelling, a system of shapes made with a single hand corresponds to the letters of the alphabet, is taught in ASL classes. Deaf and hard-of-hearing people use fingerspelling for names of people and [44]places, when information needs to be accurate. They often use a combination of signs, fingerspelling, as well as several invented signs.

[45]For the hearing population, learning sign a definite challenge but one with many rewards.

37. Choose the most logical order of sentences to introduce the first paragraph.

    A. 1, 2, 3

    B. 2, 1, 3

    C. 3, 1, 2

    D. 1, 3, 2

38. Choose the word that best fits the sentence.

    A. take

    B. study

    C. read about

    D. talk about

39. Choose the best wording for the phrase.

    A. may wish

    B. chose

    C. may think

    D. would like

40. Choose the best form.

    A. its

    B. its,

    C. it's

    D. it's,

GO ON TO THE NEXT PAGE

41. Choose the answer that best fits the sentence.

    A. as well as
    B. instead of
    C. omit
    D. orientation,

42. Choose the best phrase to complete the sentence.

    A. English, although . . . Language.
    B. English, even though
    C. English; although
    D. English. Although ASL is . . . Language

43. Choose the best format for the sentence.

    A. Fingerspelling, a system . . . classes.
    B. omit "made with a single hand"
    C. Fingerspelling, . . . hand, . . . alphabet and is
    D. Fingerspelling . . . alphabet. This

44. Choose the best form of punctuation.

    A. places, when
    B. places; when
    C. places. When
    D. places when

45. Choose the best method of completing the sentence.

    A. For the hearing . . . rewards.
    B. Insert "learning to sign is" instead of "learning sign a "
    C. For . . . population learning . . .
    D. For . . . challenge but . . .

What is your favorite flavor of ice cream? When compiling a list of typical American desserts, [46]it is high on the list. Have you ever thought of its origin? It is said, but never substantiated, that [47]Nero emperor of Rome, ate snow mixed with honey, nectar, and fruit pulp. [48]China's rulers in the T'ang period (A.D. 618–907) ate similar delicacies of flavored ice or snow. Long before ice boxes or refrigerators were in use, [49]American colonists brought recipes for ice cream from Europe. This dessert became popular in America, especially after George and Martha Washington purchased a "cream machine for ice" in the [50]mid 1770s. This machine [51]allowed them to produce ice cream for their family and guests. It became a popular treat served at many parties. At this same time, Thomas Jefferson brought a handwritten recipe for vanilla ice cream home from Paris. Dolly Madison often served ice cream. In 1813, during James Madison's second inauguration, she served strawberries with ice cream at the festivities. Initially, vanilla and lemon were the most common flavors. Later, fruit flavors such as strawberry, raspberry, and pineapple came into popularity.

[52]Interestingly enough ice cream helped to further liberate women from the confines of the home. Popular thinking had professed that ladies should not eat in public. In the late 1790s, however, shops appeared that sold ice cream. These "pleasure gardens" were acceptable places where women could go for a treat. Gradually, popular thinking changed.

Ice cream recipes began to appear in cookbooks, and ladies began making their own. On September 9, 1843, a patent was issued to a Philadelphia [53]resident, Nancy M. Johnson, for her invention of an "artificial freezer" for ice cream. It consisted of a crank, dasher, tub, cylinder, and lid. This was the first of many machines of this kind. Another Pennsylvanian, Jacob Fussell, built an ice cream factory in a rural area and sent his product packed in ice to urban areas. This was the beginning of the wholesale ice cream business.

During the Civil War, chocolate was a rarity. After the war, however, both chocolate candies and chocolate ice cream became extremely popular. [54][1]The ice cream sundae appeared at soda fountains [55]having ice cream syrups, and many other toppings. [2] Selling ice cream sodas on Sunday was prohibited. [3]To get around this restriction, the sundae was invented.

The prohibition act of 1920 caused those bar owners who wanted to remain in business to switch from serving liquor and beer to serving ice cream. Thus Americans increased their consumption of ice cream from 260 million gallons in 1920 to 365 million gallons in 1929. The first soft serve was invented in 1938 and called Dairy Queen because they thought their product would be the queen of dairy products. Although you will find many kinds of soft serve ice creams, Dairy Queen is still available.

In the 1930s, grocery stores [56]first began selling ice cream, but you had to eat it fast. The first refrigerator with a separate freezer wasn't available in most homes until 1939. Today, we have to walk only as far as the freezer section of the refrigerator in our home kitchens.

46. Choose the word that makes the sentence clearer.

    A. it

    B. ice cream

    C. dessert

    D. that

47. Choose the punctuation mark that is correct.

    A. none

    B. ;

    C. ,

    D. :

48. Choose the correct form to use when referring to dates.

    A. *Leave as is.*

    B. *Give no reference to dates for Nero and for the Chinese rulers.*

    C. *Give reference dates for both Nero and the Chinese rulers.*

    D. *Give a date reference for Nero and not for the Chinese rulers.*

49. Choose the best wording for this sentence.

    A. American colonists

    B. Colonists

    C. People from Europe

    D. Americans

50. Choose the best form to write a date.

    A. mid 1770s

    B. mid-1770s

    C. mid seventeen seventies

    D. 1770s

51. Choose the word that best completes the sentence.

    A. allowed

    B. enabled

    C. helped

    D. encouraged

52. Choose the punctuation that is most appropriate.

    A. none

    B. —

    C. ,

    D. *

53. Choose the punctuation that is most appropriate.

    A. resident, Nancy M. Johnson,

    B. resident Nancy M. Johnson

    C. resident, Nancy M. Johnson;

    D. resident: Nancy M. Johnson,

54. What should the correct sentence order be?

    A. 1, 2, 3

    B. 2, 3, 1

    C. 3, 1, 2

    D. 1, 3, 2

55. Choose the best word arrangement for this sentence.

    A. *Leave as is.*

    B. *Move the underlined words so they appear after "appeared" and before "at."*

    C. *Move the underlined words so they appear after "soda" and before "fountain."*

    D. *Move the underlined words so they appear after "sundae" and before "appeared."*

56. Correct the answer that best clarifies the sentence.

    A. *Leave as is.*

    B. *Omit the word "first."*

    C. *Omit the word "began."*

    D. *Omit "first began."*

GO ON TO THE NEXT PAGE

Astronomers have detected a minute star-like object that is too small to be a star, [57]but that has a disk of dust and gases surrounding it. To date, this is the smallest object that has been found with a disk. [58]They think it might [59]eventually become a miniature solar system that might eventually form planets. [60]It is surmised that these newly created planets might even be capable of supporting life forms. This celestial body is about 15 times the size of Jupiter. It isn't really a star, but a brown dwarf, a star that has failed. [61]When comparing temperature with other solar [62]bodies, the brown dwarf is cool, at only 3,600 degrees Fahrenheit, and emits infrared light.

Astronomers are now turning their sights from supernovas, quasars, and giant galaxies, the largest objects in the cosmos to the smallest and dimmest objects, of which there are far more. Their instruments used to study these objects are bigger [63]and bigger telescopes. The Spitzer Space Telescope is one of this new generation of instruments, launched into space to orbit the sun in 2003. It is the [64]forth of this type designed and created by NASA and the last of its Great Observatories. This Observatory is created to detect infrared, or heat radiation, emitted from celestial bodies. Because the Earth's atmosphere blocks infrared light, astronomers have been forced to go to space using satellites to study those objects emitting infrared light. It is hoped that many new discoveries will be made using these satellite observatories.

57. Choose the correct punctuation after the word "bodies" in this sentence.

   A. none
   B. —
   C. ,
   D. ;

58. What is the best word to introduce this sentence?

   A. They
   B. Astronomers
   C. Scientists
   D. PhDs

59. What word might best replace the first "eventually" in this sentence?

   A. *Leave as is.*
   B. sooner or later
   C. in time
   D. ultimately

60. How should this sentence be edited?

   A. *Leave as is.*
   B. *Omit the sentence.*
   C. *Rewrite to lengthen.*
   D. *Rewrite to shorten.*

61. How should this sentence be edited?

   A. *Leave as is.*
   B. *Change "and emits" to "emitting.*
   C. *Omit the sentence.*
   D. *Omit "When . . . bodies,."*

62. What is the correct spelling for this word?

   A. bodies
   B. bodys
   C. bodys'
   D. bodies'

63. How should this sentence be edited?

   A. *Leave as is.*
   B. *Omit the second "and bigger."*
   C. *Change the first "and bigger."*
   D. *Change the second "and bigger."*

64. What is the correct spelling of this word?

   A. forth
   B. forthe
   C. fourthe
   D. fourth

[65][1]The best-selling game of all time, [66]Monopoly, came close to never being [67]published! [2]Currently found in at least [68]28 countries and published in 19 languages, [69]it is so widely played that there are several records [70]published in the *Guinness Book of Records*. [3]It was created by borrowing heavily from another game, patented in 1904, called "The Landlord's Game," which included the purchasing of public and private property and public utilities.

After the 1929 crash of the stock market, an unemployed engineer named Charles Darrow began to design a game. It was a way to keep his mind active, use the spare time he had in excess, and possibly find a way to earn money. He didn't believe in credit or borrowing money, [71]so this was incorporated into the rules. Each of the players in the game began with a great deal of money, [72]so they could control as [73]investments or speculation. Because Atlantic City had many pleasant memories for Darrow, he decided to use street names and public works as properties [74]from there in his game. He constructed the game using a piece of linoleum as his board. [75]On it he painted symbols and lettering by hand. Even though it was not [76]artistic and in some respects, not at all attractive, it was an instant hit with family and friends. It seemed as though every person who played wanted [77]their own set. Darrow began to produce the sets, charging $4 [78]a piece. Word of mouth spread, and he began to [79]recieve orders from all over the country. Because of the great demand and problems with distribution, he took the game to Parker Brothers, who rejected it in no uncertain terms. Among the reasons they gave were that the game rules were [80]to complicated and it took too long to play; they stated over fifty other areas that made the game unacceptable for their purposes.

Darrow was disheartened at the rejection and decided to distribute the Monopoly games on his own. He took the games to FAO Schwartz in New York City and Wanamaker's Department Store in Philadelphia and convinced them to sell the game. The results were amazing. [81]Both stores sold out of the games [82]immediately; Parker brothers reconsidered and bought the rights to produce and sell the game of Monopoly. The results were the same for Parker Brothers, except [83]it was more dramatic. [84]You see Parker Brothers was on the verge of bankruptcy, and sales from this one game alone saved the company. For Christmas 1934, Parker Brothers sold every game [85]that it could manufacture. The phenomenon didn't stop there. The orders for the games were so numerous that they had to be stacked in huge baskets in the hallways. Never in Parker Brothers' history had any product been in so much demand. In the early months of 1935, they were selling more than 20,000 sets of Monopoly a week. [86]Both Darrow, originally an unemployed, bankrupt engineer and Parker Brothers, a nearly bankrupt toy

company, had no more financial worries. The public proved to Parker Brothers that complicated rules and extended periods of play made no difference where [87]an outstanding, engaging game was concerned.

65. Choose the sentence order that makes the paragraph most interesting.

- **A.** 1, 2, 3
- **B.** 2, 3, 1
- **C.** 2, 1, 3
- **D.** 3, 1, 2

66. Choose the punctuation that best completes the thought.

- **A.** time, Monopoly,
- **B.** time Monopoly,
- **C.** time Monopoly
- **D.** time; Monopoly,

67. What is the best punctuation to use at the end of the sentence?

- **A.** !
- **B.** .
- **C.** ?
- **D.** —

68. How do you express numbers written in text?

- **A.** *Keep as is.*
- **B.** *Spell out with words.*
- **C.** *It doesn't matter — express number whatever way you want.*
- **D.** *Omit them altogether.*

69. Choose the word that best completes the sentence.

- **A.** it
- **B.** Monopoly
- **C.** the game
- **D.** that

70. Choose the best wording that will avoid redundancy.

- **A.** published
- **B.** in print
- **C.** written
- **D.** *Omit "published."*

GO ON TO THE NEXT PAGE

71. Choose the phrase that makes the sentence the clearest.

    A. so this was incorporated . . .
    B. so that was incorporated . . .
    C. so this idea was incorporated . . .
    D. so that there was incorporated . . .

72. How should this sentence be edited?

    A. so
    B. because
    C. that
    D. and so

73. What is the correct conjunction that should be used in this sentence?

    A. investments or speculation
    B. investments and speculation
    C. investments but not speculation
    D. speculation but not investments

74. What is the appropriate prepositional phrase for this sentence?

    A. from there
    B. *Omit phrase.*
    C. from their
    D. from Atlantic City

75. What word order will make the sentence clearest?

    A. *Keep as is.*
    B. He hand-painted symbols and letters on it.
    C. Hand-painted symbols and letters
    D. Symbols and letters hand-painted.

76. What punctuation is correct for this sentence?

    A. artistic and in some respects,
    B. artistic and, in some respects,
    C. artistic; and in some respects,
    D. artistic: and in some respects,

77. Which pronoun is the correct choice?

    A. their
    B. his/her
    C. its
    D. there

78. Which spelling is correct for this sentence.

    A. a piece
    B. apiece
    C. a peice
    D. apiece

79. Which spelling is correct?

    A. recieve
    B. receeve
    C. recive
    D. receive

80. Which form of "to" is correct?

    A. to
    B. two
    C. too
    D. 2

81. How can you avoid redundancy?

    A. both stores
    B. each of the stores
    C. *Omit "both."*
    D. Both

82. What punctuation is needed to separate the clauses in this sentence?

    A. immediately;
    B. immediately
    C. immediately,
    D. immediately:

83. Which pronoun and antecedent are the correct for this sentence?

    A. it was
    B. they were
    C. it were
    D. they was

84. How should a parenthetical expression be punctuated?

    A. You see,
    B. You see
    C. You see;
    D. You see —

85. How can you avoid redundancy in this sentence?

    A. that it
    B. that
    C. it
    D. *Omit both words.*

86. How can you write a more interesting sentence?

    A. Both
    B. *Omit the word.*
    C. So both
    D. Then both

87. How can you make a sentence more interesting using multiple adjectives?

    A. an outstanding, engaging
    B. a outstanding, engaging
    C. outstanding engaging
    D. outstanding, engaging,

Why are the letters on a computer keyboard and the previous writing machine, the typewriter arranged in such a strange way? In 1782, three partners developed a strange-looking machine they called a "Type-Writer." This was the first machine developed for retail sales. Soon after it went on the market, problems developed. [88]The dexterous fingers of typists caused the keys to jam. If the keys were struck too closely in succession, they would stop working altogether. Charles Sholes spent a great deal of time trying to change the design of the machine so that the keystrokes could be accelerated, but was unsuccessful.

Finally, he had an inspiration. If he was unable to speed up the keystrokes, he would search for a way to slow down the typists. He was determined to design the most [89]inconvenient awkward and confusing arrangement of typewriter keys possible. Sholes spent weeks researching this problem and finally arrived at what is now called the QWERTY keyboard, after the first six keys of the typewriter's third row from the bottom. This arrangement of keys is still in use today. [90]It can be found on computer keyboards, which have replaced the typewriter. The versatility and speed of the computer has made the typewriter nearly a thing of the past.

88. How can you combine these two sentences?

    A. The dexterous fingers of typists caused the keys to jam. If the keys were struck too closely in succession, they would stop working altogether.

    B. If the keys were struck too closely in succession, by the dexterous fingers of typists they would jam.

    C. If the dexterous fingers of typists struck the keys too closely in succession, they would stop working altogether.

    D. The dexterous fingers of typists caused the keys to jam because they struck the keys too closely in succession.

GO ON TO THE NEXT PAGE

89. How should this sentence be punctuated?

    A. inconvenient awkward and confusing

    B. inconvenient, awkward and confusing

    C. inconvenient awkward, and confusing

    D. inconvenient, awkward, and confusing

90. How can you make this sentence accurate?

    A. *Leave it alone.*

    B. *Add the word, "keyboards" after "typewriter."*

    C. *Replace "It" with "This arrangement."*

    D. *Omit the word "keyboards" in the sentence. Change "computer' and "typewriter" to plural rather than singular.*

IF YOU FINISH BEFORE TIME IS CALLED, CHECK YOUR WORK ON THIS SECTION ONLY. DO NOT WORK ON ANY OTHER SECTION IN THE TEST.

Answer Key for English Expression Practice Test

1. C	31. A	61. B
2. B	32. C	62. A
3. C	33. A	63. A
4. D	34. B	64. D
5. B	35. C	65. A
6. C	36. D	66. A
7. A	37. D	67. B
8. B	38. B	68. B
9. D	39. D	69. A
10. B	40. A	70. D
11. B	41. A	71. C
12. B	42. A	72. A
13. C	43. C	73. B
14. C	44. A	74. A
15. C	45. B	75. B
16. B	46. B	76. B
17. D	47. C	77. B
18. B	48. C	78. B
19. D	49. B	79. D
20. A	50. A	80. C
21. B	51. B	81. D
22. A	52. C	82. A
23. A	53. A	83. B
24. C	54. B	84. A
25. A	55. D	85. C
26. A	56. B	86. B
27. D	57. C	87. A
28. D	58. B	88. B
29. B	59. C	89. D
30. D	60. B	90. B

1. **C.** Concept tested: rules of English usage. "Is regarded as" is used correctly. (A) The use of "being" after "regarded as" is inappropriate. (B) Omitting the entire phrase is a possibility, but not the best answer. (D) Omitting these words causes an incorrect reference to the present tense.

2. **B.** Concept tested: precise use of language. "Heartfelt" means "deeply felt, sincere." (A) "Vigorous" means "done with force and energy," usually in reference to physical activities. (C) "Serious" means "excessive or impressive in quantity or degree; thoughtful or subdued;" inappropriate answers for this question. (D) "Profound" means "marked by intellectual depth or insight." Several of these choices seem appropriate as answers, but do not have the emotional component needed.

3. **C.** Concept tested: rules of English usage. "During" refers to actions taking place at the time of the Civil War. (A) "Due to" is too informal when used to introduce a prepositional phrase. (B) "Because of" is too informal when used to introduce a prepositional phrase. (D) "In" is a preposition referring to a position.

4. **D.** Concept tested: rules of English usage. "Because" is appropriate, because the statement that follows supports the ideas stated at the beginning of the sentence. (A) "In that" is a colloquial expression. (B) "Because of" doesn't make sense in the sentence. (C) "That" should not be used as a preposition.

5. **B.** Concept tested: vocabulary. "Conditions of slavery" is specific to the topic of the paragraph. (A) "Situation" can be used when referring to a job, location, or condition. (C) "Livelihood" refers to a career or vocation. (D) "Tradition" refers to customs or beliefs handed down from one generation to another.

6. **C.** Concept tested: rules of capitalization and punctuation. "Southerners" is used as a proper noun in reference to a group of people in a specific part of the country. Proper nouns are always capitalized. The comma is necessary to separate the introductory clause from the remainder of the sentence. (A) "Outraged Southerners" has no comma separating the two clauses in the sentence. (B) "Outraged southerners" is incorrect, because Southerners should be capitalized. (D) "Outraged southerners;" is incorrect, because the semicolon is used incorrectly, and Southerners should be capitalized.

7. **A.** Concept tested: rules of English usage. "The fact that" is correct, because the remainder of the sentence states the known information. (B) "In fact" doesn't fit in the sentence construction. (C) "Omit this phrase" is incorrect, because the remaining sentence would be awkward. (D) "It's a fact that" is wordy and overstated.

8. **B.** Concept tested: parenthetical expressions. Parenthetical expressions are set off by a comma(s). "However" is used to signal that important information follows. (A) The comma after "However" is missing. (C) "Omit this word" could be possible, but this is not the best answer. (D) "It seems that" is awkward and doesn't really make sense in the sentence.

9. **D.** Concept tested: redundancy. "As a young man" is incorrect, because the phrase that follows, "in his early 20s" is more specific in stating information. To use both phrases is redundant. The other three answers are redundant.

10. **B.** Concept tested: clarity in writing. Phrases that add information to the sentence are set off with comma(s). (A) "In his early 20s" is incorrect, because the comma after the phrase is missing. (C) "In his early 20s;" is not correct, because the semicolon is incorrectly used. (D) "Omit this phrase" is incorrect, because the information indicates a specific period of time in George Washington's life.

11. **B.** Concept tested: colloquial/informal language. Omit this phrase, which is a colloquialism. The other three answers are incorrect, because the phrase should be omitted.

12. **B.** Concept tested: parenthetical expressions. "Which . . . true" is a parenthetical expression set apart from the rest of the sentence with a comma(s). (A) The comma after "wood" is missing. (C) The semicolon is incorrectly used. (D) Colons are used when information is to follow.

13. **C.** Concept tested: vocabulary/redundancy. The reason for his pain was stated in the previous sentence. (A) "Condition" means a state of being. (B) "Situation" means location or circumstances. (D) "Circumstance" refers to surrounding conditions, facts, or events that must be considered along with other facts or events.

14. **C.** Concept tested: rules of English usage. "After meeting with six dentists" describes Washington's actions. (A) "After trying . . . " is incorrect, because we try new foods or concepts, not people. (B) The phrase is needed to show the extent of George's efforts. (D) "After seeking . . . " indicates that he searched, but doesn't give the results of the search.

15. **C.** Concept tested: vocabulary. "Misshapen" means badly shaped or having an ugly shape. (A) "Distorted" means unnatural or twisted in shape. (B) "Pushed out" is too informal and casual. (D) "Abnormal" means deviating from the normal and suggests a grotesque appearance.

16. **B.** Concept tested: vocabulary. "Repaired" means restored to good condition. Parts were broken or worn and in need of replacement. (A) "Reworked" means reprocessed for further use. (C) "Remade" means made anew or in a different form. (D) "Adjusted" means changed or adapted usually using the original pieces.

17. **D.** Concept tested: use of commas in a series. You separate the items in a series with commas. All other answers are incorrect.

18. **B.** Concept tested: vocabulary, informal/formal language. "Concept" is correct, because more formal language is needed. (A) "Idea" is synonymous with concept, but less formal. (C) "Thought" is the process of thinking, and (D) "Circumstance" means an existing condition.

19. **D.** Concept tested: clarity in description. Answer D is correct, because the word arrangement makes it the clearest, most precise answer. All others are awkward, because of the placement of the word "fangs."

20. **A.** Concept tested: vocabulary. Answer A is correct, because "exploits" means the selfish use of someone/something for one's own ends. (B) "Antics" are tricks or playful pranks. (C) "Behavior" is a way of acting or behaving, and (D) "Habits" are acquired behavior patterns.

21. **B.** Concept tested: vocabulary. "Reality" is correct, because it means a real thing or fact. (A) "Actuality" can be substituted for "reality," but is not as good an answer. (C) "Real creature" is an actual object and it is too informal. (D) "Real" is less formal and means existing as a fact, not imaginary.

22. **A.** Concept tested: vocabulary. "Exclusively" is the correct answer, because it means "excluding all others." The other answers all are synonymous and indicate a possibility of including others, in this case, other countries.

23. **A.** Concept tested: agreement of clauses. Answer A is correct, because it is a clause stating a negative that corresponds to the second clause in the sentence, also a negative. All other answers have initial positive statements that are not in agreement with second negative clause.

24. **C.** Concept tested: punctuation between clauses. "Comma" is the correct answer. (A) A semicolon is used to separate main clauses, but this sentence does not have two main clauses. (B) Punctuation is needed to separate these two clauses. (D) The dash is not used to separate clauses.

25. **A.** Concept tested: pronoun reference. Answer A is correct, because it is understood that "they" refers to the bats. The other pronouns suggested in answers (C) and (D) are incorrect. (B) To repeat "the bats" is redundant.

26. **A.** Concept tested: possessive forms. "Its" is correct. (B) "It's" is incorrect, because this is the form for the contraction, it is. (C) "Its'" is never used. (D) "It has" means something different. (Note that "it's" never means "it has.")

27. **D.** Concept tested: comparison of adjectives. "Omit this word" is correct, because Southernmost means most southern, and using the word "very" does change the concept. It only repeats the idea and is redundant.

28. **D.** Concept tested: redundancy. "Of the planet" is used earlier in the sentence. To repeat it is unnecessary.

29. **B.** Concept tested: Sentence clarity. Answer B is the sentence that expresses the idea in the clearest most understandable way. It states a theory about the spot that is more accurate than giving the information about the orbit and tilt as factual causes for the hot spot. (A) has too much information and needs to be divided. (C) gives the impression that the astronomers aren't surprised about the tilt of the planet. (D) doesn't make clear distinction between theory and fact.

30. **D.** Concept tested: creating reader interest. Answer D arouses the reader's curiosity. (A) "Those people" is redundant. (B) "Omit people" leaves the word" those," which is not specific enough. (C) "Omit those" is not specific enough.

31. A. Concept tested: using precise language. The implication is that there are many types of winter thrills; however, the search is for the greatest possible winter thrill. (B) "Ultimate winter thrill of thrills" is overstated and redundant. (C) "Penultimate winter thrill" is not correct, because "penultimate" means "next to the ultimate," or a "secondary" thrill. (D) "Penultimate thrill of winter" is less than the most thrilling.

32. C. Concept tested: avoiding sentence fragments. Using a comma avoids a sentence fragment. (A) "Currently several companies that produce outdoor gear" is incorrect, because the group of words is a fragment. (B) "Currently, those companies that produce outdoor gear" states that companies that produce outdoor gear also produce the avalanche beacon. This is not true. (D) "At this time outdoor gear production companies" is awkward, because three adjectives modify the noun. In addition, the phrase refers to all companies, not several.

33. A. Concept tested: sentence order in a paragraph. The order of ideas makes sense. (B) "Place this sentence before the previous sentence" doesn't make sense, because it would mention the switch before the transmit signal is explained. (C) "Place this sentence after the following sentence" is likely to confuse readers. (D) "Remove this sentence" is not correct, because necessary information explaining the use of the device would be missing. The reader would be confused.

34. B. Concept tested: precise language. A grid format is created on the ground. (A) "Working on a grid" is unclear. Is being drawn or used as a formation? (C) "Making a grid" suggests that a grid is being constructed, which may or may not be true. (D) "Using a grid" could mean searchers are manually handling a grid of a sort.

35. C. Concept tested: use of commas. Answer C is correct, because subordinate clauses should be set off with a comma. All other punctuation is incorrect.

36. D. Concept tested: redundancy. Removing the phrase is correct, because "at the surface" is redundant. (A) "On the surface" is redundant. (B) "Near the surface" is incorrect, because something near the surface of the snow is not necessarily visible. (C) "Under the surface" is incorrect, because something under the surface it is not usually visible.

37. D. Concept tested: establishing a logical sentence order within a paragraph. (D) The first sentence is a good introductory sentence. Sentence 3 shows a change in interest from deaf to hearing people. The second sentence shows how the hearing can acquire this language. The other answers are not as logical as the first grouping.

38. B. Concept tested: precise language. "Study" indicates a desire to learn the language to be able to use it. (A) "Take" means remove, or informally, to study. This is not the best answer. (C) "Read about" doesn't indicate a desire to learn, nor does (D) "talk about."

39. D. Concept tested: vocabulary. Answer D indicates a stronger position than wishing. (A) "May wish" indicates a want, but not strong enough to act upon. Answer B is the wrong tense. Answer C creates awkward verbiage.

40. A. Concept tested: possessive form. Answer A is a possessive form of it. (B) The comma is incorrect. (C) The apostrophe indicates a contraction. (D) Both the apostrophe and the comma are incorrect.

41. A. Concept tested: figures of speech. Answer A is synonymous with "in addition to." (B) This is the opposite of the idea stated. (C) Do not omit. (D) No comma is needed.

42. A. Concept tested: use of comma. The comma is needed to show a change of ideas. (B) "Even though" shows an incorrect relationship between the two clauses. (C) The semicolon is used incorrectly. (D) To insert a period leaves the original sentence and a fragment.

43. C. Concept tested: clarifying ideas in a sentence. The sentence splits into two, making the concept clearer and easier to understand. Answer A is a complex and confusing sentence having too many ideas expressed. (B) "A single hand" is important to the definition of fingerspelling. (D) This sentence clearer than the original sentence, but it is not the clearest arrangement.

44. A. Concept tested: use of parenthetical expressions. The comma is needed to set off a parenthetical expression. (B) The use of the semicolon is incorrect. (C) To put a period after "places" leaves the remainder of the words a sentence fragment. (D) The comma shouldn't be removed. It is needed to punctuate the parenthetical expression.

45. B. Concept tested: changing a sentence fragment into a sentence. The inserted words make the fragment into a sentence. (A) The group of words is a fragment. (C) The comma shouldn't be removed. It is needed to separate the initial clause from the remainder of the sentence. (D) The comma before the conjunction, but, is needed.

46. B. Concept tested: pronouns and their antecedents. "Ice cream" is the better answer, because "it" and "ice cream" are in different sentences. Usually, the pronoun and the antecedent are in the same sentence. (A) "It" might be confusing. (C) "Dessert" and (D) "that" don't make sense in the sentence.

47. C. Concept Tested: punctuation of appositives. The comma is the correct answer, because appositives are always set off by commas. The other answer choices are incorrect.

48. C. Concept tested: use of dates in text. "Give reference dates for both Nero and the Chinese rulers" is correct. (A)The paragraph should not be left as is. The dates could be left out altogether, as in answer B. However, it is more informative in this type of article to include the date. (D) Both rulers should be treated the same, either including or excluding the dates.

49. B. Concept tested: redundancy. The adjective "American" is redundant, because it is stated earlier in the article that the topic is about American desserts. It is assumed that the colonists coming to America are there permanently, which makes answer A redundant. "People from Europe" might be those who are just visiting, not arriving to stay. (D) "Americans" is less specific than colonists and therefore incorrect.

50. A. Concept tested: writing dates. "Mid 1770s is correct. In answer B, a hyphen is not needed. (C) The date should not be written in words. Answer D is not specific enough.

51. B. Concept tested: vocabulary. "Enabled" is correct, because the machine made it possible to produce ice cream. (A) "Allow" means to let something happen. (C) is incorrect, because the machine produced the ice cream, not helped to produce. (D) is incorrect, because a machine cannot encourage anything.

52. C. Concept tested: parenthetical expressions. This is the correct answer, because parenthetical expressions should be set off with commas. The other answers are incorrect.

53. A. Concept tested: punctuation of appositives. Appositives should be set off using commas. All other answers are incorrect.

54. B. Concept tested: sentence order. Answer B is in the correct order: Selling soda was prohibited; a way to get around this restriction was needed; sundaes were invented.

55. D. Concept tested: dangling modifiers. Answer D is the correct arrangement. It is clear that the underlined phrase modifies "sundae." In the other choices the answers are confusing.

56. B. Concept tested: redundancy. Omit the word "first." It means the same as "began." (A) To use both words is redundant. (C) If "began" is omitted, the sentence doesn't make sense. (D) To omit both words the sentence doesn't make sense.

57. C. Concept tested: use of commas. "None" is correct. The thought should not be broken with punctuation. The other answer choices are incorrect.

58. B. Concept tested: vocabulary. "Astronomers" is the most precise term. (A) "They" is not specific enough. (C) "Scientists" is correct, but not as exact as astronomers. (D) "PhDs might be accurate, but is not specific enough.

59. C. Concept tested: vocabulary. "In time" is correct, because it gives a positive slant that with time conditions will change. (A) "Eventually" is repeated later in the sentence. (B) "Sooner or later" is too informal. (D) "Ultimately" duplicates "eventually" too closely.

60. B. Concept tested: continuity of ideas. The information contained within, while generally on topic, doesn't specifically relate to the sentences around it.

61. B. Concept tested: continuity of ideas. "Changing "and emits" to "emitting" makes a smoother reading sentence. The other answers are incorrect.

62. A. Concept tested: spelling. "Bodies" is the correct spelling. (D) "Bodies'" is correct only when it is necessary to show possession. The other spellings are incorrect.

63. A. Concept tested: description. The current sentence is one way to describe the immense size of the telescopes. The other choices are incorrect.

64. D. Concept tested: spelling. "Fourth" is the spelling used to indicate a numeral. (A) "Forth" is used to mean "to go forward." The other answers are incorrect.

65. A. Concept tested: paragraph organization. The first sentence grabs the reader's interest; the second adds intriguing information about current interest in the game; the third gives a bit of history in regard to the origin of the game. To use other sentence orders would require rewriting.

66. A. Concept tested: appositive use. The appositive is separated from its antecedent and the remainder of the sentence by commas.

67. B. Concept tested: end punctuation of sentences. This is a declarative sentence and requires a period at the end. (A) is incorrect, because there is no emotion written into the sentence, even though the statement is surprising. The remaining answers are incorrect.

68. B. Concept tested: writing numbers in text. Numbers that can be expressed in one or two words can be spelled out.

69. A. Concept tested: noun/pronoun usage. Answer A is correct. (B) To insert the word "Monopoly" is repetitive, because it is used in the previous sentence. (C) The words in this answer are found in the previous sentence. It would be repetitive. (D) This answer doesn't make sense in this sentence.

70. D. Concept tested: redundancy. Because the statement presents the fact that there are records about Monopoly in the *Guinness Book of Records,* it is assumed that they are in print or published. To state the obvious is redundant.

71. C. Concept tested: sentence clarity. The idea referred to is the fact that Darrow didn't believe in giving credit or borrowing money. The use of "that" is colloquial and should not be used.

72. A. Concept tested: sentence editing. "So" is correct, because the first idea explains the second part of the sentence. Answer B is incorrect, because a reason doesn't follow. (C) "That" is incorrect, because it is colloquial. (D) "And so" uses unnecessary verbiage.

73. B. Concept tested: use of conjunctions. "Investments and speculation" is correct, because the player is able to use either method. (A) "Investments or speculation" is incorrect, because a player can use both options. This indicates one or the other, but not both. The other answers do not give a choice.

74. A. Concept tested: sentence clarity. Answer A is correct, because "from there" refers to Atlantic City. (C) is incorrect, because the words can't be omitted; they're needed. (C) is incorrect, because "their" is a possessive pronoun. (D) is incorrect, because the noun "Atlantic City" becomes redundant.

75. B. Concepts tested: word order for clarity. Answer B is correct, because the words in this order make it a simple declarative sentence. (A) is incorrect, because the word order is confusing and awkward. The other two answers are incorrect, because they are sentence fragments.

76. B. Concepts tested: parenthetical expressions. Parenthetical expressions should be separated from the remainder of the sentence by commas. All other punctuation is incorrect.

77. B. Concept tested: agreement of pronoun and noun. "His/her" is correct, because the pronoun and noun, everyone must agree in number. "Every person" and "his/her" are both singular. The other pronouns can't be applied in this sentence.

78. B. Concept tested: spelling. "Apiece" is correct. The compound word means "one at a time." (A) "A piece" is incorrect, because it is the same as saying "each piece." The other two spellings are incorrect.

79. D. Concept tested: spelling. "Receive" is correct. The phrase "i before e except after c" is the rule that applies. The other answers are incorrect.

80. C. Concept tested: the form of "to." "Too" means "and" or "also." (A) "To" is a preposition, used in a prepositional phrase. The remaining answers refer to numerals.

81. D. Concept tested: redundancy. "Both" is correct. It refers to the stores, and it is redundant to include both words. (A) "Both stores" is redundant. (B) "Each of the stores" is also redundant. (C) to omit "both" is incorrect, because the sentence will not make sense without the word, "both."

82. A. Concepts tested: punctuation between clauses. Use a semicolon to separate main clauses not joined by a coordinating conjunction. All other answers are incorrect.

83. **B.** Concept tested: pronoun/antecedent agreement. "They were" is the correct answer, because "they" refers to "results," And both are plural. (A) "It" is singular, which is incorrect. (C) "It" is singular, but "were" is plural. This is an incorrect combination. (D) "They" is plural, but "was" is singular. This is an incorrect combination.

84. **A.** Concept tested: punctuation of parenthetical expression. "You see," is correct. Parenthetical expressions are set off from the remainder of the sentence using commas. All other answers are incorrect.

85. **C.** Concept tested: redundancy. The pronoun "it" is needed, while the adverb "that" is not. (A) "That it" is redundant. (B) "That" alone doesn't make sense in the sentence. (D) Omitting both words causes the sentence to lose meaning.

86. **B.** Concept tested: omitting redundancy. Omit the word "both" is correct. The remaining answers are redundant.

87. **A.** Concept tested: punctuation of multiple adjectives. "An outstanding, engaging" is correct. (B) "A" is an incorrect use of an article. (C) It is incorrect to omit all punctuation. (D) is incorrect, because the comma after "engaging" should not be there.

88. **B.** Concept tested: sentence combining. Answer B is the correct, because the information is combined in such a way that thought is clear and makes sense. (A) isn't correct, because there is information in the sentences that is repeated in addition to new information in each of the sentences. (C) is incorrect, because it isn't clear what would stop working, the fingers or the keys. (D) is incorrect, because the words "the keys" have been repeated in the sentence.

89. **D.** Concept tested: punctuation of a series. "Inconvenient, awkward, and confusing" is correct. In a series of three or more terms, use a comma after each term except the last. All other answer choices are incorrect.

90. **B.** Concept tested: accuracy of information within a sentence. Adding the word "keyboards" after "typewriter" is correct. The computer keyboard didn't replace the typewriter; it replaced the typewriter keyboard. Other answer choices do not make that correction.

PART III

WRITTEN EXAM: THE BIOGRAPHIC INFORMATION QUESTIONNAIRE

About the Biographic Information Questionnaire

What You Should Know

The biographic questionnaire is one part of the exam for which you cannot study. Its purpose is to assess your experiences in life and use the results as a predictor of how you might perform in a variety of different jobs. The questions are both general and specific, and there are no right or wrong answers. You will be asked questions about past interests, your activities throughout your life, and information about school, work, and other personal areas. The questions are multiple-choice, but on some of them, you may be asked to expand upon your answer. You will find some of these questions in the samples in this chapter.

Although it might be difficult to ascertain what a question might be measuring, others might be very obvious. While it may be difficult to analyze what is being measured, it doesn't mean you shouldn't be cognizant of how you answer the questions. Keep in mind that there are several areas that are being evaluated, such as

- Assertiveness
- Personal commitment
- Creativity and/or imagination
- Teamwork
- Decision-making abilities
- Flexibility
- Goal orientation

There are, of course, many other areas that will be evaluated. Like most psychologically oriented tests, there are checks and balances built into the questions that are scattered throughout the test that can highlight inconsistencies in your answers, so whatever you do, don't lie!

The Biographic Information Questionnaire on the exam consists of approximately 105 questions, and you have 75 minutes in which to complete it.

Biographic Questionnaire Review Section

Following are some sample questions that will give you an idea of the types of questions you might find on the actual test. Work quickly, and then go back and check your answers.

1. How old are you?

   A. under 21 years old
   B. 21–24 years old
   C. 25–29 years old
   D. 30–34 years old
   E. 35+ years old

2. What has been your primary area of residence up until now?

    A. northeast United States

    B. southern United States

    C. central United States

    D. western United Stated

    E. outside the continental United States

3. In what kind of community did you grow up?

    A. major metropolitan city (such as New York, Tokyo or London)

    B. medium-size city

    C. small city

    D. suburb

    E. rural community

Please indicate the city:_____

4. What is the highest level of education that your father obtained?

    A. completed elementary school

    B. completed some high school

    C. received high school diploma

    D. completed some college

    E. college degree or higher

5. What is the highest level of education that your mother obtained?

    A. completed elementary school

    B. completed some high school

    C. received high school diploma

    D. completed some college

    E. college degree or higher

6. How many siblings do you have?

    A. 0

    B. 1

    C. 2

    D. 3

    E. 4 or more

7. In reflecting on your upbringing, how would you characterize your father's parenting style?

    A. completely lacking in structure and/or rules

    B. rarely providing structure and/or enforcing rules

    C. sometimes providing structure and/or enforcing rules

    D. usually providing structure and/or enforcing rules

    E. always providing structure and/or enforcing rules

8. In reflecting on your upbringing, how would you characterize your mother's parenting style?

    A. completely lacking in structure and/or rules
    B. rarely providing structure and/or enforcing rules
    C. sometimes providing structure and/or enforcing rules
    D. usually providing structure and/or enforcing rules
    E. always providing structure and/or enforcing rules

9. Which type of school did you attend for the majority of your academic experience?

    A. liberal arts or sciences public school
    B. vocational or technical public school
    C. religious private school
    D. non-sectarian private school
    E. military school

10. What was your age at the time of your high school graduation?

    A. 16 years or less
    B. 17
    C. 18
    D. 19
    E. 20 or more years

11. How many years of college or other post-secondary education have you completed?

    A. less than one year
    B. 1 year
    C. 2 years
    D. 3 years
    E. 4 or more years

12. In what academic area did you major?

    A. natural or physical sciences (such as biology or math)
    B. social sciences (such as economics or psychology)
    C. language arts (such as communications or Russian)
    D. fine or performing arts (such as photography or dance)
    E. other

13. What was your standing in your college graduating class?

    A. top 2 percent
    B. top 10 percent
    C. top third
    D. middle third
    E. bottom third

14. During the last four years of your schooling, what primary means of transportation did you use?

    A. walking or biking
    B. private car
    C. taxi or car service
    D. bus
    E. train or subway

If you did not work while attending school, please skip questions 15–17 and go directly to question 18.

15. If you were employed only on school days during the last four years of your schooling, how many hours did you work per week?

  A. 5 or less
  B. 6–10
  C. 11–15
  D. 16–19
  E. 20 or more

16. If you were employed on weekends only or on school days and weekends, during the last four years of your schooling, how many hours did you work per week?

  A. 5 or less
  B. 6–10
  C. 11–15
  D. 16–19
  E. 20 or more

17. What type of employment did you engage in during your last four years of schooling?

  A. academic or clerical (research, filing, computing, and so on)
  B. food services (waiting tables, cooking, dish washing, and so on)
  C. sales (telemarketing, retail sales, wholesale buyers, and so on)
  D. technical, trades, or construction (welding, plumbing, painting, and so on)
  E. other

If you did not do volunteer work while attending school, please skip questions 18–19, and go directly to question 20.

18. How many hours a week did you devote to volunteer work during the last four years of your schooling?

  A. 1–2
  B. 3–5
  C. 6–9
  D. 10–14
  E. 15 or more

  Give examples: _____

19. Which of the following best describes the nature of the volunteer work?

  A. religious or charitable (such as for a church or synagogue)
  B. educational or social services (such as for a school, museum, or a women's shelter)
  C. political (such as for a specific candidate)
  D. health-care related (such as for a hospital or clinic)
  E. environmental (such as at an animal shelter or a park)

20. In the past five years, how many countries outside the United States have you visited?

    A. 0
    B. 1
    C. 2
    D. 3
    E. 4 or more

List them: _____

21. How many friends do you have who are not of your ethnic, cultural, or religious background?

    A. 0
    B. 1
    C. 2
    D. 3
    E. 4 or more

22. When personal acquaintances, friends, or family members give you a compliment, what is the compliment usually about?

    A. your resilience
    B. your flexibility
    C. your charisma and energy
    D. your attention to task
    E. your intelligence

23. When work colleagues, supervisors, or instructors give you a compliment, what is the compliment usually about?

    A. your resilience
    B. your flexibility
    C. your charisma and energy
    D. your attention to task
    E. your intelligence

24. In the past year, how many times have you written a letter to the editor or spoken to your boss about departmental changes?

    A. 0
    B. 1
    C. 2
    D. 3
    E. 4 or more

Describe some of these situations: _____

25. When trying to resolve an issue with a colleague or acquaintance, which approach are you most likely to take?

    A. reach a compromise
    B. collaborate to find a shared solution
    C. compete to find the best solution
    D. accommodate the other person's point of view
    E. avoid the conflict altogether

26. When making a decision, which approach are you most likely to take?

    A. use intuition or gut response
    B. seek and analyze available data
    C. make a pro and con list
    D. think outside the box for the most creative solution
    E. ask others for their opinions

27. In the past year, how many social gatherings have you attended?

    A. 0
    B. 1
    C. 2
    D. 3
    E. 4 or more

If you answered B, C, D, or E to the preceding question, please answer the following

At these gatherings, how often do you meet someone new with whom you maintain contact after the event?

    A. almost always
    B. often
    C. sometimes
    D. rarely
    E. never

28. At home, how often to you take time out to reorganize your room(s)?

    A. almost always
    B. often
    C. sometimes
    D. rarely
    E. never

29. In the last six months, how often have you felt overwhelmed by a task in a work or school situation?

    A. never
    B. once
    C. twice
    D. three times
    E. four or more times

Describe a specific situation: _____

30. In preparing for the FSE, how many specific courses have you taken to improve your job-knowledge skills?

    A. 0
    B. 1
    C. 2
    D. 3
    E. 4 or more

If you answered B, C, D, or E above, list the names of those courses:_____.

PART IV

WRITTEN EXAM: WRITTEN ESSAY

About the Written Essay

What You Should Know

The written essay is your opportunity to show your ability to analyze a topic that is presented to you, to organize your thoughts, and to develop clear, readable written work. You are given 50 minutes to complete your essay, and you will be asked to choose one topic from a selection of three topics on which to write your essay. The topics may include the following subject areas.

- Customs and culture
- Economics and finance
- Education
- Employment issues
- History
- International affairs
- Religion
- Social issues

You receive a booklet when you begin the test; you handwrite the essay in that booklet. It is important to present a clear point of view and provide enough arguments to support your viewpoint. Grading takes into account your ability to analyze the topic, support your arguments, structure sentences, and correctly use grammar and syntax. Spelling and punctuation are important, but to a lesser degree than the other criteria.

Following are several sample topics on which you can practice organizing your thoughts. Make a comprehensive outline for each topic, indicating your viewpoints and make a list of supporting arguments. An in-depth outline can help you visualize the entire essay, which you can also write, if you want the practice. If some of the sample topics are not subjects you know about, consider doing some research into these topics in order to develop a broader viewpoint.

When you see these words, do exactly what is indicated (describing, listing, and so on).

Written Essay Review Section

Read the following essay topics and answer each in no more than 50 minutes.

Essay 1

In today's political environment, we have seen the emergence of popular entertainers — singers, musicians, movie stars, and so on — taking center stage to promote and raise money for the candidates of their choice. Some people feel that these entertainers should stick to their own business, while others believe that they have a right, and perhaps even an obligation, to speak their minds. In your view, what do you think the role of entertainers should be in politics? Do they exert undue influence because of their popularity and easy access to the media? Carefully explain the rationale for your position.

Essay 2

Most exams today require students to write an essay, much like this one. Because of the sheer number of essays to be graded, some universities are experimenting with a computerized grading system. Students feel that a machine cannot comprehend a student's argument. On the other hand, the argument goes, a computer can determine whether the student addressed a specific question and can judge the essay's structure. In your view, how can this situation be resolved? Carefully explain the rationale for your position.

Essay 3

There are numerous viewpoints on the subject of cloning. One side feels that the long-term benefits of cloning — primarily a search for medical cures — is worth the effort, but with some restrictions. Others argue that there is a strong potential for abuse in this era of corporate corruption, dishonesty, and misunderstanding. In your view, aside from religious and moral considerations, who should best make the determination whether cloning is legalized: doctors, politicians, or religious leaders. Carefully explain the rationale for your position.

Essay 4

There are two words that politicians take care to avoid: foreign aid. Instead, decision makers often sidestep the issue. Many believe that it is the United States' obligation as the wealthiest nation in the world to help those who are poorer. Others feel that charity begins at home and question whether the people of those countries that receive aid actually benefit directly. Furthermore, they question whether there are any benefits for the United States. In your view, is foreign aid helpful? To whom? Carefully explain the rationale for your position.

Prewriting: How to Begin a Writing Assignment

Writing is a process. The formula good writers follow consists of prewriting, writing, and rewriting, or revising and editing. This allows their work to emerge in a series of small manageable steps. Much of what you will read in this chapter will cover these basics, and it is designed to help you with the Written Essay portion of the FSOE. In this chapter, you learn about and develop skills that will make you a more effective writer.

The Steps in Writing

Although it is a process, writing doesn't progress as neatly from one step to the next as does, for example, baking a cake or changing a tire. Roughly speaking, when you write, you

1. Decide on a topic (or have a topic assigned to you).
2. Explore ideas about the topic through thinking, reading, listening, and so on.
3. Formulate a thesis or main idea and decide what points you want to make to support it.
4. Select details and examples (from reading, research, personal experience).
5. Decide on the order in which you'll present your ideas and examples.
6. Write a first draft; edit and revise for content, style, and writing mechanics; write a final draft.

At any time during this process, you may need to stop and go back several steps. For example, when you're selecting details and examples, you may realize your topic is too broad or your thesis statement weak. Or, when you're organizing your points, you may see that the thesis you thought you were developing isn't the one that you are developing. Often the act of writing itself generates new ideas you may want to pursue. Even as late as your final draft, you may decide that the organization isn't working, or you may spot a flaw in your argument that causes you to throw out much of what you've written and rework the rest. The most realistic way to view writing is not as a straight line but as a back-and-forward movement. Take that into account when deciding how long you'll need to finish a writing assignment.

Types of Writing

The writing you're required to do in your lifetime varies — for example, timed writings and essay questions on exams; autobiographical essays for college applications; high-school and college papers on a variety of subjects; business letters, proposals, and reports related to your work. In most of your writing you'll be doing one of the following:

- Describing a person, place, or thing
- Telling a story or recounting an incident
- Reporting information
- Providing instructions or explaining a process
- Arguing a position or proving a point
- Analyzing something — a text, a theory, an attitude, or an event

The techniques you use will overlap. For example, if you're writing a descriptive essay about your Aunt Gladys, you might narrate an incident that reveals her personality.

Understanding Your Assignment

Most — although not all — college writing assignments focus on argument and analysis. But within an essay arguing a position, you might use descriptive and narrative techniques. In a paper taking a stand against capital punishment, you might include a vivid description of a gas chamber, or recount the steps of an execution, or even narrate an incident. In choosing your approach to any writing task, be guided by your purpose and the best way to fulfill it.

When you take the essay portion of the FSE, fulfilling it is your main purpose. Understand what you are asked to do. In an examination question, for example, if you're asked to analyze how an author's techniques contribute to his theme, and if you describe the theme thoroughly but don't discuss the techniques, then you've failed to fulfill the assignment. Or if in a psychology class, you're asked to compare and contrast two recent theories about selective amnesia, and you write five pages on one of the theories and only half a page on the other, you probably haven't done what is required.

Writing on the job is no different. For example, if you need to write a testing protocol for a new product, you should include such things as a detailed description of the testing samples and the control group, the conditions of testing, materials and equipment, all the steps of the tests, relevant formulas and equations, and the methods to be used in evaluating results. If after the testing your manager asks for a summary of the results, you should provide them as clearly, honestly, and succinctly as you can. You may need to include a brief explanation of the tests, but you won't want to give a blow-by-blow account.

Whether you're writing in school or at work, make sure that you understand your task. Then, in planning what you'll write, aim everything you say at achieving that purpose.

Understanding Your Audience

For whom are you writing? Before you begin, think about your audience. A reader is at the other end of your writing, and you should keep that reader in mind. In the case of this exam, you should be writing for those people who are evaluating your capabilities to become a Foreign Service Officer.

Student writers sometimes think that their audience is a stuffy instructor who will be impressed by big words and long sentences. But most teachers know good, clear writing when they see it. Most can distinguish between solid content and inflated trivia. If you have little to say but dress it up in overblown prose with commas in all the right places, you won't fare as well as someone who has something to say and says it clearly, even with a few mechanical errors.

The reason you're writing and the audience you're writing for are closely related, so be realistic. If you're writing a letter to a surfing magazine praising a new board, you'll use different language and a different tone than you will in a college paper on Mikhail Gorbachev's success in attempting to modernize Russia in the late 1980s. Although both audiences want to understand and be interested in what you write, they'll expect and respond to different styles. Changing your language, style, or tone to meet specific circumstances is fine. But don't make the mistake of thinking that you can be straightforward in the letter to the surfing magazine while you should strive to sound important in the paper on Gorbachev.

Ask yourself some specific questions about your audience before you begin. Among some things to consider

- **Are you writing for people in a particular field, such as psychology, English literature, or genetics?** Can you assume knowledge of the terminology and concepts you'll be using, or do you need to define them in the paper? Will you need to provide extensive background information on the subject you plan to discuss, or will a brief summary be enough?

- **What expectations does your audience have?** An audience of marine biologists will have different expectations from an article on marine biology than will a general audience, for example.

- **Are you writing for someone who insists on certain writing practices or who has pet peeves?** One instructor may require a five-paragraph essay, or another may forbid the use of intentional sentence fragments. Be aware of any requirements or restrictions. On grammar, punctuation, and usage questions, if you aren't sure about a particular instructor, you're safest taking a conservative path.

- **What is the reading level of your audience?** Instructions and explanations written for fourth graders shouldn't include college-level vocabulary, for example.

- **Are you writing for an audience that is likely to agree or disagree with your point of view?** Consider this question if you're writing an argumentative or editorial piece. It can make a difference in the language you select, the amount of proof you offer, and the tone you use. An editorial for a small-town paper on the importance of family values, for example, is less likely to encounter resistance from the audience than an editorial on legalizing drugs.

Guidelines for Choosing a Topic

Your main purpose in writing is to inform, persuade, or entertain. Defining your purpose or goal is the first step. Select a topic that is narrow enough to be explained within your page limitations. A thesis, unlike a topic, is a single statement that makes an assertion about a topic. It is usually placed somewhere in the introduction of an essay. Often, a thesis sentence will give the reader a clear overview of the essay by stating the main ideas. Generally, if you choose a topic that is interesting to you, then your reader will find it interesting too.

Often you're assigned a topic to write about or asked to choose among several. When you must create your own, keep in mind these points.

- **Choose a topic appropriate to the length of your paper.** Generally, students pick topics that are too broad to be adequately covered. Narrow topics lead to close observation, while broad topics lead to generalizations and sketchy development. If you're writing a five-page paper, don't write on the history of women's rights; instead, write about one incident in the history of women's rights. Even a personal or descriptive essay will be better if you choose a narrow topic — my childhood in a small town, for example, rather than my childhood, or my uncle's barn, rather than the Midwest.

- **Avoid a topic that will tempt you to summarize rather than to discuss or analyze.** Don't cover the plot of Macbeth, but do talk about how the final scene of Macbeth illustrates the play's theme. The second topic is narrower and less likely to lead to summary. When considering a topic, ask yourself if it can lead to a reasonable thesis.

- **Choose a topic that interests you.** If you don't care about limiting cigarette advertising, don't select it as a topic for a persuasive essay. You'll have more to say and write better on something you care about.

- **If your assignment requires research, choose a topic on which you can find material.** Even when you aren't writing a research paper, make sure that you've picked a subject that you can develop with sufficient details.

- **After you've picked a topic, don't be afraid to change it if it isn't working out.** Instructors would rather you write a good essay than that you grind out pages on something you realize was a bad choice.

Topic versus Thesis

Don't confuse a topic with a main idea or thesis. The topic provides the subject; the thesis makes an assertion about that subject. Here are a few examples of topics that might be assigned to a college student:

- Compare and contrast X's poem "To a Wolf" with Y's poem "The Happy Meercat." Consider both theme and technique.
- Discuss the following statement: "No matter how much we may deplore human rights violations in China, the United States should not impose sanctions on the Chinese government." Do you agree or disagree? Support your opinion.
- Analyze Shakespeare's use of clothing imagery in *King Lear*.
- Describe an incident in your life that caused you to change an opinion or attitude.
- "The Civil War had much more to do with economics than with morality." Do you agree or disagree with this statement? Support your opinion.

Two of these topics (the second and fifth) ask the writer to argue a position. A sentence expressing that position is a thesis statement. A thesis statement for the second topic might be as follows:

Imposing sanctions on China would be a mistake because it would hurt the American economy, because sanctions are notoriously unsuccessful as a way to force change, and because the United States should not interfere in the internal policies of other countries.

While the remaining three topics don't ask the writer to take a position, for a good essay on any of these topics, the writer should formulate a thesis. A thesis statement for the first might be,

> Although both poet X and poet Y show appreciation for their subjects, poet X's "Wolf" symbolizes the separation between humans and other animals, while poet Y's "Meercat" symbolizes the connection between all living things.

With this thesis statement, the writer makes, a point about the topic and sets up a direction for the essay.

Writing a Thesis Statement

Whenever you write a paper analyzing, discussing, comparing, identifying causes or effects, or arguing a position, you should be able to write a thesis statement. You can refine and improve it as you go along, but try to begin with a one-sentence statement. A thesis statement can help you steer a straight course, avoiding the danger of digression.

Make your thesis statement say something. Don't be satisfied with weak generalities that fail to zero in on your main point. The following are examples of pseudo-thesis statements:

- Poets X and Y make important points about animals in their poems.
- "To a Wolf" and "The Happy Meercat"
- People hold different opinions as to whether it is wise to impose sanctions on China because of their human rights violations.
- Shakespeare uses quite a bit of clothing imagery in *King Lear*.

None of these statements provides a clear direction for an essay because the assertions they make are so vague; they are useless. A better thesis statement for the third example might be:

> Clothing images in King Lear reflect the development of Lear from a man blinded by appearances to a man able to face the naked truth.

Remember that the creation of a thesis statement is important to the way you approach your topic, helping you direct your thinking as well as your writing.

Avoiding Fallacies

As you write be careful to avoid logic fallacies and ideological reasoning. *Logic fallacies* are problems in thinking or connecting ideas. Common fallacies include:

- **Ad hominem:** Also called name-calling, this fallacy is an attack either directly or indirectly on a person: Bob can't be right because he is an idiot.
- **Bandwagon/celebrity appeal:** This is a fallacy that implies the reader should agree with a premise because a majority or a particularly significant person agrees with the premise: As everyone knows, this bill will help our children.
- **Either/or reasoning:** Assuming that there can be only one cause or one solution in an issue: The only way to keep our children safe is to ban video games.
- **Slippery slope:** Assuming that because one minor fact is true, then a larger premise must be too, despite any further proof: Congressman Smith voted against tax increases last week; therefore, Congressman Smith will always be against tax increases.
- **Ad populum:** Arguing based upon emotional appeals rather than facts: All true Americans want to ban this book.
- **Circular reasoning:** Presents as reasons a restatement of the problem: There are not enough parking spaces because there are too many cars.

Ideological reasoning is the use of cultural, religious, or moral values and beliefs to prove a position. Although there is nothing wrong with making personal judgments in this way, you should always be aware that your audience might not share your ideological views. To reach the greatest number of individuals you should avoid making ideological reasons the foundation of your arguments.

The Main Idea in Narratives and Personal Essays

Narrative and personal essays also require a main or controlling idea to help you focus and direct your writing. For example, consider this topic:

Describe an incident in your life that caused you to change an opinion or attitude.

Before you begin writing, create a sentence that will both identify the incident you plan to narrate and describe the change it caused. Below are some examples of main idea statements.

- The divorce of my parents when I was seven changed my view that adults were infallible and always in control of their own lives.
- When I was six, my cat Edward died; and I began to mistrust the reassurances of doctors, a mistrust that has remained with me ever since.
- Changing high schools when I was fifteen made me realize for the first time that the fear of an experience is often worse than the reality.

When you write your paper, you may decide to suggest your main idea indirectly rather than state it. But making yourself create a statement is still a good idea.

Prewriting: How to Research And Organize

After you have narrowed your topic and established a working thesis, you can start researching your essay. You may want to begin by writing what you know about the topic before you head to the library or the Internet. Generally, information that is assumed to be common knowledge does not have to be identified. However, you should identify, either by quote or citation, all specific phrasing that comes from another writer. Paraphrasing is a valuable way to summarize long passages or ideas from other writers.

Write an outline to focus and develop the main ideas that support or explain your thesis. You can organize your ideas in a variety of spatial or chronological ways. If you make your outline detailed, the body of the essay should be easy to write. Although a written outline can seem like extra work, it is a valuable, almost essential, key to writing a good first draft.

Finding Examples and Evidence

When you have a topic, you begin thinking of what you'll say. Write a thesis statement to organize your thinking. Before you start writing, take notes. For personal essays, write down your thoughts, observations, memories, and experiences. When analyzing a text, take notes on the significant sections or underline them. For most other essays, read materials with an eye to finding details, examples, and illustrations to support your main idea.

If you want to use quotations, write them down accurately. Remember that you'll need to footnote tiny facts, ideas, or quotations you borrow from other sources, so be sure to include bibliographical information in your notes. Some of what you write down will probably never appear in your essay. Your notes might even include questions that occur to you as you read, possibilities you want to explore, warnings to yourself, or reminders to check further on certain points. This stage of preparing a paper is not only to ensure that you have examples and evidence but also to help you think in more detail about your topic and thesis.

Brainstorming, Taking Notes, and Outlining

Begin the process by trying free-writing on the computer. You can get ideas down quickly and legibly and save them as a brainstorming file; later, you can import parts of this file into your first draft. Take notes on the computer, too, being sure to include the information you'll need to cite references. Word-processing programs can format and place footnotes when you're at the point of preparing your final draft, but of course, you are responsible for accurately recording the sources of your information. If your writing project requires a bibliography, start a list of your references. Later, you can easily add to and rearrange the list.

Most programs have a feature that allows you to create a formal outline according to a style you choose, such as roman numerals for headings, alpha characters for first-level subheadings, and so on. If you go back into your outline to add a heading or subheading, the program will automatically update your outline designations. Changing an outline on your computer is so simple that you can experiment with different organizational plans.

Using the Computer for Research

With a computer, you can gain access to thousands of documents and databases, some in portable form on CD-ROMs (disks that store large amounts of information) and some directly online. You can call up journal and newspaper articles, abstracts, a variety of encyclopedias and dictionaries, and much more. Through the Internet, you can view databases on many subjects and have access to library archival materials. The challenge is to know what there is and how to search for it. So much information is available online that you may feel overwhelmed and frustrated. Before you use the Internet to do serious research, it's a good idea to get some training. How-to books and classes are available, as are Internet directories that steer you in the right direction. Once you are online, search systems (or search engines) — to which you enter key words — help you navigate. When you use information from electronic sources in a paper, consult a current style guide (such as the *MLA Handbook for Writers of Research Papers*) on the correct forms for citing it in footnotes and a bibliography.

The Importance of Specific Details

A frequent mistake in writing is failing to provide specific examples, evidence, or details to support an idea or thesis. In an essay about a poem, for example, it isn't enough to say that the author's language creates a dark, gloomy atmosphere; you must cite particular words and images that demonstrate this effect. In an essay arguing that magnet schools in cities improve education for minority students, you must provide some evidence — statistics, anecdotes, and so on. In a timed writing on the statement, "We learn more from our failures than our successes," don't merely reflect on the statement; you should cite examples from your life, or from the news, or from history.

Remember that essays filled with general unsupported statements are not only unconvincing, but also uninteresting.

Quoting, Paraphrasing, and Avoiding Plagiarism

As you take notes, be aware that when you write your paper you must cite any sources you use, so record the information you'll need for footnotes. Consult a style guide for proper footnoting and preparation of a bibliography. You'll be guilty of plagiarism if you don't properly give credit for words or ideas that you borrow from others.

Most people understand that they can't steal exact words from a source, but some believe that paraphrasing — simply borrowing an idea — is acceptable. Generally, it isn't. Although you don't need to footnote well-known ideas such as evolution or easily accessible facts such as the date of the first moon landing, you should document less generally known ideas or opinions (for example, a news analyst's assessment of a Supreme Court decision), and less accessible facts (such as the number of motorcycles sold in the United States in a given year). Deciding what to footnote is sometimes a gray area, but play it safe. If you have doubts, cite your source.

When should you use quotations in a paper, and when should you paraphrase information instead? If you want to make a point about an author's language or style — as in the analysis of a literary work — use quotations.

But don't quote an entire stanza if you are going to comment on only two words, and don't give up your responsibility to discuss a character simply by quoting a descriptive passage from a novel.

If your interest is in the information a source conveys rather than in the author's expression, consider paraphrasing (putting the information in your own words) rather than quoting, particularly if the relevant passage is long and includes material you don't need. The question to ask is, "Why am I choosing to include this quotation?" If you have a good reason — an author's language or tone, for example, or a particularly apt expression — go ahead. But often you're after only the information or part of the information.

Consider the following passage:

> Community-based policing has given rise to several important questions, among them the following: Should police officers address social problems that extend beyond particular crimes? Some experts on police reform say yes, while others say no. Although there is agreement that having police officers walk regular beats can decrease community suspicion and deter lawbreakers, the experts who are against greater involvement feel that giving police a broader responsibility by expecting them to deal with problems such as urban decay and irresponsible parenting is unrealistic and ultimately undesirable.

If you're writing about attitudes toward police reform, why not paraphrase the point that relates to your topic as shown in the following paragraph?

> Police-reform experts disagree about many issues, including whether or not police should involve themselves in social issues that go beyond their direct responsibility to deter crime and apprehend lawbreakers.

Don't pad a paper with quotations to add to its length (you'll irritate the instructor) and don't quote heavily to prove that you've read a source and have evidence for your points. Paraphrasing works just as well. One caution, however. Paraphrasing a source requires correct citation (footnoting) just as quotation does.

Reviewing the Types of Writing Assignments

All assignments are not identical, and you can use different strategies as you approach each writing task. The main purpose of your project may be research, argument, analysis, or narrative. In each of these areas, you can learn some basic skills that will make the work easier.

The Research Paper

Don't regard a research paper as unlike other writing assignments. As in other essays, you should have a topic, a thesis, an introduction, good organization, unified and coherent paragraphs, transitions, and so on. A research paper should not consist of footnoted facts loosely strung together.

However, unlike other essays, a research paper depends on the use and citation of several sources of information, such as reference books, books related to your subject, relevant journal and magazine articles, speeches, and lectures. During the information-gathering period, get to know your library well. If available, check electronic databases. Learn how to locate a variety of materials that will give you a thorough (not one-sided) view of your topic. When you do find information, take careful notes that include bibliographical information about your source.

Practices for footnoting and preparing a bibliography vary. Therefore, when you're assigned a research paper, ask your instructor to recommend a style guide. Several general guides are available, as well as more specific ones designed for particular fields, among them language and literature, biology, business, history, and law.

Essays Arguing a Position from a Single Text

If your assignment is to write about a single text — for example, to take a position on an article in favor of regulating the Internet — read the text more than once. Look up terms you're uncertain about. Mark points that seem unclear or issues that may require research, and include outside research if is allowed by the assignment. (If you do use material from other sources, be sure to cite them, just as you would in a research paper.)

Determine the strongest and weakest arguments in the article. After studying the text carefully, decide whether you agree or disagree with the author's position. Remember that when you write your paper, you should provide a brief, fair summary of that position, whether you're agreeing with it or not. In an argumentative essay you must support your own viewpoint *and* answer the opposition.

Essays Analyzing a Literary Work

When you're asked to analyze a literary work, or one aspect of a literary work, stay close to the text. Read it and, if possible, reread it. Your first job is to interpret meaning, which can take some time. Once you feel comfortable with your interpretation, take notes or mark the text with an eye toward finding support for your topic and thesis. You'll be using quotations in your paper, so indicate those passages or lines that might be particularly effective.

Generally, when you write an essay on a nonliterary text, you focus on content, concentrating on the author's information and the quality of his or her arguments. When you write about a literary text, however, you must also pay close attention to the author's technique. If you don't already know such terms as *meter, image, metaphor, simile, diction, flat character,* and *irony,* check a glossary of literary terms. In your notes, include specific words and images from the text, observations about structure (a poem's rhyme scheme, for example, or a novel's subplot), point of view, and tone. Remember, however, that when you discuss formal features like these in your essay, you should relate them to a point you are making, usually about the author's theme or purpose. Don't risk having your reader ask, "So what if the rhyme scheme changes in the last stanza?"

Narrative, Descriptive, and Autobiographical Essays

For some essays, you'll use your own thoughts, observations, and experiences, without reference to a text. But as with essays of argument and analysis, you need to gather information to develop your main ideas, and taking notes is a good way to do it. Before beginning an essay describing your Aunt Gladys, for example, write down all the details you can about her, including any anecdotes that reveal her characteristics. At this point, don't worry about organizing your observations. Remember that you're gathering information. If you haven't yet written a sentence stating a main idea, try to do so now. (For example, "Although Aunt Gladys prides herself on being no trouble to anyone, she finds ways to get everyone in the family to do what she wants, or Aunt Gladys looks like a little old lady, but she acts like a teenage girl.") Without a controlling idea, your essay will be a list of details with nothing to unify them or give them purpose.

When a college application asks for an essay about yourself, your purpose will be to describe the traits, experiences, interests, achievements, and goals that show you're a good candidate for college admission. First, take notes about yourself — whatever you can think of. Be sure to consider things that emphasize your individuality. In going over your notes later, you may decide not to include the no-hit Little League softball game you pitched when you were nine, or every fast-food job you've ever had; but by making a complete list, you can look for patterns that will help you organize your essay. When it comes time to put your points in order, throw out unnecessary details, consolidating and summarizing — for example, mentioning that you held five fast-food jobs (but not specifying each employer) while attending high school and becoming class valedictorian.

Writing

A common misconception about writing is that the first draft must be perfect. However, even excellent writers create multiple drafts before they feel content with their writing. In the first draft, focus on introductions, connecting ideas within paragraphs, and conclusions.

A good introduction catches the reader's attention and then provides a general orientation to the topic. You can interest the reader by using quotations, anecdotes, questions or addressing the reader directly. Paragraphs develop a single idea in a series of connected sentences. A unified paragraph stays focused on a single idea and is coherent and well developed. Your final statement should bring all of your points to their logical conclusion. You can leave the reader pondering your essay by using a quotation, a reference back to a point or question made in the introduction, or a story that emphasizes your thesis.

Working from a Thesis Statement

The first thing to look at when you're ready to organize your paper is your main idea or thesis statement. Putting yourself in a reader's place, imagine how you would expect to see the main idea developed. Then look at the notes you've taken. If you used your thesis statement as a guide in gathering information, you should see a pattern.

Look at the following thesis statement:

> Imposing sanctions on China would be a mistake because it would hurt the American economy, because sanctions are notoriously unsuccessful as a way to force change, and because the United States should not interfere in the internal policies of other countries.

This statement suggests that the paper will be divided into three main parts; it even indicates an order for those sections. When you go through your notes, decide where each note most logically fits. For example, a note about U.S. clothing manufacturers' increasing use of Chinese labor would fit into section one, and a note about the failure of sanctions in the Middle East in section two.

Of course, things aren't usually this neat. Your thesis statement might not be this precise, or the kind of essay you're writing might not lend itself to such an easy division. But starting from the moment you look at your topic and decide on your main idea, you should be thinking about ways to develop it. This thinking leads you to your organizing principle.

A review of some common methods of organization will help you. Remember, however, to avoid an overly rigid approach. After you begin to write, you may realize that your plan needs to be changed. Writing itself, often generates new ideas, or suggests a different direction.

Spatial or Chronological Organization

Some topics lend themselves to organization based on space or time. A descriptive essay might work well if you begin with a distant view and move closer: First describe how a barn looks from the road, for example, then describe the view you see when you stand directly in front of the barn, then describe the view (and smell and sounds) when standing inside the barn door, and completing your description with what you see when you climb the ladder into the loft.

In the narration of an event and in some kinds of technical writing describing a process, you write about events in the order they occur. Often dividing your material into stages avoids the "and then, and then, and then!" effect. If you were writing about making a ceramic vase, you could divide the process into three main stages: selecting and preparing the clay, forming and refining the shape of the vase on the potter's wheel, and glazing the piece and firing it in a kiln. The detailed steps in making the vase could then be organized sequentially under these sections.

Dividing a Subject into Categories

Just as you can divide a process into stages, you can divide a subject into categories. When you look over your notes, and using your thesis statement as a guide, see if logical groupings emerge. Look at the following topic and thesis statement, written by a fictional student.

- **Topic:** Write a paper addressing an environmental concern and suggesting ideas for a solution.
- **Thesis:** The United States is losing its forests, and the solution is everyone's responsibility.

Note that the second half of this thesis statement is weak: *the solution is everyone's responsibility* is a vague assertion.

In looking over his notes, the student quickly identifies those that relate to the first part of the thesis statement.

> Less than 1 percent of U.S. old-growth forests remain, U.S. consumption of wood is up 3 percent since 1930, and so on.

However, when he looks at the rest of his notes, he finds he has everything from "Logging bans have been effective in many areas" to "Don't use disposable diapers," to "Agricultural waste can be effectively processed to make building materials that provide excellent insulation."

At this point, he decides to create categories. He finds that many notes are related to simple, everyday actions that can help reduce wood and paper consumption (no disposable diapers, e-mail instead of memos, cloth bags instead of paper bags, recycling newspapers, and so on). Still others cover alternatives for wood, such as agricultural waste, engineered wood manufactured by the forest products industry, the use of steel studs in construction rather than wooden ones, a method of wall forming called "rammed earth construction," and so on. Then he notices that several notes relate to government actions, such as logging *bans, wilderness designations, Forest Service reforms, and so on.* He decides to use three general classifications as a principle of organization:

I. Problem

II. Solutions

    A. Consumer actions

    B. Alternatives to wood

    C. Government regulations

He may decide to change the order of the classifications when he writes his paper, but for now he has a principle organization.

If some notes don't fit into these classifications, he may want to add another category, or add some subsections. For example, if several notes deal with actions by major conservation groups, he may want to add a division under "Solutions" called "Conservation group activities." Or, if he finds some notes relating to disadvantages of wood alternatives, he may add some subtopics under B, for example, price, stability, public perception.

Dividing material into categories is one of the most basic forms of organization. Make sure the categories are appropriate to the purpose of your paper and that you have sufficient information under each one.

Organizing Essays of Comparison

Sometimes, students have problems with topics that ask them to compare and contrast two things. After gathering information on each thing, they fail to focus on the similarities and dissimilarities between them.

When your topic involves comparison, you can organize in either of two ways. First, you can discuss each thing separately and then include a section in which you draw comparisons and contrasts between them. With this organization, if you were comparing and contrasting two poems, you would write first about one — covering, for example, theme, language, images, tone, and rhyme scheme — and then about the other, covering the same areas. In a third section, you would make a series of statements comparing and contrasting major aspects of the poems. If you choose this method, make your separate discussions of the poems parallel — that is, for the second poem, address points in the same order you used for the first poem. Also, in the third section of the paper, avoid simply repeating what you said in sections one and two.

A second way of organizing requires you to decide first which aspects of the poems you want to compare and contrast (theme, language, and imagery), and then to structure your essay according to these. For example, if you begin with theme, you state the themes of both poems and compare them. Then you compare the language of the two poems, then the imagery, then the tone, and so on. Two advantages of this type of organization are, first, you are forced to focus on similarities and dissimilarities and less likely to include material that isn't pertinent and, second, you avoid repetition by eliminating a separate compare-and-contrast section.

You can also combine these two types of organization. For example, you may want to discuss each poem's theme separately, and then move into a point-by-point comparison of the other aspects of the poem (language, imagery, tone, and so on).

Inductive or Deductive Patterns of Organization

In a logical argument, the pattern in which you present evidence and then draw a general conclusion is called *inductive.* This term can also be used to describe a method of approaching your material, particularly in an essay presenting an argument. You are using this method in an essay even when you state the general conclusion first and present the supporting evidence in successive paragraphs. In fact, in essays it is customary to begin with the general conclusion as a thesis statement:

- **Evidence:** The student action committee failed to achieve a quorum in all six of its last meetings.

  During the past year, the student action committee has proposed four plans for changing the grievance procedure and has been unable to adopt any of them.

  According to last month's poll in the student newspaper, 85 percent of the respondents had not heard of the student action committee. Two openings on the committee have remained unfilled for eight months because no one has applied for membership.

- **Conclusion:** The student action committee is an ineffective voice for students at this university. (Note that, in an essay, this would be a thesis statement.)

Another type of organization borrowed from logical argument is called *deductive*. With this pattern you begin with a generalization and then apply it to specific instances. In a timed writing, you might be given a statement such as, "It's better to be safe than sorry" or "Beauty is in the eye of the beholder," and then asked to agree or disagree, providing examples that support your view. With such essays, you aren't proving or disproving the truth of a statement, but offering an opinion and then supporting it with examples. For example, if you begin with a generalization such as "Beauty is in the eye of the beholder," you could cite instances such as different standards for human beauty in different cultures, or different views of beauty in architecture from era to era. You could also use examples from your own experience, such as your brother's appreciation of desert landscapes contrasted to your boredom with them.

Order of Examples and Evidence

Within any overall pattern of organization, you must decide on the specific order of your examples and evidence. The best plan is to save your most important point or most convincing piece of evidence for last. The last position is the most emphatic, and a reader will expect you to build to your strongest point. Saving the best for last isn't a rule; you must decide, based on your thesis and the evidence and examples you've collected, which order works best. But do remember that you want to avoid having your essay trail off with a trivial example or weak argument.

Connecting Paragraphs in an Essay

Your essay should move from paragraph to paragraph smoothly, each point growing out of the preceding one. If you are shifting direction or moving to a different point, prepare your reader with a transition. Achieving continuity in your essay is similar to achieving continuity in a paragraph.

Outlining

Creating an outline, either a formal or an informal one, helps you stay with your organizational plan. Sometimes an outline helps you see problems in your original plan, and you can eliminate them before you've spent time writing.

If you prefer writing papers without an outline, try an experiment. Create an outline *after* a paper is finished to see if your organization is clear and logical. This exercise may make you decide that outlining is a good idea.

Informal Outlines

An *informal outline* can be little more than a list of your main points. You can refine it by following each main point with notations of the evidence or examples that support it. You are, in effect, grouping your notes. A simple outline like this is often all you need. It is especially valuable for timed writings or essay exams. Thinking your approach through before you begin — and jotting down your thoughts — will help you avoid rambling and moving away from the assignment.

Formal Outlines

You may want to prepare a more *formal outline*. Sometimes you may even be asked to submit an outline with a writing assignment. Following are a few guidelines:

Use roman numerals for main topics. Alternate letters and Arabic numerals for subtopics. Indent subtopics.

I.

  A.

  B.

    1.

    2.

      a.

      b.

Make outline topics parallel in form. Make subtopics parallel in form also. For example, if you use a sentence for the first topic, use sentences for all subsequent topics, but if you use a noun for the first subtopic, use a noun for the following ones.

Watch the logic of your outline. The main topics generally indicate the basic structure of your essay. The second level of your outline (A, B, C) covers the major ideas that contribute to the larger units. The next level of subtopics is for narrower points related to these ideas. Don't stick irrelevant ideas in your outline under the guise of subtopics. Make sure each element logically fits under its heading or you're defeating the purpose of an outline.

Each topic and subtopic should have at least one mating topic or subtopic; that is, no I without a II, no A without a B, and so on. Remember that topics and subtopics are divisions of your subject, and you can't divide something into one part. If your outline shows solitary topics or subtopics, reevaluate to see whether you are misplacing or poorly stating your headings. The information should perhaps be worked into an existing larger category or divided into two topics or subtopics.

Sentence Outlines and Topic Outlines

In a *sentence outline,* all elements are stated in complete sentences. In a *topic outline,* the elements may be presented as single words or as phrases. Study the following examples.

Here's an example of a sentence outline:

  I. Many high school classes do not prepare students for large university classes.

    A. Nontracked high school classes don't challenge more able students to achieve at the highest level.

      1. Less competition leads some students to "get by" rather than excel.

      2. Inflated grading of good students in nontracked classes can lead to false expectations.

    B. High school classes are not designed to encourage individual responsibility, which is required in large university classes.

      1. Required attendance in high school may lead students to react to less rigid attendance requirements by cutting classes.

      2. High school teachers assign daily homework and reading assignments, whereas university professors generally make long-term assignments.

      3. High school teachers frequently spend more time with individual students than do professors in large universities.

  II. Some high schools offer programs to help students prepare for university classes.

And now, an example of a topic outline:

  I. Lack of preparation of high school students for university classes

    A. Nontracked high school classes

      1. Less competition

      2. Mated grades

    B. Less individual responsibility in high school classes

        1. Required attendance

        2. Homework and daily assignments

        3. Individual attention from teachers

  II. Programs to prepare high school students for university classes

Structuring Your Paper

The first thing to remember when beginning to write is that you don't have to create a perfect first draft. Count on rewriting. Your first draft may well be a mixture of planning and improvising — letting yourself move in a direction you hadn't originally intended. Remember that writing is not a straightforward process, that even when you begin a first draft you may make changes in your thesis statement or in your organizational plan.

The exception to the rule about first drafts is in timed writing assignments like the FSE written essay, for which you may have time for only one draft. Spend a few moments planning your answer, noting examples you intend to use, and then move ahead. Graders of these assignments are looking for substance, support for ideas, and clear writing.

Avoid definition of a term that doesn't require defining or that leads nowhere: "The novel *Silas Marner* by George Eliot is about a man who is a miser." What is a miser? According to the definition in *Webster's New World Dictionary,* a miser is "a greedy, stingy person who hoards money for its own sake."

Suggestions for Introductions

An introduction should lead naturally into the rest of your paper and be appropriate to its subject and tone. Some suggestions for openings follow, but use judgment in applying them. Although beginning with an anecdote can be effective for some papers, don't force one where it doesn't belong. A story about your indecisive father is not the best way to begin a paper analyzing the character of *Hamlet*.

- **Use a relevant quotation from the work you are discussing.**

  "I am encompassed by a wall, high and hard and stone, with only my brainy nails to tear it down. And I cannot do it." Kerewin Holmes, one of the main characters in Keri Hulme's novel *The Bone People,* describes herself as both physically and emotionally alone in a tower she has built by the New Zealand Sea. Throughout the novel, Hulme uses concrete images — the tower, muteness, physical beatings, the ocean — to suggest her characters' isolation from each other and the community around them.

- **Provide background or context for your thesis statement.**

  Until the second half of this century, Americans spent the country's natural resources freely. They mined for minerals, diverted rivers, replaced wilderness with cities and towns. In the process, they cut down forests that had been in place for thousands of years. Now, in the 21st century, the reality that progress has its price is obvious to almost everyone. Only ten percent of old-growth forests in the United States remain intact, with demand for wood products expected to grow by 50 percent in the next 50 years. The country is in danger of losing its forests altogether unless citizens pursue solutions from everyday recycling to using wood alternatives to actively supporting government regulations.

- **Ask a question that leads to your thesis statement.**

  Is the United States still a country where the middle class thrives? Strong evidence suggests that the traditional American view of a successful middle class is fading. At the very least, the prospects for someone who stands in the economic middle have significantly changed since the 1970s. Twenty-five years ago middle-class people expected to own their own homes in the suburbs and send their children to college. Today, for many people, these expectations have become more like distant dreams. Two factors — a growing disparity in wages within the labor force and rising prices for real estate and goods — suggest that the middle class is a less comfortable place to be than it was for the previous generation.

- **Begin with a relevant anecdote that leads to your thesis statement.**

  Doug was the star in my high school senior class. He captained the football team, dated the best looking girls, charmed the teachers, and managed to get As and Bs seemingly without studying. When he headed off to a big Midwestern university, we weren't surprised. But when he was home again a year later on academic probation, many of us wondered what could have happened. Doug told me candidly that his year at the university was far removed from anything he'd experienced in high school. Quite simply, his small, noncompetitive high school classes hadn't prepared him for a large, impersonal university where the professors didn't know his name, let alone his role as a big man on campus. I believe programs to help students like Doug make the transition from high school to college could help reduce the high failure rate among college freshmen.

- **Speak directly to your readers. Ask them to imagine themselves in a situation you create.**

  Imagine being escorted into a room and asked to disrobe every time you want to take an airplane trip. Picture someone in a uniform grilling you about your background or even hooking you up to a lie detector. Such scenarios seem impossible in America, but experts agree that the United States may be forced to take extreme measures to combat increasing domestic terrorism.

Your own particular topic may suggest to you any number of creative beginnings. Try to go beyond the obvious. For example, which of the following two openings for an essay on the qualities of a good mate is more likely to catch a reader's interest?

- **Student 1:** It is important to look for many qualities in the person you choose to spend your life with.
- **Student 2:** Finding a mate is hard enough. Finding a mate you're happy with may seem close to impossible.

The Paragraph

A paragraph develops one idea with a series of logically connected sentences. Most paragraphs function as small essays themselves, each with a main topic (stated or implied) and several related sentences that support it.

How many paragraphs do you need in your paper? That depends on what you have to say. The idea that an essay should consist of five paragraphs — an introduction, three paragraphs of examples, and a conclusion — is much too rigid, although students first learning to write are sometimes taught this. You may well have more than three examples or points to make, and you may have an example or point that requires several paragraphs of development in itself. Don't limit yourself. Let your particular topic and supporting points guide you in creating your paragraphs.

Paragraph Length

Paragraphs vary in length. For example, short paragraphs (one to three sentences) are used in newspaper stories where the emphasis is on reporting information without discussion, or in technical writing where the emphasis is on presenting facts such as statistics and measurements without analysis. Written dialogue also consists of short paragraphs, with a new paragraph for each change of speaker. In an essay, a short paragraph can also be effectively used for dramatic effect or transition.

> But the reconciliation was never to take place. Her grandmother died as Jane was driving home from the airport.

Generally, however, avoid a series of very short paragraphs in your essays. They suggest poor development of an idea.

On the other hand, paragraphs a page or more in length are difficult for most readers, who like to see a subject divided into shorter segments. Look carefully at long paragraphs to see whether you have gone beyond covering one idea or are guilty of repetition, wordiness, or rambling. Don't arbitrarily split a long paragraph in half by indenting a particular sentence, however. Make sure that each paragraph meets the requirement of a single main idea with sentences that support it.

Paragraph Unity

A unified paragraph is one that focuses on one idea and one idea only. Look at the following example of a paragraph that *lacks* unity.

Identification of particular genes can lead to better medicine. For example, recently scientists identified a defective gene that appears to cause hemochromatosis, or iron overload. Iron overload is fairly easily cured if it is recognized and treated early, but currently it is often misdiagnosed because it mimics more familiar conditions. The problem is that when not treated in time, iron overload leads to a variety of diseases, from diabetes to liver cancer. The identification of the faulty gene can prevent misdiagnosis by allowing physicians, through a screening test, to identify patients who carry it and treat them before the condition becomes too advanced. *It is interesting that most people don't realize the exact role of iron in the body.* They know that it is important for their health, but few are aware that only about ten percent of the iron in food is normally absorbed by the small intestine. Most of the rest is tied up in hemoglobin, which carries oxygen from the lungs.

The first sentence of the paragraph presents the main idea that identification of genes leads to improved medical care. This idea is developed by the example of how the identification of a gene causing iron overload can lead to better diagnosis and early treatment. In the italicized sentence the paragraph begins to wander. It is a topic sentence for a different paragraph, one about the role of iron in the body and not about a benefit of genetic research.

Sometimes a sentence or two buried in the middle of a paragraph can break its unity, as in the following example.

Moving out of my parents' house and into an apartment didn't bring me the uncomplicated joy that I had expected. First of all, I had to struggle to make the rent every month, and the landlord was much less understanding than my parents. Then I realized I had to do my own laundry, clean up the place now and then, and fix my own meals. *One nice thing about my mother is that she is an excellent cook. She even attended a French cooking school before she married my father.* It's true that I liked the greater freedom I had in my apartment — no one constantly asking me what time I'd be home, no one nagging me about cleaning up my room or raking the front lawn — but I wasn't thrilled with spending most of a Saturday getting rid of a cockroach infestation, or Sunday night doing three loads of smelly laundry.

Notice how the italicized sentences interrupt the flow of the paragraph, which is really about the downside of leaving home and not about the writer's mother.

To test the unity of your paragraphs, locate your topic sentence (if you have left it unstated, be clear on your paragraph's main idea) and then test the other sentences to see if they are developing that particular idea or if they are wandering off in another direction.

Paragraph Coherence

Along with developing a single idea, a paragraph should be well organized. You can use many of the same principles — chronology, inductive and deductive patterns, and so on — that you use to organize complete essays.

After you've decided on the order of your details, make sure the connections between sentences in the paragraph are clear. The smooth, logical flow of a paragraph is called paragraph coherence. Write each sentence with the previous one in mind.

Connecting Sentences through Ideas

Connect your sentences through their content, by picking up something from one and carrying it into the next. For example, follow a sentence that makes a general point with a specific, clear illustration of that point. Look at the following example.

The gap in pay between people with basic skills and people without them seems to be widening. In one comparison, the pay difference between women of varied mathematical skills had grown from $0.93 an hour in 1978 to $1.71 an hour in 1986.

Here, the second sentence is a clear illustration of the point made in the first sentence. But look at how coherence can be lost in a paragraph.

The gap in pay between people with basic skills and people without them seems to be widening. Women are now playing a more important role in the work force than they have since World War II, when many had to fill the positions of men who were overseas. The pay difference between women of varied mathematical skills has grown considerably, from $0.93 an hour in 1978 to $1.71 an hour in 1986.

In this example, the second sentence is not clearly connected to the first. Sentence three returns to the subject, but the continuity of the idea has been weakened.

You can also use one sentence to reflect or comment on the previous sentence, as in the following example.

The idea that in America hard work leads to financial success has been one of our most successful exports. For decades immigrants have arrived on American soil with a dream that here they can have what was impossible in their home countries, where they were limited by class structure or few opportunities.

Be sure in reviewing your paragraph that such reflections logically follow from the previous statement. Here, immigrants arriving with the preconceived notion that they will succeed, is tied to the point in the first sentence that the American dream has been a successful export.

You can also connect sentences by asking a question and following it with an answer or making a statement and following it with a question.

Why should the government invest in research? Research leads to technological advances that create employment, as was shown in the years following World War II.

Polls indicate that many Americans favor regulation of the Internet. Are they willing to pay both with their tax dollars and their freedoms?

The sentences in these two examples are linked by words as well as by ideas. In the first example, the word "research" has been picked up from the question and repeated in the answer. In the second example, the pronoun "they" in the question has its antecedent ("Americans") in the previous statement.

Connecting with Words and Phrases

Achieving paragraph coherence by connecting ideas is your first step. But as indicated in the last two examples, words and phrases can help strengthen the connection between sentences.

- Use a pronoun whose antecedent appears in the previous sentence: *Gabriel Garcia Marquez* suspends the laws of reality in his novels. *He* creates bizarre and even magical situations that reveal character in surprising ways.

- Repeat a key word or phrase: The idea of a perfect society, though never realized, continues to intrigue political *philosophers*. None of *these philosophers* seems to agree on where perfection lies.

- Use a synonym: According to my research, *physical beauty is* still considered a more important asset for women than for men. *Looks* are everything, according to several girls I spoke to, while the boys I interviewed felt that their athletic prowess and social status were at least as important as their appearance.

- Use word patterns, such as *first, second, third,* and so on: The reasons for the dean's announcing his decision today are clear. *First,* students will recognize that he is listening to their concerns. *Second,* faculty will applaud the end of a disruptive period of indecision. *Third,* wealthy and influential alumni though not particularly pleased by all the details of the plan will be overjoyed that the controversy will be off the front page of the paper.

- Use transitional words and phrases. Many words and phrases signal connections between sentences in a paragraph or between paragraphs in a paper. Look at the italicized words in the following sentences. The italicized words or phrases explicitly connect the second sentence to the first by creating a particular relationship.

  - The main character worships her. *Later,* his adoration turns to hatred.

  - The church stood at the top of the hill. *Below* stretched miles of orchards.

  - She treated him well. *For example,* she bought him a car and new clothes.

  - The product promised he'd grow new hair. *But* all he grew was a rash.

- Hamlet disdained Ophelia. As *a result,* she killed herself.
- Elizabeth was angry at Darcy. *In fact,* she wanted nothing to do with him.
- The plan is too expensive. *Furthermore, it* won't work.
- No one volunteered to help. *In other words,* no one cared.

Vary the transitional words you use.

Following is a list of words classified according to the relationships they suggest.

- **Time or place:** above, across from, adjacent to, afterward, before, behind, below, beyond, earlier, elsewhere, farther on, here, in the distance, nearby, next to, opposite to, to the left, to the right
- **Example:** for example, for instance, specifically, to be specific
- **Contrast:** but, however, nevertheless, on the contrary, on the other hand
- **Similarity:** similarly, in the same way, equally important
- **Consequence:** accordingly, as a result, consequently, therefore
- **Emphasis:** indeed, in fact, of course
- **Amplification:** and, again, also, further, furthermore, in addition, moreover, too
- **Restatement:** in other words, more simply stated, that is, to clarify
- **Summary and conclusion:** altogether, finally, in conclusion, in short, to summarize

Conclusions

How should you end your paper? Writing a proper conclusion is like tying a ribbon around a gift package. It's the last thing you do, but it also gives your final effort a finishing touch. If your ending works, your reader will feel satisfied.

What to Avoid

Before you can write your conclusion you should know what to avoid. Here are some common errors.

- **Don't introduce a new topic.** For example, if your essay has been about the loss of forests and possible solutions for the high consumption of wood products, don't end with a paragraph about another environmental concern, such as the disappearance of the California condor.
- **Don't trail off with a weak statement or a statement leaving your reader up in the air**. The Internet, free of regulation, has opened a world of information and ideas to everyone. Children enjoy learning at the computer.
- **Don't simply repeat your thesis or main idea in the same words.** Thus, as stated earlier, clothing imagery shows the changes in King Lear throughout the play.
- **Don't apologize for or suggest doubts about your thesis.** For a variety of reasons, middle-class expectations in the 1990s differ from those in the 1970s. It is possible, however, that the difference is not particularly illuminating about life in the United States.

You may use a brief concluding sentence instead of a formal conclusion in a simple or short paper (up to five pages, for example). Formal conclusions can sometimes be superfluous and even insulting to the reader's intelligence, particularly if the conclusion is a long summary of what he or she just read. Instead, end your paper with your best point, using a strong final sentence.

Suggestions for Conclusions

The two most important things a conclusion should do is give your readers a sense of completion and leave them with a strong impression. You can do this with a single statement or with a paragraph. If you do write a concluding paragraph, consider the following possibilities.

- **End with an appropriate quotation.**

  Throughout the novel the characters suffer both from their isolation and from their attempts to end it. Kerewin burns her tower, Joe beats his son and goes to prison, and Simon — who barely survives the beating — must painfully find his way back to those he loves. Recurring images dramatize their journeys, which end in a reconciliation between being alone and being part of a community. Kerewin describes the home that will now take the place of her lonely tower: "I decided on a shell-shape, a regular spiral of rooms expanding around the decapitated Tower . . . privacy, apartness, but all connected and all part of the whole."

  Notice that in this example, the writer also pulls loose ends together and briefly refers to the thesis.

- **Without directly repeating your thesis, come full circle by relating the final paragraph to a point you made in your introduction.**

  Preserving old-growth forests and finding substitutes for wood should concern everyone who cares about the environment. The days when Americans could view this country as an unlimited provider of resources are as gone as roaming herds of buffalo and pioneers in covered wagons.

- **End with a story related to your thesis.**

  On a recent trip to the airport, I stood at the ticket counter behind an angry woman. It seems she'd forgotten her photo ID and was being told by the attendant that she couldn't fly without it. After calling the clerk a storm trooper and threatening to sue the airline, she turned to me indignantly. "You tell me. Do I look like the kind of person who would blow up a plane?" I didn't answer, since the question seemed rhetorical. I wondered, though, how in the future this woman would react to a fifteen-minute interview about herself, or to a uniformed attendant patting her down.

Another way to conclude a paper is to summarize your points. But because summaries aren't particularly interesting conclusions, consider one only if your paper is fairly long and if one would be helpful to your reader. Keep summaries brief and avoid wishy-washy final sentences, such as "For all these reasons, the Internet should not be regulated."

Revising and Editing

After the review is completed, edit and revise the essay. Editing, which can be done with most computers and word processors, involves looking at the grammatical and mechanical content of your work. Revising means looking not only at grammar, but also the overall effect of the essay. Editing and revising ensure that the final draft is appropriate for the assignment and audience, grammatically and mechanically correct, well organized and supported, and well crafted.

Titles

Because titles are important, choose one that is interesting and informative. Consider the formality of the writing assignment and the audience when selecting a title for your work. Try reading your draft aloud, and if possible, ask someone you trust to review your essay.

While you're writing an essay, if you have a good idea for a title, write it down. But often the best time to choose a title is when you've completed a first draft and read it over. You'll have a more complete picture of your essay. Be creative, but don't overdo it. For example, if you're writing a paper about deforestation, "Knock on Wood" might seem clever, but it doesn't accurately fit the topic.

Use good judgment when you choose a title. Consider the tone of your essay and your audience. "No More Mr. Nice Guy" might be a good title for a personal essay on the loss of your gullibility, but think twice before using it as the title of your analytical paper on Shakespeare's character *Macbeth*. (It's true, however, that one instructor who had received dozens of papers with unimaginative titles reacted well to the student who called hers "Dial M for Murder: The Character of Macbeth.")

The best advice is to take a middle road. Avoid both dullness and strained cleverness. Consider a good quotation from a work you are writing about, an effective phrase from your own essay, or an appropriate figure of speech:

- "Sleep No More: The Role of Macbeth's Conscience" rather than "Macbeth's Conscience"
- "I'm Nobody: Finding Emily Dickinson in her Poetry" rather than "Emily Dickinson and her Poetry"
- "Gaining Safety or Losing Freedom: The Debate over Airport Security Measures" rather than "Airport Security Measures"
- "Only Skin Deep?" rather than "The Importance of Beauty to Today's Woman"
- "Fit to be Tried: An Examination of the McNaughton Rule" rather than "Judging Legal Sanity"

Reviewing the First Draft

When you read your first draft, you will probably make your most extensive revisions. Here are a few suggestions that can help you in reviewing your first draft.

- If possible, leave some time between writing the first draft and reviewing it. Your objectivity will improve.
- Try reading your paper aloud to yourself; sometimes your ear catches problems your eye misses.
- Ask someone to read your draft and offer suggestions. Choose a reader you can trust to be honest and fair. And remember: You are looking for an objective opinion, not simply reassurance. Judge your reader's suggestions carefully, and decide for yourself their value, and whether or not to act on them.
- Remember that nothing is unchangeable. Until preparation of your final draft, you can change your thesis, your organization, your emphasis, your tone, and so on. A review of your first draft should *not* be limited to minor mechanical errors.
- Use a revision checklist to make sure you've reviewed your draft thoroughly.

Preparing the Final Draft

You may be able to move directly from your revised first draft to a final draft, but careful writers often prepare several drafts before they are ready to call a piece finished. Within your time constraints, follow their example. As you rewrite, you may continue to discover wordy constructions, poor connections, awkward sentences, and so on. Only when you're satisfied that you've done your best should you prepare the final draft.

Writing and Editing a Draft

The computer allows you to produce a legible first draft that's easy to change by using a few basic functions, such as *delete, insert, merge, block,* and *move.* When you try making changes to a handwritten draft, on the other hand, you can end up with something so messy it's indecipherable. If you want to change a word-processed draft but aren't certain whether you'll want to keep the changes, save both your original and your revised drafts under different file names and decide later which you want to use or import parts of one into the other. You can also re-order the paragraphs in a paper with a few keystrokes.

You can do much of your editing directly on the screen. If you think of a better way to say what you've just said, make the change immediately and move on. For more global editing, however, many writers like to print out sections or complete drafts, mark them up by hand, and then go back to the computer to input the changes. This method has advantages. Working on the screen limits you to a small section of text; scrolling back and forth in the document can be confusing, and it's difficult to get a beginning-to-end picture of what you've written. Another advantage of printing out your document is that it forces you to slow down and read carefully. Sometimes, because you can write so quickly on a computer, your fingers may get ahead of your thoughts. Remember that good writing requires deliberation and judgment, and that you should always review a computer draft closely.

Spell-Checking, Grammar-Checking, and Search-and-Replace Functions

A spell-check function is useful for catching misspelled words, typos, and accidental repetitions (such as, the the). But be careful. The checker won't signal a word that is actually a word, even if it isn't the one you intended — for example, when you inadvertently type form for from. Spell-checking also doesn't distinguish between homonyms, so if you have trouble with its and it's, it won't help you. Consider the spell-checker as an aid, not a replacement for your own careful proofreading. Unfortunately, on the FSE, the essay is handwritten, so you're left to your own spelling skills.

Grammar or style-checkers require even more caution because grammar and style are less clear-cut than spelling. Many writers don't use these functions at all, and unless you already have a good grasp of grammar, they can be confusing or misleading. For example, the checkers will catch pronoun agreement and reference errors but not dangling participles or faulty parallelism. Some checkers flag possible homonym confusions, usage problems (literal used incorrectly, for example), and passive constructions, but they also signal every sentence beginning with But, all contractions, and every sentence ending with a preposition — "errors" that current usage generally permits. If you use a checking function, do so critically. Don't automatically change a passive construction, or restructure a sentence ending with a preposition, for example, simply because the checker flags it.

A search-and-replace feature in word-processing programs lets you correct a particular error throughout your paper automatically. If you find you've misspelled a person's name, you can spell it correctly and ask the program to locate every instance of the name in your 25-page document and replace it with the correct version. Just be sure that the error is one that you want replaced in the same way every time.

Layout of the Final Draft

With word processing, you can produce a final draft that looks professional. Choose from different type fonts, use bold-face type and italics, center titles with a stroke, create headings of different sizes, and use bullets or other symbols to highlight your points. You can create properly formatted and numbered footnotes, and place them correctly by selecting a footnote option and consistent page numbers by selecting automatic page numbering. If it's appropriate, you might want to present some materials in tables, charts, or graphs — which are easy to create with most programs. You can even import graphics. One note of warning: Don't confuse a good-looking paper with a well-written one. Although your readers may be favorably disposed toward documents that are nice to look at, word-processing features can't compensate for meager content or poorly expressed ideas.

Checklist

Good writing often comes after revision and rewriting. If you can view your work critically, you will be able to improve it. Use the following checklist before you write a final draft.

Purpose, Audience, and Tone

These three elements deal with the overall effect of your essay and should guide you throughout your writing.

- If I am writing in response to an assignment, does my essay fulfill all parts of the assignment?
- Is my topic too broad?
- Do I state my thesis or main idea early in the paper? If I don't state a thesis or main idea, is it clearly implied so that there can be no mistake about my purpose?
- Is my thesis or main idea interesting? If this is an essay of argument, is my thesis statement fair? Do I take opposing viewpoints into account?
- Have I thought about my audience? Does my audience have any special requirements? Is my tone appropriate to my audience and purpose?
- Is my tone consistent throughout the essay?

Examples, Evidence, and Details

These are specific details in the writing process. When you read your essay, you can determine whether you have used these elements well.

- Have I adequately developed my thesis or main idea? Do I use specific details rather than generalities?
- Are my examples and evidence accurate, relevant, and convincing?

- Do I use quotations appropriately? Is too much of my paper quotation? Do I paraphrase carefully?
- Do I cite sources for the words and ideas of others?

Structure

Use an outline to determine the structure of your paper, but be aware that you may need to alter it as you write. Keep in mind the following:

- Do I have a principle of organization? Do I avoid repetition and digressions?
- Is my organization appropriate to my topic and thesis?
- Do I adequately introduce and conclude my paper?
- Are my paragraphs well developed, unified, and coherent?
- Does one paragraph grow out of another? Do I use transitions?
- Are my examples, evidence, and details in the best order? Do I save the strongest point for last?

Language and Style

Rely on a dictionary and your word-processing tools to help you with language and style. Ask yourself some questions.

- Have I chosen my words carefully? Am I sure of meanings?
- Is my language appropriate to my purpose, tone, and audience?
- Have I avoided wordy expressions? euphemisms? cliches?
- Have I avoided pretentious language?
- Have I used idioms correctly?
- Have I followed the guidelines of current written usage?
- Have I avoided sexism in the use of nouns and pronouns?
- Have I preferred the active to the passive voice of the verb?

Sentence Construction

Use your editing and revision skills to make sure your sentences are well constructed. Keep the following in mind:

- Are my sentences correct? Have I avoided both fragments and run-ons?
- Are my modifiers in the right place? Do I have any dangling modifiers?
- Do my subjects and predicates agree in number?
- Do I keep parallel constructions parallel?
- Have I avoided short, choppy sentences?
- Do I combine sentences effectively?
- Are my sentences varied in length and structure? Do I avoid monotony?

Grammar

Use this book to augment your grammar skills and keep the following in mind:

- Have I checked spelling (including correct plural forms, hyphenation), capitalization, correct use and consistency of verb tenses, agreement (nouns, verbs, pronouns), pronoun cases, pronoun antecedents, use of adjectives with linking verbs, comparative degrees of adjectives and adverbs?
- Does my punctuation make my meaning clear? Have I followed punctuation rules?
- Commas with nonrestrictive elements; no commas with restrictive elements

- Commas with interrupting elements, with introductory phrases and clauses when necessary, between series items, between independent clauses
- Correct use of periods and question marks
- Correct use (and not overuse) of exclamation points
- Correct use of semicolons and colons
- Correct use (and not overuse) of dashes and parentheses
- Correct use (and not overuse) of quotation marks
- Correct use of other punctuation with quotation marks

PART V

ORAL ASSESSMENT

About the Oral Assessment

What You Should Know

You will be invited to the Oral Assessment portion of the FSOE only if you pass the exam and written essay. This portion represents the next stage of your candidacy for a position in the Foreign Service. Although this portion involves working with other candidates, this is not considered a job interview, but merely another examination.

There are three major sections in which you will participate.

The Group Exercise

In group exercise, you will work together with three to six other candidates on a project. Keep in mind that this is not a competition with the other candidates; it is a time for you to demonstrate your ability to work with others and convince the assessors that you will become an effective Foreign Service Officer. This exercise has three segments:

- **Preparation:** You are given 30 minutes to read through a packet of materials that pertains to the exercise in which you will be participating.
- **Presentation:** In the second segment of the group exercise, you are joined by four assessors (Foreign Service Officers) who observe you as you discuss the project with the other members of the group.
- **Discussion of a sample project:** When the presentation segment is complete, you work together to discuss the project and determine among you which project you are going to select and how you will allocate your resources.

Keep in mind that all of these sections are critical to your evaluation, so your active participation is extremely important.

The Structured Interview

In the second portion of the oral assessment, you participate in an interview by two assessors. The interview is conducted on an individual basis and consists of three modules that last about one hour.

- **Experience and motivation interview:** In this module of the interview, you are asked to give a clear overview of who you are: your personality, accomplishments, and skills — and to demonstrate a strong knowledge of the Foreign Service.
- **Hypothetical scenarios:** In this module, the assessors give you a brief scenario of a hypothetical situation in an embassy setting, and you are asked to demonstrate your problem-solving abilities, judgment, planning, and so on.
- **Past behavior interview:** The final module of the interview section asks you to respond to a series of questions from the assessors, using example from your own life, in order to demonstrate your ability in work-related situations.

Case Management

This final section of the oral assessment is 90 minutes long. In this section you are evaluated for your management skills, interpersonal skills, and quantitative abilities. You are also required to display strong writing and English skills. You are given tasks to complete based on the information given you. It is recommended that you spend 30 minutes reading and analyzing the material you receive, 45 minutes writing the memo, and the final 15 minutes reviewing and revising what you've written.

Assessment Criteria

The purpose of the oral assessment is to evaluate you based on a variety of categories, including

- Written communication
- Oral communication
- Information integration and analysis
- Planning and organizing
- Judgment
- Resourcefulness
- Initiative and leadership
- Experience and motivation
- Working with others
- Composure
- Quantitative analysis
- Objectivity and integrity
- Cultural adaptability

These categories are self-explanatory, and when you measure these thirteen items against the major exercises in the oral assessment, you can see how they are demonstrated in each of the situations in which you'll find yourself. These are the only criteria by which you will be evaluated by the assessors, and it is up to you to demonstrate your strengths as you move through each of the steps of the assessment.

At the end of the complete oral assessment, each of the assessors enters your scores into a computer. Each of the three sections of the assessment carry equal weight. After the scores are tabulated, you are notified whether you have reached the passing score.

- If you are unsuccessful, you are also notified and given a private interview with two assessors.
- If you are successful, you will be briefed on the subsequent steps to complete the hiring process, including a medical exam, security background investigation, and a final suitability review. During this briefing, you can also ask questions about the Foreign Service to get a better idea of what you can look forward to in the diplomatic corps.

Finally, assuming you have completed all of the pre-employment requirements, you will probably be put on a waiting list (the Register List), while you await a job offer. Your listing will remain on this register for up to 18 months, after which your candidacy will expire.

When you apply for the FSOE, you will receive a booklet that will spell out portions of this in greater detail. If you have additional questions, you can go on the Internet to www.careers.state.gov/officer, where you get greater insight into what you can expect as a Foreign Service Officer in the diplomatic corps.